HASIDISM AND POLITICS

T0373447

THE LITTMAN LIBRARY OF
JEWISH CIVILIZATION

Dedicated to the memory of
LOUIS THOMAS SIDNEY LITTMAN
who founded the Littman Library for the love of God
and as an act of charity in memory of his father
JOSEPH AARON LITTMAN
and to the memory of
ROBERT JOSEPH LITTMAN
who continued what his father Louis had begun
יהא זכרם ברוך

'*Get wisdom, get understanding:*
Forsake her not and she shall preserve thee'
PROV. 4: 5

The Littman Library of Jewish Civilization is a registered UK charity
Registered charity no. 1000784

HASIDISM AND POLITICS

◆

The Kingdom of Poland
1815–1864

◆

MARCIN WODZIŃSKI

The Littman Library of Jewish Civilization
in association with Liverpool University Press

The Littman Library of Jewish Civilization
in association with Liverpool University Press
4 Cambridge Street, Liverpool L69 7ZU, UK

www.liverpooluniversitypress.co.uk/littman

Managing Editor: Connie Webber

Distributed in North America by
Oxford University Press Inc., 198 Madison Avenue,
New York, NY 10016, USA

First published in hardback 2013
First issued in paperback 2016

Catalogue records for this book are available from the
British Library and the Library of Congress

ISBN 978-1-906764-94-4

Publishing co-ordinator: Janet Moth
Copy-editing: Bonnie Blackburn and Connie Webber
Proofreading: Mark Newby
Index: Jane Read
Designed and typeset by Pete Russell, Faringdon, Oxon.
Printed in Great Britain by
CPI Group (UK) Ltd., Croydon, CR0 4YY

To my wife Agatka

◆

*The translation of this book was facilitated by
a grant from the*

CENTER FOR RESEARCH ON THE
HISTORY AND CULTURE OF POLISH JEWS
AT THE
HEBREW UNIVERSITY OF JERUSALEM

◆

Preface and Acknowledgements

I SHOULD LIKE TO OFFER some words of thanks to the many people and institutions whose assistance made this book possible. First of all, I am grateful to the Center for Research on the History and Culture of Polish Jews at the Hebrew University of Jerusalem for supporting my endeavours in this field. I should also like to thank the Hanadiv Charitable Foundation of London (now the Rothschild Foundation Europe) as well as the Polish Committee of Scientific Research for their research grants; the YIVO Institute for Jewish Research, which supported my work in its initial stages through the Professor Bernard Choseed Memorial Fellowship; and the Dubnow Institute of Leipzig, which provided me with hospitality and support as I started preparing my typescript. I also received financial assistance from my alma mater, the Institute of Polish Philology at Wrocław University. I express my deepest gratitude to all these institutions, and even more to all those who represent them.

Further thanks are due to the institutions that allowed me access to their collections. Among them are the library of Wrocław University; the state archives in Częstochowa, Grodzisk Mazowiecki, Kalisz, Katowice, Kielce, Lublin, Łódź, Płock, Radom, Sandomierz, and Włocławek; the Warsaw Central Archives of Historical Records; the National Library and the Library of the University of Warsaw; the Jerusalem Central Archives for the History of the Jewish People; the National Library of Israel and the Library of the Hebrew University; and the library and archive of the YIVO Institute for Jewish Research in New York.

Among the many individuals to whom I am indebted I should mention Israel Bartal, without whose keen interest in my work and support this book would not have been written; Moshe Rosman, for recommending this book for publication and early advice; David Assaf, Gershon Bacon, Gershon Hundert, Marek Urbański, and Scott Ury for their many valuable critical remarks; Agnieszka Jagodzińska, who helped me find and acquire the illustrative material; and finally Andrzej Chwalba, Maciej Mycielski, and Shaul Stampfer, who agreed to read the typescript. I was further greatly helped by the weekly discussions of the research group Towards a New History of Hasidism, hosted in 2007–8 by the Institute of Advanced Studies at the Hebrew University of Jerusalem, of which I had the honour to be a fellow. Again I should like to thank cordially all those mentioned (and, with apologies, those not mentioned).

*

In the interests of full disclosure, as the contemporary idiom has it, I should say that parts of this study have been previously published elsewhere, as listed below; however, all previously published material has been amended and re-edited.

Excerpts from Chapter 1 have appeared as 'Cywilni chrześcijanie. Spory o reformę Żydów w Polsce, 1789–1830' [Civil Christians: Controversies over the Reform of Jews in Poland, 1789–1830], in Grażyna Borkowska and Magdalena Rudkowska (eds.), *Kwestia żydowska w XIX w. Spory o tożsamość Polaków* [The Jewish Question in the Nineteenth Century: Controversies over Polish Identity] (Warsaw, 2004), 9–42, and later in English as 'Civil Christians: Debates on the Reform of the Jews in Poland, 1789–1830', in Benjamin Nathans and Gabriella Safran (eds.), *Culture Front: Representing Jews in Eastern Europe* (Philadelphia, 2008), 46–76.

Chapter 2 has been published in part as 'Rząd Królestwa Polskiego wobec chasydyzmu. Początki "polityki chasydzkiej" w Królestwie Kongresowym (1817–1818)' [The Government of the Polish Kingdom and Hasidism: The Beginnings of 'Hasidic Politics' in the Congress Kingdom (1817–1818)], in Krzysztof Pilarczyk (ed.), *Żydzi i judaizm we współczesnych badaniach polskich* [Jews and Judaism in Contemporary Polish Research], iii (Kraków, 2003), 65–77, and as 'Chasydzi w Częstochowie. Źródła do dziejów chasydyzmu w centralnej Polsce' [Hasidim in Częstochowa: Sources for Hasidic History in Central Poland], *Studia Judaica*, 8/1–2 (2005), 279–301.

Parts of Chapter 4 have been published as 'State Policy and Hasidic Expansion: The Case of Włocławek', *Jewish Studies at the Central European University*, 5 (2006–7), 171–85, and 'A Rabbi Informer and the Hasidim of Będzin: Dimensions of Hasidic Politics', *East European Jewish Affairs*, 39/2 (2009), 153–66.

Portions of Chapter 5 have been published as 'Hasidism, *Shtadlanut*, and Jewish Politics in Nineteenth Century Poland: The Case of Isaac of Warka', *Jewish Quarterly Review*, 96/2 (2005), 290–320, and in 'How Modern is an Anti-Modernist Movement? Emergence of the Hasidic Politics in Congress Poland', *AJS Review*, 31/2 (2007), 221–40.

Parts of Chapter 7 have been published as 'Haskalah and Politics Reconsidered: The Case of the Kingdom of Poland, 1815–1860', in David Assaf and Ada Rapoport-Albert (eds.), *Yashan mipenei ḥadash*, ii: *Maskilim, mitnagedim verabanim* [Let the Old Make Way for the New, ii: Haskalah, Orthodoxy, and the Opposition to Hasidism] (Jerusalem, 2009), 163–97* (English section).

Contents

List of Illustrations

Note on Transliteration

THE transliteration of Hebrew in this book reflects consideration of the type of book it is, in terms of its content, purpose, and readership. The system adopted therefore reflects a broad approach to transcription, rather than the narrower approaches found in the *Encyclopaedia Judaica* or other systems developed for text-based or linguistic studies. The aim has been to reflect the pronunciation prescribed for modern Hebrew, rather than the spelling or Hebrew word structure, and to do so using conventions that are generally familiar to the English-speaking reader.

In accordance with this approach, no attempt is made to indicate the distinctions between *alef* and *ayin*, *tet* and *taf*, *kaf* and *kuf*, *sin* and *samekh*, since these are not relevant to pronunciation; likewise, the *dagesh* is not indicated except where it affects pronunciation. Following the principle of using conventions familiar to the majority of readers, however, transcriptions that are well established have been retained even when they are not fully consistent with the transliteration system adopted. On similar grounds, the *tsadi* is rendered by 'tz' in such familiar words as bar mitzvah. Likewise, the distinction between *ḥet* and *khaf* has been retained, using *ḥ* for the former and *kh* for the latter; the associated forms are generally familiar to readers, even if the distinction is not actually borne out in pronunciation, and for the same reason the final *heh* is indicated too. As in Hebrew, no capital letters are used, except that an initial capital has been retained in transliterating titles of published works (for example, *Shulḥan arukh*).

Since no distinction is made between *alef* and *ayin*, they are indicated by an apostrophe only in intervocalic positions where a failure to do so could lead an English-speaking reader to pronounce the vowel-cluster as a diphthong—as, for example, in *ha'ir*—or otherwise mispronounce the word.

The *sheva na* is indicated by an *e*—*perikat ol*, *reshut*—except, again, when established convention dictates otherwise.

The *yod* is represented by *i* when it occurs as a vowel (*bereshit*), by *y* when it occurs as a consonant (*yesodot*), and by *yi* when it occurs as both (*yisra'el*).

Names of individuals have generally been left in their familiar forms, even when this is inconsistent with the overall system. Similarly, names of institutions are generally given in the familiar modern Hebrew forms, though if an alternative Ashkenazi or Yiddish form is widespread, that form is indicated in parentheses.

Place Names

Since place names are so complicated and ideologically loaded in eastern Europe, I have used the Polish form for all localities in territories of the former Polish–Lithuanian Commonwealth, excepting cities that have well-known English names (Warsaw, not Warszawa; Vilna, not Vilnius or Wilno; Danzig, not Gdańsk—but Kraków rather than Cracow, in keeping with modern convention). Where hasidic courts have markedly different Polish and Yiddish names, I give both, Polish then

Yiddish: Góra Kalwaria (Ger), Mszczonów (Amshinov), Opatów (Apt). Where there is only a minor difference, I use the Polish name alone (for example Kock, not Kotsk). Readers unfamiliar with Polish should be aware that the Polish *c* is pronounced 'ts', *sz* or *ś* are pronounced 'sh', *ch* is pronounced as in 'loch', and *cz* and *ć* are pronounced 'tsh'.

Sources

This study is based primarily on the rich collections relating to the history of Polish hasidism that are to be found in central and provincial Polish state archives, supplemented by documents from other institutions. A selection of many of these documents, mostly in Polish, has recently been published,[1] and an online version is available on the website of the Austeria Publishing House, <http://www.austeria.pl/ UserFiles/zrodla_chasydyzm_fragment.pdf>. These published sources are indicated throughout by an asterisk (*) followed by the number of the source as it appears in the volume.

---

[1] In *Źródła do dziejów chasydyzmu w Królestwie Polskim, 1815–1867*, ed. Wodziński.

Abbreviations

AGAD	Archiwum Główne Akt Dawnych
AmL	Akta miasta Lublina (1809–74)
AmP	Akta miasta Płocka (1808–67)
APK	Archiwum Państwowe w Kielcach
APL	Archiwum Państwowe w Lublinie
APŁ	Archiwum Państwowe w Łodzi
APP	Archiwum Państwowe w Płocku
APRG	Anteriora Piotrkowskiego Rządu Gubernialnego
CWW	Centralne Władze Wyznaniowe
KRSW	Komisja Rządowa Spraw Wewnętrznych
KWK	Komisja Województwa Kaliskiego
MDSC	Artur Eisenbach, Jerzy Michalski, Emanuel Rostworowski, and Janusz Wolański (eds.), *Materiały do dziejów Sejmu Czteroletniego* [Sources on the History of the Four Year Sejm], vi (Wrocław, 1969)
RGR	Rząd Gubernialny Radomski

MAP 1
Partitions of the
Polish–Lithuanian Commonwealth,
1772–1795

Territories lost to

☐ Russia

▨ Prussia

▦ Austria

·—·—· Boundary between the
Korona and the Duchy
of Lithuania

0   50   100   150 miles

0   100   200 km

Połock

1772

Witebsk

Dnieper

Mścisław

Mińsk

Słuck

Dniepr

Pińsk

Pripyat

1793

RUSSIA

Kiev

Żytomierz

Dniepr

Kamieniec Podolski

Dniestr

Iaşi

OTTOMAN LANDS

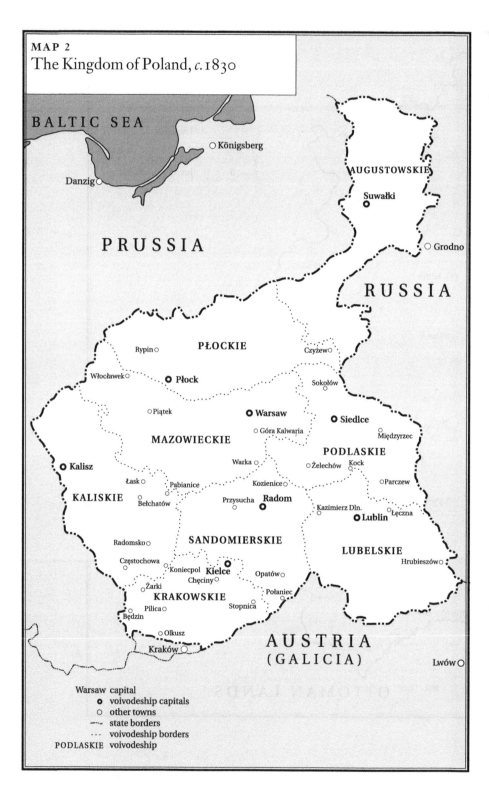

MAP 2
The Kingdom of Poland, *c.* 1830

BALTIC SEA

○ Königsberg

Danzig ○

PRUSSIA

AUGUSTOWSKIE

Suwałki ◉

○ Grodno

RUSSIA

Rypin ○   PŁOCKIE   Czyżew ○

Włocławek ○   ◉ Płock

Sokołów ○

○ Piątek   ◉ Warsaw   ◉ Siedlce

○ Góra Kalwaria   Międzyrzec ○

MAZOWIECKIE   PODLASKIE

◉ Kalisz   Warka ○   ○ Żelechów Kock

Łask ○   ○ Pabianice   Kozienice ○   ○ Parczew

KALISKIE   ○ Bełchatów   Przysucha ○ ◉ Radom   Kazimierz Dln. ○ ○ Łęczna

                                                                    ◉ Lublin

Radomsko ○   SANDOMIERSKIE   LUBELSKIE

Częstochowa ○   Hrubieszów ○

          ○ Koniecpol Kielce ◉   Opatów ○

          Chęciny ○

     ○ Żarki   Połaniec ○

          KRAKOWSKIE   Stopnica ○

     ○ Pilica

Będzin ○

     ○ Olkusz

Kraków ◉   AUSTRIA
                    (GALICIA)   Lwów ○

Warsaw capital
     ◉ voivodeship capitals
     ○ other towns
     –··– state borders
     ··· voivodeship borders
PODLASKIE voivodeship

Introduction

IN PART, this book continues my previous study of the Haskalah and the hasidic movement in the Kingdom of Poland (sometimes also known as 'Congress Poland' because it was created by the Congress of Vienna) in the long nineteenth century.[1] One reason I have returned to the same period and geographical region is my assumption that the appearance and growth of any major social movement entails changes in social structures, in how social groups relate to one another, in cultural perceptions, and even in the economic matrix. Hasidism was no doubt the largest and most important new movement to emerge within east European Jewry in those turbulent times, which in the Polish territories were marked by abrupt social, economic, and cultural transformations (industrialization, urbanization, the replacement of traditional estate structures by new social strata, changes in political status, and the evolution of modern ideologies). How did hasidism participate in these transformations? I believe that one way to approach this issue is by investigating the changes in social relations and perceptions that these developments brought about; or, in other words, how the new social formations that arose in the Polish lands defined and redefined themselves in relation to each other.

The various social groups and institutions reacted to hasidism in different ways, and the ways in which hasidim reacted to them were similarly varied. The most important players in this social nexus were (*a*) the Haskalah or Jewish Enlightenment and its successor integrationist camp, which strove to become 'modern' by integrating with the surrounding society; (*b*) the traditional non-hasidic Jewish community, frequently and wrongly identified with the *mitnagedim*, an anti-hasidic group; and (*c*) the state and its institutions and political elites representing the state or states. In my previous book I tried to explore in some detail what the hasidic movement meant for the first of these players, i.e. the Haskalah and its successors. In this study I turn my attention to the last of the three, by considering the political history of the Kingdom of Poland and its relationship with the hasidic movement. This is thus the second part of what I hope will be a trilogy about hasidism and the context in which it developed.

Another element that very much shapes this book, and which it shares with its predecessor, is an anti-essentialist perspective on hasidism. An

[1] Wodziński, *Haskalah and Hasidism*.

essentialist approach privileges some characteristics of a historical phenomenon, in this case hasidism, by making them the constitutive elements of the
definition of that phenomenon, while rejecting or marginalizing other characteristics as auxiliary or 'alien'; I disagree with that. I will try to show that
hasidism was defined as much by its incessant social interactions as by its
mystical inspirations and theological doctrines. Hasidism's skirmishes with
the Polish state and with local supporters of the Jewish Enlightenment—not
to mention its internal political disputes—were as much a part of the history
of the movement as the traditionalist language that its leaders used to try to
contain change.[2]

In all other respects, however, the present study is independent of my
earlier book. It poses new questions and deploys different historiographical
approaches, chief among them those of political history.

The political perspective on hasidism is hardly new: even some of its
nineteenth-century critics, such as Nahum Sokołów in the Kingdom of
Poland and Wilhelm Feldman in Galicia, among many others, perceived it as
having its origins as a political entity.[3] The later historiography, however,
came to be dominated by two other approaches. One school championed a
three-stage theory of the development of east European Jewry: from traditional society, to liberal progressivism, to its final flowering in post-liberal
mass politics.[4] Characterizing the earlier stages as mere way-stations of this
supposed dialectic, this school concentrated on the emergence of hasidism as
a mass political movement. Historians who took this approach produced a
great many studies of the various factions within hasidism, and other Orthodox groups as well, but their prime focus was a relatively late stage in the
political development of the hasidic movement and the emergence of Orthodox parties in the contemporary politics of Israel. Of special interest are the
studies of the best known of the Orthodox political parties, Agudat Yisra'el
(Agudas Yisroel) and Mahazikei Hadat (Makhzikey Hadas).[5] As a rule, these
studies describe political events at the end of the nineteenth and the first
half of the twentieth century, the era of mass politics and modern political
movements.

The second common approach was the traditional 'great man' historiography, which ascribed policy and politics to outstanding leaders. This school

---

[2] See more on this in a thought-provoking essay by Adam Teller, 'Hasidism and the
Challenge of Geography', 6–8.

[3] See e.g. Sokołów, *Zadania inteligencji żydowskiej*, 4–5; id., 'Do pracy i zgody!'; Feldman,
'Korespondencja "Izraelity"'; id., 'Z piśmiennictwa'.

[4] This concept is best articulated in Frankel, *Prophecy and Politics*, 1.

[5] On Agudat Yisrael see Bacon, *The Politics of Tradition*; on Mahazikei Hadat see Manekin,
'Tsemiḥatah vegibushah shel ha'ortodoksiyah hayehudit begalitsiyah'. See also other interesting studies of this type, e.g. Ravitzky, 'Munkács and Jerusalem'; Salmon, *Religion and Zionism*.

focused, for example, on the controversy in hasidic literature over Napoleon's role in the messianic scheme of salvation, with tsadikim involved on both sides.[6] It also studied how Polish tsadikim appealed to Moses Montefiore,[7] or the influence of the tsadik Menahem Mendel Schneersohn of Lubawicze (Lubavitch) at the meetings of the Rabbinical Commission in St Petersburg in 1843.[8] The drawback of many of these studies is that they tend to over-simplify the politics of the age,[9] and to limit research to hasidic leaders.[10] This approach, the result of a specific paradigm of the history of hasidism as the story of the tsadikim and a more general understanding of politics as an elite undertaking, remains dominant in the historiography of hasidism. It is a per-spective that seems inadequate today, not only because political historians generally have significantly expanded and refined their understanding of their subject matter, but also because we increasingly understand hasidism as a mass movement that reached far beyond the hasidic court.

Each of these approaches has its limitations. The former correctly grasps the collective nature of political agency, but fails to understand the politics of an age before the emergence of mass organizations in the late nineteenth century. The latter is more convincing on the movement's beginnings, but fails to analyse the political activity of hasidim other than the machinations of its leaders.

The present study tries to fill the gaps. It studies hasidic politics in the early nineteenth and even the late eighteenth century, but instead of simply identifying the movement with its leaders it attempts to elucidate the com-plicated nature of the relations between the political representatives and

---

[6] The events have been described many times, the best-known literary version being a novel by Martin Buber, *For the Sake of Heaven*. A collection of hasidic stories related to Napoleon and his times can be found in *Napoleon utekufato*, ed. Mevorach, 181–9. For a good introduction to the historical literature on the subject, see Levine, '"Should Napoleon Be Victorious . . . ": Politics and Spirituality in Early Modern Jewish Messianism'.

[7] Assaf and Bartal, 'Shetadlanut ve'ortodoksiyah'; H. M. Rabinowicz, 'Sir Moses Montefiore and Chasidism'.

[8] See Stanislawski, *Tsar Nicholas I and the Jews*, 78–81; Lurie, *Edah umedinah*; a hasidic ver-sion of the events is included in Schneersohn, *The 'Tzemach Tzedek'*. For more on hasidic historiography, mainly generated by the Schneersohns, and its characteristics, see Rapoport-Albert, 'Hagiography with Footnotes'.

[9] The most notorious is equating Jewish political activity with bribery; see Levine, '"Should Napoleon Be Victorious . . .'", 14. Some studies are also 'presentist', projecting the activities and mindset of the author's period on to earlier people and events. Worse still, other historians impose their own ideological and political narrative. Raphael Mahler was a master of this technique: his vision of 'hasidic leadership of Jewish passive resistance', inspired by both Zion-ism and Marxist ideology, remains surprisingly influential to this day—see Mahler, *Hasidism and the Jewish Enlightenment*.

[10] One of the few publications breaking with this tendency is Deich, *Tsarskoe pravitel'stvo i khasidskoe dvizhenie v Rossii*. However, this is only a collection of documents dealing mainly with the activities of a 'learned Jew' and maskil, Moses Berlin.

those whom they represented. It takes a similar approach to the other political actors, demonstrating how negotiations between maskilim and the government represented the politics not of the Haskalah (meaning, the interests of all those whose lives were touched by the drive for enlightenment), but only of its politically active representatives; and when hasidic leaders did the same, they represented themselves, and not necessarily their movement.

Naturally, this raises the key question of the legitimacy of political representation in non-democratic systems. Current political science portrays the distinction between representatives and the masses as a dichotomy between elitist and ethnic political cultures,[11] but no such clear-cut division can convey the diverse and complex relations between collective players (such as the hasidic community and the government bureaucracy), which were never monolithic. So, for example, in speaking of 'the state' we should distinguish between, on the one hand, the highest ruling bodies of the Kingdom of Poland (the king, the viceroy, and some of the members of the government) and, on the other, the state officials responsible for implementing (or not implementing) legislation and political strategy imposed from above. Each political grouping had its own multilayered structure, conflicting objectives and interests, procedures, and so on. They were driven not only by structural factors but also by individual motives, sometimes very far removed from our ordinary conception of state politics. No individual is fully systematic, methodical, or consistent, and such lack of consistency is particularly marked when considering large groupings of any kind; this observation is as true of our historical subjects as it would be today. That is why history is shaped not only by great forces, but also by many silent factors that leave few traces of their origins but have profound effects.

My plan for this study was determined in part by my choice of territory (the Kingdom of Poland, one of the smallest political entities in nineteenth-century eastern Europe) and in part by my firm intention to put the phenomenon studied in its proper context. For many decades, histories of the Jews of the nineteenth century in central and eastern Europe concentrated on the Russian empire, marginalizing Galicia, Hungary, the Kingdom of Poland, the ephemeral Grand Duchy of Warsaw, and the Free City of Kraków. Only recently has the significance of the local context and diversity of those political creations been somewhat better researched. This is also true of studies on hasidism and its links with politics in eastern Europe. The inadequate understanding of the social and political context has had negative consequences, for how can one comprehend the political actions of a Polish, Russian, or Galician *shtadlan* (Jewish political intercessor) without first studying the political and legal conditions under which he operated? Fundamental differ-

[11] See e.g. Putnam, 'Studying Elite Political Culture'; Nelson, 'Ethnicity and Socioeconomic Status as Sources of Participation'.

ences between Warsaw, Brody, Vilna, Odessa, and St Petersburg have been ignored or misinterpreted, so that real mechanisms, motivations, causes, and effects have been overlooked and misunderstood. In politics, the link between, on the one hand, the strategy and actions of the historical agent who is the focus of the narrative and, on the other, the non-Jewish context in which he is operating is so profound that it is simply impossible to understand one without the other.

My aim in formulating this study also included a desire to focus on the Kingdom of Poland during its constitutional (1815–30) and semi-autonomous (1831–64) periods; a renunciation of a general east European 'panoramic' perspective; and an emphasis on the connection between the two implications of the term 'Jewish politics'—state politics related to Jews and Jewish politics related to the state. More specifically, I wanted to resolve a number of problems concerning the political relations between the Kingdom of Poland and the hasidic collective. What was the policy of the state towards hasidism? Who made that policy, what were its objectives, and what were its results? Who else was involved? And finally, how did the hasidim themselves, both the rank and file and the leaders, participate in this political game, and what were the consequences?

The last question leads to the critical issue of the definition of 'hasidic politics'. While the first element of the question—state policy towards the hasidic movement—is not especially problematic, the second, namely the political involvement of the hasidim themselves, is much harder to define. Once hasidism had become a significant social force, its supporters were involved in political conflicts in almost every community and participated in politics almost daily. However, it is important to note that they only sometimes acted as hasidim.

When can we say that they did act as hasidim, and what does that mean? This touches on the very difficult and still unsatisfactorily examined issue of 'hasidic identity', which unfortunately cannot be fully discussed here. Traditionally, historians have seen hasidism as a form of primeval identity, i.e. one that precedes and informs secondary identities and social roles: in this view, everything a hasid does has to be in some degree 'hasidic'. But this seems a mistaken or at least a doubtful assumption. It does not proceed from factual analysis and theoretical reflection, but from an oversimplified understanding of pre-modern identity and its connections with social roles.[12] Even a casual glance at the complex political relations within Jewish communities shows that dividing lines did not run entirely between hasidim and non-hasidim.

[12] Sociologists who impose modern (or postmodern) fluid or situational identities on pre-modern societies which they assume to be simple fall prey to a somewhat arrogant assumption, identifying their vision of the past with the past itself. For the most influential sociological concepts of fluid identity see Giddens, *Modernity and Self-Identity*.

Hasidic society itself was divided not only into the 'courts' surrounding the different tsadikim, but also according to many diverse attitudes, exactly like its non-hasidic counterpart. For example, in elections for community leaders, the voices of hasidim (but not 'hasidic voices') came out for various candidates, none of whom may have been hasidim or promoted as hasidic candidates.[13] Just as the Catholic community in the United States is divided among supporters of the Democratic and Republican parties without any association with Catholic identity, so members of the hasidic community in the nineteenth-century Kingdom of Poland could make different political choices on many issues in which hasidic identity played little or no part.

What, then, is hasidic politics? When does hasidic identity become essential to defining political roles? Attempts to come up with a definition relying on distinctive features differentiating hasidic politics from political activity undertaken by non-hasidim are, unfortunately, very problematic because they depend on a subjective evaluation of the strength of these features and the connections between them. In Chapter 7, I examine some of these connections and juxtapose characteristic hasidic and maskilic political activity, but I do not venture to define 'hasidic' politics on the basis of these findings.

In my view, we can more safely term political activity 'hasidic' if it fulfils at least one of two conditions: (*a*) the activity either represents, or is perceived to represent, a clearly defined interest of the hasidic community or a part of it; (*b*) someone on one side of the political conflict defines himself, or is defined by adversaries, as hasidic, so that the hasidic identity is important in the judgement of at least one side of a political conflict (even if that does not necessarily reflect the real objectives of the group). An example of political activity defined by the first, objective, condition, i.e. based on interest of the hasidic group, might be the defence of the right of hasidim to use the community *mikveh* (ritual bath) or to establish a *shtibl* (prayer room) independent of the community; an example of the second, subjective, condition, i.e. based on the definition or self-definition of one side as hasidic, might be the numerous conflicts surrounding the nomination of a hasid as the communal rabbi.

However, as will become clear, hasidic political activity in the nineteenth-century Kingdom of Poland was significantly more complicated even than this, escaping clear definition and encompassing very broad forms of activity. In fact, the known cases of hasidic political engagement form a certain continuum. From straightforward, defensive interventions undertaken by hasidim in response to activity aimed at them as hasidim, they range through practices undertaken by hasidim with the goal of gaining political benefit for

---

[13] Of many examples, the communal elections in Piątek are perhaps the best; see AGAD, KWK 3224. Unfortunately, a consistent analysis of such political behaviour has not yet been undertaken.

the hasidic community to interventions by hasidic political representatives at the state level in which the defined beneficiary was not only hasidim but the entire Jewish community. The scope of the description and analysis of the present book will be all forms of hasidic political activity, including those meant to benefit this whole community. I have included this more general form of activity in the discussion since, as I show in Chapter 5, it was the natural consequence of earlier forms of political engagement which were unquestionably hasidic and basically still served clearly defined, though indirect, hasidic political goals. Moreover, the political activity initiated by the tsadikim on behalf of the entire Jewish community came from a belief fundamental to hasidism which saw the tsadikim as leaders of the entire people of Israel. In this sense, even if this activity did not realize hasidic political interests directly or indirectly, the fact that the activity was undertaken at all was a direct consequence of the activists' hasidic identity.

I should also explain that, because of the goals I set myself, large sections of this study are more descriptive than analytical. The first goal is corrective. Some of the events I describe have already been extensively researched, such as the investigation into the nature of hasidism conducted by the highest state officials in the years 1823–4. Unfortunately, the existing literature on this subject is in many respects unsatisfactory since it is full of errors and consists of a mixture of fact, speculation, and even outright fiction. That is why it seems particularly important to retell the events, as carefully as possible, on the basis of all sources that can still be found. (Sadly, some of the archives available to pre-war historians no longer exist.)

Another objective that led to the descriptive character of much of this study was my intention to examine in the greatest possible detail 'at source'. By this I mean not only basing myself on existing sources but subjecting such sources to close reading and thorough analysis in order to reconstruct as precisely as possible all the decision-making mechanisms, micro-factors, procedures, and so forth that were involved in a given situation. My aim is to establish the part played in decision-making mechanisms and administrative processes by representatives of the Jewish community, including the hasidim, as well as their knowledge of the state apparatus and their ability to influence it. I also examine in detail the complex links between all the above-mentioned social groups, their concepts, perceptions, and misperceptions and the ways in which these influenced their political relations. My conviction is that the political culture that developed in consequence was, paradoxically, both an established reality with which the agents concerned had to contend and at the same time in a state of continuous evolution.[14] Note that I understand

---

[14] Even though I am clearly influenced by the trend of political history that perceives political acts as symbols 'caught in a net of meanings', I do not use the term 'political culture' in this study because of its vagueness. On controversies over the uses and abuses of the term, especially in historical and political studies, see Formisano, 'The Concept of Political Culture'.

'political culture' as incorporating not only a particular content (ideas, assumptions, and meanings attributed to political behaviour), but also the forms of in which that content was expressed or implemented. That is why a considerable part of this study consists of painstakingly detailed reconstructions of the relations between ideas, people, and administrative procedures.

A third and final objective of the descriptive component of this study is to put to the test my scepticism about grand historical narratives. Although historians are usually aware of the danger of these broad generalizations, there are still too many studies faithful to the narratives of Simon Dubnow and Raphael Mahler, especially in studies on hasidism. I am convinced that the only way to avoid these problematic influences is to strive consciously, when reading each source, to liberate historical reflections from the traditional paradigms.

The book has an introduction, seven chapters, and a conclusion. The first chapter is a general introduction to the issues that shaped Polish policy towards Jews: I focus on the most general policy objectives and their implementation, as well as on the way the Jewish community was perceived. In Chapters 2–4 I present, in chronological order, the political developments in the Kingdom of Poland throughout its autonomous and semi-autonomous existence (1815–64) as they affected hasidim. Chapter 5 is devoted in its entirety to an analysis of hasidic political activity as a reaction to the policies directed at hasidim. Here, the actions of Rabbi Isaac of Warka, the best-known hasidic political activist in nineteenth-century Poland, are especially interesting as a case study of direct and indirect hasidic involvement in elite politics. Chapter 6 analyses communal hasidic politics, and the relationship between the hasidic elite and the hasidic masses, shifting its focus from the state level to communal politics and the relations between 'elite' and 'ethnic', or popular, political participation. The final chapter analyses the influence of the Haskalah on government policy towards hasidim, and the political involvement of hasidism and adherents of the Haskalah alike.

CHAPTER ONE

To 'Civilize' the Jews: Polish Debates on the Reform of Jewish Society, 1788–1830

AMID THE RAPID AND COMPLEX political transformations of the Polish–Lithuanian Commonwealth in its final years, Polish political elites vigorously debated projects for social and state reform. Of the many questions that generated discussion during this period, the issue generally referred to as 'the reform of the Jews', but meaning the reform of the socio-occupational structure of Jewish society, was regarded as one of the most pressing, along with reforms in the status of the peasantry and town dwellers.

In 1772 the Polish–Lithuanian Commonwealth lost 37 per cent of its population and 29 per cent of its territory to Russia, Austria, and Prussia in what came to be known as the First Partition. The king, Stanisław August Poniatowski, who had been on the throne since 1764, was already aware of the need for modernization, but this sudden shock brought home the need for profound change. The Sejm debated proposed reforms several times after 1772 and introduced certain changes, but the most comprehensive, and, as it turned out, the last attempt at reform was the Four Year or Great Sejm of 1788–92.

In the favourable international climate of these years—favourable in the sense that Russia was involved in its own wars at this time—reform-minded political circles in the Polish–Lithuanian Commonwealth succeeded in getting the Sejm to debate radical reforms of the state, the military, and public finances, as well as many areas of social and economic life. Wide-ranging changes were introduced, of which the most important, even spectacular, was the constitution of 3 May 1791—the first in Europe, and preceded internationally only by that of the United States.

But the achievements were short-lived. In 1792 the neighbouring powers, supported by internal opponents of reform, intervened militarily to cripple the Sejm, and the Second Partition, of 1793, by Prussia and Russia alone, doomed the Commonwealth altogether. The insurrection of 1794, led by Tadeusz Kościuszko, tried to oust the occupying forces and undo the 1793

Figure 1.1 Stanisław August Poniatowski (1732–98), last king of
Poland–Lithuania (1764–95), actively engaged in the debate on the reform of
Jewish society in the Polish–Lithuanian Commonwealth.
Copperplate engraving *c*.1765 by T[eofil Gottlob] J[akob] Marstall[er].
Biblioteka Narodowa w Warszawie, Zbiory Ikonograficzne, G. 10514
(zb. Czetwertyńskich)

partition, but by the end of the year the insurrectionary forces were forced to
surrender. In 1795 the three powers divided the lands between them, bringing the Polish–Lithuanian Commonwealth to an end.

A form of Polish statehood, and with it the project of social reform, was
reborn in 1807 when Napoleon, after his successful Prussian campaign,
formed the Duchy of Warsaw out of the territories that Prussia had gained in
the second and third partitions. The Duchy was enlarged in 1809 when after
a victorious war against Austria it regained West Galicia (Austria's share of

the third partition), as well as a small part of East Galicia, taken in 1772. But the Duchy, though nominally independent, remained Napoleon's creation and a French protectorate, upon which French legal institutions, notably the Code Napoléon, were imposed. Most significant for the Jews was Napoleon's infamous decree of March 1808, which made some of the rights that had been gained by the Jews of France in the French Revolution conditional on cultural and social integration.

The Duchy of Warsaw fell in 1813 after Napoleon's disastrous Russian campaign, and in 1815 the Congress of Vienna created a new, autonomous Polish state. This new Kingdom of Poland became the main stage on which the events discussed in this book were to be played out.[1]

Although the Kingdom was under Russian rule, the tsar was not an absolute ruler in Poland but merely a constitutional monarch; his powers were limited by prerogatives of the Sejm, the Administrative Council (i.e. the government), and the viceroy (*namiestnik królewski*), as well as by an independent judiciary. The Sejm's legislative power was limited to being able to reject laws submitted by the king or the viceroy, but it could bring ministers to a judiciary tribunal if they were deemed to be acting illegally; moreover, its members enjoyed immunity from prosecution, then a new and important principle in Europe. The government was wholly appointed by and accountable to the king, but the constitution was such that royal decrees did not become law until they had been countersigned by the responsible minister. The Kingdom of Poland, while not formally sovereign, thus had a large measure of independence. Within its territory (see Map 2) it was ruled by Polish institutions using Polish emblems of state; its inhabitants were Polish, not Russian, citizens, and they enjoyed considerable civic freedom. Besides having its own legislature and judiciary, the Kingdom also had its own schools, currency, and even army, so that its character was entirely Polish. Polish was the sole official language (correspondence with St Petersburg was in French), and state functionaries had to be citizens of the Kingdom.

This wide-ranging independence did not last long, however. Following the abortive November uprising in 1831, Tsar Nicholas I revoked the constitution, gradually restricted the competence of the Warsaw government, and transferred some of its functions to St Petersburg. This marked the end of the Kingdom's constitutional period (1815–30) and the start of its autonomous

[1] Brief introductions to the subject can be found in Ajnenkiel, Leśnodorski, and Rostocki, *Historia ustroju Polski (1764–1939)*; Kieniewicz, *Historia Polski 1795–1918*; and id. (ed.), *Polska XIX wieku*. Current attitudes and the present state of research are reflected in Chwalba, *Historia Polski 1795–1918*, 257–87, 319–84, and Zdrada, *Historia Polski 1795–1914*, 94–137, 293–322. Essential literature in English includes Wandycz, *The Lands of Partitioned Poland, 1795–1918*; Davies, *God's Playground*; and the classic study of Reddaway, Penson, Halecki, and Dyboski (eds.), *The Cambridge History of Poland*.

period (1831–64). When the January uprising of 1863–4 also failed, the Kingdom lost nearly all its remaining powers. Although it was never fully integrated with the Russian empire and retained a distinct legal and political status until the very end, its autonomous politics are rightly regarded as having ended in the aftermath of the January uprising.

Each political development in this tempestuous period provoked great public debate, and each time the question of the Jews' place in Polish society was raised anew. Reforms discussed during the Four Year Sejm were not implemented, mainly because of the collapse of the state, but discussion continued, albeit in a radically different form. The fall of the Commonwealth created a major turning-point in the debate, dividing it essentially into two stages, before and after 1795. Both when the Duchy of Warsaw was formed and again in the constitutional period of the Kingdom of Poland, the place and organization of Jewish society became a lively issue. The last of the great public discussions of that time, between 1818 and 1822, produced hundreds of pamphlets, treatises, newspaper articles, and a few literary works, which together form one of the richest documentary collections concerning the debate on the Jewish Question in nineteenth-century Europe.[2]

These were by no means merely abstract debates. They touched on basic questions about the whole of Polish–Lithuanian society, not only factors affecting the daily life of the Jews, and had a real impact on policy. In the final years of the Commonwealth and the first three decades of the nineteenth century, the leaders of the Polish Enlightenment had a decisive influence on the shape and direction of state policy, including of course its treatment of the Jewish Question. The reformers included prominent state officials, above all King Stanisław August, as well as eminent politicians and ideologues such as Stanisław Staszic, Hugo Kołłątaj, Julian Ursyn Niemcewicz, Stanisław Kostka Potocki, Adam Jerzy Czartoryski, Aleksander Linowski, Marcin Badeni, Wincenty Krasiński, Kajetan Koźmian, Józef Zajączek, Nikolai Novosiltseff, and Tadeusz Mostowski. Mid-level ministerial officials such as Gerard Witowski or Jan Alojzy Radomiński also influenced the debate. The proposals of these highly placed figures affected official ways of thinking, and some

[2] There is a good critical edition of the sources for the so-called Jewish Question during the Four Year Sejm in MDSC vol. vi, but not for the further stages of the debate. For the secondary literature on the main works on the Jewish Question during the Four Year Sejm see Gelber, 'Żydzi a zagadnienie reformy Żydów na Sejmie Czteroletnim'; Ringelblum, *Projekty i próby przewarstwienia Żydów w epoce stanisławowskiej*; Eisenbach, *Emancypacja Żydów*; Michalski, 'Sejmowe projekty reformy położenia ludności żydowskiej w Polsce'; Zienkowska, 'Citizens or Inhabitants?'; and Hundert, *Jews in Poland-Lithuania in the Eighteenth Century*, 211–31. The most important works on the debate and reforms of the constitutional period are Wishnitzer, 'Proekty reformy evreiskogo byta v Gertsogstve Varshavskom i Tsarstve Polskom'; Gelber, 'She'elat hayehudim bepolin'; id., 'Di yidn-frage in kongres-poyln'; Mahler, *Divrei yemei yisra'el*, v. 153–72; and id., *A History of Modern Jewry, 1780–1815*, 303–13.

eventually became law. These lively discussions and the projects that emerged from them thus decisively influenced both short-term policy and long-term strategy towards the Jewish population.

While state policy and strategy regarding Jewish society as a whole of course affected the hasidim too, would-be Polish reformers of Jewish society obviously wondered how the emerging hasidic movement would bear on their plans. The question was whether it would correspond to their ideas of a reformed Jewish society and could serve as an instrument of reform or what its influence on the process of reform might be.

1. The Framework of the Debate

What were the main assumptions and fundamental ideas that shaped Polish government policy towards the Jews? What did government circles expect of Jewish society, and in what direction did they intend to influence it? What was the time frame proposed for reform? These questions are not easy to answer, not only because those in authority and their subordinates offered few clear statements on these topics, but also because the rich body of writings that emerged from these debates has still not been properly studied in its entirety, and its fundamental ideas have thus not been coherently formulated. Although both Polish and Jewish historians have discussed the matter at great length, their work has rarely gone beyond reconstructing the facts. Research is somewhat more advanced only with regard to the period of the Four Year Sejm, and especially its political and social context. A further problem is that historians have tended to treat the Four Year Sejm, the Duchy of Warsaw, and the early years of the Kingdom of Poland as separate subjects, so that continuity of process and proportionality of elements have been lost.[3] This treatment is all the more surprising since in all three phases of the debate many of the participants were the same, and the legislative proposals in the Kingdom of Poland were largely based on those of 1788–92. The unfortunate consequence of this situation, however, is that our knowledge is only partial. We have relatively reliable knowledge of arguments, published drafts, and the society and politics of the period, but we know little about the nature of the reform plans themselves, their evolution, their primary goals, and above all about what, according to the reformers, the outcome was to be—in other words, what the reformed Jewish community was supposed to look like.

---

[3] The only two works which treat both phases of the 'Jewish debate', Eisenbach's *Emancypacja Żydów* and Mahler's *Divrei yemei yisra'el*, ignore their continuity, and the marked ideological tendency of both works limits their value. Moreover, Eisenbach's work focuses too strongly on the legal aspects of emancipation, while Mahler's discussion of the reforms of the Four Year Sejm is only superficial.

Our knowledge of the primary ideological divisions in these debates is equally unsatisfactory. Traditional historiography saw two camps on the Polish (Christian) side[4]—enlightened reformers, favourably disposed towards the Jews; and backward obscurantists who were hostile towards them—while among the Jews, the maskilim were held to favour reform while the traditionalists opposed it.[5] Historians have recently cast doubt on these black-and-white classifications, which say more about the ideology of the classifiers than about the phenomena they describe. In truth, very few Polish writers and politicians went so far as to reject Enlightenment rhetoric, and it is difficult to find anyone who did not pretend to the title of 'enlightened reformer', even if of a very conservative kind. On the other hand, the 'good reformers' were as harsh as the outright antisemites in their criticisms of the real and supposed faults of the Jewish community. The differences between them were often more technical than ideological: the former held that the Jews would reform themselves once they were granted rights; the latter wanted to grant them rights only once they had reformed themselves. Thus the difference did not concern their general diagnosis, nor the final goals of reform, nor their general ideological framework. Since Jewish views were equally not clear-cut, statements made on both sides of the Jewish debate, like the opinions of politicians in supposedly opposite camps, surprisingly often turn out to be identical. The traditional four-part schema made up of homogeneous groups is therefore misleading. There were, obviously, divisions and groups among those who drafted plans for the reform of the Polish state, but for a proper understanding of the situation it is more fruitful to identify the common elements in the thinking of the time than to focus on the differences.

2. Diagnosis

To understand the proposals of Polish reformers regarding the Jews we must first understand that the reformers' basic assumption was always that Jewish society was unhealthy and in need of fundamental change. It was held to have degenerated socially, economically, and even morally, primarily because of customs and beliefs that, 'under the guise of religion', had acquired the sanction of inviolable religious laws. In short, the reformers claimed that the evils they intended to cure were due to the corruption of Judaism itself. The differences of opinion were only over the causes of that lamentable state, and

---

[4] The use of the term 'Christian' to refer to all the non-Jewish participants in the debate, though technically correct, seems inappropriate, since the underlying tenor of the discussion defined the Jews as a 'nation', a 'people', or an ethno-religious group. I use the term 'Polish' to designate the non-Jewish participants in the debate but this isn't intended to imply that the Jewish participants weren't also Polish.

[5] See e.g. Gelber, 'She'elat hayehudim bepolin', 116; Mahler, *A History of Modern Jewry*, 304–6; Eisenbach, *Emancypacja Żydów*, 82–101.

how to change it. Some reformers, such as the liberal politicians Mateusz Butrymowicz, Tadeusz Czacki, and Walerian Łukasiński, felt that the degenerate condition of the Jews was the result of legal discrimination; others identified causes within the Jewish community itself, such as its educational system.

The conception of Jewish society as degenerate originated in part in long-established antisemitic prejudices that attributed all the supposed faults of the Jews, including their alleged practice of ritual murder, to Judaism itself.[6] But it seems wrong, or at least counterproductive, to accuse all the reformers of holding antisemitic views (even if some did), for at least two reasons. First, many of them strongly rejected such views, at least at the level of their conscious ideological decisions, and were highly critical of antisemitic publications.[7] Second, as I will claim throughout this study, it was not explicitly antisemitic opinions that influenced many of the reformers, but rather an 'antisemitic habitus'[8]—a set of automatic, subconscious ways of understanding reality and reacting to it that was culturally transmitted, and which manifested itself in everyday behaviour, in ways of thinking, and even in psychosomatic reactions. Instead of labelling all the reformers as antisemites, it seems more relevant to consider their critique of Judaism within the canon of lay Enlightenment thought, which strongly opposed all confessional influence on public life, and especially on the state. In the context of eighteenth-century Europe, this was, of course, above all a critique of Christianity, or more precisely, of the Christian churches' trespasses upon the Enlightenment concept of 'private religion'. But a logical consequence was the critique of other religions as well, and as many of the ideologues of the Enlightenment nursed strong anti-Jewish phobias (Voltaire is a particularly vivid example), Judaism of course became a target. To understand the intellectual framework of the Polish reformers' attitude to Judaism, one must bear in mind the general context of the European Enlightenment, with its critique of all public functions of religion.

Examples of such criticism were omnipresent in contemporary publications and public statements by liberal reformers in France, Austria, and Germany, as well as by maskilim in Germany, France, and later in Poland. The polemics of the French revolutionary statesman Henri Grégoire have often been mentioned, as have those of Christian Wilhelm von Dohm, who was influential in and beyond Germany. The most significant early

---

[6] The classic example is Chiarini, *Théorie du judaïsme*, modelled on the best-known early modern antisemitic treatise by Johann Eisenmenger. However, it was not only those writers who were widely considered to belong to the antisemitic camp who made use of antisemitic literature. For example, Niemcewicz, *Lejbe i Sióra*, refers extensively to 18th-c. German antisemitic literature. [7] See e.g. Czacki, *Rozprawa o Żydach i karaitach*.

[8] The term 'habitus' in this sense was introduced by Pierre Bourdieu, and is best summarized in his *Reproduction in Education, Society and Culture*.

implementation of the policies of enlightened absolutism towards the Jews was the Edict of Tolerance (*Toleranzpatent*) enacted by Emperor Joseph II of Austria.

The publications of the maskilim also played an important, and I believe underestimated, role. The eighteenth-century writings of Menahem Mendel Lefin and Jacques Calmanson in Poland serve as examples, as do works published outside Poland, including, for example, those of Zalkind Hurwicz or Solomon Maimon. In 1792 Lefin published draft legislation for the reform of Jewish society, to be put before the Four Year Sejm's Commission for the Discussion of Proposed Reforms of the Jews. Calmanson's work, first published in French in 1796, with a Polish version following in 1797 though prepared during the period of the Four Year Sejm, included a broad study of the beliefs and customs of the Polish Jews as well as a proposal for reform. These two texts, like many others, clearly articulated the belief that successful reform depended on ridding Judaism of its aberrations. Lefin saw Judaism as having two streams, the rationalist and the mystical. In his view, the former was best represented by the medieval philosopher Maimonides and the putative founder of the German Haskalah Moses Mendelssohn, while the contemporary incarnation of the latter movement was hasidism. The state should oppose the mystical stream with all its power, he held, since it represented the degeneration of a religion of reason based on the Talmud and was contrary to the basic tenets of Judaism.[9] Calmanson similarly saw hasidism as a problem; he argued that reform was necessary because of the existence of 'Jewish sects that have spread through former Poland'. Cleansing Judaism of the fanaticism of the hasidim, and especially of the Frankists (followers of the heterodoxical sect of Jacob Frank), would restore Jewish morals and customs to their original form, which according to the author resembled natural religion:

The part that to that point was only a strange mixture of superstitions and prejudices would soon incorporate in itself excellent and pure rites worthy of the Being above beings. Once the Jew was awakened from the errors that were blinding him, the errors in which gullibility had lulled him to sleep, henceforth he would see nothing more in the history of his religion than a chain of obligations in the nature of the very first ones, which on the one hand unite him with the Creator of all things, and on the other unite him with all the beings similar to him that have come forth from the very hands of the Creator.[10]

[9] [Lefin], 'Essai d'un plan de réforme'. See also Gelber, 'Żydzi a zagadnienie reformy Żydów', 331–4; id., 'Mendel lefin-satanover'; Mahler, *Divrei yemei yisra'el*, iv. 73–5, 266–8; Sinkoff, 'Strategy and Ruse in the Haskalah of Mendel Lefin of Satanow'; ead., *Out of the Shtetl*, 84–95; and van Luit, 'Hasidim, Mitnaggedim and the State in Lefin's *Essai*'.

[10] Calmanson, *Uwagi nad niniejszym stanem Żydów polskich*, 50. A shorter version appeared in French: see Calmanson, *Essai sur l'état actuel des Juifs de Pologne*.

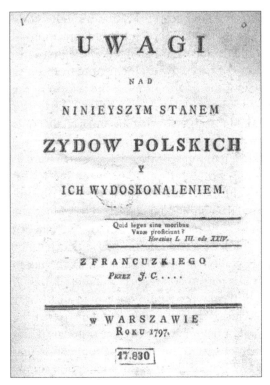

Figure 1.2 Title page of Jacques Calmanson, *Uwagi nad niniejszym stanem Żydów polskich y ich wydoskonaleniem* [Notes on the Present State of the Polish Jews and their Improvement] (Warsaw, 1797), an influential maskilic contribution to the debate on the state of Jewish society in eastern Europe that to a significant degree informed the early stages of the reforms of Jewish society in Prussian Poland and then in the Duchy of Warsaw. Zakład Narodowy im. Ossolińskich we Wrocławiu, XVIII.11612

It is difficult to substantiate the argument that the Polish reformers acquired their belief in the degeneration of the Jewish religion solely from the maskilim. The same assumption had been made many times in Enlightenment literature in France and Germany, where Jewish influence on the debate was almost non-existent. Nevertheless, the Jewish voices were very important to the Polish proponents of reform as the ultimate verification of their diagnosis: since the Jews themselves acknowledged that their community was in need of change, its deterioration must have been very advanced; and since the Jews themselves saw the sources of that deterioration in the degeneration of Judaism, then this diagnosis was surely correct.

But there was a fundamental difference between Polish and Jewish reformers. Calmanson and Lefin, following the example of other maskilim, defined precisely which elements of contemporary Judaism they considered part of the inviolable foundation of the true Jewish religion (which they termed 'Mosaic') and which beliefs and customs they saw as aberrant. For both men the religion based on the Bible and the Talmud (albeit read critically) was the true religion, and sectarianism, fanaticism, and mystical belief were deformations of it. Christian reformers accepted the differentiation between an inviolable, original core and later accretions that were therefore potentially subject to reform, but saw no need to accept the categorizations of the maskilim: they themselves would decide what belonged to the first category and what to the second. Mateusz Butrymowicz, the deputy from Pińsk to the Four Year Sejm who was one of the first to propose the reform of the Jews in Poland, wrote: 'The secular government can neither correct nor change religion, but it can and should distinguish what has incorrectly come under its rubric.' In the Judaism of the time Butrymowicz distinguished dogma, which was inviolable, from 'ceremonies, or their rites', which were to be modified. Among the 'ceremonies' to be reformed, he listed the Jewish festivals, the laws of *kashrut*, and the practice of resting on the sabbath. Butrymowicz proposed that a Sanhedrin should be convened to reduce the number of Jewish festivals, 'which were not so much about the observance of holy days as occasions for criminal idleness', and he proposed that Jews be permitted to eat non-kosher foods. Rabbis should also grant Jews serving in the military and Jewish public servants permission to carry out their duties on the sabbath.[11] Such reforms, in Butrymowicz's opinion, would in no way violate the principles of Judaism. Curiously, the author was able to list the Jewish 'ceremonies' that he felt did not belong to the essence of Judaism, but did not devote a single word to characterizing the inviolable foundation that supposedly was not subject to reform. It could be that this foundation simply was not the focus of his interest because it lay beyond the area of reform; but it seems likely, too, that his omission resulted from the basic ignorance that was so characteristic of proposals for reform. The most noteworthy point, though, is that Butrymowicz, like later reformers, did not bother to define the phenomena he described: he classified Jewish practices that he considered negative as mere 'ceremony' and therefore easy to change, with no actual understanding of their religious significance. Ultimately what mattered for such would-be reformers was not the significance of the customs to the Jews themselves, but rather their own stereotyped views of them. Around 1790 the author of an anonymous ephemeral printed pamphlet wrote:

> Away with Sabbot [*sic*], kosher, ignorance!
> Let's teach the idlers how to work.
>
> .   .   .   .
>
> Away with ritual and all superstition!
> Let them eat at the tables of Poles,
> Let them shave, wear Polish clothes.
> Improving their manners will cure much evil,
> And make a harmful people good for us.[12]

---

[11] Butrymowicz, 'Sposób uformowania Żydów polskich', 84–5; id., 'Reforma Żydów', 124–5.
[12] 'Zwierciadło polskie dla publiczności', 248.

The persistence of attempts to abolish *kashrut* (the social consequences of which were in no way commensurate with the attention it received) is explicable only when we understand that, according to Polish custom, refusal to share a common meal was a great insult. Although sharing a meal with a Jew was undoubtedly beyond the imagination of Butrymowicz and all the other Polish reformers, they must have felt personally insulted by the Jews' rejection of their (completely hypothetical) hospitality, all the more since the Jews were their social inferiors. The refusal to share meals thus violated both the Enlightenment concept of equality and the aristocratic concept of honour and social order.

The distinction between healthy and unhealthy elements of Jewish belief remained a persistent tenet of reformist ideas. Stanisław Kostka Potocki, a well-known liberal politician, Freemason, and anti-clericalist, was the minister of religious affairs and public enlightenment in the early years of the Kingdom, and as such his official duties included reforming the Jews. Justifying the Jewish policy of the European states, he wrote: 'The solicitude of today's governments for [the Jews] is not aimed at subverting their faith, but rather at the terrible and anti-social superstitions that they have incorporated into that faith.'[13]

But despite the apparent continuity between Butrymowicz's views and those of Potocki, a fundamental evolution had taken place, one which marked the transition of the debate into its second, post-partition stage. Where Butrymowicz distinguished between faith and practice, later reformers put the boundary between an even more abstract 'true religion' and morality. Reform proposals encompassed not only a change in custom, but also the reconstruction of the entire ethical system of the Jews. According to the reformers, contemporary Jewish ethics was based on religious separatism and hatred of Christians. This view was expressed most fully by Stanisław Staszic, an extremely influential ideologue, author, and politician, who was in effect the author of the 'Jewish policy' of the constitutional period.[14] Having spent several years studying in Paris, Staszic had an excellent knowledge of French Enlightenment literature, on which he drew extensively. Following Claude Fleury and his successors, Staszic accepted that the perfect Jewish religion of the biblical period had been damaged by the false influence of the Talmud,

---

[13] [Potocki], *Żyd nie żyd?*, 11–12. See also a similar opinion in AGAD, CWW 1418, p. 43; and in 'Dodatek z Prowincji'.

[14] Staszic's views on the Jewish question have not yet been analysed in detail, and most previous authors have used elements of his thought to promote their own ideology. Good examples are Kruszyński, *Stanisław Staszic a kwestia żydowska* (Staszic as a patron of anti-semitism); Leśniewski, *S. Staszic*, 325–8 (Staszic as a statesman troubled about the well-being of the Jewish people); and I. Lewin, 'Staszic a Żydzi', 49–56 (Staszic as an example of evolving antisemitism). An attempt to characterize Staszic's views objectively can be found in Eisenbach, *Emancypacja Żydów* (see the index for references); see also Szacka, *Stanisław Staszic*, 147–9.

Figure 1.3 Stanisław Kostka Potocki (1755–1821), a well-known liberal
politician, Freemason, and anti-clericalist, the minister of religious affairs and public
enlightenment in the early years of the Kingdom of Poland, and thus officially
responsible for the reform of the Jews. Woodcut by Wilhelm Berg (1877) from the
drawing of Miłosz Kotarbiński after the painting of Angelika Kauffmann, in
H. Skimborowicz and W. Gerson, *Willanów: Album Widoków i pamiątek oraz kopje
obrazów Galeryi Willanowskiéj* [Wilanów: Album of Views and Memorabilia, with
Copies of the Paintings from the Wilanów Gallery] (Warsaw, 1877). Biblioteka
Narodowa w Warszawie, Zbiory Ikonograficzne, A. 2876—table m.s. 94/95

which had nothing to do with the true Mosaic religion.[15] The differentiation
made here between good 'Mosaism', as Staszic termed it, and bad 'Judaism'
allowed for unlimited criticism of the latter:

We should say 'the Jewish religion' and not 'the Mosaic religion', because the
current belief of that population is not Mosaic; Moses did not give, and did not

[15] On Fleury's views and his influence on the 'Question juive' in France see Hertzberg, *The
French Enlightenment and the Jews*, 41–3, 253–8, 279.

know any Talmud, and he couldn't even have understood it. All of today's teaching of faith is based on the Talmud, and that is the main source of the damage . . . to Jewish morality. Moses speaks in his Books only of peoples who do not believe in God, who take the rivers, mountains, trees, and stones for gods; on the contrary, the religion of the talmudists, and thus of today's Jews, speaks of Christians, saying that Christians do not believe in God, that they are the godless idolaters about which Moses speaks in the Old Testament, and on which, after all, the entire Christian religion is grounded. With such a false though religious image of Christians, the morality of the Jews with regard to the Christians is false and harmful.[16]

Thus, according to Staszic, the Talmud was a source of Jewish separatism, anti-Christian prejudice, and dual morality. His argument that 'the religion of today's Jews must be cleansed of the Talmud', would in practice mean the rejection of the entire tradition of Judaism. Staszic's programme therefore called for the government to replace Judaism with a new religion, which he termed 'Mosaism', which was to be based closely on the Five Books of Moses but free of any talmudic influence, and to take steps to prevent it from becoming a basis for Jewish separatism and fanaticism, as he believed Judaism had been.

However absurd the idea of a religion created by the state seems today, Staszic was by no means alone in his thinking. In the 1820s the priest Luigi Chiarini, a professor at the University of Warsaw and a censor of Hebrew books, developed almost identical views. Soon the views of Staszic and Chiarini became the official policy of the Kingdom of Poland: in 1825, when the Jewish Committee (Komitet Starozakonnych, literally the Committee for the People of the Old Covenant) was created as a state institution to accomplish the task of Jewish reform,[17] these two men played a decisive role in it. Similar views were presented in literary form by the influential writer and radical politician Julian Ursyn Niemcewicz: a character in his *Lejbe i Sióra*, the first Polish novel on a Jewish theme, voiced the opinion that the Jewish people had forsaken the religion of Moses and 'drunk their fill of the wild superstitions of their fanatics'.[18]

Central to Staszic's criticism of Judaism was the assumption that talmudic beliefs were the source of Jewish separatism, and that this separatism in turn was the source of all the other negative social qualities of the Jews. The author repeatedly stated that religion could not give the Jewish people, or anyone else for that matter, the right to create institutions independent of the state; such institutions would serve autonomous goals that might not be in accordance with the intentions of the state. The new Jewish religion should

---

[16] AGAD, CWW 1418, pp. 16–18.
[17] There has not yet been a critical discussion of the activities of the Jewish Committee. From among older works, see Kandel, 'Komitet Starozakonnych', 85–103; Eisenbach, *Emancypacja Żydów*, 193–6, 258–60.   [18] Niemcewicz, *Lejbe i Sióra*, p. v.

Figure 1.4 Julian Ursyn Niemcewicz (1757/8–1841), one of the leading writers
and politicians of the Polish Enlightenment, who actively participated in the
Jewish debate during the period of the Duchy of Warsaw (1807–15) and the early
years of the Kingdom of Poland (1815–30). Portrait by Jacques François Llant
(1834); lithograph by François Le Villain. From J. Straszewicz, *Die Polen und die
Polinnen der Revolution von 29 November 1830* (Stuttgart, 1832–7), pl. 41.
Biblioteka Narodowa w Warszawie, Zbiory Ikonograficzne, A. 2927

therefore be a private religion in the strict sense of the word. Although the
ideologues of the Enlightenment proposed that all religions should have
private status, they regarded Judaism and Christian denominations as equal
only in a formal sense. Staszic asserted that since Jews would be able to join
any non-Jewish organization, the creation of such institutions as the *kahal*
(Jewish community board) or fraternal organizations from which Christians
were excluded should not be allowed. It did not occur to him that virtually all
organizations at the time refused Jews the right of membership; the assertion
that a Jew could join any non-Jewish organization, even after the reform, was
simply absurd. Imagine a Jew in a parish rosary circle! For Staszic a Christian
rosary circle was not an institution at all, whereas the Jewish equivalent—the
khevre tehilim, or association for the recitation of psalms—was something
negative. Thus it is difficult to speak of the equal treatment of the faiths.

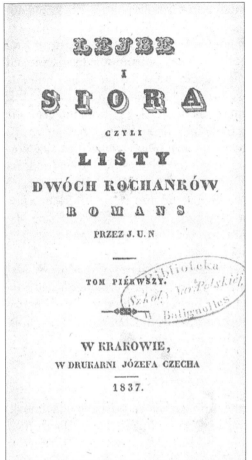

Figure 1.5 Title page of *Lejbe i Sióra*, the first Jewish novel in Poland, by Julian Ursyn Niemcewicz. Biblioteka Narodowa w Warszawie, I.38.027 (vol. i)

Staszic by no means failed to understand the realities of the day; quite the reverse. The problem was that, like most ideologues of the Enlightenment, he did not accept the existence in the state of institutions of a confessional character, and the Jews were the only estate (or quasi-estate) in the former Commonwealth whose separateness was defined by religion. The attack on Judaism was thus a criticism of estate forms of national organization. Beyond that, despite Staszic's undoubtedly strong dislike of Jews, we may suppose that his anti-talmudic tirades were not always in fact directed at the Talmud and the Jews. The harshness of his statements against the Jews may have had a compensatory function:[19] as a renegade priest known for his conflicts with

---

[19] The same was true of the writings of the enlightened men of France, where for various reasons it was not possible to direct that criticism against Catholicism. On this see Hertzberg, *The French Enlightenment and the Jews*, 283–4. It is very likely that Staszic was influenced by French literature.

the Catholic hierarchy and his distinctly anti-Catholic politics,[20] he could not allow himself openly to criticize the role of the Church in a state that was officially Catholic. (Even in the Kingdom of Poland, whose king, the tsar of Russia, professed Orthodoxy, Catholicism had a constitutionally guaranteed role as the state religion.) As a leading ideologist of the late Polish Enlightenment and a person of great public authority known for his stubbornness, Staszic did not have to worry too much about opposition from the Catholic Church, especially as despite being the established religion it had no formal secular power. However, as an active politician he was obliged to take into account potential reactions to his criticism of religious institutions and the religious foundations of the state structure. After all, his close associate Stanisław K. Potocki, an icon of the liberal and anti-clerical faction in the Polish Enlightenment, had lost a ministerial position for criticizing the Catholic Church too openly. Judaism thus became an easy target for Staszic, though not the only or even the primary one.

One way or another, Polish reformers from Butrymowicz to Staszic agreed that it was developments within Judaism that were the cause of the Jewish problem, hence the need for it to be 'returned to the original purity which had been darkened by the superstitions of the Talmud',[21] or even, in radical versions, replaced by a new 'Mosaic religion'.

3. The Goal

Just as the reformers' diagnosis of the problem was surprisingly unanimous, so was their goal: as generally formulated, it was to 'mould the Polish Jews into citizens useful to the country'.[22] This formulation was not as trite as it might seem. It was a set phrase that expressed the characteristic utilitarianism of the Enlightenment, but it also clearly showed that the reforms were meant to benefit the state and non-Jewish society rather than the Jews. Polish politicians were naturally concerned with the interests of their citizens, but why did the Jews themselves not count as citizens?

The rationalization was Jewish separatism—that is, the fact that the Jews rejected integration and strove for the consolidation of a quasi-governmental Jewish body politic. But it was really about something else as well. The separatism of which the Jews were accused resulted not only from the desire

---

[20] See e.g. Gliński, *Komisja Rządowa Wyznań Religijnych*, 41–2; Brodowska, 'Stanisław Staszic 1755–1826', 93–4; on Staszic's resignation from the priesthood, see Banaszak, 'Kapłaństwo Staszica'.   [21] APL, AmL 2158, p. 88.

[22] This formula appeared, among other places, in the title of a pamphlet by Butrymowicz: 'Sposób uformowania Żydów polskich', 78. See also Czacki, 'Refleksyje nad reformą Żydów', 206; 'Reforma Żydów', 216. A declaration typical of the time of the Kingdom of Poland is Łukasiński, *Uwagi pewnego oficera*, 8; see also Smoczyński, 'Krótki rys historyczny Żydów', 375.

to perpetuate the communal autonomy that they had long enjoyed on the Polish lands, but equally from the mentality of the Polish 'enlightened men', who treated the Jews as inferiors and had a more or less instrumental attitude towards them. The general view was that Jews were not natural subjects of the state. The reformers' essentially self-interested motives, of course, did not mean that Jews might not benefit as well, but that was not the primary aim. Any improvement in the lot of the Jews was to result from their integration as individuals into Polish society, so that the Jewish community would benefit from the reforms only to the extent that it ceased to be a Jewish community. The only politician to mention 'the happiness of the million [Jewish] people' was Scipione Piattoli, an Italian Catholic priest who was secretary to King Stanisław August and an enthusiastic advocate of the general reform of the Jews of Europe.[23]

At the other end of the spectrum stood those whose emphasis on the advantages for non-Jewish society was entirely one-sided, some of whom even expressed concern that improving the legal and educational situation of the Jews would merely allow them to exploit the Polish people more effectively. Such was the opinion of General Wincenty Krasiński, later a senator of the Kingdom of Poland, as well as of the ministerial official Gerard Witowski, both of whom were known for their animosity towards Jews.[24] In the debate over the founding of the Warsaw Rabbinical School in 1818, members of the Council of State agreed that caution was necessary so that the teaching would not strengthen a 'harmful corporation', and instead of improving the Jews would merely reinforce their ability to cheat good Christians.[25] Likewise, Marcin Badeni, an influential politician of the liberal camp, said in 1819 that 'in our case we should delay the civilization of the Jews, which could provide them with greater means for oppressing the people who are already so oppressed by them today. In carrying out or expanding civilization we must preserve the order that the civilization of Christians should be accelerated, and Jewish civilization should be delayed.'[26] Staszic went still further in advancing his particular 'anti-reform' programme. He wrote that Jews 'have a superior family arrangement, and they surpass us in the establishment of the authority of fathers and husbands and in the arrangement of marriages. . . . If we cannot in the present degree of our associations likewise change, improve, and perfect those elements in our

<hr>

[23] See e.g. Piattoli's letter to Stanisław Małachowski, 23 May 1792, *MDSC* 337. See also Zienkowska, 'Citizens or Inhabitants?', 45–52.

[24] See [Krasiński], *Aperçu sur les Juifs de Pologne*; [Witowski], *Sposób na Żydów*, 6. Krasiński was a Napoleonic general and the first president of the Senate of the Kingdom of Poland.

[25] AGAD, I Rada Stanu Królestwa Polskiego 436, p. 857. Tadeusz Mostowski, a minister of internal affairs, made a very similar statement in 1816: see Eisenbach, *Emancypacja Żydów*, 199.

[26] After Mycielski, *Marcin Badeni (1751–1824)*, 86.

Figure 1.6 Wincenty Krasiński (1782–1858), a Napoleonic general and later senator in the Kingdom of Poland known for his anti-Jewish bias, author of an important contribution to the Jewish debate, *Aperçu sur les Juifs de Pologne par un officier general polonois* (Warsaw, 1818). Lithograph portrait (first half of the nineteenth century). Biblioteka Narodowa w Warszawie, Zbiory Ikonograficzne, G. 10058 (zb. Czetwertyńskich)

nation, then we must try to weaken them among the Jewish race as well.'[27] In other words, since Poles could not better the Jews in certain of their virtues, and especially in an area as important as family life,[28] then those Jewish advantages should be eliminated. Even if such views were not widespread, they illustrate clearly the one-sided nature of the goal of the planned process.

Staszic and other Polish statesmen were worried about the Jews' 'superior family arrangement' not because of a general dislike of Jews but because they feared Jewish demographic expansion. This expansion was considered the main reason why the Jews had become a 'privileged estate', why they could maintain their separation, and why they had gradually achieved independence from the rest of society.[29] Staszic believed that an increase in the Jewish population would strengthen the development of self-sustaining institutions and encourage a growing independence from the rest of society. Radical critics, among them Niemcewicz, stirred public opinion with frightening talk of the 'Judaization' of the country or the transformation of Poland into 'Judaeo-Polonia'.[30]

[27] Staszic, 'O przyczynach szkodliwości żydów', 232; see also id., *Ród ludzki*, iii. 298–9.

[28] On the importance of the family in the social concepts of Stanisław Staszic see Kizwalter, *Kryzys Oświecenia*, 60–1.

[29] See e.g. Kołłątaj, *Listy anonima*, ii. 328, 329; *O srzodkach aby reforma Żydów w Polsce mogła bydź skuteczną*.

[30] The most influential text of this type is a satire by Julian Ursyn Niemcewicz, *Rok 3333*. Ludwik Janowski wrote in a similar vein: 'All the countries of the globe are the promised land for the children of Israel; so together with their growth in numbers, their dominance over the

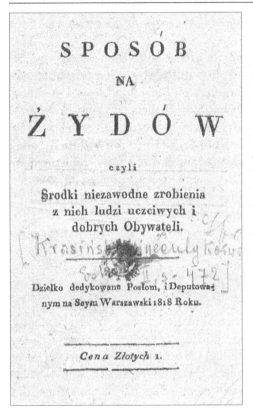

Figure 1.7 Title page of Gerard Witowski, *Sposób na Żydów* [How to Deal with the Jews] (Warsaw, 1818), one of the strongest antisemitic statements in the debate on the Jewish Question in the Kingdom of Poland in the years 1818–22. His radical anti-Enlightenment proposals aroused a massive negative reaction in the Jewish world. Biblioteka Narodowa w Warszawie, I.478.258

A still more radical opinion was voiced by the ministerial bureaucrat and sometime activist Gerard Witowski, who wrote in 1818 that since no reform would be possible, the Jews should be expelled from Poland.[31] Witowski's voice was among the first signs of frustration with a debate that had gone on for thirty years with little sign of progress, and similar frustration appears in other publications of the period. The way in which the debate dragged on led to ever more radical views and harsher criticism of the Jewish community, which was now accused of sabotaging reform.[32] The reactionary tendencies that followed the Congress of Vienna, particularly in the countries of the

whole world is approaching. Once the Jewish population equals or surpasses ours, then their time of liberation will come, then their mighty Kingdom will rise; then the God of Israel will give all the nations of the earth into their hands for destroying them, so that not a single man of the tribe of Esau survives.' [Janowski], *O Żydach i judaizmie*, 22–3. See also Staszic, 'O przyczynach szkodliwości żydów', 218, 247, and id., 'Uwagi nad projektem organizacji Żydów', AGAD, CWW 1418, pp. 9, 15 ('Eventually, will Jews turn into Poles or rather Poles into Jews?').

[31] [Witowski], *Sposób na Żydów*.

[32] See e.g. Moszko Jankiele [Julian Ursyn Niemcewicz], in *Pamiętnik Warszawski*, 1/3 (1815), 546–7.

Holy Alliance, no doubt also contributed to the growing conservatism of the Kingdom's opinion-makers.[33]

Nevertheless, such views were still an exception to the rule. Witowski's publication was countered by both Polish and Jewish activists, who vehemently rejected proposals for deportation as inhumane and absurd. A young liberal officer and writer, Walerian Łukasiński, challenged Witowski to provide even a single example of a country in which reforms had failed to bring about the desired results;[34] the reforms in Poland had not had the desired results, he said, merely because they had never been truly implemented. Stanisław Kostka Potocki also noted that in practical terms it would be easier to reform the quarter-million strong Jewish population of the Kingdom than to resettle them.[35] Throughout the period under discussion, the Enlightenment belief in the achievability and the usefulness of reform remained dominant.

4. Measures: What are 'Civil Christians'?

Polish advocates of the impending transformation of the Jewish community asserted that it should be industrious, obedient to the state, honest, clean, and, above all, identical to the surrounding Christian population in every way except for its religion. The sentiment was clearly and concisely expressed by Adam Jerzy Czartoryski, a scion of the most influential of the aristocratic families and a very influential politician himself. Commenting on draft legislation regarding the Jews in 1816, he characterized the goal of the proposed reforms as follows: 'to transform the Jews from useless and harmful members of society into good citizens attached to their country, to give them more light—namely, the morality that they lack; in a word, to make of them *civil Christians*, that is, people who for their neighbours, for the monarchy, and for the country, would acquire Christian sensibilities'.[36]

Other authors wrote of 'surrogate Christians', that is, Jews who 'in custom and lifestyle' would be identical to Christians.[37] But these declarations should not be interpreted, as they sometimes have been, as expressions of cryptomissionary aspirations. If eighteenth- or nineteenth-century politicians had believed that the aim of reform should be the mass conversion of the Jews, they would not have been shy of saying so.[38] And, indeed, a few of them did;

---

[33] See Kizwalter, *Kryzys Oświecenia*.

[34] Łukasiński, *Uwagi pewnego oficera*, 8–9.   [35] [Potocki], *Żyd nie żyd?*, 16.

[36] AGAD, CWW 1418, pp. 40–1. My emphasis. In an earlier publication, '"Civil Christians"', 54, I erroneously attributed this statement to Kajetan Koźmian, another important participant in the debate. I am grateful to Lidia Jerkiewicz for drawing my attention to this error.

[37] See e.g. [Witowski], *Sposób na Żydów*, 8; [Świtkowski], 'Uwagi względem reformy Żydów', 137.   [38] Michael Stanislawski correctly indicated this in his *Tsar Nicholas I and the Jews*, 46.

Figure 1.8 Woodcut of Kajetan Koźmian (1771–1856), a member of the
Council of State in the Kingdom of Poland and a well-known conservative writer of
the late Enlightenment involved in the debate on the reform of the Jews, among
other projects; author of an important memoir. Woodcut; from *Kłosy*, no. 609 (1877),
p. 129. Biblioteka Narodowa w Warszawie, Zbiory Ikonograficzne, G. 24981

but they were a small minority, and often inconsistent in their views.[39] Most
reformers did not equate reform with conversion. Although some supported
missionary efforts, they fought bitterly against linking that mission with
general plans for reforming the Jews. In that respect, Staszic is representative.[40] An example is his response to the prosecutor general, Józef Kalasanty
Szaniawski, during the aforementioned discussion on founding a rabbinical
school—a totally new system for creating rabbis. Opposing the creation of
such a school, Szaniawski remarked that since the Holy Alliance promoted
Christianity it seemed unfitting to establish a school that would strengthen
Judaism; to which Staszic, who on his part had called for 'preparing the
Jews for the civilization of Christian associations',[41] replied that the best way
to raise Jews' cultural level would be to educate their clergy. He added that
'although the spreading of Christianity is the tendency of the European powers, it is not their intention to force those who profess other religions to
accept Christianity'.[42] And it was Staszic, let us remember, who was most
influential in shaping the state's Jewish policy.

[39] See Eisenbach, *Emancypacja Żydów*, 181.
[40] See AGAD, I Rada Stanu Królestwa Polskiego 436, pp. 860–1; CWW 1418, p. 3.
[41] AGAD, CWW 1418, p. 3.   [42] AGAD, I Rada Stanu Królestwa Polskiego 436, pp. 860–1.

Figure 1.9 Adam Jerzy Czartoryski (1770–1861), scion of the most
influential Polish aristocratic family and himself a very influential politician.
Originally close to Tsar Alexander I and a follower of the pro-Russian faction in
Polish post-partition politics, during and after the anti-tsarist 1830–1 uprising he
became one of the leaders of the conservative camp of the Polish insurrectionist
movement. Mezzotint signed 'Peint par J[oseph] Abel Gravé à Vienne par
A[ndreas] Geiger 1799'. Biblioteka Narodowa w Warszawie, Zbiory
Ikonograficzne, G. 9735 (zb. Czetwertyńskich)

To a great extent, the aversion to missionizing was fired by an obsession
with the consequences of Frankism,[43] as the mass conversion of numerous
followers of Jacob Frank in 1759 had raised the spectre of a Fifth Column of
false converts bent on destroying Christian society. For the first time in
Polish history, the Jews were assigned the leading role in a conspiracy theory
of history, supplanting in this role the recently suppressed Jesuits.[44] Proposals
for the mass conversion of Jews were therefore decidedly unpopular.

[43] See e.g. 'List przyjaciela Polaka'; 'Dwór Franka'; 'Zwierciadło polskie dla publiczności',
254–5; 'Katechizm o Żydach i neofitach'; [Janowski], *O Żydach i judaizmie*, 20–8; [Krasiński],
Aperçu sur les Juifs de Pologne, 27–30; 'O Żydach w Polszcze'.

[44] See Tazbir, 'Conspiracy Theories'. Proposals to resolve the 'Jewish question' through mass
conversion had already become unpopular by the 1770s. See Goldberg, 'Changes in the Attitude of Polish Society', 56.

Within mainstream Enlightenment ideology, moreover, the concept of 'Christianity' had nothing at all to do with religion. Christianity was regarded as simply representing the best of all known forms of social organization and ethics, as well as the highest form of culture, and therefore the 'civil Christian' was the ideal being; that is, one who accepted the culture and morality of the Christian world without the unnecessary (and, in the opinion of the radicals, harmful) ballast of religious beliefs. The Jew, transformed into a 'civil Christian', was thus to be the ideal creature of enlightened reform and the ideal subject of the enlightened state.

As to details, it was agreed above all that this imagined, enlightened Jewish community would renounce the external markers of its separateness, take on Polish attire and the Polish language, and abandon its judicial and administrative separateness. There was even discussion of whether the rabbinate should be completely dismantled, or merely have its sphere of competence limited to strictly religious matters—yet another reflection of the typical ignorance of Jewish religious life and the complicated relationship between halakhah and everyday aspects of life. Likewise, there was the question of whether the *kahal* should be preserved, and if so, in what form. It was generally agreed, however, that the final result should be the dismantling of the corporate power of Jewish religious institutions that allowed Jewish society to be a 'state within the state'. Jews were also to accept the Polish educational system; be forbidden to produce or trade in alcohol; and be directed instead towards 'useful' activities. Likewise, *kashrut*, early marriage, and quick burial of the dead were to be prohibited, along with such conspicuous displays of wealth as the use of expensive fabrics. However, the reformers' prime objective was to force the Jews to accept not only Christian customs, but also Christian norms of morality, 'for as there is one God, there is only one morality'.[45] Of course, in the conception of enlightened men, Christian morality was the same as natural and universal morality. The Jew thus should not differ from his Christian neighbour in profession, language, attire, or even customs and morality. The only difference allowed was the difference in beliefs, on the condition, of course, that these beliefs (rather than a religion) would not require external expression, and would therefore remain strictly private.

5. What Does 'to Civilize' Mean?

All this sounds like a programme of total assimilation. This accusation has often been made against Polish reformers, particularly in nationalist-oriented Jewish historiography. It appears to be justified, since the Polish reformers stated their goal of 'remaking the Jews into Poles' repeatedly and

---

[45] AGAD, CWW 1418, p. 35.

without mincing their words, while liberal proposals to leave the Jews a certain margin of religious and cultural separateness were isolated and unpopular.⁴⁶ But it would be a mistake to write off the reformers' intentions as total assimilation, for at least two reasons. First, the very term 'assimilation' is not useful because it is loaded, and because it contains a value judgement, it blurs rather than clarifies the picture. Second, and more important, although the reformers did advance many concepts that are popularly put under the rubric of assimilation, they themselves did not use that term (as further discussed below), and nor does it properly describe their programme. In other words, they were proposing something other than mere assimilation.

In publications from the period of the Four Year Sejm, the terms used most often to describe the goals of the Enlightenment were 'reform', 'improvement', and sometimes 'refinement'. The term 'assimilation' did not appear, and in fact was generally unknown until the second half of the nineteenth century.⁴⁷ 'Reform' and 'improvement' were generally not loaded terms, and could signify any change in the situation of the Jewish community. But around 1815 a new term came into use, a term that was indicative of a fundamental change in the discussions about the Jews: that term was 'civilization', and it marked a transition into a second, post-partition stage of the debate.⁴⁸ At the turn of the century this concept was not strongly established in the Polish language and its meaning was still somewhat nebulous; its international career had begun only at the end of the eighteenth century, when it was borrowed from French public discourse. The term was still used so imprecisely that the meaning of the verb 'to civilize'—that is, to refine or to polish—often overlapped with the adjectives 'civil' and 'civic', the latter meaning 'of the citizenry' as opposed to 'clerical' or 'military'.⁴⁹ The concept of 'civil Christians' could thus include both 'secular Christians' and those who were 'civilized into Christians'.

Despite this lack of clarity the concept of 'civilization' soon became a permanent part of the public debate. 'Civilized' was usually taken to mean

---

⁴⁶ Two of the most important of these voices were Józef Pawlikowski (*Myśli polityczne dla Polski*, 101–15), and Walerian Łukasiński (*Uwagi pewnego oficera*). On Pawlikowski see Goldberg, 'Changes in the Attitude of Polish Society', 57.

⁴⁷ An exception was a pamphlet in French by Wincenty Krasiński, a Napoleonic general and the first president of the Senate of the Kingdom of Poland, who in 1818 used the term 'assimilation' in reference to the Jews—albeit, significantly, French Jews. See [Krasiński], *Aperçu sur les Juifs de Pologne*, 38.

⁴⁸ Here I must correct Artur Eisenbach, who believed that the term 'civilization' appeared in the debate as early as the period of the Four Year Sejm (Eisenbach, *Emancypacja Żydów*, 104–5). On the evolution of concepts related to the reform of the Jews in the Russian empire see Klier, *Imperial Russia's Jewish Question*, 66–83.

⁴⁹ See e.g. Wolfowicz, 'Więzień w Nieświeżu o potrzebie reformy Żydów', 142: 'The Jewish civilitas [*cywilność*], which is in essence a *status in statu*.' As an example of the multitude of meanings of the term at the beginning of the 19th c. see e.g. Linde, *Słownik języka polskiego*, i. 343.

'cultured', broadly conceived: the word 'culture' itself did not appear in Polish public debate until several decades later. The term was not, however, purely descriptive. 'Civilization' implied the essential concepts of progress and the hierarchy of various civilizations, so it involved a clear value judgement. 'To civilize' meant to raise from a demeaning state of barbarism and cultural primitivism to a superior, and above all more modern, culture of a higher level; 'civilization' was 'modern and progressive culture'.[50] At the top of the hierarchy was of course the enlightened civilization of western Europe, synonymous with 'Christian civilization', which was to be imitated, though not necessarily in the religious sense. Arguments over civilization and civilizing progress were not, of course, exclusive to the Jewish debate in Poland. Such debates have taken place and continue to take place today in many countries that are subject to the influence of Western society (especially American cultural imperialism). Indeed, at the beginning of the nineteenth century in Poland, the major debate on 'civilization' was primarily about Poles and other segments of Christian society, not about the Jews. Polish politicians and ideologues debated 'civilizing' the broad masses of the population, especially in the villages, through education. Staszic became famous for his experiments at 'civilizing' his own private town of Hrubieszów, through socio-economic and political reforms.

Debate on 'civilizing' the Jews thus fell well within the general framework of Polish and European conceptions of the Enlightenment, but the far-reaching consequences for the Jews were very different. While the Polish population (regardless of its social stratification), once 'civilized', would still be culturally Polish, though at a higher cultural level, 'civilizing' the Jews would render them an indistinguishable part of another people. Paraphrasing a famous statement of the Russian maskil Judah Leib Gordon, who advised his fellow Jews 'to be a Jew at home and a human being in the street', one can say that the Polish reformers sought to make them into Jews at home and Poles, instead of human beings, in the street.

The concept of the 'civilizing of the Jewish people' emphasized that, despite its delay in this area, Poland was and always had been part of the civilization of the West, while the Jews remained outside that civilization and at a lower level of development. In part, aside from its obvious compensatory function, the reflexive scapegoating of the Jews, albeit represented as an 'enlightened' programme of 'reform', excused the difficulties of Polish society as a whole, which was forced to struggle with such wild and backward bodies within. This was clearly expressed in a language of symbolic violence,

---

[50] A discussion of the changing conceptions of the term can be found in Jedlicki, *Jakiej cywilizacji Polacy potrzebują*, 27–8, 34–5, and Serejski, 'Początki i dzieje słów "kultura" i "cywilizacja" w Polsce'.

i.e. one that by misrepresenting reality created power relations reaffirming the domination of the hegemonic party, in this case the superiority of Polish high culture over 'uncivilized' Jewish society. As we shall see, the use of symbolic violence was one of the most persistent characteristics of the paternalistic language of reformers in their relation to the reformed Jewish society, including hasidism.

It seems to have been Staszic who injected the concept of 'civilizing' into the Jewish debate: he often wrote about 'the civilization of Christian associations' (that is, of the social organizations of Christian societies), as well as about the soothing and enlightening effects of 'civilization'.[51] The concept soon became widespread and, I believe, is the best indicator of the character that the Jewish debate assumed in the period after 1795. The appearance of the 'civilizing' concept in this period was no coincidence. Since the Four Year Sejm took on the task of state reform, reform proposals naturally centred on state and society. The fall of the Commonwealth in 1795 and the violent political changes that followed led to the general reformulation of the conceptual categories of public discourse. In place of the state and 'the political nation', the nation as defined by its spirit and culture became the primary category in Polish literature. Society became a rather nebulous concept, grounded more in the cultural life of the nation than in state structures.[52] Of course the concept of 'nation' was still an open category, much closer to a community of culture than of blood; in this sense, early nineteenth-century conceptions of nation were more connected to the old Enlightenment conception of society than to the views of the nationalists at the end of that century. Nevertheless, the change that took place at the start of the nineteenth century in the categories used to describe the world was radical and widely felt. This was why after 1795 the old assumption that the Jews needed to become 'citizens useful to the country' gave way to an insistence that they 'become civilized'; that is, they were to cast off the outdated Jewish culture and to accept without reservation the higher, 'modern' Polish culture. Polish reformers assumed that the Jewish world, marked by its own language, morality, customs, forms of social organization, and cultural life, was primitive and therefore destined to give way to the enlightened culture of Europe. But as long as this backward Jewish society existed alongside Polish

---

[51] See e.g. AGAD, CWW 1418, pp. 3, 5; Staszic, 'O przyczynach szkodliwości Żydów', 217, 231, 234, 236–7, 243. On Staszic's conception of civilizing see Serejski, 'Początki i dzieje słów "kultura" i "cywilizacja" w Polsce', 240–1. It should be added here that the term had also appeared sporadically in other publications before it was introduced into the debate by Staszic. See e.g. Czacki, *Rozprawa o Żydach i karaitach*, 222. I am grateful to Lidia Jerkiewicz for this reference.

[52] On the evolution of the concept of state and society in Polish discourse in this period see A. Walicki, *Philosophy and Romantic Nationalism*, 64–85, and Jedlicki, *Jakiej cywilizacji Polacy potrzebują*, 26–7, 37.

society it was also delaying the civilization of Polish society as a whole; so that the only way that Jews could become 'citizens useful to the country' was to renounce Jewish culture and accept Polish culture. In a manner typical of cultural imperialism, the alleged cultural inferiority of the Jews was used to justify the use of every kind of coercion against them: the proposed actions were in Kajetan Koźmian's words 'only seemingly harsh for the Jews, and in reality will be most beneficial for them'.[53] In other words, the total linguistic, cultural, structural, and national assimilation that the reformers proposed to impose on the Jews would rescue them from their primitive state. Character-istically, this view gained ground in Polish public opinion precisely at the time of an analogous debate within Polish society over replacing tradi-tional patterns of behaviour and social organization with imported Western models.

In one way or another, the need to 'civilize' the Jews became the reform-ers' main thrust after 1795, and especially after 1815, so the proposals for reform put forward in this period were focused on this concept. The pro-posals called for the Hebrew and Yiddish languages to be abandoned; a ban on the publication and distribution of books promoting traditional rabbinical culture; support for publications in Polish promoting Polish culture; support for secular education; and the promotion of norms of behaviour character-istic of the Christian majority.

The most complete proposal for reform was prepared by the Jewish Committee, a state institution established in 1825 precisely for the purpose of 'civilizing the Jewish people'. The committee perfectly illustrated the government's 'civilizing' policy in the constitutional period. Luigi Chiarini, the prominent ideologue of nineteenth-century antisemitism who chaired the committee, gave its proposals their final shape,[54] but the especially radical character of Chiarini's antisemitism should not lead us to conclude that the committee's draft proposals were unrepresentative of general opinion among the reformers. Quite the contrary: even if Chiarini's proposals and rhetoric were more extreme, they were still in principle within the Enlightenment mainstream of the debate on the reform of the Jews. One might even say that his main contribution to the development of the 'rationalist' antisemitism of the nineteenth century was precisely that he took Enlightenment reform proposals to their extreme. Thus the committee was representative of the direction in which the debate developed, precisely because of the persistent antisemitic undercurrent in all its activities.[55]

[53] AGAD, CWW 1418, p. 71.
[54] On Chiarini see Ages, 'Luigi Chiarini: A Case Study in Intellectual Anti-Semitism'; Raskin, *Ks. profesor Alojzy Ludwik Chiarini w Warszawie*.
[55] It should be noted, however, that the relationship between the committee's policy and Chiarini's views was highly complex. First, Chiarini was not the only creator of the committee's

According to the committee's recommendations, the reform was to be divided into two stages, a concept probably derived from the early Polish maskil Jacques Calmanson, who had proposed very similar stages.[56] The goal of the first stage was to limit the dangers that Jews posed to a Christian society, while the second stage involved radical moral and cultural reform. The basic instruments of reform were to be (*a*) a school for Progressive rabbis, and elementary schools for Jewish children that followed a regular curriculum rather than that of the traditional *ḥeder* but nevertheless offered some an element of Jewish education; (*b*) a moral treatise, to be drawn up by leading Jewish figures, which would draw on quotations from Jewish religious texts to bring the Jews closer to Christian 'pure morality'; (*c*) a translation of the Talmud into French, the idea being that when the ridiculous notions of the Talmud were accessible to wider society throughout Europe, Jews would simply be shamed into accepting reform; (*d*) a course on ancient Hebrew history to be taught at Warsaw University in order to educate Christian specialists in the field of Jewish culture, thereby permitting development of a cadre of knowledgeable advisers with an impartiality that Jews could never have; (*e*) the establishment of a committee for the censorship of Hebrew and Yiddish books and periodicals alongside a single authorized Jewish publishing house whose publications would support the cause of propagating the moral reform of the Jews.

Many of the planned institutions did in fact come into being. The most famous of these, the Warsaw Rabbinical School, was established the following year, 1826 (its creation had already been approved in 1818), because education of a new spiritual leadership was considered a high priority: 'In the history of virtually all nations we see that the true and godly education and the civilizing that made the people happy occurred only after the priesthood itself took up the task of study and became more enlightened.'[57] Chiarini personally chaired the Department of Hebrew Antiquities at the university and began the translation of the Babylonian Talmud into French (taking care, above all, to extract personal financial gain from this enormous project).

policy, and Haskalah circles were consulted on many of the committee's proposals. Beyond this, on many points the committee's proposals expressed the views not just of Chiarini but also of Staszic and other reformers, some of them far from outright antisemitic, such as those of Jan Alojzy Radomiński or Stefan Witwicki.

[56] See Calmanson, *Uwagi nad niniejszym stanem Żydów polskich*, 37–53. Notwithstanding these similarities, one should note the very important distinction that Haskalah was concerned with improving the condition of the Jews whereas the Poles were concerned with improving the condition of the Poles; the Haskalah viewed many aspects of Jewish tradition as outdated and harmful to the Jews; the Poles viewed Jewish tradition as a whole as harmful to the Poles. For a comparative analysis of the Polish and Jewish proposals for reform, see Wodziński, '"Civil Christians": Debates on the Reform of the Jews in Poland'.

[57] AGAD, CWW 1444, p. 14.

The Censorship Committee was officially founded in 1822 (but had in fact existed since the establishment of the Kingdom of Poland). Preparation of the treatise on morality was to be entrusted to Abraham Stern, the most famous of the Polish maskilim; when he refused, the task was given to Abraham Buchner, a teacher of Hebrew and Bible at the new rabbinical school, consultant to the Government Commission for the Religious Denominations and Public Enlightenment, and a prolific, albeit controversial, Haskalah author.[58] Secular elementary schools for Jewish children came into existence in 1820. The government actively promoted the publication of works in Polish at least as early as the beginning of the 1820s, when government agencies ordered the publication of catechisms for the Jewish faith and prayer books and textbooks for Jewish schools.[59] Another important element of the government's educational plan was sponsoring *Dostrzegacz Nadwiślański / Der Beobachter an der Weichsel*, a fortnightly periodical first published in 1823 with one column in Polish and another in German written in Hebrew characters (in later issues, Yiddish); the publisher was Antoni Eisenbaum, and for a long time it remained the only Jewish newspaper to have been published in eastern Europe, though publication ceased in 1824, less than a year after it had started. The censorship of Hebrew books, another aspect of the government's activities, involved supervision both of current publishing activities, thereby limiting the publication of certain types of rabbinic literature (particularly mystical tracts), and of public and private Jewish libraries. As a result, thousands of books considered contrary to 'the civilized spirit of European societies' were taken out of circulation.[60] At the same time, however, the Kingdom of Poland became one of the leading centres of Haskalah publication, luring authors primarily from Russia, where printing Haskalah literature was much more difficult.[61]

The Jewish Committee and the institutions associated with it thus constituted the first serious attempt to realize the initiatives of the reform programme in its radical form for 'civilizing' the Jewish people. This seems to have been the fullest possible expression of the 'civilizing' tendency of the Polish authorities, and the final proof of their intentions. The committee was active for less than four years, but its achievements were the clearest

[58] Buchner, *Katechizm religijno-moralny dla Izraelitów*. This treatise has never been analysed. More on Buchner in Mahler, *Hasidism and the Jewish Enlightenment*, 214–18, 239–42, 322, and Wodziński, 'Good Maskilim and Bad Assimilationists'.

[59] A complete list of Jewish textbooks from the years 1817–64 can be found in Shatzky, *Yidishe bildungs-politik in poyln*, 224–8.

[60] Typical incidents, with the attendant investigations, took place, for example, in Będzin in 1842–3 (AGAD, CWW 1481, pp. 236–418). See also reports of similar actions in AGAD, CWW 1463, pp. 262–96.

[61] Werses, 'Hasifrut ha'ivrit bepolin', 163. On the readership of Haskalah writings in the Kingdom of Poland see Zalkin, 'Hahaskalah hayehudit bepolin', 408–9.

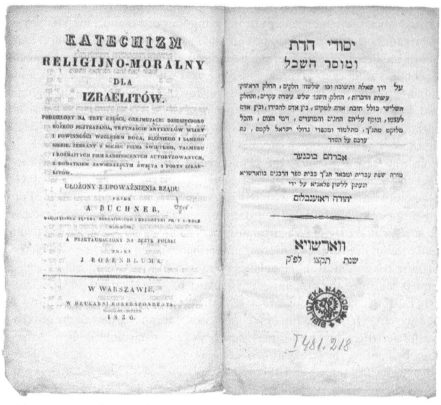

Figure 1.10 Title page of *Katechizm religijno-moralny dla Izraelitów—Yesodei hadat umusar hasekhel* [A Religious and Moral Catechism for the Israelites] (Warsaw, 1836), by Abraham Buchner (1789–1869), a teacher of Hebrew and Bible at the Warsaw Rabbinical School, a consultant for the educational authorities, and a prolific, albeit very controversial, Haskalah writer. Biblioteka Narodowa w Warszawie, I.481.218

expression of the changing political context that was to characterize the next decade. During the anti-tsarist uprising of 1830–1 the committee was suspended. It was reinstated after the defeat of the uprising, but its role was rapidly reduced. After 1834 it was active only sporadically, and in 1837 it was finally dissolved.[62] The new authorities, directly controlled from St Petersburg, now embarked on a new Jewish policy that was no longer intended to 'civilize' the Jews, let alone 'civilize' them to conform to Polish culture. After 1831 the politics of the authorities of the Kingdom of Poland no longer reflected the presuppositions of Polish political thought: policies were now

[62] AGAD, I Rada Stanu Królestwa Polskiego 285. A discussion of the basic elements of the committee's plan and the reasons for its failure are located in AGAD, Sekretariat Stanu Królestwa Polskiego 199, fos. 64–187. See also Szmulewicz, *Dzieje Komitetu Starozakonnych w Warszawie 1825–1837*.

formulated not in Warsaw but in St Petersburg and were not formulated with a view to achieving the strategic goals of the Polish political environment. The loss of partial sovereignty after 1831 thus effectively brought to an end Poland's deliberations on the Jewish Question. The 'civilizing' concept remained a prominent debating point, but it lost all political significance.

6. Conclusions

Many Polish reformers envisaged that Polish Jews should become 'civil Christians', that is, distinct from their Polish Christian neighbours only in their private religious beliefs. The proposed new 'Mosaic' religion was to be essentially devoid of religious ritual and with a minimum of institutional structures; supra-local bodies were unthinkable. This was a state-sponsored campaign to purge Judaism of its content so as to facilitate the reform of Jewish society.

This vision of 'reform' was the result of a development that had begun long before, in the Four Year Sejm of the 1780s, though at that time it was oriented towards social rather than cultural reform. The fall of the Commonwealth brought radical change to that concept.

At the beginning of the nineteenth century a new and essential element entered the debate, namely the concept of 'civilization'. According to this concept, the Jews, like other underprivileged groups such as the peasants and burghers, were held to exist at a lower cultural level than the nobility, and so needed to be 'civilized'. The concept soon completely redefined the entire Jewish debate, and the goal of 'civilizing' totally replaced reform. The Jewish Committee expressed that aim clearly even in its first report, in 1826:

The only way to accomplish a thorough and lasting reform of the Jewish people is through the spread of pure moral and religious enlightenment . . . All mechanisms and regulations, though they may be correct in and of themselves, will not bring lasting benefit, because, acting only on the ill effects, they cannot destroy the nucleus itself . . . Given this state of affairs, we must think not of the organization of the Jews, but above all of their radical improvement.[63]

Traditional historiography has correctly found that the demand for the Jews to 'civilize themselves' eventually became a useful justification for perpetuating the disadvantageous political and legal position of the Jewish population and the existing social order.[64] This report provides a good example of this

---

[63] AGAD, I Rada Stanu Królestwa Polskiego 285, pp. 18–19.
[64] See e.g. Mahler, *Hasidism and the Jewish Enlightenment*, 1755–88, and Eisenbach, *Emancypacja Żydów*, 316–31. Views of this type were particularly strongly articulated in the works of lesser historians—for example Kandel, 'Żydzi w Królestwie Polskim po 1831 r.'; Warszawski, 'Yidn in kongres-poyln (1815–1831)'.

tendency. The committee saw no need to introduce correcting 'mechanisms and regulations' or to consider the organization of the Jews; rather, it urged that work should be done for their moral improvement. Of course, moral improvement was supposed to lead eventually to civic improvement, at least as the liberals saw it. Nonetheless, with the emphasis on moral reform the prospect of change in the civic status of the Jews, and of other non-conformist social groups, became very vague and distant.

It seems, however, that the ill will of the ruling circles and their acolytes towards Jews cannot explain everything. First of all, plans for legal reform were generally abandoned only after 1831, when matters had in any case been taken out of Polish hands. Second, this process had a more general character. It did not concern the Jews alone; it went on, through various phases, for half a century; and it was not only plans for political reform that were abandoned. As the political discourse evolved, the concepts of the Four Year Sejm and the political writings of that period became increasingly outdated. In the public debate of the late Enlightenment, after the fall of the Polish–Lithuanian Commonwealth, the emphasis shifted ever more clearly from state and society to culture and nation, and state concerns became subordinate to cultural ones. This shift became ever more readily apparent after 1815, as Romantic literature accelerated the maturation of the modern concept of nation. The alienation of the nation from the state became increasingly obvious. Many bureaucrats active in the administration of the Kingdom of Poland did not identify with the state that they ran, and in social perception the gap between state and nation steadily widened. This tendency was manifest even in the Kingdom's early years and even among politicians who were enthusiastic about the new state, and it deepened with each political crisis. A natural consequence was that plans to integrate the Jewish community into state institutions were abandoned, while initiatives to bring the community closer to 'Polishness', the Polish nation, and society conceived of as a 'community of Polish culture' were cultivated. The reform thus lost its political and legal character and became increasingly a matter of identity and culture.

This fundamental conceptual shift and the resulting reorientation of projects for Jewish reform had an important influence on the development of policies towards the hasidic movement. The actions of the Polish authorities towards the hasidim in the Duchy of Warsaw and then the Kingdom of Poland were not only shaped by the state's general appraisal of the movement's potential harm or benefit to Poland, or of the possibilities of making the hasidim into 'citizens beneficial to the country'; it also scrutinized their capacity to become 'civilized', and even made it the primary object of scrutiny. That meant deciding whether they could be induced to reject Jewish culture, which the authorities perceived as inferior, in favour of European culture, preferably in its Polish version. As we can infer, this consideration became fundamental in shaping the relations between the Kingdom of Poland and the hasidic movement, especially before 1830. This chapter has outlined the ideas that shaped policy, but as we shall see in the next three chapters, the link between ideas and action was far more complicated.

CHAPTER TWO

Origins: Controversies over Hasidic Shtiblekh

THE PROMINENCE of the Jewish Question in the political debates of the last years of the Commonwealth, as well as in the later journalism of the Duchy of Warsaw and the Kingdom of Poland, does not mean that there was a similarly lively interest in hasidim; quite the opposite, in fact. The main reason was that, when the debate was crystallizing in the 1780s and 1790s, hasidim were still few in number in central Poland and not yet politically active. The reason for the development will be considered in detail later, but by way of introduction it seems relevant here to offer a brief characterization of the origins of what was later to become a significant movement.

The cradle of Polish hasidism (from the Hebrew *ḥasid*, meaning 'pious') was Podolia and Volhynia, the south-eastern borderlands of the Polish–Lithuanian Commonwealth, where from the 1740s to 1760 the putative creator of the group, Israel ben Eliezer (*c.*1700–60), also known as the Besht (an acronym of Ba'al Shem Tov, or Master of the Good Name) was active. This group, whose members came to be known colloquially as hasidim, emerged from and coexisted with other, similar, Jewish mystical groups that had arisen earlier, and was often confused with them. Like other Jewish mystical groups of this period, the hasidim borrowed abundantly from Lurianic kabbalah. The elements that fundamentally distinguished them from related groups were a decidedly anti-ascetic attitude and an interest in the broad propagation of mystical ideals and practices. Particularly important were the ideas of *devekut*, or cleaving to God (*unio mystica*), and of *tikun olam*, or each person's responsibility to do good deeds that have the divine power to 'repair the universe'. Though one anti-hasidic critic wrote that the 'sickly bud' of hasidism did not promise to develop well, the doctrinal base and organizational success of hasidism began to take shape as early as the 1770s. Supporters of this new form of religiosity acquired more and more followers in Red Ruthenia, Ukraine, and the Grand Duchy of Lithuania, as well as in central Poland—in other words, in almost all the territory of the old Polish–Lithuanian Commonwealth.

The traditional historiography accepts that this group (certainly not yet a movement) originated in central Poland with the activities of Samuel Shmelke Horowitz of Nikolsburg, who remained one of the distinguished hasidic leaders of his generation and served as the rabbi of Ryczywół from around 1750 to 1766 (in some versions, until 1761).[1] But speculation about a hasidic centre in Ryczywół has little basis, since it is not certain that Shmelke had become a student of Dov Ber, the Maggid of Międzyrzec Korecki (Mezhirech)—the second of the great teachers of hasidism—before Shmelke transferred to Sieniawa in eastern Poland in 1766.[2] There is somewhat better information about Shmelke's students, especially Levi Isaac, the 'tsadik of Berdyczów (Berdichev)', who worked in central Poland from 1772 to 1785 as the rabbi of Żelechów. The known public activities of Levi Isaac, as well as his later influence on hasidism in Żelechów at the end of the eighteenth century and the early decades of the nineteenth century, allow us to conjecture that this small town had already become a centre of hasidic activity during Levi Isaac's time, though defining its scale is completely impossible. There is also information about other supporters of hasidism in central Poland in the 1770s and 1780s. Better known are Rabbi Aron of Opatów, publisher of the first short collection of works attributed to the Besht; the tsadik Abraham Joshua Heschel; and Rabbi Ariel, active in Nowy Dwór. Still more numerous references confirm the presence of hasidim in central Poland in the 1790s. Literature on the beginnings of hasidism includes many combinations of hasidic leaders and locations, but such references do not necessarily support the conclusion that *concentrations* of hasidim existed in those locations. A good example is the supposed 'hasidic centre' in Praga near Warsaw in 1781, well known in the literature. The only evidence of such a centre is a letter from Abraham Katzenellenbogen, the rabbi of Brześć Litewski (Brest Litovsk), to the tsadik Levi Isaac of Berdyczów, which recalls a dispute between them in the Praga synagogue in 1781, to which 'members of the sect' listened. Ignacy Schiper, and other historians after him, concluded that a

---

[1] On the beginnings of hasidism in central Poland see Schiper, *Przyczynki do dziejów chasydyzmu w Polsce*, 19–73; Rubinstein, 'Reshitah shel haḥasidut bepolin hamerkazit'; and T. M. Rabinowicz, *Bein peshisḥa lelublin*, 23–100; see also Dynner, '*Men of Silk*', 25–53.

[2] Mordecai Wilensky (*Ḥasidim umitnagedim*, i. 84), and other historians after him, assume that Shmelke became a hasid in his youth. Hasidic hagiography, however, does not mention that Shmelke had any contact with the Besht, the putative founder of hasidism, though it delves into legendary instances of Shmelke's father, Tsevi Hirsch of Czortków, encountering him. Thus it seems reasonable to assume that the hasidic sympathies of Shmelke emerged only after the Besht had died in 1760. On Shmelke, see T. M. Rabinowicz, *Bein peshisḥa lelublin*, 21–46; Biladi, 'Toledotav shel tsadik'. It should also be remembered that Dov Ber of Międzyrzec acquired the position of unchallenged leader among the hasidim only around 1766, so it is not obvious that there was any earlier contact between Dov Ber and Shmelke seeking hasidic advice. See Rapoport-Albert, 'Hasidism after 1772', 94–101.

significant group of hasidim[3] must have existed in Praga, though the letter does not say that the listeners were from Praga, or that they were more than a handful.

There is more credible evidence of hasidim around the start of the nineteenth century, when relatively numerous and influential hasidic leaders appeared in Kozienice, Lelów, Przysucha (Pshiskha), Chełm, Wieniawa, and Lublin. Their well-documented activities suggest that the followers who gathered around them created the first centres in which hasidism achieved significant social influence. This does not mean, of course, that hasidism had become a mass movement by the turn of the century, or even that it was yet a movement at all. Quite the contrary: as the integrationist Daniel Neufeld later wrote, hasidism was still only a 'curiosity' (*dziwowisko*); the structures and institutions of the hasidic social movement were still in their infancy.[4] Still, the pilgrimage sites that grew around the tsadikim, and their concentration in certain areas (particularly the lands of the 1795 Austrian Partition) permit the conclusion that by the early nineteenth century there were already centres in which hasidim played a significant and sometimes even a decisive role in the community's social life. This does not mean that they constituted a majority of the local population.

Somewhat later sources, from the 1820s, tell of pilgrimages of 500 or 600 people to the most popular hasidic centres during the High Holy Days.[5] Twenty years earlier there would no doubt have been significantly fewer; even so, we can conclude that the hasidic movement was already off to an excellent start when the turbulent transformations caused by the Napoleonic Wars created fertile soil for its further growth. When the Kingdom of Poland was created in 1815, supporters of hasidism certainly made up less than 10 per cent of its Jewish population, but they were an established and growing social force.

1. Before the Kingdom of Poland

Hasidism did not interest either the administration or the press of the Polish–Lithuanian Commonwealth until the beginning of the 1790s. The first and only voice to speak of hasidism during the period of the Four Year Sejm—half a century after the Ba'al Shem Tov began to be active—was a famous pamph-

---

[3] This information first appears in Dubnow, *Geschichte des Chassidismus*, i. 246–7. On the 'hasidic centre' in Praga near Warsaw see e.g. Schiper, *Przyczynki do dziejów chasydyzmu w Polsce*, 24; T. M. Rabinowicz, *Bein peshisha lelublin*, 99; Dynner, *'Men of Silk'*, 95–6.

[4] The issue of the numerical strength of hasidism in the Kingdom of Poland in the first half of the 19th c. is discussed in Wodziński, 'How Many *Hasidim* Were There in Congress Poland?'.

[5] Majmon, 'Luźne kartki'; AGAD, KRSW 6635, fos. 16–17; see also Mahler, *Haḥasidut vehahaskalah*, 495–7.

let by a maskil from Podolia, Menahem Mendel Lefin of Satanów.[6] Lefin made hasidism the main target of his campaign to reform the Polish Jews, encouraged the government to fight energetically against the supporters of hasidic doctrine, and presented it as a plague infecting not only the Jewish population but the whole society of the Commonwealth. Despite its apocalyptic tone and its powerful patron (Prince Adam Kazimierz Czartoryski), Lefin's publication passed without notice; not until the end of the nineteenth century did the first historians of hasidism revisit it. Later publications of the maskil Jacques Calmanson and the Polish reformer and statesman Tadeusz Czacki that mentioned hasidim met exactly the same fate, though both authors intended their works to influence the plans to reform the Jewish people, then actively under way.[7] At no time did any of the institutions of the Polish–Lithuanian Commonwealth take any kind of action against hasidism. The situation is all the more striking in that the so-called Jewish Question was then one of the most extensively discussed topics; at least one Polish and two Jewish participants in these debates were aware of the existence of hasidism and concerned with its progress, and the group had already been developing in the lands of Poland–Lithuania for five decades.

Something very similar happened after the final fall of the Polish–Lithuanian Commonwealth in 1795. From 1795 to 1807, the central Polish lands that would later make up the Duchy of Warsaw and the Kingdom of Poland were divided between Prussia and Austria. Wielkopolska, part of Mazovia, northern Podlasie, and the western borderlands of Małopolska and the Siewierz principality fell to Prussia in the Second (1793) and Third (1795) Partitions; from these lands were created the provinces of Northern Prussia, New East Prussia, and New Silesia. Austria did not participate in the Second Partition of 1793, but in 1795 occupied northern Mazovia, the Sandomierz district, southern Podlasie, and the Lublin region, which comprised the territory known as Western Galicia.

During the fifteen years of its rule over central Poland, the Prussian government never once seems to have occupied itself with the question of hasidism, but the Austrian authorities did. In January 1798, the authorities of Sandomierz district (*obwód*, later *powiat*) took an interest in 'how hasidim differ from other Jews'.[8] Unfortunately, why they did so cannot be determined for lack of sources, nor can we know if the interest continued; still, it is

---

[6] [Lefin], 'Essai d'un plan de réforme'. The best analysis of this text is in Sinkoff, 'Strategy and Ruse in the Haskalah of Mendel Lefin of Satanow'; ead., *Out of the Shtetl*, 84–95; van Luit, 'Hasidim, Mitnaggedim and the State in Lefin's *Essai*'.

[7] Calmanson, *Essai sur l'état actuel des Juifs de Pologne*; Czacki, *Rozprawa o Żydach i karaitach*. See the discussion in Ch. 1 above.

[8] AGAD, Sekretariat Stanu Królestwa Polskiego 199, fo. 462ᵛ. Documents concerning this case have not been preserved; neither have other sources on the anti-hasidic investigations in 18th-c. Galicia mentioned here. In the 1820s they were incorporated into the archives of the

the first trace of official interest in hasidism in central Poland. In August 1798 the same authorities began an investigation into a conflict between a hasidic ritual slaughterer (*shoḥet*) and a rabbi, and the resulting boycott of kosher meat in Połaniec.[9] But the investigation, initiated by the *kahal*'s imposition of a candle tax on hasidic slaughterers and leaseholders, did not concern hasidism itself (though the official leading the investigation did point out the traits of hasidism that he considered harmful to society), but rather the financial and administrative violations committed by those who were the subjects of the complaint. Also in 1798, an imperial decree for Western Galicia allowed for the establishment of private groups for prayer, which it called *miniam* (instead of *minyan* or *minian*), on condition that they paid a yearly fee of 25 florins.[10] We do not know the immediate context which inclined the Austrian authorities to issue this decree. Its direct model was certainly the analogous decree for Eastern Galicia issued by Emperor Francis II in 1792.[11] Neither the 1792 nor the 1798 decree specifies whether it includes hasidim, nor even mentions them, but the decrees seem to constitute some of the earliest evidence of the conflict most typical of the emergence of the hasidic community, that is, the conflict surrounding the establishment by hasidim of their own prayer rooms, known as *shtiblekh* (sing. *shtibl*).

The basic reason for the conflict was that the hasidim aimed to separate themselves from the Jewish community at large by creating their own *minyanim* (prayer groups) and private *shtiblekh* where they could pray independently of the community.[12] The conflict had theological and halakhic as well as social and even economic dimensions. The Sephardi liturgy itself (or, more exactly, the Sephardi liturgy as modified by the Safed kabbalist known as the Ari (Rabbi Isaac Luria) and referred to as *nusaḥ ari*), which the hasidim used instead of the Ashkenazi liturgy traditionally used by Polish Jews, was not in itself controversial; rather, the controversy was over the social implications of its adoption, which the established community considered an act of arrogance because it was a rejection of the established tradition. Luria's prayer book had been used for at least a century by elite pietistic groups, the most famous being that of Brody, so that this hasidic innovation had a long

state-funded Jewish Committee, then into the Archiwum Oświecenia Publicznego which was completely burned down by the Nazis during the Warsaw Uprising in 1944.

[9] The investigation in Połaniec is one of very few clashes between the hasidim and their opponents in late 18th-c. central Poland that has been researched. See Kuperstein, 'Inquiry at Połaniec'.

[10] See *1.01; AGAD, KRSW 6628, k. 198–201. See also *Sr. k.k. Majestät Franz des Zweyten politische Gesetze und Verordnungen*, xiii. 101–3, no. 35.   [11] Ibid. i. 89.

[12] See the classic study by Louis Jacobs, *Hasidic Prayer*. See also Wilensky, 'Hassidic Mitnagedic Polemics'; Nadler, *The Faith of the Mithnagdim*, 50–77. For a comprehensive description of hasidic liturgy and its difference from the Ashkenazi liturgy see Wertheim, *Law and Custom in Hasidism*, 128–214.

Figure 2.1 A hasidic *shtibl* in late nineteenth-century Galicia according to the artistic vision of Viennese painter Isidor Kaufmann; actual images of *shtiblekh* from the period are, unfortunately, unknown. Raphael Posner, Uri Kaploun, and Shalom Cohen (eds.), *Jewish Liturgy: Prayer and Synagogue Service through the Ages* (Jerusalem, 1975)

tradition. *Mitnagedim*, however, very accurately perceived in it a threat to tradition as well as an attempt to undermine the authority of the *kahal* (the Jewish community). That the hasidim followed a different ritual was perceived as a pretext for the creation of their own *shtiblekh* in private homes or small halls, their gradual withdrawal from community obligations, and then the assertion of an autonomy that went far beyond the use of a different prayer book. Those who opposed this development stressed its financial consequences for the community synagogues: a decline in the income from the reading of the Torah (because as the number of those bidding for the honour decreased, so did the size of the bids), from donations, from the sale of seats, from community taxes, and from fees for special services.[13] An Austrian

---

[13] Interestingly, there was a very similar case concerning the economic aspects of the hasidic movement and anti-hasidic regulations of the *kahal* in Vilna; see Wilensky, *Ḥasidim umitnagedim*, i. 208–9. The issue reappeared later on numerous occasions, among them as one of the central points of debate during the Rabbinical Commission in St Petersburg in 1843; see Lurie, *Edah umedinah*, 71.

Figure 2.2 Emperor Francis II
(1768–1835), last emperor of the
First Reich (1792–1806), first
emperor of Austria (as Francis I)
after the defeat of the Habsburg
monarchy in the Napoleonic Wars,
and an architect of the conservative
turn in the policy towards Jews in
Galicia. Copperplate engraving
by Jan Ferdynand Krethlow, from
the original of Johann Zitterer.
Biblioteka Narodowa w Warszawie,
Zbiory Ikonograficzne, G.9560

imperial degree of 1798 aimed to reduce the level of conflict by regulating the establishment of private *shtiblekh*, but it did not resolve the fundamental issue of the relationship between the hasidim and the *kahal* and in fact actually excluded the *kahal* entirely from the decision-making process. Moreover, as was typical of Habsburg fiscalism, the establishment of such *shtiblekh* was seen as an opportunity for increasing the imperial income: the government levied an annual charge, notionally to contribute towards the future state funding of Jewish schools. The decree therefore did nothing to resolve the economic source of the conflict, which was that the establishment of private *shtiblekh* was detrimental to the community's finances. (Actually, the basis for applying the new law seems not to have been clear to the provincial administration. In the following year, the authorities re-examined the issue and concluded that the right to assembly for hasidim should be conditional on their meetings taking place in community synagogues.[14] This was thus exactly the opposite of the previous year's ruling.)

Galician officialdom revisited the hasidic issue at least twice more in 1799. The enigmatic matter of 'the prohibition or protection of hasidim' was examined in the Sandomierz district on 28 July 1799,[15] and on 15 March it

[14] See AGAD, Sekretariat Stanu Królestwa Polskiego 199, fo. 462ʳ. Materials concerning this issue were later collected in the archives of the Voivodeship Commission of Kraków in Kielce and of the Voivodeship Commission of Mazovia in Warsaw. This suggests that the matter was investigated quite extensively.

[15] AGAD, Sekretariat Stanu Królestwa Polskiego 199, fo. 462ʳ. There are a number of parallels between this regulation and the information provided by a well-known anti-hasidic

was decreed that hasidim were forbidden to collect funds to support poor Jews in Palestine.[16] The Austrian government had thus intervened at least five times in the matter of hasidism in central Poland in 1798 and 1799.

The striking difference between Prussian and Austrian officials in their interest in and knowledge of hasidism can above all be explained by the fact that there were no hasidim in the lands taken by Prussia in 1772: Western Prussia and the Noteć River District[17] were in that respect quite different from central Poland or Galicia.[18] Until Prussia occupied central Poland in 1795, the Prussian authorities most likely did not know of the existence of hasidim. In contrast in Galicia, the territory that fell to Austria in 1772, centres of hasidism are known to have existed as early as the 1770s and 1780s, above all in Zbaraż, Leżajsk (Lizhensk), and Złoczów, and somewhat later in Rymanów, Sasów, and Łańcut. The Austrian government thus came into contact with hasidism at least two decades before the occupation of central Poland. Hasidim were the subject of an investigation in Rzeszów in 1788, so the government, or at least some officials, knew of the existence of hasidism well before the annexation of central Poland in 1795.[19]

Of course, we have to be somewhat cautious in drawing further conclusions about the Austrian government and hasidism. Though the above-

preacher, Israel Löbel, who claimed that in 1799 he had met Emperor Francis II, convinced him of the subversive nature of hasidism, and persuaded him to ban it in the Habsburg empire. See Löbel, 'Glaubwürdige Nachricht von der in Polen und Lithauen befindlichen Sekte', 333; there is an annotated Hebrew translation in Wilensky, *Ḥasidim umitnagedim*, ii. 326–38. There is a record in the protocols of the imperial chancellery for the year 1799 confirming that the governor of Eastern Galicia, Johann Jakob Graf von Gaisruck, proposed anti-hasidic regulations, but his proposal was not accepted. See Allgemeines Verwaltungsarchiv Wien, Hofkanzleiprotokolle Galizien 1799, pp. 210–12 (I am grateful to Dirk Sadowski for this information). Since the emperor issued no anti-hasidic decrees at that time, Israel Löbel's claim is discredited. See also Manekin, 'Hasidism and the Habsburg Empire'.

[16] AGAD, Sekretariat Stanu Królestwa Polskiego 199, fo. 255ʳ. It is not clear what kind of 'regulation' it was. It was definitely not an imperial decree, as no such text appears in the collection of all the imperial laws and decrees for the year 1799; see *Sr. k.k. Majestät Franz des Zweyten politische Gesetze und Verordnungen*, vol. xiv.

[17] Throughout the territory of Royal Prussia there was a law *de non tolerandis Judaeis*. In the districts of Malbork, Chełmno, and Pomorze Nadwiślańskie, there were only 3,600 Jewish inhabitants; the Jewish community of the region of Noteć numbered between 11,000 and 16,000. There is no information about hasidic activities in these territories. See Kemlein, *Żydzi w Wielkim Księstwie Poznańskim 1815–1848*, 45–9.

[18] It should be explained here that the Austrian documents on hasidic issues, and the corresponding lack of such documentation from the Prussian administration, is known to us mainly thanks to the archival research conducted for the Jewish Committee by the ministries of the Kingdom of Poland in the mid-1820s. Thus it is possible that the shortage of information on anti-hasidic investigations in Prussia is a result of a lack of familiarity with the post-Prussian archive on the part of the officials of the Kingdom of Poland rather than a reflection of the absence of such investigations and documents.

[19] On Rzeszów see Mahler, *Hasidism and the Jewish Enlightenment*, 73.

mentioned decrees demonstrate that there was some willingness on the part of the imperial government to get involved in such matters, it is doubtful whether such interest extended beyond the lower ranks of the provincial administration (and one of the decrees did not speak specifically of hasidim at all). Moreover, it is difficult to speak of real interest, since although government officials in Western Galicia troubled themselves in matters concerning hasidim several times in only two years, they took no steps to investigate or to regulate them more generally. Still more telling is the fact that in the remaining ten years of Austrian rule in central Poland, the authorities did not occupy themselves with hasidism even once. The first real interest, and thorough investigations with real conclusions, date from 1814, when Austria had already lost control over central Poland.[20] It thus seems that, in spite of the many incidents of local significance mentioned above and a somewhat better grasp of the subject, the relationship of the Austrian authorities to hasidism did not differ substantially from the attitude of the other regimes of central Poland (and of other regions of eastern Europe) at the end of the eighteenth century and the beginning of the nineteenth.[21] This relationship may generally be described as one of neglect and marginalization. We have seen that all the consecutive governments of this part of Europe more or less ignored the hasidim. The authorities of the Polish–Lithuanian Commonwealth and the Prussian partition administration displayed no interest in hasidim (though they had good reason to do so),[22] and the Austrian government was unusually reserved on this issue. Moreover, if we can trust the extant sources and research from the early nineteenth century, the matter of hasidism did not come up even once during the period of the Duchy of Warsaw (1807–15). The first traces of government interest in hasidism in central Poland date only from the period of the Kingdom of Poland, more than five decades after the appearance of the first documented traces of hasidic presence in the region.

---

[20] See Mahler, *Hasidism and the Jewish Enlightenment*, 73–5.

[21] The Austrian administration's lack of interest in hasidic matters is well illustrated by the protocols of the imperial chancellery for Galicia (Allgemeines Verwaltungsarchiv Wien, Hofkanzleiprotokolle Galizien), where for the years 1786–99 there is hardly a word about 'Chusiden, oder sogenannten frommen Juden'. I am grateful to Dirk Sadowski for this information.

[22] An interpretation by Israel Halperin ('Rabi levi-yitsḥak miberditshev', 342), recently reiterated by Glenn Dynner ('How Many *Hasidim* Were There Really in Congress Poland?', 101), suggests that a note in one of the projects of the Four Year Sejm about 'all of their sects' ('Żydom i wszystkim ich sektom') relates to hasidism, but this seems unlikely, as 'Jewish sects' was a common phrase in Polish official documents long before the emergence of hasidism (see e.g. *Instrukcja sejmiku ziemi zakroczymskiej posłom na sejm walny dwuniedzielny warszawski* (1712), in Biblioteka PAU i PAN (Kraków) MS 8354 (Teki Pawińskiego 15), fo. 45[r–v]); see also *Sejmy i sejmiki koronne wobec Żydów*, ed. Michałowska-Mycielska, 361.

Certainly many factors, changing with subsequent governments and the accompanying context, contributed to this indifference over a period of several decades, but the most important were the numerous internal and external problems of the successive states. For the Polish–Lithuanian Commonwealth in a state of permanent crisis and decline, for the new Prussian and Austrian regimes, and, finally, for the Duchy of Warsaw fighting for its survival (during the course of seven years, the Duchy participated in three great European wars whose campaigns rolled through its lands), the development of a new Jewish 'sect' was truly a marginal phenomenon. Also not without significance is the fact that the number of supporters of hasidism in central Poland was certainly very limited, comprising at most a small percentage of the Jewish population (though locally, as in Połaniec, the group may have been significantly stronger); even Jews themselves did not always consider hasidim an element of any significance.[23] One should also remember the inertia of the state administration, which did not undertake to deal with any new issue gladly. Actually, considering how little the elites of European society would have known about Jews, one can surmise that governments simply had insufficient information about hasidism to develop a reasoned policy. Tadeusz Czacki, the Polish politician and author engaged in reform of the Jewish population, indirectly confirmed this. In his 1807 *Tractate on Jews and Karaites* he explained the attitude of the government of Poland–Lithuania towards hasidism in the following words: 'It was expected in the Polish government that the hasidim would soon die out if nobody asked about them.'[24] The wording may be insensitive, but the authorities simply waited for the matter to resolve itself. One can have no doubt that the motives of subsequent governments in central Poland, whether Prussian, Austrian, or again Polish, were similar. Ignorance, together with an indifference to internal Jewish matters, was an essential factor in the attitude of east European governments (and certainly many others) towards the Jewish population, including the hasidim.

A fundamental consequence of this was that the government of the Kingdom of Poland, when it addressed the issue of hasidism, had no foundation on which to build a policy. There existed almost no legislation, or even custom, to which it could refer. The only legislation in place was the law regarding *minyanim*, which formally applied to the post-Austrian part of the Kingdom until 1817 and occasionally aroused the interest of the regional and central governmental administration (on which more below). Besides that, there was absolutely nothing that could help the authorities to acquaint

---

[23] See Wodziński, 'How Many *Hasidim* Were There in Congress Poland?'. See also Dynner, 'How Many *Hasidim* Were There Really in Congress Poland?', and my response, 'How Should We Count *Hasidim* in Congress Poland?'.   [24] Czacki, *Rozprawa o Żydach i karaitach*, 106.

themselves with hasidism or help them develop a position on the group. Moreover until 1819, when the Berlin maskil David Friedländer published a work on the reform of the Polish Jews that touched briefly on hasidism, there was essentially no literature they could draw on. Lefin's earlier pamphlet, of 1791 or 1792, had been almost completely forgotten, and Calmanson's effort of 1796 had fared little better. In 1820 the Polish official Jan A. Radomiński published a tractate on the reform of Polish Jews that was marginally concerned with hasidism. Finally, in 1821, Julian Ursyn Niemcewicz published his famous 'hasidic' story, *Lejbe i Sióra*.[25] But even these publications did not fundamentally change the state of knowledge about hasidism. None even showed much familiarity with it: the pamphlets by Friedländer and Radomiński made little more than passing reference to hasidism (in spite of the great erudition of both authors in Jewish matters), and Niemcewicz's story was clearly polemical and satirical. At about the same time, Franciszek Karpiński, a well-known and well-educated Polish sentimental pre-Romantic poet, published a memoir concerning his encounter some time previously with Lithuanian hasidim. He evidently did not know the publications by Lefin and Calmanson and had not even heard of hasidism.[26] So it is not surprising that in the first years of the Kingdom there were difficulties in identifying the group and its supporters, who in local sources and documents of the government administration were called hasidim, Hussites, *kitajowcy*, or Michałki (the terms will be discussed below), or even not named at all.

2. Nameless: The First Ruling on Hasidic *Shtiblekh*

The functioning of a new Jewish group seems to have emerged as an issue for the government for the first time in 1817. As before, the problem was the establishment of hasidic *shtiblekh*. Usually in such cases, a government investigation was initiated following a request from the *kahal* authorities to the city or voivodeship (province; Pol. *województwo*) to force the hasidim to attend the community synagogue rather than pray separately, and to pay all necessary dues. The earliest such request came to the Voivodeship Commission of Sandomierz at the beginning of 1817 from a *kahal* unknown to us. Following

---

[25] For a comprehensive analysis of Polish opinions on hasidism in 1818–22, see Wodziński, *Haskalah and Hasidism*, 73–7.

[26] Karpiński, *Pamiętniki*, 154. The meeting with the men, whom Karpiński calls *kitajowcy* or 'men of silk', took place around 1800–1. Karpiński's testimony, though written more than twenty years later, is interesting because the encounter was so early, and because it contains descriptions from which inferences can be drawn. For example, we can probably infer the identity of an unnamed rabbi who explained to him the general hasidic attitude towards mourning a father's death: he was probably R. Jacob Aryeh of Nieśwież (Nezhiz) (d. 1837), whose father, Mordecai of Nieśwież, had died in 1800, just before Karpiński and R. Jacob Aryeh met.

that complaint, the commission addressed a query to the Government Commission for Religious Denominations and Public Enlightenment (i.e. the
Ministry for Education and Religion), asking whether private prayer rooms
could be tolerated, and if so, whether the fee of 25 florins introduced by the
Austrian authorities in 1798 should be maintained.[27] The question was taken
up by Stanisław Staszic, a member of the Government Commission, who at
that time almost monopolized issues relating to the Jewish population since
he also directed the Department of Industry and Art at the Government
Commission for Income and Assets (i.e. the Ministry of Finance and the
Treasury Department).[28] On Staszic's advice, the government responded that
since the constitution ensured freedom of ritual for all believers, permission
to establish private prayer rooms should be given without charge, and this
decision was conveyed not only to the Voivodeship Commission of Sandomierz but also to all voivodeship commissions throughout the Kingdom.[29]
Although this decree did not mention hasidism directly, and the state officials
who had issued it were probably not aware that the question concerned
this group, it was actually the first government regulation concerning hasidism in the Kingdom of Poland. By abolishing the 1798 Austrian decree, it
gave hasidim full freedom to set up private *shtiblekh* independent of *kahal*
authorities.

   In accordance with administrative practice in the Kingdom, the decree—
as with other decrees of little importance—was not published and was soon
forgotten by the Government Commission that had issued it, by the voivodeship commissions that had been informed about it, and even by Staszic
himself, who had signed it for the Minister for Religious Denominations and
Public Enlightenment, Stanisław Kostka Potocki. The ruling thus had no
practical significance for later policies towards hasidic *shtiblekh* or the position of hasidim in their conflicts with hostile community authorities. But the
decision is nevertheless significant, since it casts light on later government
rulings on hasidism. The 1817 ruling accepts the constitutional basis of freedom of religion,[30] and in the spirit of the law allows for the creation of private
hasidic *shtiblekh*, as did Viceroy General Józef Zajączek and the Administrative Council in more extensive investigations into hasidism in later years.
The ruling legitimately calls into question the thesis dominant in the literature, that constitutional freedom was an empty phrase in the Kingdom of

---

[27] See *2.01; AGAD, CWW 1430, pp. 1–2.   [28] See *2.02; AGAD, CWW 1430, p. 3.
[29] See *2.03, *2.04; AGAD, CWW 1430, pp. 4–6; see also APK, RGR 4405, p. 1.
[30] Article 11 of the constitution that Alexander I granted in 1815 stated: 'The Roman
Catholic religion, professed by the majority of the Kingdom of Poland's citizens, will be an
object of special protection on the part of the Government, which cannot, however, harm the
freedom of other faiths, all of which, with no exceptions, may practice all their rituals in public
under the protection of the Government.'

Poland and that any concessions to the hasidim were a result of pressure from the group's wealthy and influential supporters.[31] Above all, the belief that the law was repeatedly violated is simply wrong. It results in part from Polish national myths (the anti-tsarist uprising in 1830–1 was to be justified by the Kingdom's supposed lawlessness), and in part from a false view of the realities of nineteenth-century Europe. During the constitutional period from 1815 to 1830, the Kingdom was a lawful state according to European standards of the time, and violations of constitutional order by the highest organs of state happened relatively rarely, or at least no more often than in other constitutional monarchies. The 1817 decision was justified with reference to constitutional freedoms, and could not have been influenced by supporters of hasidism, who knew nothing about it. It shows clearly that the constitutional basis of religious freedom was indeed a factor in the politics of the time, including the government's attitude towards hasidism, at least in the constitutional period. That the argument was significant is shown by the fact that it played a role in government investigations. It was not dependent only on 'Jewish swords' (as Jewish bribes were called in old Poland), and deserves proper consideration.

Of course, other factors are also likely to have influenced the government's decisions, perhaps even decisively. After 1815 the debate on the planned reform and emancipation of the Jews entered a new phase. Among the reformers' most frequent demands was to weaken the authority of the *kahal*, or simply to rescind the autonomy of Jewish institutions; one of the radical advocates of this idea, as we saw earlier, was Staszic. Such reformers would have seen independent *shtiblekh* as a welcome competitor to the *kahal*. Staszic stated this intention in so many words a few years later, in a report to a delegation concerned with the issue of the 'sect of hasidim'.[32] In the Enlightenment plan to 'civilize' the Jews, hasidism was thus paradoxically perceived as potentially beneficial.

3. *Kitajowcy*: Investigation in Płock

Far from resolving the conflict over the *shtiblekh*, however, the ministerial decision of 1817 made things worse. Provincial and central governmental authorities alike had to intervene in a dramatically growing number of conflicts of this type. As early as 1818, there is evidence of such conflicts in Płock

---

[31] Glenn Dynner offers the examples of Berek Sonnenberg and his wife Temerl; see Dynner, *'Men of Silk'*, 97–109. See also Mahler, *Hasidism and the Jewish Enlightenment*, 316; Boim, *Harabi rebe bunem mipeshisḥa*, ii. 585–94.

[32] See *11.73; CWW 1871, pp. 187–90; Wodziński, 'Sprawa chasydymów', 240–1. Mahler maintained that using hasidism to subvert and divide the traditional Jewish community was the Kingdom's only policy regarding hasidism (see Mahler, *Hasidism and the Jewish Enlightenment*, 328–9). In the light of more recently discovered sources, however, this claim seems baseless.

(more below) and in Chęciny; in 1820 in Łask; in 1821 in Radzyń, Suwałki, and Chmielnik; and in Raczki and Złoczew in 1822, Szydłowiec in 1826, Włocławek in 1827, Pyzdry in 1828, Częstochowa and Pilica in 1830, Radomsko in 1831, in Włocławek again in 1835, in Lublin in 1836, and so on. Moreover, the overwhelming majority of these incidents specifically concerned hasidic *shtiblekh*. Government investigations were thus increasingly concerned not just with the abstract right to organize private *shtiblekh*, but with the character and legality of the hasidic groups establishing them. The 1818 incident in Płock occasioned the Kingdom of Poland's first official investigation into the movement.

During this period, Płock was the capital of one of eight voivodeships in the Kingdom. Intensive cultural and economic development had led to significant demographic growth, thanks to which Płock, north of Warsaw, became an increasingly significant population centre after years of stagnation. In 1827, 34.8 per cent of its residents (3,412 individuals) constituted a sizeable and influential Jewish community. Of course, this large group of residents attracted the attention of the administration, which under the direction of the distinguished Napoleonic General Florian Kobyliński—eager both to achieve reform in the interests of modernization and to exercise power over the local population—led to numerous 'civilizing' projects, including attempts to combat illegal *shtiblekh*. At first glance this seems paradoxical, given that reformers also saw *shtiblekh* as a way of reducing the power of the *kahal*; but the truth is that the situation was full of inconsistencies. One would not expect that the provincial authorities in Płock, for example, would follow the strategic thinking of the ministry, nor even necessarily have a clear understanding of what was happening on their own doorstep. What we do know is that on 2 May 1818, local police closed the hasidic *shtibl*. It is not known how the Płock authorities knew of its existence, or why they decided to close it, though it appears that Kobyliński had somehow found out about the gathering of Jews in private homes for prayer services and on 18 April 1818 had ordered their closure, an order that was implemented a couple of weeks later.[33] But neither Kobyliński's instruction to the mayor nor the mayor's response specifically mentioned hasidim (although the mayor did have a list of all the private prayer rooms in Płock). It is thus possible that the closing of the hasidic *shtiblekh* was part of a broader action aimed at all private *minyanim*.[34] Three days after the closing of the *shtibl*, ten hasidim, 'in the name of all', appealed to the Voivodeship Commission to revoke the decision.[35] The hasidim invoked the constitutional freedom of religion

---

[33] On the investigation in Płock in 1818 see Gliński, *Komisja Rządowa Wyznań Religijnych*, 175–7; Wodziński, *Haskalah and Hasidism*, 104–7; Dynner, '*Men of Silk*', 59–65; so far the most comprehensive analysis is Wodziński, 'Rząd Królestwa Polskiego wobec chasydyzmu'.

[34] See APP, AmP 199, fos. 86–9.   [35] See *4.01; AGAD, CWW 1869, pp. 10–11.

(possibly in reference to the 1817 decision) and justified the need for their people to gather for their own services on the grounds that, being more pious, they could not pray in the community synagogue, which was full of 'craftsmen, traders, etc.' who prayed very hurriedly so they could return to their occupations. The Voivodeship Commission supported the police ban, but at the same time referred the matter to the Government Commission for Religious Denominations for approval.[36] Kobyliński's position was that private services should be banned if they led to the creation of a sect. More-over, religious services should be conducted only in public places because people not attending the synagogue would not hear announcements of gov-ernment regulations. He further mentioned that illicit gatherings undoubt-edly attracted secret contributions which diminished the general funds; and that the 'known universal tendency of the Jewish nation to disorder' meant that services celebrated in unclean places offended religious sentiment. He specifically named the 'sect' that aimed to create separate prayer rooms as *kitajowcy*, who, he said,

offer no justification deserving of merit for holding services separate from other Jews, mentioning only that they devote a longer time to services than other Jews, and so the service in the synagogue with the general public, according to their opinion, is too short. This objection is groundless because nobody is forbidden to pray for a longer period of time in the synagogue and, finally, the rabbi may be compelled to lengthen the service, since this is not contrary to religious dogma.[37]

Kobyliński did not have any information on the topic of the group described, other than the arguments and characteristics of hasidism included in the petition from Płock. Some of Kobyliński's arguments against hasidic *shtiblekh* resemble those put forward by the Jewish community boards (especially the impossibility of communicating government rulings to the hasidim and illegal contributions diminishing community income), which suggests that the unknown denunciation that initiated the police action may have in fact come from such a source.

Kobyliński's letter reveals doubts concerning the status of hasidism that are characteristic of all similar incidents. The letter defines the group as a sect but at the same time questions its separateness. These contradictory percep-tions could lead to two mutually exclusive conclusions. If hasidism was a sect, and thus distinct from traditional Judaism, it could be persecuted as an illegal religious organization (more about this in the next chapter); yet limiting its right to assembly would contravene the constitutional guarantee of freedom of religion. On the other hand, if the hasidim did not differ from other Jews, then it could be concluded that they were not entitled to hold separate

[36] See *4.02; AGAD, CWW 1869, pp. 1–4.   [37] Ibid.

services; but if they were like other Jews then they were no more threatening than other Jews, so there would be no reason to limit their other activities. In effect, the same arguments were used to support contradictory claims. Both competing interpretations had their supporters, and some of them (Staszic, and later Radomiński) referred to both, depending on the context.

Kobyliński's letter was seemingly the first thing that made the Government Commission aware of the existence of hasidism, though it had known of the existence of a suspicious 'sect'. At first, both the authorities and the hasidim themselves used the word *kitajowcy*; not until September 1818 did a report by Abraham Stern explain to the Government Commission that *kitajowcy* and hasidim were one and the same. He said the name came from *kitaj*, the fine silk or cotton fabric of the clothing worn by hasidic men.[38]

After receiving Kobyliński's report, the Government Commission asked the Płock Voivodeship Commission for better information on the suspect '*kitajowcy* sect'.[39] The commission soon presented a report maintaining that the group seemed dangerous and that the government should take note of it. '*Kitajowcy* distinguish themselves in their rituals from other Jews and they live in mutual hatred with them, but are so numerous that in almost all cities of the voivodeship they have separate local prayer rooms.'[40] The commission also noticed that they should quickly concern themselves with 'the *kitajowcy* sect', as the group was causing growing unrest in Jewish communities. In addition, the degree of hatred between hasidim and their opponents was so great that reconciling the two and forcing them to pray together seemed impossible. The commission therefore concluded that if hasidic beliefs were not dangerous to society, hasidim could be allowed to gather independently.

This conclusion differs radically from that reached seventeen days earlier, when the Voivodeship Commission recognized the need to ban the *shtiblekh*. Kobyliński did not, however, reverse his stance completely and adopt a positive attitude to hasidism; he suggested only that the government should take steps to regulate the status of the new 'sect' and its prayer rooms. Overall, the Voivodeship Commission seemed to have no consistent policy towards the group—which was hardly surprising, since it really knew nothing about it. At this stage, as in later investigations of hasidism, even officials who tried honestly and skilfully to solve the emerging problems posed by the hasidim were hampered by lack of knowledge, anti-Jewish prejudice, and, especially, 'enlightened' ideas of 'civilizing' the Jews.

Concerned by the news from Płock, the Government Commission decided to monitor the new phenomenon more closely, and summoned Ezekiel Hoge (1791–1860) and Abraham Stern (1769–1842) 'to tell them

---

[38] On hasidic laws and customs concerning dress, see Wertheim, *Law and Custom in Hasidism*, 291–5.
[39] See *4.03; AGAD, CWW 1869, p. 5.   [40] See *4.04; AGAD, CWW 1869, pp. 6–9.

how to distinguish the sect of *kitajowcy* from others and whether they cannot hold services together in synagogues'.[41] At the time Hoge and Stern were the government's most highly regarded advisers on the Jewish Question; both were maskilim, though Hoge was the more radical.

The reports that Hoge and Stern prepared are the first evidence we have of advocates of Haskalah in the Kingdom of Poland participating in anti-hasidic polemics.[42] Hoge's report has unfortunately not survived, but it cannot have been sympathetic to the hasidim, since it was entitled 'The Opinion of Hoge against Hasidim'.[43] Hoge was undoubtedly qualified to write such a report: he came from a hasidic family, but he had abandoned the court of the tsadik Jacob Isaac Horowitz, known as the Seer of Lublin, because he considered the latter's beliefs irrational. After becoming involved in the Haskalah, Hoge was for several years an active and influential adviser to the government on Jewish affairs. He was baptized in 1825 and left Poland soon after. During his last years, which were spent in England, he returned to Judaism.[44]

Abraham Stern, the most famous of the Polish maskilim and also an internationally famous engineer and inventor, was commissioned by the government to write opinions on various Jewish social issues. His report on hasidism appeared on 29 September 1818. This extensive text was for many years the best work on hasidism to come out of the Polish Haskalah, but at the same time the most critical.[45] According to Stern, hasidism was not a new religion but rather the invention of a band of charlatans, the essence of which was to reinforce ignorance and to exploit simple Jews. In his view the majority of Jews in Poland were disdainful of hasidism but did not have the means to counter its expansion; and therefore the Government Commission should not permit hasidim to establish separate prayer rooms but should force them to participate in services in the regular communal synagogues.

Almost immediately after receiving this report, the Government Commission instructed the Voivodeship Commission that 'this sect does not differ

---

[41] See *4.04; AGAD, CWW 1869, pp. 6–9.

[42] Wodziński, *Haskalah and Hasidism*, 86–94.   [43] See AGAD, CWW 1871, p. 130.

[44] See Frenk, 'Yekhezkel hoge oder "haskel meshumad"'; Lask Abrahams, 'Stanislaus Hoga—Apostate and Penitent'. For more on his alleged role in the 1824 anti-hasidic investigation see the next chapter.

[45] See *4.07; AGAD, CWW 1871, pp. 43–6; AGAD, KWK 702, pp. 137–41; AGAD, KRSW 6634, fos. 239–42; Mahler, *Haḥasidut vehahaskalah*, 477–81; Wodziński, *Oświecenie żydowskie w Królestwie Polskim wobec chasydyzmu*, 268–71; id., *Haskalah and Hasidism*, 260–3. More information on the report can be found in Mahler, *Hasidism and the Jewish Enlightenment*, 318–22, and Wodziński, *Haskalah and Hasidism*, 88–9. Mahler, who had access to an unsigned copy of the report in the collection of the Government Commission for Internal Affairs (see AGAD, KRSW 6634, fos. 239–42), wrongly believed that the author of the report was Abraham Buchner.

Figure 2.3 Abraham Jakub Stern (1769–1842), the most influential of the
Polish maskilim, a mathematician, inventor, and engineer of international fame,
and a harsh anti-hasidic critic involved in several government investigations
related to hasidism. The National Library of Israel in Jerusalem,
Shvadron Collection

in its religious beliefs from other Jews, therefore services can be held in
public synagogues together with others. From a religious viewpoint, then,
the *kitajowcy* did not have a good reason for their demand to meet freely in
private homes on the pretext of religious services.'[46] In other words, Stern
had won the day as the conclusions of the Government Commission were
identical with his recommendations. Though the ministerial decision was
signed by Minister Stanisław Kostka Potocki, there is no doubt that Staszic
at least participated in the decision-making process, as the Government
Commission sent him a copy of the document.

    However, this ministerial ruling did not end the matter, as Viceroy General
Józef Zajączek, the highest authority (in the absence of a king), soon
became interested. He learned of the investigation into hasidism and of the
ruling of the Government Commission from a weekly report of the Voivodeship Commission of Płock, and on 10 November 1818 he ordered the Government Commission to review the decision concerning the *shtiblekh* with

[46] See *4.08; AGAD, CWW 1869, p. 15; see also pp. 12–13.

Figure 2.4 Józef Zajączek (1752–1826), a Napoleonic general and then
viceroy of the Kingdom of Poland, personally involved in several investigations
in the matter of hasidism. Portrait by Walenty Śliwicki, lithography from the
printing shop of Aleksander Chodkiewicz, 1820–30, in A. Chodkiewicz, *Portrety
wsławionych Polaków* [Portraits of Famous Poles] (Warsaw, 1820–30). Biblioteka
Narodowa w Warszawie, Zbiory Ikonograficzne, A. 2877, pl. 21

particular reference to freedom of religion and differences in ritual between
the '*kitajowcy* and Jews'.[47]

Initially, Potocki rejected the viceroy's position. Adamant in his support
for Stern's report, he again repeated its conclusions. Concerning the '*kitajowcy*
or hasidim', Potocki wrote to Zajączek, the principle of religious liberty
could not be applied because:

1. According to evidence from the hasidim themselves, they differ from Jews only
   in the length of time devoted to services, which is not a sufficient reason to allow
   them separate synagogues.

2. There are *kitajowcy* or hasidim in other cities too, and they do not demand
   separate synagogues; even the Płock *kitajowcy* admit that only for the past ten
   years have they met separately in homes.

3. Allowing them to have separate synagogues may encourage the formation of
   numerous sects among Jews, which would hamper enlightenment; even the
   rabbinical school planned for Warsaw cannot guarantee the desired results.[48]

[47] See *4.09; AGAD, CWW 1869, p. 16.   [48] See *4.10; AGAD, CWW 1869, pp. 16–19.

In conclusion, Potocki stressed again that the problem posed by hasidism was not one of religion but rather one of public order; so the principle of religious liberty did not apply, and police regulations should settle the issue. Stern's report was attached to the ministerial opinion.

On 24 November 1818 the issue came up at the meeting of the Administrative Council, as the government was known.[49] The discussion was again based on Stern's report, together with an opinion prepared by Staszic in Potocki's absence from the meeting. Again, Potocki's position on the matter was thus at least as much the work of his adviser Staszic as his own. But Staszic's position was rejected: first the viceroy and then the Administrative Council repeated their earlier opinion in favour of hasidic prayer rooms. To be sure, Zajączek recognized that hasidism brought 'various eccentricities and superstitions' to Judaism, but he held that the believers of a religion tolerated in the Kingdom could not be denied the freedom to follow their own ritual. The viceroy therefore made the following recommendation in the Administrative Council:

Since the rituals of the hasidim or *kitajowcy* do not contradict regulations or laws in any way, we therefore find no reason why they should be excluded from the freedoms and liberties shared by other believers in the country and authorize the Government Commission for Religious Denominations and Public Enlightenment to apply the regulations where necessary; the Government does not find any harm in the holding of services in the prayer rooms of the sect under discussion.[50]

The decision of the viceroy was conveyed to the Government Commission for Religious Denominations, and the Government Commission sent it on to the Voivodeship Commission of Płock. Two weeks later Kobyliński told the government authorities that he regarded the ruling of the viceroy as a mistake since the previous ministerial decision did not limit religious freedom at all but merely prevented public unrest and conflict among those of the 'Jewish denomination'. Kobyliński also requested an explanation regarding the freedom of hasidim to gather freely for services in private homes and asked if they should be forced to restrict themselves to a single location. However, the Government Commission for Religious Denominations did not intend to concern itself further with the issue of hasidism, and bluntly informed Kobyliński that this question came under the jurisdiction of the Government Commission for Internal Affairs and Police and that questions should be directed there.[51]

We do not know the ruling of the Government Commission for Internal Affairs on this issue, nor even if Kobyliński sent his questions on to them.

[49] See *4.11; AGAD, Rada Administracyjna 6, pp. 484–5; see also AGAD, CWW 1869, p. 20.
[50] AGAD, CWW 1869, p. 20.   [51] See *4.12–*4.14; AGAD, CWW 1869, pp. 18–25.

The Government Commission for Religious Denominations had clearly lost interest, and the answer given to Kobyliński no doubt left Potocki and Staszic disappointed with this setback to their project of 'reforming the Jewish people' (even though one year earlier Staszic had arrived at an identical decision regarding the *shtibl* in the Sandomierz voivodeship). However, it is difficult to say that this was a clash of competing ideas, since neither Staszic nor Potocki, let alone Zajączek, possessed even basic information about hasidism, and Staszic's ideas were often subject to radical change. In both cases the ruling regarding hasidic *shtiblekh* was an expression of a more general idea to reform the Jewish people and their relationship to the Kingdom. It had little, if anything, to do with hasidism itself.

What was this more general idea? As we know, Staszic consistently treated all forms of Jewish political, social, cultural, and religious life as signs of a destructive separatism against which the state had to take radical action. Such an attitude, while clearly evidence of strong anti-Jewish prejudice, also derived from physiocratic ideas that saw Jewish society as parasitic because it did not contribute to national wealth by increasing agricultural production. In that view, the Jewish social order had to be dismantled in order to direct Jews to more productive professions. Staszic, like many other Polish reformers, built on these radical conclusions and spoke against respect for Jewish constitutional rights, against legal assurances of state care to Jews,[52] against appointing any kind of Jewish representative bodies (even religious ones),[53] and even opposed their freedom to perform religious rituals, since they fell outside the control of the state. Hasidic *shtiblekh* were, then, for him another form of Jewish separatism reducing the state's control over the Jews. The change in his attitude between 1817 and 1818 is also telling. In the 1817 incident, the intervention of the Voivodeship Commission of Sandomierz and of Staszic, representing the Government Commission, was apparently a reaction to an anti-hasidic denunciation by the *kahal*. Although the decision benefited the hasidim, its aim was to weaken the *kahal*, not to protect the new 'sect'. In Płock in 1818 by contrast, the opposing sides were not the hasidim and the *kahal* (the *kahal* was not mentioned even once in government

---

[52] See for example Staszic's disapproval of the liberal project Organizacja Ludu Starozakonnego, submitted by the senator Nikolai Novosiltseff to the State Council at the personal request of Emperor Alexander I (AGAD, CWW 1418, pp. 1–38; I Rada Stanu Królestwa Polskiego 283, pp. 217–68; Eisenbach, *Emancypacja Żydów*, 186). The very first sentence of the Staszic report is: 'One of the biggest mistakes of the ancient Poles was that they allowed Jews to enter their country at the time when all others, especially the wise Russians, were expelling them.'

[53] Staszic opposed the establishment of any Jewish representative bodies (see e.g. AGAD, CWW 1411, p. 27) and fought against the institution of the provincial rabbinate, which he viewed as strengthening the power of Jewish religious institutions (see AGAD, KRSW 6629, fo. 127; CWW 1444, pp. 22–4).

correspondence), but rather the hasidim and government institutions. In that situation, Staszic's sympathy of course lay with the government. Hasidism was not perceived as a dissident movement weakening the hegemony of the *kahal*, but as a form of Jewish collective life that had to be opposed.

Zajączek's position is less clear. We actually know relatively little about his views on the Jewish Question besides the fact that he shared contemporary prejudices and stereotypes.[54] He seems to have been somewhat sceptical in his approach to plans for reforming the Jews, but that might have been due as much to a sense of realism as to his anti-Jewish prejudices. To his mind, the persecution of hasidim in the name of abstract plans for the transformation of Jewish society was merely an unnecessary incitement to social unrest, especially because it did not lead to any effective changes in Jewish society. An awareness of Staszic's bias in this area might also have influenced Zajączek's attitude. In 1817 Zajączek refused to agree to Staszic's request to be entrusted with writing the opinion of the Council of State on Nikolai Novosiltseff's proposal *The Organization of the Jewish People*.[55]

We also do not know if the supporters of hasidism had any influence on Zajączek's decision.[56] Of course the possibility cannot be excluded, but it was unlikely to have been a critical factor. The route by which the viceroy received information about the investigation in Płock (through a weekly report from the Voivodeship Commission) does not suggest the participation of hasidim. The viceroy's notes to the Government Commission do not indicate that he knew anything about hasidim beyond what was mentioned in the weekly report, so that there is no circumstantial evidence to substantiate any claim of hasidic influence during this phase of the conflict. To be sure, hasidim were active throughout the investigation, but their activity was limited to the Płock voivodeship, and did not extend to the government authorities.[57] When the hasidim intervened later on (for example, in the 'affair of the hasidim' in 1824, described in the next chapter), their activity did leave traces in the sources, whereas nothing of the kind exists for 1818. Of course, the lack of evidence is not a decisive argument; for example, giving the viceroy a bribe in any form would not have been done openly: the rich texture of life often leaves no trace in archival material. To repeat, we simply

---

[54] See Koźmian, *Pamiętniki*, iii. 21–2.

[55] See ibid. iii. 20; Gelber, 'She'elat hayehudim bepolin', 108.

[56] Dynner ('*Men of Silk*', 63, 277) points to the fact that a well-known patron of hasidism, Berek Sonnenberg, was a private banker of General Zajączek, so a direct hasidic influence on his opinion was possible.

[57] See *4.06; AGAD, CWW 1869, p. 14, where Kobyliński complains that he is flooded with petitions from hasidim throughout the voivodeship requesting permission to open their prayer houses. The Voivodeship Commission had thus ordered the closing of hasidic *shtiblekh* not only in Płock, but in the entire voivodeship.

know too little to explain Zajączek's favourable attitude towards hasidim convincingly.

4. Michałki: *Shtiblekh, Mikveh*, and Burial Societies

The decision of the highest state authorities in the matter of Płock was un-equivocally favourable to the hasidic community, but its effects seem minimal and limited exclusively to the Płock voivodeship. Between 1818 and 1824, when the second great investigation into hasidism took place, the decision of the viceroy was not referred to even once in the numerous conflicts concern-ing hasidim, either by government institutions or by the hasidim themselves. For example, when in 1821 the Jewish community board of Suwałki asked the Government Commission for Religious Denominations to ban prayer gatherings in private homes, because 'in our congregation an opposition faction has formed, which does not go to synagogues, but gather for Jewish services only in private homes', Staszic, in the name of the Government Commission, banned such gatherings.[58] Similarly, in 1822, in response to an enquiry from the Voivodeship Commission of Kraków regarding the legality of private prayer rooms and the tax imposed on them that the Austrian government had introduced in 1798, Stanisław Grabowski (1780–1845), the new Minister for Religious Denominations and Public Enlightenment, ban-ned such gatherings, completely ignoring the 1817 and 1818 rulings.[59] A similar incident took place in Łask in 1820.[60] Local *kahal* leaders there presented to the Voivodeship Commission a charge that a new 'sect' that had arisen in wartime (between 1807 and 1813) had organized a separate prayer room for itself and did not participate in the synagogue. *Kahal* leaders asked the commission to prohibit the sect's separate services and offered as argu-ments the following: (*a*) Judaism forbids the organization of services outside the synagogue; (*b*) those from the sect who do not participate in the syn-agogue do not hear new government decrees announced there; (*c*) abandon-ing prayer in the synagogue contributes to a decline in community income from the collection box and from the reading of the Torah. The arguments here resemble those used elsewhere, for example in several instances in the Sandomierz voivodeship in 1817 and 1818, as mentioned above. The Voivodeship Commission turned for an opinion to the local maskil, Dr M. Schönfeld, and sent his report, which was hostile to the *kahal* leaders and rejected all their arguments, to the Government Commission for Religious Denominations. The Government Commission requested the opinion of

[58] See AGAD, CWW 1818, pp. 4–22.
[59] See *9.01, *9.02; AGAD, CWW 1432, pp. 197–202.
[60] See AGAD, CWW 1555, pp. 6–8, 17–20; KWK 702. See also Wodziński, *Haskalah and Hasidism*, 82–3, for a comprehensive analysis of Schönfeld's report and Hoge's polemics.

Ezekiel Hoge; the latter noted the hasidic context of the conflict, pointed out mistakes in the religious texts Schönfeld cited, and rejected his conclusions. He also added that, in his opinion, 'past conflicts in this city between Jews stem from the sect known as hasidim, who want to distinguish themselves from common Jews and who, as is known, are the most harmful Jews in the country'. We do not know the final decision of the Government Commission on this issue; however, characteristically, none of the officials referred to the viceroy's 1818 ruling on the hasidic *shtiblekh* in Płock.

The reason for this state of affairs can be discerned relatively easily. The ruling of the viceroy was communicated only to the Voivodeship Commission of Płock and to local representatives of the districts.[61] The seven remaining voivodeship commissions did not receive the ruling, and as the ruling was not published, only the Płock voivodeship knew about it. Moreover, the Government Commission clearly did not attach any great weight to the ruling and soon forgot about it. This attitude seems to have resulted directly from the general relationship to hasidism, which the authorities still perceived as an issue of local character and little consequence, in no way connected to the fundamental issues of state policy towards the Jewish population. It is not therefore surprising that the authorities involved in ongoing investigations in the Kraków and Kalisz voivodeships asked the same question which the decision of the viceroy had already answered. The three investigations going on at more or less the same time in Olkusz and Częstochowa illustrate this as well.

Olkusz is a small but important city, known since the fourteenth century as a centre for the mining of lead, zinc, and silver, and also for its sizeable Jewish population. After 1795 Olkusz found itself within the borders of Western Galicia. In 1809 it became part of the Duchy of Warsaw, and in 1815 of the Kingdom of Poland. In 1827 Olkusz numbered 1,213 residents, of whom 261 (21.5 per cent) were Jews. In 1817 the court in Olkusz heard a case concerning an assault on a man called Jakub Brüll by Michał Friedman and others.[62] According to Brüll, the aggressor supposedly belonged to the Michałki sect, and the brawl resulted from 'the forming of a new denomination in the Jewish religion called Michałki, and the split among the Olkusz residents of the Jewish faith'. Although the case was presented as one of assault, the court ruled that it also concerned the constitutional principle of religious tolerance and applied to the Voivodeship Commission for help in determining the legality of the formation of a new 'sect' and whether its aggression towards members of the 'Jewish faith' (*starozakonnego wyznania*

---

[61] See *4.12, *4.13; AGAD, CWW 1869, pp. 21–4.
[62] See Majmon, 'Luźne kartki'; Schiper, *Przyczynki do dziejów chasydyzmu w Polsce*, 101; Dynner, *'Men of Silk'*, 75–8.

Figure 2.5 The central square of Olkusz, depicting the run-down condition of this once important lead- and silver-mining town. Despite attempts to revitalize the mining industry in the early years of the nineteenth century the town never regained its influential position. According to Stanisław Staszic, the reason for the run-down condition was the Jews, who, after the destruction of Olkusz in the 1794 war, 'were the first to sneak into the town, since when the ruins have been a place of poverty and stench'. Watercolour by Zygmunt Vogel (1792). Gabinet Rycin Biblioteki Uniwersytetu Warszawskiego, Zb. Król., T.175, no. 218

mojżeszowego) was subject to the regulations of the penal code.[63] The commission authorized the local district commissioner, Dominik Raczyński, to lead an investigation with the purpose of resolving the following questions:

1. (*a*) Does a sect known as Michałki actually exist among Jews in Olkusz? (*b*) How long ago was the sect organized and by whom?
2. How many people belong to the sect?
3. How far have branches of the sect spread?
4. Who is the founder of the sect?
5. How much does the sect differ from the Jewish religion?
6. What is the essential goal of the sect, and does it embrace depraved customs as moral principles?[64]

Commissioner Raczyński summoned the plaintiff Jakub Brüll and the rabbi of nearby Pilica, Joshua Landau, since Olkusz had no rabbi of its own at the time.[65] Brüll testified that the Michałki were the same sect that referred to

---

[63] See *5.01; APK, RGR 4399, pp. 1–2.   [64] See *5.02; APK, RGR 4399, pp. 3–4.
[65] See *5.04; APK, RGR 4399, pp. 16–21.

itself as Hussites (or hasidim).[66] Their leader in Olkusz was named Michał Friedman, which was why Brüll had called them Michałki. Asked about the differences between 'normal' Jews and hasidim, Brüll explained that hasidim followed the ritual in the Sephardi prayer book (actually, as we have seen, according to the liturgical rite of Isaac Luria) instead of the Ashkenazi prayer book that was in general use. Asked further about the harmful nature of hasidism, he requested a delay of four days, in order 'not to say anything false', after which he testified that he and others he questioned knew of nothing other than the different prayer book. Rabbi Landau testified very similarly, also mentioning the different prayer book, and minimizing all other dissimilarities. Recommended by Brüll as an expert in the topic, Süskind (Zyskind) Rozenheim added two interesting details.[67] According to Rozenheim, 'This sect of Hassites, by decree of the most glorious emperor for the former Austrian government, was banned, and no Hassite was free to stay overnight, but local elders had forgotten this decree.' On the harmfulness of hasidism, he added: 'some Hassites become prophets, such as one in Stopnica, whose name I do not know, attracting less enlightened Jews and ordering them to pay and calling it an offering'. Rozenheim was referring to the well-known tsadik Meir Rotenberg, but since Rotenberg had moved from Stopnica to Opatów the previous year his information on hasidism was not current. After hearing these three testimonies, Commissioner Raczyński compiled a report in which he repeated Rabbi Landau's view that 'no Michałki sect exists, only Hussites, who differ from other Jews only in that they use a different book for their prayers and pray in a separate place, not disturbing those who do not belong to the Hussites'.[68] He also stressed that the information that Brüll had presented was coloured by personal antagonism since he and Friedman were opponents in a court case, and further

---

[66] In 19th-c. central Poland the sound of the vowel sign *kamats gadol* was pronounced both in Yiddish and Hebrew as *u:*, while consonants in final sounds became voiceless; hence *khusit* or *khusyt* instead of *ḥasid* in contemporary standard Hebrew or *khosid* in YIVO standard Yiddish. Since many of the dialects of the Polish language lost the phonemic opposition between the voiced *kh* and the voiceless *h* and, eventually, lost the voiced *kh* altogether, for a Polish-speaking interlocutor the Yiddish (or Hebrew) word *khusit/khusyt* was identical with Polish *husyt* (Hussite), i.e. a member of a Bohemian religious movement founded by the Christian reformist Jan Hus. This form was frequently recorded in Polish literature in the 19th c., and even today it is the most common name for the hasidim in Polish folk culture; it appears in Brzezina, *Polszczyzna Żydów*, 72, 336, and in Cała, *Wizerunek Żyda w polskiej kulturze ludowej*, 18, 25, 36, 45, 56–7, 59, 68–72, though the English edition of the latter book, *The Image of the Jew in Polish Folk Culture*, lost this linguistic feature.

[67] The wealthy and influential tax farmer Zyskind Rozenheim was in conflict with local hasidim and their leader Michał Friedman at least as early as 1816, when the hasidim managed to dismiss a cantor and ritual slaughterer, Majer Blumberg, whom Rozenheim supported. At the same time, the hasidim tried unsuccessfully to put Rozenheim under a *ḥerem* (ban of excommunication): see Archiwum Państwowe w Katowicach, Akta miasta Olkusza 151, pp. 3–16.

[68] See *5.05; APK, RGR 4399, pp. 14–15.

recommended that the district commission in Stopnica should check whether some kind of 'Jewish prophet' really was active there, as Rozenheim had claimed. The Voivodeship Commission did send an order to that effect to the commissioner in Stopnica, but there was no further result and the incident evidently ended there. The commission did not turn the matter over to the central authorities, but accepted the opinion of Raczyński regarding the harmlessness of hasidism and that of Landau that the only difference between the hasidim and other Jews was their method of prayer. No report was submitted from Stopnica, and the Voivodeship Commission forgot about the matter.

What is striking here is the reluctance on the part of both the Jewish community representatives and the government bodies to explore the subject further. That all Rabbi Landau's answers were conciliatory is especially telling since he was the son of the well-known maskil from Prague, Israel Landau, and the grandson of Ezekiel Landau, the famed rabbi of Prague and a known critic of hasidism.[69] The fact that Jakub Brüll, who had brought the original accusation, was evasive in his responses and also requested a four-day adjournment when asked to provide details of the differences between the hasidim and other Jews is similarly telling; we can surmise that the delay was needed not to get more specific information, as he claimed, but rather to discuss the matter with others who were similarly opposed to the hasidim. The negotiations were most clearly favourable towards the hasidim, because in the end Brüll did not present any specific accusations. Equally ineffectual was the testimony of Rozenheim, the 'expert witness', who not only was unable to name the accused tsadik but could not even say where he lived. We can surmise either that those questioned were afraid to have state authorities intervene in an internal Jewish conflict and therefore held back at the last minute,[70] or that the investigation itself was sufficiently effective as an instrument of pressure that those opposed to hasidim could gain the concessions they wanted in return for not pressing the matter. Both scenarios appear relatively often in Polish government investigations into Jewish affairs (not only those connected to hasidism),[71] so we can safely presume that at least one of them applies here.

[69] On the family relations see Kestenberg-Gladstein, *Neuere Geschichte der Juden in den böhmischen Ländern*, i: *Das Zeitalter der Aufklärung, 1780–1830*, 126; 'Rabanim ugedolei torah be'olkush', 27. On the Landau family in Opatów see Hundert, *The Jews in a Polish Private Town*, 116–33. The most comprehensive analysis of Ezekiel Landau's anti-hasidic pronouncements is in Flatto, 'Hasidim and Mitnaggedim: Not a World Apart', and ead., *The Kabbalistic Culture of Eighteenth-Century Prague*, 86–93.

[70] See Lederhendler, *The Road to Modern Jewish Politics*, 12–14, on the communal regulations prohibiting appeals to the non-Jewish legal court.

[71] See also a very similar result of an anti-hasidic denunciation in Połaniec, in Kuperstein, 'Inquiry at Polaniec', 37–8.

Not surprisingly, the district commissioner did not proceed further: since both plaintiff and witnesses were reluctant to give more details, the investigator was basically helpless. Both the district commissioner and the Voivodeship Commission were also clearly relieved to abandon the investigation, a response which in itself was an expression of the more general lack of interest in hasidism by the provincial authorities. When the Olkusz court petitioned the Voivodeship Commission for further information about hasidism so that they could settle the conflict between Brüll and Friedman, they were bluntly informed that 'it is not known when and from whom some sect of Hussites among the Jews was grafted onto the group', and that it could offer no further information.[72] Hasidism still was not perceived by provincial officials as a significant issue, other than as part of a more general Jewish Question in Poland which central and voivodeship officials were debating at that time. The court gladly agreed that the case resulted from a personal conflict and that the only difference between the hasidim and their opponents was the difference in prayer books, something completely trivial from the point of view of the Polish administration.

An incident in Częstochowa in 1820 reveals almost identical attitudes on the part of both Jewish representatives and the state administration, though the conflict there had a completely different origin, development, and character. Though Częstochowa, an average-sized city in the south-western part of the Kingdom, is known mainly as the Catholic centre of devotion to the Virgin Mary, traces of Jewish settlement there date back at least to the beginning of the eighteenth century. By 1827 Jewish residents already numbered 1,141, or 18.5 per cent of the population. At some point this number also included hasidim. In 1820 a group of local hasidim demanded the right to use the local *mikveh*, or ritual bath, but opponents (usually called 'talmudists') claimed that the bath was intended exclusively for use by women and that the hasidic attempt to use the *mikveh* contradicted religious law and was indecent.[73] In response, the hasidim argued that the bath belonged to the entire community, and everyone had a right to use it; they complained that forbidding them to use it meant they had to bathe in the Warta river, with the attendant danger of exposure to illness (the incident occurred in October and November).[74] When the conflict became acute, the *kahal* closed the *mikveh*

---

[72] See *5.07; APK, RGR 4399, p. 23.

[73] See more on the events in Częstochowa and on a report submitted by the maskil Dr Schönfeld in Wodziński, *Haskalah and Hasidism*, 83–4; see also Wodziński, 'Chasydzi w Częstochowie'.

[74] See *7.10, *7.11; AGAD, KWK 702, pp. 17–19; see also Wodziński, 'Chasydzi w Częstochowie', 291–2. Traditionally, immersion in the *mikveh* was obligatory for married women after menstruation and for proselytes during the ceremony of conversion, as well as for the ritual cleansing of dishes bought from non-Jews. The hasidim, however, following the customs of other mystical groups, also made it obligatory for men on the sabbath and during

completely—equally burdensome for both sides—and even forbade the burial of a dead child from a hasidic family, which led the hasidim to request the mayor's intervention. The mayor ordered the community to give the hasidim access to the *mikveh*, but referred the matter to the Voivodeship Commission of Kalisz for a comprehensive examination.[75] The next day, hasidim went to the *mikveh* but were chased away by a crowd that had gathered in front of it, though the police defended them. The hasidim then asked the Voivodeship Commission to intervene. The commission ordered an investigation and again requested an opinion from Dr Schönfeld on hasidism and the right of hasidim to use the Jewish bath.[76] Both the commission and mayor received numerous letters from both hasidim and the *kahal*, in consequence of which the mayor withdrew his permission for hasidim to use the bath and asked the commission for a speedy decision. The following questions were asked of hasidim and representatives of the *kahal*: (*a*) 'How long has the *kitajowcy* sect existed in Stara Częstochowa?'; (*b*) 'Do they pay taxes in common with Jews of the Mosaic faith and how?'; (*c*) 'Who has contributed to the *mikveh*?'; (*d*) 'How do they differ from Jews of the Mosaic faith in paying for religious rituals?'[77] The hasidim and *kahal* gave completely different answers to the first three questions. The hasidim stated that they had already existed as a group in Częstochowa for sixteen years, that they paid all taxes, and that they had contributed to building the *mikveh*. The *kahal*, on the other hand, maintained that hasidim had been in the city for only ten years, that a *shtibl* had existed for only five, that the hasidim did not pay taxes, and that the *mikveh* had been built with money from five donors, who had intended it exclusively for use by women. To the fourth question the hasidim responded that the only way in which they differed from the other Jews was in the length of their services, and that they could give examples of non-hasidic men who also used the *mikveh*. The *kahal* testified that it would soon present information on the fourth issue. Of course, no information was ever submitted, just as in Olkusz. Again, Jews were reluctant to involve non-Jewish institutions in an internal religious conflict, though it cannot be ruled out that in both Olkusz and Częstochowa, as among Polish Jews in general, there was as yet little clear understanding of differences between hasidim and other Jews, so that the *kahal* really did not have reliable information to convey.

religious festivals. For more on hasidic customs using the *mikveh*, see Wertheim, *Law and Custom in Hasidism*, 215–16.

[75] See *7.01, *7.02; AGAD, KWK 702, pp. 33–4; see also Wodziński, 'Chasydzi w Częstochowie', 284–5.

[76] See *7.03, *7.04, *7.13; AGAD, KWK 702, pp. 19–20, 22, 31–2; see also AGAD, CWW 1542, pp. 6–8; Wodziński, 'Chasydzi w Częstochowie', 285–7, 293.

[77] See *7.09; AGAD, KWK 702, pp. 38–42, 67–72; see also Wodziński, 'Chasydzi w Częstochowie', 290–1.

Soon after, the Voivodeship Commission also received an opinion from Dr Schönfeld, who presented very superficial characteristics of hasidism without any kind of conclusion, and in the matter of the *mikveh* took the side of the hasidim. He wrote that there was no 'indecency' in the use of one bath by women and men (they were not, it should be stressed, using it at the same time), and that the two groups (the hasidim and those who identified with the *kahal*) could agree to an appropriate division of hours. He wrote further that hasidim had even more right to use the *mikveh* than other Jews because they observed ritual more strictly; their obedience to the religious laws on ritual purity was indeed praiseworthy.[78] The Voivodeship Commission recognized that it was not in a position to make a decision on this issue, so it sent Schönfeld's report, the protocols of the questioning, and the petitions of the hasidim to the Government Commission for Religious Denominations and Public Enlightenment to request a ruling on two points: (1) Could the ritual bath serve both talmudists and hasidim without further conflict if certain hours were designated for the first group and others for the second, since both groups assisted in its maintenance? (2) Could the ritual bath now be subject to police inspection for the prevention of disease resulting from a lack of cleanliness?[79] The Government Commission showed no interest in the matter; on the basis of the documents submitted, Minister Grabowski proclaimed (*a*) that hasidim had the same right to the *mikveh* as everyone else and (*b*) that the question regarding the supervision of sanitation should be transferred to the police. But in fact the parties had already reached an understanding which allowed hasidim to use the *mikveh*, and the incident was forgotten.[80]

As in Olkusz, the local and provincial authorities had carried out all the required procedures scrupulously, and had equally meticulously avoided committing themselves to any decision of a general nature. The Voivodeship Commission transferred the matter to the Government Commission without revealing its own position; the Government Commission made a decision exclusively on the basis of the scant documentation, and so did not enter into the essence of the conflict. And as in Olkusz, representatives of the *kahal*, the traditional majority, refrained from submitting more complete testimonies which would have incriminated the hasidim and exposed them to further government investigation. In the face of the intervention of the state authorities, the *kahal* had to capitulate and allow the hasidim access to the *mikveh*,

---

[78] See *7.17; AGAD, KWK 702, pp. 73–86; see also Wodziński, *Oświecenie żydowskie w Królestwie Polskim*, 271–5; id., *Haskalah and Hasidism*, 269–73.

[79] See *7.18; AGAD, CWW 1542, pp. 4–5; see also AGAD, KWK 702, p. 44; Wodziński, 'Chasydzi w Częstochowie', 298–9.

[80] See *7.15, *7.20, *7.21; AGAD, KWK 702, pp. 51–2, 56–7, 65–6, 87; see also AGAD, CWW 1542, pp. 9–10; Wodziński, 'Chasydzi w Częstochowie', 300–1.

because the '*mikveh* was necessary for women of talmudist belief according to their religion and it had been closed for fourteen days; thus, those who could not wait further for a decision regarding its opening requested the use of the bath [for the sake of the women], which the *kitajowcy* always allowed'.[81]

In 1823 there was another investigation into hasidism in Olkusz. In 1822–3 the authorities of the Kingdom had implemented one of the most important elements of the projects to reform Jewish society, the closure of institutions that in the opinion of the reformers strengthened Jewish separatism, and in 1822 the *kahals*, the basis of Jewish autonomy in the Kingdom, were abolished. Some of their functions were transferred to the Jewish community boards that had been created in 1821. The community boards were supposed to be institutions analogous to church boards (collective bodies of wardens in Catholic, Protestant, and Orthodox parishes) that were created at that time. In both cases the goal was the same: to limit the competence of religious authorities and to transfer their authority in non-religious matters (such as collecting taxes and maintaining registers of births, marriages, and deaths) to the state. This was, then, a typical Enlightenment state reform. All religious fraternities, especially burial fraternities (*ḥevrot kadisha*), which were of course a prime source of revenue and power for the *kahal*, were closed down shortly afterwards. During the formal dissolution of the burial fraternity in Olkusz, state authorities questioned representatives of the local Jewish community: 'Besides this fraternity, are there any associations unknown to the government in the Jewish congregation in Olkusz?' The group, among whom were hasidim, non-hasidim, and opponents of hasidim, testified to the mayor that 'an association of Hussites is located in Olkusz, but it is not known if it has the approval of the government'.[82] This response suggests that the Jews were themselves uncertain regarding the status of hasidism, no doubt a result of the 1818 inquiry and the government's later contradictory decisions, all of which left the status of hasidim equivocal. To add to the confusion, the Kraków voivodeship allowed the creation of hasidic *shtiblekh* on the basis of an 1822 ruling by Stanisław Grabowski, then minister for religious denominations, which banned the establishment of prayer rooms in cities with synagogues but allowed them elsewhere, and which permitted prayer in private homes.[83] Given this complicated legal situation, it is not surprising that the Jews were perplexed. The hasidic *shtibl* of Olkusz was closed, but the district commissioner soon ordered it to be reopened.[84] He also asked the Voivode-

[81] See *7.20; AGAD, KWK 702, pp. 56–7.

[82] See *9.02; AGAD, CWW 1420, pp. 22–3; see also Archiwum Państwowe w Katowicach, Akta miasta Olkusza 151, p. 32.

[83] See *9.02, *10.04; AGAD, CWW 1432, pp. 201–2; AGAD, CWW 1420, pp. 18–19; see also APK, RGR 4014, pp. 11–12.

[84] See Archiwum Państwowe w Katowicach, Akta miasta Olkusza 151, pp. 36–7.

ship Commission if the 'corporation of Hussites' was subject to the law regarding the dissolution of Jewish religious fraternities; the Voivodeship Commission sent the question on to the Government Commission for Religious Denominations, at the same time informing the Commission that hasidim distinguished themselves from other Jews by 'rituals of service, not participating in the synagogue, and not using kosher meat' (the latter comment is perhaps a reference to their refusal to regard the meat slaughtered under community auspices as kosher).[85]

The Government Commission of course made no decision; it simply ordered the Voivodeship Commission to conduct an investigation. When questioned, Joshua Landau (now the rabbi of Olkusz, previously of Pilica) provided very general information about the beginnings of hasidism and the differences between hasidim and other Jews, referring again to the differences in prayer. Similarly, the hasid questioned, Perec Szternfeld, said that hasidim distinguished themselves from 'simple Jews' only by their prayer book. In contrast to the earlier investigations, this time no clearly anti-hasidic voice was heard, so the result was positive for the hasidim. Both the district commissioner and the Voivodeship Commission conveyed to the Government Commission the opinion that hasidism was merely a popularized prayer group with no harmful intentions, so that it was not affected by the ruling requiring the dissolution of harmful Jewish fraternities.[86]

Compared with previous interventions, the 1823 issue, though in itself very minor, clearly triggered greater interest and engagement on the part of both local and voivodeship authorities. This was no doubt the result of two mutually reinforcing factors. First, it suggests that the growing number of such interventions made the government realize that this was a large issue. Second, the question surfaced during the dissolution of the burial fraternities, one of the most important measures to reform Jewish society to be undertaken by the Kingdom of Poland. As we know, one of the central premisses of the reform programme was to fight against Jewish separatism and the institutions that maintained it; religious fraternities, especially burial fraternities, were perceived as one of those institutions. Though any connection between hasidim and religious fraternities was accidental, hasidim began to get caught up in the central political line that the authorities were adopting towards the Jewish population. Slowly, hasidism ceased to be a peripheral question of provincial authorities refereeing local Jewish squabbles: as the issues widened, it became a matter of mainstream concern.

Unfortunately, we do not know what opinion the Government Commission reached on the latest Olkusz incident. Most likely, it never expressed an

---

[85] See *10.04; AGAD, CWW 1420, pp. 18–19; see also APK, RGR 4014, pp. 11–12.

[86] See *10.05–*10.08; AGAD, CWW 1420, pp. 18–19; AGAD, CWW 1433, pp. 116–21; see also APK, RGR 4014, pp. 17, 19–20.

opinion, either because it recognized that the issue required no further action or because even as early as 1823 it was known that a thorough investigation of the issue of hasidim throughout the Kingdom was already under way, so that it postponed its decision until more general regulations had been enacted.

5. Conclusions

Though hasidism appeared in the lands of central Poland as early as the mid-eighteenth century, the governments that controlled these territories between 1772 and 1830 became aware of it only slowly; in consequence it was not until nearly the end of that period that the existence of hasidic groups became an issue in Jewish politics. This was above all a result of the fact that during most of this time hasidism was still an elite, ecstatic group; even when it became a broader movement it was still not an especially large one. To a still greater degree, the lack of official interest in hasidism was caused by the very complicated general history of the states of central and eastern Europe at the start of the nineteenth century. The Polish–Lithuanian Commonwealth, the Habsburg monarchy, and the Duchy of Warsaw, threatened almost incessantly by war and engaged in great political reforms, rarely had time for contemporary social politics; in reality, the only official apparatus that worked efficiently was the Treasury, which levied heavy taxes to fill the war chests. Successive ruling powers had neither the opportunity nor the desire to concern themselves more deeply with the social contingencies of a population that fate had brought within their borders, especially with one that, like the Jews, was unwanted. But this was a double-edged sword. Times of unrest, of course, weakened the authority of the *kahal*, whose 'derivative power', as Eli Lederhendler accurately defined it, resulted from the prerogatives granted it by the state and its representatives at all levels of power (and in private cities, by the landowner).[87] As the examples above show, hasidic groups with pretensions to autonomy often appeared just when state authority was weakening: in Łask in 'the times of greatest war', in Częstochowa between 1805 and 1810 (the *shtibl* was created in 1815, five to ten years after the group had emerged), and in Olkusz around 1815. Undoubtedly, the appearance of hasidic groups and their independent *shtiblekh* triggered local conflicts, but the number of complaints to which the growing autonomy of the hasidic movement gave rise was surprisingly small. *Kahal* representatives, unsure of how long the new regimes would last and how interested they would be in community matters, probably did not seek state intervention because they did not think it would be effective. Only after 1817 did the number of state interventions grow quickly, a consequence which was, of course, tied to increasing confidence in the state's power to endure, though not necessarily in the state itself.

[87] Lederhendler, *The Road to Modern Jewish Politics*, 12, 163.

But Jewish communities complaining to the authorities about challenges to their authority did not always think it appropriate to inform the authorities that their allegations related to hasidism.

The political engagement of hasidim at this time can be characterized as grass-roots politics. Hasidim sought the aid of the non-Jewish authorities in conflicts with the non-hasidic majority, or defended themselves against the *kahal* when it appealed to the state, but did not appear interested in broader political activity. Even in 1818, when the investigation into the legality of hasidism was ongoing in Warsaw, requests to the provincial authorities for permission to open *shtiblekh* are the only recorded trace of hasidic engagement. Until 1823 it is difficult to speak of more ambitious nationwide political aims. As a social force, hasidism was still not large enough to take political initiatives independently and on a larger scale, even in matters relating exclusively to hasidic society. The day when hasidim would have sufficient political maturity to launch initiatives on a broader front of Jewish issues was still far off.

It is possible to say that the degree of hasidic involvement in politics in the Kingdom of Poland was in a certain sense proportional to the recognition of the political significance of hasidism and the involvement in such matters of the central authorities. In both cases politics remained at the community level. Though the first large investigation in the matter of hasidism took place in 1818, when for the first time the question of the legality of hasidic *shtiblekh* was determined at a central level, it cannot be said that there was a consistent 'hasidic policy'. Above all, the authorities fundamentally viewed these matters as singular incidents of local significance only, without ties to the general politics of the Jewish Question. Only Staszic, and after him Potocki, saw the controversy surrounding the establishment of *shtiblekh* as a small part of a more general issue of Jewish separatism. Characteristically, however, the issue for both politicians was the establishment of these independent prayer rooms, not hasidism per se, because hasidism was still imperceptible to the Polish administration. Even the alarmist report of the well-known maskil and anti-hasidic critic Abraham Stern, and the popularity of Julian Ursyn Niemcewicz's anti-hasidic novel *Lejbe i Sióra*, did not change this general attitude. Moreover, Viceroy Zajączek and the Administrative Council did not share Stern's and Niemcewicz's negative view of the *shtibl*, while Stanisław Staszic, the minister most critical of the hasidim, managed in short order to come out with completely contradictory decisions (a tendency of his), so that his political views had little if any effect. In essence, the 1818 decision of the Administrative Council and viceroy, along with the formal decrees and directives from ministries, voivodeship commissions, and local authorities between 1817 and 1822, were chaotic in the extreme, had no influence on subsequent government policy, and played no essential role in the internal affairs of the hasidic movement. Several factors account for this: (*a*) a lack of inherited legislation to which the administration of the Kingdom could appeal, other than the 1798 Habsburg decree on *minyanim* in Western Galicia, which made no clear reference to the hasidim; (*b*) the general inertia and lack of desire to take on new issues, typical of all administrations; (*c*) stereotypical and schematic thinking on the Jewish Question in categories that did not reflect internal Jewish religious divisions; (*d*) a general ignorance of Jewish issues and an unwillingness to learn; (*e*) a lack of knowledge of other investigations and decisions in matters related to hasidism, and so a lack of awareness of the general scale of the phenomenon (this was, of course, a result of the weakness of the state administrations); (*f*) as in similar matters, unwillingness on the part of Jewish society to disclose the deeper nature and scale of the conflict to state authorities, even when the struggle was no longer an internal Jewish conflict and when one of the sides had turned to the state administration for help, because of the negative attitude to this in Jewish law.

In the end, however, the growing wave of interventions in issues related to hasidism and the fact that the question of the legality of hasidism became tied up with the issue of religious fraternities—one of the central themes of Enlightenment reforms in Poland—led the authorities of the Kingdom to take a deeper interest in the topic. That was in 1823.

CHAPTER THREE

The Great Inquiry, 1823–1824

THE MOST IMPORTANT episode in the political history of hasidism in central Poland was the government investigation conducted in the years 1823 and 1824. Despite its importance, the investigation has never been properly described, and the literature on the subject, though extensive, is comprised of works in which incomplete knowledge of the facts is mixed with pure confabulation,[1] biased interpretations given as fact,[2] unclear allusions,[3] second-hand testimonies,[4] or hasidic hagiography.[5] At best, these accounts are sketchy descriptions or focused on selected threads of the investigation.[6] The task of this chapter is, above all, to set out what we know about the investigation on the basis of the extant sources—and what we do not know. This should help to eliminate at least some of the worst errors that still persist in works on Polish hasidism.

1. Hussites: The Beginnings of the Investigation

In September 1823 Viceroy General Józef Zajączek received a report written by Colonel Dulfus, the head of the gendarmerie in Parczew, a small provincial town in the Podlasie voivodeship:

I have the honour to report to His Enlightened Lordship the Prince Viceroy that in the town of Parczew, in the district of Radzyń . . . a group of young Jews has formed a sect of Hussites. Those assembled do not go to services [in the synagogue] but rather only meet in private homes, where, until midnight, they make noise, and so debauchery happens, encouraging and attracting others from different places to

---

[1] An especially glaring example is Frenk, 'Yekhezkel hoge oder "haskel meshumad"'. Frenk's confabulations were reiterated by later historians.
[2] Many of these interpretations are in Mahler, *Hasidism and the Jewish Enlightenment*, 317–37; see also Schiper, *Żydzi Królewstwa Polskiego w dobie powstania listopadowego*, 24–5; id., *Przyczynki do dziejów chasydyzmu w Polsce*, 102–3. [3] Tsederbaum, *Keter kehunah*, 130.
[4] Feinkind, 'Dysputa żydowska za czasów Stanisława Staszica'; Lask Abrahams, 'Stanislaus Hoga—Apostate and Penitent'; Wilensky, *Ḥasidim umitnagedim*, ii. 354.
[5] Alfasi, *Gur: hameyased ḥidushei harim*, 86; Bromberg, *Migedolei haḥasidut*, 42–3; Boim, *Harabi rebe bunem mipeshisḥa*, ii. 633–6.
[6] Wodziński, 'Sprawa chasydymów'; id., *Haskalah and Hasidism*, 90–1, 107–13; Dynner, 'Men of Silk', 109–13.

Figure 3.1 Parczew. The photograph on this postcard, possibly taken during the First World War, vividly depicts the semi-rural nature of the hamlet as late as the 1910s. Private collection of Marek Wojciechowski

join them, concealing their activities without witnesses. They have a rabbi in the town of Przysucha [Pshiskha] on the Vistula who supports them with advice and to whom they turn to confer about their interests.[7]

We do not know where Colonel Dulfus obtained this information, nor do we know why he wrote his report. Disturbed by the emergence of such a harmful, new, and strange sect that evidently appealed to young men, the viceroy ordered the Government Commission for Internal Affairs and Police 'to get to know the circumstances and the general situation corresponding to the rulings made in this area'.[8] In the name of the minister of internal affairs, Stanisław Staszic therefore wrote to the Government Commission for Religious Denominations and Public Enlightenment with a request for information relating to this 'sect of Hussites' and for suggestions of effective means of maintaining control.[9] The president of that commission, Minister Stanisław Grabowski, had never heard of Jewish Hussites, i.e. of Jewish supporters of the fourteenth-century figure Jan Hus and the religious-social Hussite movement established by his supporters, and therefore ordered the

[7] See *11.01; AGAD, CWW 1871, p. 4; see also Wodziński, 'Sprawa chasydymów', 229.
[8] See *11.02; AGAD, KRSW 6634, fo. 230.
[9] See *11.03; AGAD, CWW 1871, p. 2; see also AGAD, KRSW 6634, fo. 231; Mahler, *Haḥasidut vehahaskalah*, 475.

Figure 3.2 Stanisław Grabowski (1780–1845), son of the last Polish king, Stanisław August Poniatowski, a political activist, from 1820 minister of religious affairs and public enlightenment, embodiment of the reactionary turn in the politics of the Congress Kingdom. Lithograph by Józef Sonntag(?), before 1825. Biblioteka Narodowa w Warszawie, Zbiory Ikonograficzne, G. 33789 (zb. Potockich)

Voivodeship Commission of Podlasie to conduct a detailed investigation. The correspondence unequivocally shows that neither Zajączek, Staszic, Grabowski nor any of their officials knew that the investigation was related to hasidism. And so, following its standard procedures, the government attempted to investigate these hitherto unknown Jewish Hussites.

The Voivodeship Commission of Podlasie performed its task with exceptional diligence. It immediately ordered all the district commissions within its jurisdiction to conduct detailed investigations in the towns under their own jurisdiction regarding the nature of the new sect, its beliefs and customs, and the number of its followers. In the course of two months the Voivodeship Commission assembled and sent to the Government Commission reports of two of the four districts, Biała Podlaska and Siedlce, as well as twelve reports from the mayors of Adamów, Garwolin, Łaskarzew, Łuków, Maciejowice, Osieck, Parysów, the city of Siedlce, Stężyca, Stoczek, and Żelechów. The quality and credibility of the reports vary.[10] The mayors of Adamów, Garwolin, Łaskarzew, Maciejowice, Osieck, Parysów, Stężyca, and Stoczek wrote in one-sentence notes that there were no 'Hussites' in their towns. In the cases of Stężyca, Stoczek, and Łaskarzew, there is no doubt that this was the truth, as not a single Jew lived in these towns at that time. Hasidim were rarely found in towns that were so poor that a basic religious

---

[10] See *11.04–*11.14, *11.16–*11.18, *11.20; AGAD, CWW 1871, pp. 3, 7–33, 35–6. The statistical data gathered in these reports are analysed in Wodziński, 'How Many *Hasidim* Were There in Congress Poland?'.

infrastructure, such as a prayer room or *mikveh*, was lacking, or so small that it was impossible to gather a *minyan* for prayer. Such was the case in Osieck; as the mayor explained, there were only seventeen families, but among these paupers there was 'no Jewish sect called Hussites'. He further said that it was difficult to provide the information he had been asked to supply about the Jews: 'as their deviousness is known to all, it is not possible to investigate their rituals'. The mayor of Garwolin commented that in his town 'not even a synagogue exists, or a *kahal*; Jews gather for their prayer services only privately, in private homes, so small is their number'. The mayor of Parysów noted that there were several Jewish families but no group of hasidim.[11]

The reports from areas where the mayors and district commissioners did find groups of hasidim are somewhat more specific, and some of them offer fascinating detail. The commissioner of the Biała district reported interesting information, obtained from both hasidim and non-hasidim, that hasidism originated with Israel of Międzybóż (Medzibezh), the Ba'al Shem Tov in the 1740s, who had published a commentary on Psalms 149 and 150 called *Tsava'at haribash* (this work is in fact an anthology of hasidic teachings and is only attributed to the Besht). He further explained that hasidim prayed with song and dance, and that the ties of friendship between members of the community was strong; and that since 'they spend their days praying . . . they regard themselves more highly than other Jews not belonging to this sect'. The commissioner of the Siedlce district complained that obtaining reliable information about the sect was very difficult, but he nonetheless offered precise information: hasidim differ from other Jews in that they have a different liturgy and different customs in ritual slaughter. At the same time he regarded hasidim as descendants of families that were 'the most distinguished religious clergymen'. The positive tone here suggests that the wording may have come from the hasidim themselves. The mayor of Żelechów emphasized the separatism of the hasidim: their not associating with 'common Jews'; not attending their synagogues; having their own distinct teachings and spiritual leaders;[12] spending sabbaths and festivals only within their own groups; and having their own mystical beliefs and practices. The mayor of Łuków reported that according to information obtained from Jews and converts, hasidim were no different from other Jews, but were 'particular only in being more learned in their religion, more pious and more scrupulous, for which reason they consider themselves to be distinguished from other Jews; other Jews they call "simple Jews"; they [hasidim] are not distin-

---

[11] See *11.11–*11.13; AGAD, CWW 1871, pp. 28, 31–2.

[12] The statement that hasidim have 'their separate leaders, of whom one is the highest (like the one in Żelechów)' is followed by the explanation that this refers to 'Balcin [Ba'al Shem] i.e. Moszko Mączycki'. This is a corrupted version of the name of the tsadik from Żelechów, Moses b. Benjamin of Stężyca, a disciple of Jacob Isaac Horowitz of Lublin.

guished by their origin, but they distinguish themselves by their piety and religious scruples, forming their own group'. When officers of the town council of Siedlce questioned a man whose home was used as a hasidic *shtibl*, Abram Dawidowicz (that is, Abram ben David) Kohen, he testified that hasidim observed the same rituals and the same prayers as other Jews and that they were distinguished only by their greater piety and longer services. Usually they prayed separately, but, he said, 'sometimes we pray together in synagogue with other Jews' and 'any Jew is free to come and pray together with us'. Asked about permission for the establishment of the *shtibl*, he responded that 'under the Austrian government, we had permission, and now, as is the custom, we practise according to the older custom'. This last comment probably relates to the ruling about *minyanim* from 1798, which was known to the hasidim and which actually legalized the *shtiblekh*.[13]

The most interesting and most extensive information on hasidism comes from three different sources in Parczew, where an especially detailed investigation was conducted. The investigation was led by the commissioner of the Radzyń district, who asked about the origins, numbers, activities, and harmfulness of the 'sect' and about the 'debauchery, depravity, and disturbance committed in the city' as mentioned in the Dulfus report.[14] According to the official record, the mayor and deputies of the town council, the board of the Jewish community (*dozór bóżniczy*; in 1822, the *kahals* of the Kingdom of Poland were disbanded and their functions taken over by new bodies known as Jewish community boards), and local hasidic leaders all testified that there were two groups of hasidim in Parczew. The first group, which was less extreme than the second, in the sense that it had better relations with non-hasidim, was made up of followers of the tsadik of Radzyń, Jacob Simon Deutsch; the members of the second were the supporters of the tsadik of Przysucha (Pshiskha), Simhah Bunem. According to the mayor, the followers of Jacob Simon Deutsch prayed in the synagogue together with the other Jews but also met separately as a group to study religious texts or simply to talk, tell stories, drink, or spend time together; they were quiet, and besides their singing, dancing, jumping, and being joyous, could not be distinguished from other Jews. The followers of the tsadik of Przysucha, in contrast, generally did not participate in community services. They gathered in their own *shtibl*, in which 'throughout the entire night they make a great deal of noise, conducting their prayers with singing, jumping, and dancing. Repeated observations show that in the same place that they gathered for services they also played games and drank, after which they ran around the

---

[13] See *11.05, *11.09, *11.16, *11.18, *11.20; AGAD, CWW 1871, pp. 7–10, 22–5, 35–6. For a discussion of the Austrian ruling of 1798 see Ch. 2, §1.

[14] See *11.17; AGAD, CWW 1871, pp. 11–21.

Figure 3.3 Simhah Bunem of Przysucha (Pshiskha) (1765–1827), an influential hasidic leader, depicted here in a style typical of nineteenth-century hasidic images. From Yitshak Alfasi, *Gur: hameyased ḥidushei harim, ḥayav, maḥshevotav vetorato* (Tel Aviv, 1954), 32, ill. 3. Private collection of the author

streets singing, jumping, and shouting.' After being fined several times by the mayor and local police for such nocturnal misbehaviour, some measure of quiet was restored. The mayor and deputies of the town council also added that the hasidim of this latter group actively encouraged new members to join them. Those who did so often acted against the will of their parents, abandoned their wives and children without any means of livelihood, and even stole from their families so that they would have money for travelling to visit the tsadik and supporting the extravagances of the hasidic court. When asked by the commissioner, municipal deputies testified that in three instances legal proceedings against hasidim had reached the courts, and that there were other cases known to them that had not been tried.

The Jewish community board (i.e. the traditional *kahal* elite) confirmed most of the allegations made by the mayor and the municipal deputies: that the hasidim of both groups did not differ in faith from other Jews, and that supporters of the tsadik of Przysucha 'already do not listen to their parents, while others forget about the needs of [their] wives and children, do not want to be employed in a trade, and often go for several weeks, and even for months, to the rabbi; because of this, the wives of some poorer Hussites are not able to feed their children and often go asking for bread'.

Four hasidim from the Przysucha group were summoned to testify, but naturally they denied all the charges. According to their testimony, it was possible to find among them those who committed such offences, but in no way were these 'misdeeds the principle of our association', and those guilty of such acts should be fined appropriately. This attempt at denial is so routine as to be of no great interest, but the testimony of the mayor and deputies of the town council and of the Jewish community board is, in contrast, very interesting indeed. The fact that the municipal officials were well informed about hasidism in Parczew suggests either that they had prepared for the investigation or, more probably, that the activity of the Przysucha hasidim was a subject of controversy in which the municipal powers were actively engaged. This allows us to hypothesize that the report on Parczew by Colonel Dulfus, which began this general investigation in Poland, had come about because the tension in the town was such that neither the local gendarmerie nor the local authorities could control the situation. The mayor and the Jewish community board were both clearly less troubled by the original group of hasidim, the followers of Jacob Simon Deutsch, because their behaviour was less disruptive (possibly also because they were older). By contrast, the followers of Simhah Bunem were accused of aggressive proselytizing, disruptive and indecent behaviour, drunkenness, breaking up families, and thievery (though, confronted with the testimony of the hasidim, the deputies of the town council did admit that 'to be sure, not everyone does this'). Reading the report of Colonel Dulfus in this light we see that it was ostensibly not concerned with hasidim as such, but rather with a new proselytizing group, comprised mainly of young people who had a 'rabbi in the city of Przysucha on the Vistula' (Przysucha does not lie on the Vistula). This again suggests that the report by Dulfus was a reflection of the local context, and that tensions within the Jewish community in Parczew were so great as to require the involvement of civic institutions. On the basis of the existing documentation, however, it is difficult to determine who was actually behind the report to which Dulfus lent his name. It could have been the mayor, as he was the most indignant at the lack of order caused by the new hasidim, but the mayor did not need Dulfus to write such a report as he could have done so himself. It might have been the Jewish community board, or it might have been a strategic move on behalf of the followers of the tsadik Jacob Simon Deutsch of Radzyń, who felt themselves threatened by the aggressive proselytizing of the Przysucha hasidim. Moreover the tsadik of Radzyń was the main hasidic voice in the nationwide campaign against the Przysucha hasidim, so one cannot exclude the possibility that the entire affair was simply another phase in that ongoing battle.[15] In any case, the idea advanced in the literature that the initiative came from Haskalah circles is completely unfounded.[16]

[15] The conflict over the Przysucha school of hasidism has been broadly described in the historical literature. See e.g. Aescoly, *Hahasidut bepolin*, 82–9; T. M. Rabinowicz, *Bein peshisha lelublin*, 275–85.   [16] See e.g. Schiper, *Przyczynki do dziejów chasydyzmu w Polsce*, 102.

2. Hasidism Is Banned

At the beginning of December 1823 the Voivodeship Commission sent all the reports (with the exception of the reports of the district commissions for Siedlce and Biała, which went later) to the Government Commission for Religious Denominations. The only term used to define the group under investigation was *husyci*, i.e. Hussites (only the mayor of Stoczek wrote 'Husset or Sage'), but the officials of the Government Commission nevertheless began to suspect that the investigation might relate to hasidism. This shows that in 1823 ministerial officials (or at least some of them) already had some knowledge of hasidism; they were able to recognize it on the basis of a general description and identify it as a 'sect' within Judaism. To make certain, however, the Government Commission wrote to the Jewish community board of Warsaw, the Committee for the Censorship of Hebrew Books and Periodicals, and the Płock rabbi Ozyel Rubinstein,[17] enquiring 'if this name is a transformation of the sect known as hasidim', and also requested all additional information about the sect.[18]

Several days later, a letter from the district commissioner of Biała Podlaska spoke unambiguously of the 'hasidim sect or Hussites'.[19] Nevertheless the Government Commission waited to hear from the Jewish community board in Warsaw and the Committee for Censorship before taking action. The answers of both institutions arrived, after some urging, in February 1824. The Jewish community board, comprising known *mitnagedim* and maskilim, limited itself to philological notes confirming the identity of 'Hussites' as hasidim.[20] In contrast, the Committee for Censorship presented an extensive report signed by Adam Chmielewski, Józef Hayim Halberstam, and Abraham Stern (but lacking the signature of Jakub Tugend-hold) in which they wrote that there had been a similar investigation in 1818 and that Stern had at that time prepared a report in which 'everything that may relate to this sect had been explained, thoroughly and precisely, not omitting even the least detail'.[21] The original report of 1818 was submitted together with the new report.[22] As will be remembered, this violently anti-hasidic text had

---

[17] Ozyel Rubinstein, the son of R. Yerakhmiel Fishel of Płock, communal rabbi of Płock from 1823 to 1825, collaborator with the governmental Committee for the Censorship of Hebrew Books and Periodicals, a follower and an active propagator of the ideas of the Haskalah.

[18] See *11.21; AGAD, CWW 1871, pp. 7–8; see also Schiper, *Żydzi Królestwa Polskiego w dobie powstania listopadowego*, 24–5.   [19] See *11.20; AGAD, CWW 1871, pp. 7–8.

[20] See *11.28; AGAD, CWW 1871, pp. 50–1; see also Schiper, *Żydzi Królestwa Polskiego w dobie powstania listopadowego*, 25.   [21] See *11.27; AGAD, CWW 1871, pp. 41–2, 47.

[22] See *4.07; AGAD, CWW 1871, pp. 43–6; see also AGAD, KWK 702, pp. 137–41; AGAD, KRSW 6634, fos. 239–42; Mahler, *Haḥasidut vehahaskalah*, 477–81; Wodziński, *Oświecenie żydowskie w Królestwie Polskim*, 268–71.

called for a total ban on the creation of *shtiblekh*, on pilgrim-ages to tsadikim, and all other kinds of hasidic activity.

However, the committee—and, it later turned out, Stern himself—did not stop there. In its lengthy letter, it clarified, first, the terminological issue that the Government Commission had raised because it complicated the identification of hasidism; next, it clarified that hasidism was not a separate denomination, which would have justified separate legal status, but rather 'a free association under the pretence of piety, which leads to proselytization, delusion, deception, the seduction of the gullible and those with less sense, and to the spurning of all kinds of decency and morality, as well as to the thwarting of all kinds of praiseworthy intentions of the government with regard to the education of youth'. Stern went on to explain that hasidim lived not only in the voivodeships of Podlasie and Kraków (which the letter of the Government Commission mentioned as well), but also in the voivode-ships of Lublin, Mazovia, and Płock. The list omits three voivodeships: Augustów, Kalisz, and Sandomierz. The letter ends with a discussion of measures for fighting hasidism, including a complete ban on *shtiblekh* and pilgrimages—in fact, the same measures as those called for in 1818.

The letters from the Podlasie voivodeship and Stern's report provided the Government Commission for Religious Denominations with the infor-mation necessary to formulate an appropriate ruling. On 12 February 1824, Minister Grabowski sent each voivodeship commission a directive that repeated almost word for word Stern's recommendation not to allow 'the gathering of Jews in private homes for services, but to encourage participa-tion in synagogues, and not to allow pilgrimages to and meetings with individuals suspected of being leaders or members of this sect'.[23] At the same time, however, the directive recommended the avoidance of 'pressure', i.e. any form of enforcement.[24] Stern's 1818 report was attached to the ruling. On the very same day, 12 February 1824, information about the directive was sent to the Government Commission for Internal Affairs together with a general note summarizing Stern's 1818 report.[25] Staszic, in the name of the minister of internal affairs, sent each voivodeship commission an additional instruction 'to implement the directive with the goal of keeping a watch on the specified sect and preventing its expansion', and also ordering, in the voivodeship commissions of Sandomierz and Podlasie, a special investi-

---

[23] See *11.29; AGAD, KWK 702, p. 136.

[24] The Government Commission circulated the report without naming its author. This was a source of misunderstandings, and later of speculation by Raphael Mahler, who, as noted in the previous chapter, forcefully but wrongly suggested that the report was written by Abraham Buchner. See Mahler, *Hasidism and the Jewish Enlightenment*, 321–2.

[25] See *11.30; AGAD, KRSW 6634, fo. 238; see also AGAD, CWW 1871, pp. 48–9; Mahler, *Hahasidut vehahaskalah*, 475–6.

gation of hasidic activity in Przysucha and Parczew.[26] Also on the same day, the report that had been requested the previous September was sent to the viceroy.

On 15 March 1824, Viceroy Zajączek also decided to take steps to fight hasidism, using 'the most effective methods employed so far',[27] on the grounds that the principles of hasidism were 'contrary to decency and also to the intended reform of the Jews but instead instilled prejudice, alienated Jews from all education, and condoned fraud and violent methods (without regard to legality) to increase the number of proselytes through the pretence of religion', and that the hasidim were 'becoming harmful to the country'. The formulation used by Zajączek suggests that for the first time the subject of hasidism was being unequivocally connected to the central questions of the policy towards Jews, that is, to the intended 'reform of Jews' and to measures to minimize the dangers that Jews were presumed to pose to the country. Though hasidism was not yet an important theme in government policies with regard to Jewish society, this moment might be recognized as a turning-point in the political history of hasidism in the Kingdom of Poland: not only did the politics of the government regarding hasidism and their legal position began to change but, above all, the political awareness and activity of leaders of the hasidic movement changed.

In a letter to the Government Commission for Religious Denominations, the viceroy issued a directive requiring, in those places where the 'hasidic sect' existed, the appointment of rabbis 'of the regular Jewish denomination'; seeing the 'participation of sectarians in synagogues' they would oblige them, 'through gentle persuasion and religious teachings, to recognize the mistakes of their sect and be inclined to reject it'.[28] The viceroy approved the avoidance of the repressive measures suggested by Stern and the Government Commission for Religious Denominations. In addition, he ordered special supervision of the 'rabbi from Przysucha' (the government still had not determined the name of the tsadik) and instructed the police to supervise the ban on hasidic gatherings in private homes and on pilgrimages. According to Zajączek, hasidism was a form of Jewish superstition and could therefore be combated by 'enlightenment' brought about by proper religious education (a task to be undertaken by rabbis) and friendly persuasion.

The Government Commission for Religious Denominations issued a decree to the voivodeship commissions, repeating the ruling of the viceroy and asking the Government Commission for Internal Affairs to require the police to ensure that 'Jews [did] not gather for services in private homes'.

---

[26] See *11.31–*11.33; AGAD, CWW 1871, pp. 58–9; see also AGAD, KRSW 6634, fos. 244ᵛ–245ʳ; AGAD, KWK 702, pp. 131–2; Mahler, *Haḥasidut vehahaskalah*, 482.

[27] See *11.35; AGAD, KRSW 6634, fo. 249; see also AGAD, CWW 1871, pp. 52–3 [copy]; Mahler, *Haḥasidut vehahaskalah*, 484–5.   [28] Mahler *Haḥasidut vehahaskalah*, 484–5.

Staszic responded, however, that his previous order was exactly to this effect, so there was no need for further action.[29] Shortly after the voivodeship commissions passed on the appropriate order to the district commissioners in March 1824, the ban on the gathering of hasidim for prayer in *shtiblekh* had come into effect throughout the entire Kingdom.

3. Counteroffensive

Naturally, the hasidim did not submit willingly to this ministerial order. The mayors and voivodeship commissions were soon sending reports to the Government Commission for Religious Denominations complaining of hasidic non-compliance and of their own inability to implement the new law for lack of effective means. Stern's proposals and the directive of the viceroy were such that action was limited to appeals to conscience; lacking appropriate means of enforcement, it was no wonder that this was not effective. The frustrated mayor of Sokołów Podlaski described the mocking hasidic reaction: 'When the mayor urged the hasidim to attend the same synagogue as other Jews, one of them responded, "and who will see to it that the mayor goes to church?"'[30]—a response that suggests brash self-confidence on the part of the hasidim of Sokołów. In an effort to curb the separatist tendencies, the mayor even proposed forbidding hasidim to conduct ritual slaughter separate from that of the community, a practice they had introduced on the grounds that the regular kosher meat was not kosher by their standards. The Jewish community board of Sokołów similarly urged the use of 'enforcement measures', since 'in spite of the introduction of prohibitions [as authorized in the new directives] and other unpleasant steps, they [the hasidim] do not want to retreat from their folly'.[31] Both the mayor and the Jewish community board were thus in agreement with the commissioner of the voivodeship of Biała Podlaska that there needed to be administrative penalties; appealing to people's conscience might be effective where the number of hasidim was small but not in centres like Sokołów where there was a large concentration of hasidim and correspondingly significant disruption to community life. (Anti-hasidic petitions had been investigated there as early as 1821.) All these proposals were forwarded by the Voivodeship Commission of Podlasie to the central authorities in Warsaw, and other voivodeship commissions presented identical proposals. Rajmund Rembieliński, the president of the Voivodeship Commission of Mazovia, and Wincenty Kowalski, the deputy president of the Voivodeship Commission of Kalisz, also mentioned the impossibility

---

[29] See *11.36–*11.38; AGAD, CWW 1871, pp. 54, 56–7; AGAD, KRSW 6634, fo. 248ʳ; AGAD, KWK 702, p. 135; Mahler, *Haḥasidut vehahaskalah*, 485–6.

[30] See *11.40; AGAD, CWW 1871, pp. 104–6.

[31] See *11.44; AGAD, CWW 1871, pp. 102–3.

of carrying out the ministry's orders in light of the fact that the law regarding rabbis had not yet been passed.[32] Despite long debate and numerous legislative proposals, the principle of appointing state rabbis was not yet legally regulated, so the question of rabbinical appointments remained entirely in the hands of the Jewish communities. Furthermore, despite calls for appointing rabbis who were more 'enlightened', no method had been proposed for determining a possible candidate's degree of 'enlightenment'; as Rembieliński put it, the 'will of the Government Commission can in no way be fulfilled'. The question of the hasidic *shtiblekh* was thus directly tied to the project of 'civilizing' the Jewish people: until the status of the rabbinate was regulated there was no way of eradicating the *shtiblekh*. Indeed, next to the abolition of the *kahal* and other institutions fundamental to the alleged Jewish separatism, the reform of the rabbinate was the most important undertaking of the government in its policy towards the Jewish population. Although a decision to establish a rabbinical school had been taken as part of this process in 1818, the issue dragged on, mainly for financial reasons, but possibly also because some officials were reluctant to initiate government involvement in Jewish education. The eventual establishment of the rabbinical school in 1826 and its regulation by law was seen as a significant achievement of government policy on the enlightenment of the Jews. It is very probable that repeated references to the 1818 project in the investigation under discussion and the passing of the law on rabbis were significant factors in this development, especially since in the later stages of the investigation the issue of hasidic superstitions (i.e. religious practices that they considered contrary to reason and socially harmful) and the establishment of the rabbinical school were more strongly linked and merited the support both of ministers Grabowski and Staszic and of Viceroy Zajączek.[33]

Government correspondence from this time unequivocally shows (*a*) that hasidim did not respect ministerial orders, especially in places where the movement was strong, and that they even mocked the ineffectiveness of the local administration; (*b*) that the government, especially at the voivodeship level, was increasingly aware of the appeal and growth of hasidism and of the impossibility of remedying the situation with the existing methods; and (*c*) that no measure to control the spread of hasidism would be effective unless it was linked to a more general plan for the reform of Jewish society. From the first moment that the anti-hasidic law was on the rule books it was continually being broken: as we have seen, it proved impossible to enforce. In

---

[32] See *11.39, *11.41, *11.45, *11.49; AGAD, CWW 1871, pp. 60–4, 86, 97–101.

[33] See *11.73; AGAD, CWW 1871, pp. 187–90; see also Wodziński, 'Sprawa chasydymów', 240–1. On the founding of the rabbinical school in Warsaw see Sawicki, 'Szkoła Rabinów w Warszawie (1826–1862)'; S. Lewin, 'Beit-hasefer lerabanim bevarshah bashanim 1826–63'.

the usual course of things, administrative inertia might have caused the issue to burn itself out; this time, however, the situation took a rather unusual turn in that the leaders of the hasidic movement, anxious to strengthen their position with regard to the community boards, took the initiative and forced the authorities to re-examine the entire issue.

On 9 May 1824, two prominent representatives of the hasidic movement submitted a letter to the Government Commission for Religious Denominations and Public Enlightenment.[34] The first of the signatories was (Hayim) Fayvel Kamienicer (or Kamienicki) Wolberg, a rich entrepreneur from Warsaw affiliated with the wealthy Jewish Sonnenberg family and one of the most influential hasidim of Przysucha (Pshiskha).[35] The second was Alexander Zusya b. Abraham Kahana of Warsaw, a close collaborator of Simhah Bunem of Przysucha, and later of Isaac Kalisz of Warka, rabbi of Siedlce from 1826 and then of Płock from 1829. Kamienicer and Kahana requested that the Government Commission should re-examine the issue, and that the ban on hasidic *shtiblekh* should be suspended pending a final decision. The Government Commission did not respond, probably because it had no intention of re-examining the issue; two weeks later therefore, Kamienicer and Kahana sent an almost identical letter to Viceroy Zajączek,[36] who forced the government to act. Both petitions claimed that the accusations directed against the hasidim were false, and that the investigations into hasidism in the Russian empire in 1805 and in the Kingdom of Poland in 1818 had both favoured the hasidim (authorized copies of the relevant documents were attached but have not been preserved). They also stressed that hasidim were more inclined 'to virtue and morality' than other Jews, and also 'to spreading enlightenment among their co-religionists and becoming dignified in society'. The petition to the viceroy was significantly broadened to include characteristics of hasidic doctrine: the authors paid special attention to the spontaneity and sincerity of their prayer and their scrupulousness in fulfilling their religious obligations, in particular the obligation to love one's neighbour. The economic contribution of hasidism was also stressed ('our leaders instruct us to be efficient, to acquire knowledge and ingenuity, and we eagerly try to do so'); the accusations directed against hasidim were damaging to their reputation and so also to their economic activity. Subsequent requests by Kahana to hasten the investigation did not expand upon the arguments already made, although he allowed himself to emphasize more strongly that hasidism was tolerated in the Russian empire and in

---

[34] See *11.42; AGAD, CWW 1871, pp. 65–9.
[35] For basic information on Kamienicer see Alfasi (ed.), *Entsiklopediyah laḥasidut*, iii. 729. On Kahana see Grynszpan, 'Rabanim: kovets masot al rabanei plotsk', 93–6; Boim, *Harabi rebe bunem mipeshisḥa*, i. 275–82; see also *Sefer me'ir einei hagolah*, i. 93–4, no. 189.
[36] See *11.43; AGAD, CWW 1871, pp. 71–8.

Austria (as he put it, 'Is the Polish government alone to be intolerant of them?'). He also stressed that what the Enlightenment saw as 'superstition' was actually what makes people moral and good, and that it therefore deserved support rather than condemnation.[37]

The hasidic petitioners wrote what the government wanted to read, or, more precisely, what they imagined the government would want to read. From this standpoint the letters were efficiently written. The emphasis on the command to love one's neighbour was perhaps aimed at convincing government officials that hasidim did not share the anti-Christian prejudice attributed to the rest of Jewish society. Similarly, the emphasis on the spontaneity and joy of hasidic ritual practice was meant to convince officials that hasidim were far from practising the exaggerated ritualism attributed to Jews (which was regarded as one of the sources of their separatism). The 1818 decision of the government favourable to hasidim and legalizing their *shtiblekh* and the 1804 Imperial Jewish Statute in Russia were skilfully presented as the result of an anti-hasidic investigation.[38] Particularly interesting is the ambiguous relationship of the petitioners to secular enlightenment and modernization. Both petitions unequivocally attribute the anti-hasidic accusations to 'hypocritical people' who 'do not observe Jewish law and in their religious beliefs are weak', and who therefore supported the Haskalah and the modernization of Jewish society. This description is legitimate enough, in that the government ruling did rely on the report of the maskil Abraham Stern, but it is rather difficult to say of him that his religious beliefs were 'weak' (religiously, Stern was observant and very attached to traditional forms of Jewishness, including external signs, as can be seen from Figure 2.3). In fact, however, this view was mistaken because the investigation originated in a community conflict in Parczew that did not involve maskilim; in a second investigation only one maskil other than Stern participated, Jakub Tugendhold, who testified in defence of hasidism. But the hasidic view was that their chief opponents were the maskilim, so accordingly they contrasted these 'hypocrites', 'weak in religion' (and so potentially immoral) and supporters of modernization, with the 'virtuous and moral' hasidim. This formula was consistent with the anti-Enlightenment tendency in the politics of the European powers after 1815, and in the Habsburg monarchy significantly earlier, in the early years of the reign of Francis II. The increasingly

[37] See *11.49, *11.52; AGAD, CWW 1871, pp. 86, 88–90.

[38] '§854. If the sect is divided and apostasy occurs to such a degree that one group does not want to be with the other in one synagogue, then in such a case one of the groups should be allowed to build for itself a synagogue and select a rabbi.' AGAD, Sekretariat Stanu Królestwa Polskiego 199, p. 354. For a comprehensive analysis of the 1804 Jewish Statute in Russia, see Klier, *Russia Gathers Her Jews*, 116–43; Ettinger, 'Takanot 1804' (which also gives the Hebrew translation of the statute).

cautious stance of the Austrian government towards the Haskalah had political benefits both for hasidim and for other traditional Jews in Galicia, in that instead of having to waste their energies trying to demonstrate that they were not 'superstitious' and not opposed to Enlightenment they could present themselves as believers in traditional values and supporters of the monarchy.[39]

However, this formula did not fit with the political reality of the Kingdom of Poland in the constitutional age, a period when the Enlightenment tradition of the Four Year Sejm was still invoked and the government worked towards the reform of the Jewish people in an Enlightenment spirit, or at least with an Enlightenment rhetoric. Though the later Enlightenment was more conservative, and most certainly not liberal, the fundamental concept underlying its politics was still distant from the reactionary ideology of states in the Holy Alliance.

Kahana and Kamienicer, though not aware of all the ideological intricacies of the fall of the Enlightenment in Poland, accurately sensed the general political direction. They therefore not only contrasted hasidim with the maskilim who were 'weak in belief' but also stressed that hasidism was not in fact opposed to education and modernization. They placed still greater emphasis on hasidic industriousness, which corresponded well with the government's plans to make Jews 'useful citizens of the country' and with the 'productivization' projects begun at the same time. We can see, then, that they identified correctly the interests of the officials whom they were addressing and exploited them in constructing their own argument. Given that the political climate was very complicated, this level of understanding is admirable—and especially as this campaign marked the political debut of the Polish hasidim in actions on a broad scale: Alexander Zusya Kahana, who directed the entire campaign, was only 29 years old, and as yet had no experience of public life (it would be a further two years before he became the rabbi of Siedlce, in 1826).

Almost immediately—just a week later—the viceroy sent a letter to the Government Commission for Religious Denominations, in which he mentioned the letter of Kamienicer and Kahana and said that if the Government Commission 'as a result of earlier orders was convinced that the hasidic sect had no principles harmful to decency and wished to have their own synagogues only to distinguish themselves from other Jews, we allow that maintaining such synagogues should not be forbidden'.[40] The viceroy's reaction is astonishing for two reasons. First, he said that the results of the investigation did not, in his opinion, justify upholding the charges. However, in a decision

---

[39] See Mahler, *Hasidism and the Jewish Enlightenment*, 69–103.
[40] See *11.46; AGAD, CWW 1871, p. 70.

of March 1824 written in response to the results of the same investigation he had written that 'there is already no doubt that the principles of the sect are against decency and even against the intended reform of the Jews',[41] and the other institutions participating in that investigation had been equally negative towards hasidim. Now he was blatantly contradicting those earlier conclusions. Secondly, he was permitting the reopening of the hasidic *shtiblekh* even though this was not an issue raised in the letters sent to him. The hasidim had indeed requested this concession to be made on a temporary basis, but the request had been addressed to the Government Commission, so formally the viceroy should not have known about it. This suggests unequivocally that the viceroy's decision was the result of arguments other than those documented in the sources, perhaps of behind-the-scenes contacts or, conceivably, simple bribes (for more on corruption and its significance see Chapter 5, §5).

The Government Commission for Religious Denominations rejected the viceroy's conclusion. Again summarizing the information in Stern's report, Minister Grabowski responded that the 'sect' kept its supporters in darkness and slavish obedience to their leaders, who, above all, financially exploited the simple people. Therefore, he argued, 'this sect . . . cannot be regarded as harmless and should at least be suspended until its rabbis and superiors are more enlightened and acquire better moral principles'.[42] The enlightenment of the rabbis, it went without saying, would follow only after the creation of a state rabbinical school; once again, the status of hasidism was linked with the general reform of Jewish society. The response was decided, and in places even sharp. However, under renewed pressure from the hasidim, the ministry began to consider establishing a committee to research the entire issue. Viceroy Zajączek was not even informed about these plans. The hasidim now had to negotiate between the interests of the viceroy, who supported them but was weak, and those of the minister, whose ambitions they had thwarted by trespassing on his prerogative and who certainly did not intend to give in to the viceroy. Since constitutionally the decisions of the king (or his viceroy) were invalid without the counter-signature of the appropriate minister, it was Minister Grabowski, as president of the Government Commission for Religious Denominations and Public Enlightenment, who would decide the issue. At the same time, Grabowski would not want to risk significant conflict with Zajączek in defence of his politics regarding hasidim, since none of those involved perceived hasidism as a question of the first priority; but equally it is also difficult to imagine that the viceroy would relish confrontation on this issue, especially since Grabowski, as the son of Stanisław August Poniatowski and also a close associate of many influential

[41] See *11.36; AGAD, CWW 1871, p. 54; see also AGAD, KWK 702, p. 135; Mahler, *Haḥasidut vehahaskalah*, 485–6.   [42] See *11.47; AGAD, CWW 1871, pp. 84–5.

Russian politicians, had significant political support at the imperial court in St Petersburg. The matter had reached an awkward impasse.

Support for hasidic demands came from an unexpected quarter. The Government Commission, involved in censorship proceedings relating to a book that contained 'gross instances' of intolerance, asked Jakub Tugendhold, a maskil and censor of Hebrew books, whether hasidim used this book.[43] Tugendhold provided a lengthy answer, in which he not only rejected this suspicion but also charged Abraham Stern with the deliberate presentation of a misleading report in the name of the entire Committee for the Censorship of Hebrew Books and Periodicals, a report in which Stern unjustly charged hasidim with fanaticism, which, Tugendhold claimed, was a description of the group's opponents: 'I would even say that if the High Government initiated a general reform of the Jews, they should begin with the class of zealous talmudists, who certainly demonstrate more unruliness than hasidim.'[44] Tugendhold's argument is close to that of Kamienicer and Kahana, who also maintained that hasidim were more open to enlightenment and more modern than other Jews. It is possible that Tugendhold's remarks reflect an agreement reached with representatives of the hasidic community, especially given that he had testified in defence of hasidism several times in this period and also co-operated with the Warsaw representatives of the movement in an alliance against tax leaseholders' heavy-handed exploitation of the tax on kosher meat.[45]

After receiving Tugendhold's opinion and Kahana's subsequent follow-up to the two co-authored letters, Grabowski ordered the Office of Education and Denominations (a division of the Government Commission for Religious Denominations and Public Enlightenment) to prepare an opinion as to whether to grant the requests of the hasidim and temporarily allow prayer meetings in private homes. The opinion and the subsequent decision of the Government Commission ruled in favour of the hasidim, and Grabowski instructed the voivodeship commissions that 'persecution and harsh treatment of these believers had no place; also, until a final decision had been made, these believers can gather for services in private homes, taking care to preserve the peace and order, however'.[46] At the same time he decided to

[43] The book under consideration by the Government Commission cannot be identified. For more on Tugendhold's attitude towards hasidism, see Wodziński, 'Jakub Tugendhold and the First Maskilic Defence of Hasidism', and *Haskalah and Hasidism*, 142–52.

[44] Tugendhold's report has not been preserved, but extensive excerpts were incorporated into the anonymous summary of the investigation; see *11.56; AGAD, CWW 1871, pp. 131–64.

[45] See AGAD, CWW 1723, pp. 95–8, for interesting information about the co-operation between Jakub Tugendhold and Abraham Abish of Końskowola, a disciple of Jacob Isaac Horowitz of Lublin, a prominent hasidic leader himself and a deputy rabbi in Warsaw.

[46] See *11.49–*11.51; AGAD, CWW 1871, pp. 91–2; see also AGAD, KRSW 6634, fo. 263; Mahler, *Haḥasidut vehahaskalah*, 487–8; AGAD, KWK 702, pp. 144–5; APL, AmL (1809–74) 2419, pp. 57, 62.

Figure 3.4 Jakub Tugendhold (1794–1871), an influential Polish maskil and political activist, and an early example of maskilic conciliatory attitudes towards hasidism. From Joachim Nirnstein, *Proverbia Salomonis: Przysłowia Salomona. Wyjątek z Pisma Świętego z hebrajskiego tekstu spolszczył wierszem* [Proverbs of Solomon: Excerpts from the Hebrew Text Translated into Polish] (Warsaw, 1895). From the private collection of the author

renew the investigation into hasidism in order to determine its nature once and for all.

4. Deputation: Stanisław Staszic against the Tsadikim

For the purposes of the investigation, Minister Grabowski summoned five hasidic leaders to Warsaw: the tsadikim Simon Oderberg 'of Chęciny' (at this time he was not living in Chęciny but in Śmieszowice near Żelechów); Simhah Bunem of Przysucha; Moses Eliakim Bria of Kozienice; Meir Rotenberg of Opatów (Apt); and Fayvel Kamienicer, the Warsaw entrepreneur who was a follower of the tsadik of Przysucha. The list seems quite random, including as it does the tsadikim Simhah Bunem and Moses of Kozienice,[47] who were known from earlier investigations; one of the most influential tsadikim of this period, Meir of Opatów; a minor local hasidic leader from Chęciny; and a wealthy hasidic entrepreneur from Warsaw. The committee established to interrogate them consisted of Stanisław Staszic as chair; Senator and General Curator Dawid Oebschelwitz; the well-known Enlightenment political activist and philosopher Józef Kalasanty Szaniawski; the classical writer, critic, translator, follower of the Enlightenment, and state official Józef Lipiński; and the well-known historian, journalist, and politician Wawrzyniec Surowiecki. Shortly after the committee was established, Mark Aurelius de Müller, Councillor of the Imperial Court, known as a specialist in Jewish issues, was also invited to join.[48] The committee was thus very diverse in its composition, including as it did the foremost members of the last generation of the Polish Enlightenment, from both the liberal (Surowiecki) and conservative (Szaniawski) factions active in the educational and religious politics of the constitutional period. Moreover, Oebschelwitz and Szaniawski were among the closest collaborators of the anti-liberal Grabowski (Oebschelwitz was also a protégé of Nikolai Novosiltseff, a friend of Grabowski), while Lipiński and Surowiecki were former workers in the ministry connected with the dismissed Stanisław Kostka Potocki, who had currently withdrawn to the margins of political events. In other words, the committee consisted of protégés both of the new anti-liberal minister and his liberal predecessor, creating a situation of open conflict.

The committee was supposed to convene to interrogate the tsadikim at the end of July; accordingly, the ban on the gathering of hasidim for prayer was suspended until the final decision was taken. Even before their first meeting, the committee members and the officials assigned to assist them

---

[47] The ministry came to know Moses Bria of Kozienice in 1819, when a denunciation of his activities on the outskirts of Warsaw reached the government. See AGAD, CWW 1424, pp. 11–13.

[48] See *11.54, *11.55; AGAD, KRSW 6634, fo. 262; see also AGAD, CWW 1871, pp. 92–3 [copy]; Mahler, *Haḥasidut vehahaskalah*, 486–7.

Figure 3.5 Stanisław Staszic (1755–1826), author and politician, and an
extremely influential ideologue of the Polish Enlightenment, actively engaged
in planning for the reform of the Jews in Poland. He was the author of the
'Jewish policy' of the constitutional period (1815–30) in the Kingdom of Poland.
Drawing by W[ładysław] B[arwicki], lithograph by A. Jarzyński, 1917; in
W. Barwicki, *Gwiazdy myśli polskiej. 36 portretów* [Stars of Polish Thought: 36
Portraits] (Lublin, 1917), vol. i, pl. 6. Biblioteka Narodowa w Warszawie,
Zbiory Ikonograficzne, A. 2877, A. 492

began to gather information. The most interesting document we have from
this period is an anonymous report sketching out the goals of the committee
and possible further political action regarding hasidism.[49] We can surmise
that its author was Jan Alojzy Radomiński, director at this time of the Division of Public Enlightenment, the office that co-ordinated the work of the
committee in the name of the Government Commission for Religious Denominations. An author with a real interest in the Jewish Question, he published one of the most interesting opinions in the ongoing debate in 1820.[50]

[49] See *11.60; AGAD, CWW 1871, pp. 124–9.
[50] [Radomiński], *Co wstrzymuje reformę Żydów w kraju naszym?*. For literature on the debate,
see Ch. 1 n. 1. For more on Radomiński's pamphlet, see Wodziński, *Haskalah and Hasidism*, 74–
6; for more on Radomiński, see 'Radomiński, Jan Alojzy', in *Polski Słownik Biograficzny*, xxix.
731. That Radomiński was the author is suggested both by the fact that he was director of the
division at the time and signed many other documents related to this issue and by the fact that
the study draws extensively on his pamphlet, citing fragments from it without attribution.

Notwithstanding the government's current position, his considered position was that the reform of the Jews, up to then realized only to a modest extent, was 'one of the most necessary and most important tasks for our country', and that the new investigation was an excellent opportunity 'to obtain a deeper understanding of Jewish ideas, gain the favour of the different parties, and influence the welfare of the Jews and of our country'. The opinion of De Müller, presumed to be an expert on the subject, was solicited to confirm this view; he stated that 'government [of the Jewish community] by hasidim may certainly contribute to the general reform of the Jews, so condemning them out of hand would be counter-productive'. Radomiński thought that the government could gain the favour of the hasidim in two ways. First, it could 'exploit the Jewish disagreement and offer protection to the persecuted, since they requested it'. This would encourage competition between the groups for government support, which would in turn give the government influence in internal Jewish matters; moreover, the example set by the hasidim would encourage others to accept new patterns of education and socialization within the majority society. 'Consider what can be achieved among talmudists and other Jews if hasidim are seen to be co-operating with the government. As the rivalry between them increases, the easier it will be for the government to implement policies that benefit Jews and our country alike.' Radomiński also suggested gaining the support of the hasidic leaders, on the grounds that hasidim followed their leadership blindly. He doubted that the investigation would facilitate acquaintance with the underlying principles of hasidism since the hasidim would not give straight answers to questions, but he was aware that other Jews would not do so either. In his view, none of this was a problem: the important thing was that the presentation of petitions and the response to them created the possibility of exerting influence, not only on the hasidic petitioners but on other Jews too. In their letters to the government the hasidic leaders had expressed various worthy intentions; now, he said, they should be forced to 'stand and solemnly confirm everything they had said'. Radomiński imagined the interrogation as a great debate that would place binding and ceremonial obligations on hasidic leaders, obligations that the government would later enforce. As a scholar well versed in Jewish issues he was familiar with the literature on a similar debate that had taken place in Lwów in 1759, after which the supporters of Jacob Frank were forced to accept baptism; he clearly saw a similarity between the Frankist strategy in 1759 and the arguments raised by the hasidim in the investigation of 1824. As we have seen, the hasidim, and especially Kahana, contrasted their own morality very strongly with the presumed corruption of Jewish society: they offered assurances of the productivity of the hasidim, appealing to the universal conviction of Christian

society about the parasitic character of the Jewish community, and in particular they tried to convince their readers of the hasidim's love for their neighbours. These assurances were unequivocally read by government officials
as a sign that the morality of hasidism was closer to Christian morality (in
their opinion, universal morality) than was the corrupt Jewish morality based
on the negative principles of the Talmud. This last argument especially called to mind the anti-talmudic rhetoric of the Frankists, and in the later stages
of the investigation, the hasidim were duly asked if they were followers of
Frankism.

In drawing the analogy with the Frankist debate Radomiński was not
advocating the religious conversion of the hasidim (this was not the ideal of
the age), but rather the idea of action leading to the rejection of separatism,
the acceptance of the 'sentiments sympathetic to Christians', and other 'civil-
izational' goals. Even so, in his imagination the investigation had to be a
turning-point in the history of Polish hasidism and the reform of Jewish
society. Of course, the strategy of getting the hasidic leaders to accept public obligations was unrealistic, not only because they would not want to do
so but also because Radomiński had a false image of the hasidic hierarchy.
He most certainly imagined it as similar to the only religious structure
intimately known to him, that of the Roman Catholic Church, a centralized
and hierarchical institution. It is also possible that he thought of hasidism
as a sect under the sway of charismatic and often despotic leaders, since the
literature he knew on the subject suggested such an image. Meanwhile,
the loose, entirely decentralized structure of the hasidic movement, with its
numerous, completely independent groups of followers of different hasidic
courts, guaranteed that none of the tsadikim would be in a position, even if
they so wanted, to accept obligations in the name of the entire movement.

Though Radomiński's plan was naive, and he himself was not even a
member of the committee, his opinion had fundamental significance for the
course of the investigation. This was because he linked the question of hasidism so strongly to the general objective of reforming Jewish society and
made future action on the hasidic question conditional on the more general
aspects of this reform. Secondly, he saw the possibility of exploiting hasidism in the conflict between the Jewish groups: each division within Judaism
weakened the community's internal solidarity, and so increased the opportunities for state action. Both assumptions were included in the final report
of the committee, undoubtedly under Radomiński's influence.

The hasidic leaders were summoned to Warsaw for the first meeting
of the committee, which was set for 27 July 1824. Moses Eliakim Bria of
Kozienice and Simon Oderberg of Chęciny did not show up at all,[51] but the

[51] At that time Simon Oderberg did not live in Chęciny, but in Śmieszowice near Żelechów,
so the summons did not reach him: see *11.70; AGAD, CWW 1871, pp. 210–11.

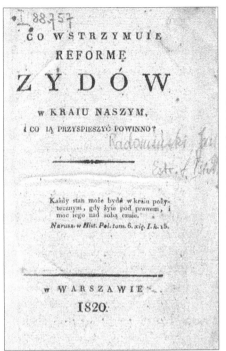

Figure 3.6 Title page of *Co wstrzymuje reformę Żydów* [What Holds Back the Reform of the Jews?] (Warsaw, 1820), by Jan Alojzy Radomiński (1789–1864), an important and possibly the best-informed Polish publication issued during the debate on the Jewish Question in the Kingdom of Poland in the years 1818–22. Biblioteka Narodowa w Warszawie, I.88.757

three others arrived in advance of the date set. Simhah Bunem of Przysucha and Meir Rotenberg of Opatów, known in hasidic tradition as arch-rivals, in fact co-operated with each other in writing the Government Commission a letter asking for the investigation to be conducted as quickly as possible because the high prices and local air in Warsaw were not good for them (something that is easy to believe). They also asked if the committee's questions could be given to them in advance in writing, 'so that our answers can come from consideration of our deep convictions, as we cannot do this orally in the presence of dignified men before whom we have the good fortune to appear for the first time'.[52] This request was not granted. However, before the investigation began, the committee met twice to allow members to acquaint themselves with the collected documentation and to formulate the questions to be asked of the people summoned.[53] Wawrzyniec Surowiecki also prepared a first draft of the report, in which he concentrated on legal issues: the existing regulations relating to hasidism; whether the movement was a sect; and, if it was, whether its leaders would be subject to three years' imprisonment, as provided for by law. Surowiecki's report unfortunately did not reach any conclusion, but one can infer from its tone that he

[52] See *11.59; AGAD, CWW 1871, pp. 114–17; see also Boim, *Harabi rebe bunem mipeshisḥa*, ii. 633–40 (photocopy and Hebrew translation); Wodziński, 'Sprawa chasydymów', 233–4.

[53] See *11.61, *11.62; AGAD, CWW 1871, pp. 130, 165–7.

Figure 3.7 Signatures of the tsadikim Simhah Bunem of Przysucha and Meir of Opatów (Apt) in their letter to the Government Commission of Religious Affairs and Public Enlightenment (1824). AGAD, CWW 1871, p. 117

was opposed to the legalization of the hasidic *shtiblekh*; indeed, he even mooted the possibility of introducing new repressive measures.[54]

Finally, after a delay of more than two weeks, the hasidic leaders were interrogated by Staszic before the assembled committee on 4 August 1824. Rabbi Simhah Bunem did not attend; he sent a medical certificate attesting to his illness and a deputy to represent him, but the latter was not interrogated.[55] Fayvel Kamienicer and Meir Rotenberg were asked almost identical questions, and their answers differed only in details. Despite its length I quote one of the two protocols of the meeting in its entirety, as this exceptional document is of immense importance for the political history of hasidism in the Kingdom of Poland:[56]

The next to be summoned was the Orthodox Jew Meier Rotenberg from Opatów. Because of his inability in the Polish language and his lack of even a comprehensible German, he was accompanied by Jakub Bereksohn Sonnenberg, an entrepreneur and owner of local factories, and Hersz Sztamm, the commissioner of Sonnenberg's factories, both adherents of this faith.

The questions were asked of Meier Rotenberg, hasidic rabbi, on 4 August 1824. Sixty-four years of age, native by birth of the town of Pacanów. He is rabbi of Opatów.

Q: Does there exist a difference between your faith and that of other Jews?

A: None whatsoever.

Q: Why do you separate yourselves for the prayers?

A: We wish to conduct our prayers with a greater degree of preparation than do ordinary Jews.

[54] See *11.63; AGAD, CWW 1871, pp. 80–3.

[55] The name of the deputy has not been recorded in the protocol, but we can assume it was Alexander Zusya Kahana.

[56] See *11.66; AGAD, CWW 1871, pp. 168–79, 181–6 [copy]; full text in Polish published in Wodziński, 'Sprawa chasydymów', 235–9.

Q: How much time daily do you devote to this?

A: At seven o'clock in the morning, but in the prayer room, there are at least ten altogether, at sunset an hour, and the third time, when the stars are in the sky less than an hour. Except holy days. We need an hour or one and a half hours for preparation, but one who has work to do is not necessarily obligated.

Q: Do you accept the entire Talmud, that is the Mishnah and Gemara?

A: That is so.

Q: Is everybody your neighbour and their souls the same?

A: That is so.

Q: Do you love your brethren?

A: Yes.[57]

Q: Do you know *Keser Shemtoch*, *Likute amorim*, and *Noah hamelech*?[58]

A: Yes, we know these works, but the Talmud is the major book that we follow. We read all the others and give them some attention.

Q: Does your denomination possess any secrets unknown to others?

A: None, except for kabbalah, which not everybody can understand.

Q: The Thirteen Principles of Moses Maimonides, [do] you hasidim accept these?

A: That is so, we do.

Q: Do you know the credo by Józef or Polish Jew?[59]

A: I do not know any book by this author. However, if I am able to remember, I could bring it immediately tomorrow, if the honourable deputation were to so permit.

Q: What are the means to cleave to God?

A: Good deeds.[60]

Q: Do rabbis have more power to intervene with God?

A: My answer is similar to that of the first person questioned, but with the

---

[57] The protocol of the Kamienicer inquiry added: 'In this place it was said to him that surely he does not include Christians among his brethren, because in the Talmud it is written that *goyim* are idolaters and cannot be treated as brethren; Fayvel denied it, saying that they do not consider Christians, who pray to the same living God, to be idolaters.'

[58] *Keser Shemtoch*, lit. *Keter shem tov* (Crown of a Good Name) (Żółkiew, 1794), an anthology of hasidic teachings attributed to the Besht; *Likutei amarim* (Collection of Teachings), better known as the *Tanya* (Sławuta, 1796), the best-known tractate by Shneur Zalman of Lyady, a prominent hasidic leader who founded the Habad (Lubavitch) school of hasidism; *Noah hamelech* can be identified as *No'am elimelekh* (Sweetness of Elimelekh) (Lwów, 1788), a commentary on the weekly Torah portion by the tsadik Elimelekh of Leżajsk (Lyzhansk).

[59] Józef was Jacob Frank's baptismal name, by which Polish sources fairly often identified him. It thus seems reasonable to assume that the question about 'Józef or Polish Jew' referred to Frank.   [60] Kamienicer replied: 'good and noble heart'. See *Pirkei avot* 2: 9.

addition that rabbis perceive themselves particularly as being learned and therefore obliged to dispel doubts.

Q: Do hasidim need a separate rabbi and a separate synagogue?

A: That is not compulsory.

Q: Can you pray in Polish?

A: The prayer can be in the holy tongue exclusively, but those who do not know
    Hebrew, for example women, can pray in Polish, that is, in the language that
    they know.

Q: What religious and spiritual power do your rabbis have for the upholding of
    discipline in your faith?

A: They have none whatsoever.

Q: Are your rabbis paid?

A: No. But if somebody comes for advice and he is wealthy, he can pay if he wants.
    But from the poor nothing can be accepted.

Q: Why do your rabbis wander around and collect money?

A: They only travel to some important rabbis, but the rabbis do not expect pay-
    ments from anybody.

Q: Do you have in your faith anything that would make you oppose the wishes of
    the government?

A: No, we do not. On the contrary, it is our duty to follow whatever the govern-
    ment tells us to do.[61]

Q: Why do you not send your children to the public schools? Because, as it is, we
    are aware there are no children of your faith in them.

A: [crossed out: If it were possible to send our children to public schools and have
    them examined there, we would certainly send our children. In addition, par-
    ents may also have this reason] Because the teachers in the schools for the Jews
    are not moral, so we prefer a Christian teacher who is moral, rather than a Jew
    who is immoral, that is, a Jew weakened in his faith.[62]

Q: Why are you neither factory owners nor farmers?

A: There are many of us in the factories; for example, Jakub Bereksohn owns fac-
    tories and Hersz Sztamm is a manager there. There are also a lot of hasidim
    and their children working in these factories.

Q: Do you have any conditions for accepting adherents and do you punish those
    who leave the faith?

[61] Kamienicer added: 'and even, if the government wished, we would go to the army and fight
like others'.
[62] Kamienicer replied: 'Because we have separate teachers; also I have a teacher for my
grandchildren who teaches them to read and write in Polish.'

A: None.

Q: What means are you aware of for encouraging people into your company, that is, into your faith?

A: None.

Q: Why do you leap and drink during worship?

A: I think that what you call leaping is exultation, which is experienced by those who are carried away by the worship; but as for drinking, such accusations are groundless and according to us would be a violation, not tolerated in our laws and worship.

Q: If a wife unaccompanied by her non-hasidic husband or a son of his who was still a juvenile were to come to your congregation, would she or he be admitted?

A: They are free to come to the synagogue; however, women generally are not hasidim. Anyway, women and children come under the authority of the father, so that if it is not the father's will that they be hasidim, they cannot be accepted.

Q: Why do you hate other Jews?

A: On the contrary! We share the same faith.[63]

Meier Rotenberg

Contrary to Radomiński's expectations, the atmosphere at the investigation was neither negative enough to gain the hasidic leaders' respect nor positive enough to convince them that the government was well disposed towards them and incline them to an alliance. It is clear that Staszic, who generally agreed with Radomiński's suggestions, was unable to free himself from paternalism towards the hasidim, an attitude that characterized all his writings on and official actions towards Jewish society (and towards others, too).[64] The suspicion expressed in the question about 'unknown secrets' reflected a widespread prejudice connected to an updated version popular at the time of the charge of ritual murder, to the effect that it was not all Jews but rather Jewish fanatical sects that were guilty of this crime. In the nineteenth century the finger was generally pointed at the hasidim.[65] The course of the investigation, then, along with the line of questioning, the long delays, and the petty harassment by both central and provincial officials confirmed the suspicions harboured by the tsadikim regarding the government's attitude to them.[66] In consequence the investigation did not bring about the

[63] Kamienicer replied: 'On the contrary! And we are not hated by all.'

[64] On the difficult character of Staszic and his numerous conflicts, see the generally sympathetic memoirs of Kajetan Koźmian, *Pamiętniki*, ii. 152–224.

[65] For more on this issue, see Wodziński, 'Blood and the Hasidim'.

[66] The voivodeship commissions examined very carefully whether the tsadikim had fulfilled their obligation and obeyed the government's summonses (*11.67, *11.68; AGAD, CWW

rapprochement between the tsadikim and the state that Radomiński and others had expected.

The questions asked of the hasidic leaders show that the committee treated the investigation seriously and came to it well prepared. They not only demonstrate familiarity with the basic canon of Jewish tradition (for example, the Talmud and Maimonides' Thirteen Principles of Faith) but also reveal a knowledge of hasidism beyond that to be found in earlier documents. For example, the question about hasidic works (*Keter shem tov, Likutei amarim, No'am elimelekh*) demonstrates that the authorities had consulted a publication by the well-known anti-hasidic preacher Israel Löbel of Słuck, as they mention these titles with the same mistakes that he made.[67] It is true that the purpose of these questions is not always clear. The questions about the Talmud and the 'creed of belief of Józef or Polish Jew' (to the extent that we may say this is actually about Jacob Frank) may have been to verify whether hasidim did or did not belong to the so-called contra-talmudists, as Frankists were called, and by implication whether they were or were not likely to reject the authority of the Talmud in favour of a more Christian morality. The questions imply a belief that the Talmud had a negative influence on Jewish society, a belief, which, as we know, was central to the reform plans of Staszic and many others. Other questions, for example about the knowledge of hasidic works (all belonging to the basic canon of hasidism) or the Thirteen Principles of Faith, were certainly rhetorical flourishes on Staszic's part, for it is difficult to imagine how answers to these questions would have served the committee. Moreover, those being interrogated also did not know the underlying intent of the questions, so in all cases they offered the most general, evasive answers.

Some of the questions were taken almost verbatim from those posed by Napoleon in France in 1806 to his Assembly of Jewish Notables and Sanhedrin—changing the subject, of course, from French Jews to Polish hasidim. These questions concerned the hasidic recognition of non-Jews as neighbours, the authority of rabbis, the rules regarding the attitude towards state authorities, and, indirectly, the attitude towards labour in the field and industry.[68] The answers are surprisingly in line with how Jewish represen-

---

1871, pp. 122–3; see also Wodziński, 'Sprawa chasydymów', 234). Simhah Bunem of Przysucha did not receive written permission to leave Warsaw and return home until more than a week after the interrogation, which he missed, claiming illness (*11.71, *11.72; AGAD, CWW 1871, pp. 123, 187–90).

[67] The title of the commentary by Elimelekh of Leżajsk is given in the same corrupted form *Noam hamelech* instead of *No'am elimelekh*. See Löbel, 'Glaubwürdige Nachricht', 315. This information could have come from Radomiński, who used Israel Löbel's pamphlet extensively in his study; see [Radomiński], *Co wstrzymuje reformę Żydów w kraju naszym?*, 63–6; see also *11.60; AGAD, CWW 1871, pp. 124–9.

[68] The corresponding questions asked by the French Assembly were: '4th. In the eyes of

tatives responded in France. The most interesting questions concerned hasidism itself, that is, the attitude towards the government and government schools, the attitude towards prayer in 'the language of the country', and the attitude towards Christians. The questions illustrate how members of the committee imagined the reform of Jewish society as well as the possible place of hasidim in these plans. Of course, the answers say more about what hasidic leaders thought the government wanted to hear than about what the hasidim themselves thought. Members of the committee were fully aware of this. Still, an interesting tension emerged between what should be said and what could not be said. Meir of Opatów and Fayvel Kamienicer realized that their answers could influence the legal obligations the government might place on hasidim, so they generally avoided definitive declarations that might not hold water in reality. Kamienicer was at times less careful (for example, stating that the hasidim would gladly perform military service); Meir of Opatów—or perhaps Jakub Bereksohn Sonnenberg 'translating' for him—demonstrated an excellent sense of argumentation. For example, in the matter of the language of prayer, Meir said that prayer in Polish is basically impossible, but those who do not understand Hebrew—for example, women—can pray 'in Polish, that is, in the language that they know'. The language understood by those who did not know Hebrew was, of course, Yiddish, and not Polish. The tsadik himself had to use a translator during the investigation because of his inability to speak Polish and his 'lack of a comprehensible German' (he was doubtless speaking Yiddish). Still, the answer was a model of diplomacy. The tsadik skilfully rejected the possibility of obligating hasidim to pray in Polish but at the same time suggested somewhat truthfully a positive relationship to the language. Similarly, the very presence of Jakub Bereksohn Sonnenberg was in itself strong evidence of the economic usefulness of hasidim and their contribution to the development of the country. This argument, we remember, was put forward by Kamienicer and Kahana in their earlier petitions but now served to counteract the accusation that hasidim did not participate in domestic agriculture and industry. The only verifiable result of the investigation was the testimony of the hasidim that night meetings, singing, and drinking were not part of their rituals and so could be subject to police prosecution. This was also mentioned in the committee's final report.

Another interesting characteristic of the investigation is that the responses of Meir of Opatów and Fayvel Kamienicer were almost identical,

Jews, are Frenchmen considered brethren or strangers?', '6th. . . . Are they bound to obey the laws and to follow the directions of the civil code? 7th. What kind of police-jurisdiction have the Rabbies [*sic*] among the Jews?', '10th. Are there professions from which the Jews are excluded by their law?'. See *Transactions of the Parisian Sanhedrim*, 133–4. For more on the Assembly and the Sanhedrin, see Schwarzfuchs, *Napoleon, the Jews and the Sanhedrin*, 45–114.

though they were interrogated separately and most certainly could not have heard each other's answers.[69] This suggests that the hasidic leaders knew the questions in advance—even though their request to have the questions in advance had been rejected by the committee—and managed to establish similar versions of their testimony. If this is so, it means that the hasidim had conducted behind-the-scenes political activity which gave them access to the list of questions. We have no information allowing us to speculate who from the hasidic side could have undertaken this intercession and which of the government officials (most certainly members of the deputation or Department of Public Enlightenment) could have acceded to this request. Surowiecki and Radomiński were known for their friendliness towards the Jewish population; moreover, Radomiński made positive references to hasidim in the report. However, a bribe may have been in play here, so these positive comments do not necessarily indicate a genuine desire to help Jewish society. And we cannot exclude the participation of Ezekiel (Stanisław) Hoge, the influential maskil who was both an official of and a consultant to the Polish authorities: according to one hasidic tradition, he appeared at the time of the investigation as a defender of hasidism—even though, according to another tradition, he had already accepted Christianity at this time (in fact, at the time of the investigation, Hoge had not yet been baptized).[70] Hoge was the personal secretary of Stanisław Staszic in the 1820s, and if he held this position at the time of the investigation discussed here he would have had access to the committee papers and could easily have copied the list of questions. This would substantiate Hoge's positive role as assumed in the traditional versions of the story of the 1824 investigation. Unfortunately, however, there is no shred of evidence that might confirm Hoge's participation in this stage of the investigation.[71]

[69] The deputation recognized that those questioned were interrogated 'individually and not summoned together': *11.61, AGAD, CWW 1871, p. 130. However, the text of the interrogation suggests that their statements might sometimes have been challenged, for example when Meir says 'My answer is similar to that of the first person.'

[70] Sources are vague and sometimes contradictory, but it can be assumed that Hoge was baptized into the Evangelical Church in Apr. 1825 (see AGAD, CWW 1723, p. 276). Note, however, that the government report of July 1824 clearly proves that his preparations for conversion were already well advanced: see *11.60; AGAD, CWW 1871, pp. 124–9.

[71] The source of the legend about Hoge's involvement can be traced back to Alexander Tsederbaum's *Keter kehunah*, 130, whose version was supposedly based on family tradition. A hasidic hagiographer of Simhah Bunem, Yehuda Menahem Boim, in *Harabi rebe bunem mipeshisha*, ii. 635–6, rejects this story as an anti-hasidic libel, but it was popularized by Ezriel N. Frenk in 'Yekhezkel hoge oder "haskel meshumad"', and later by Beth-Zion Lask Abrahams in 'Stanislaus Hoga—Apostate and Penitent'. The role of Ezekiel Hoge in the inquiry is indeed rather mysterious. The Government Commission made use of his 1818 report, in which he criticized hasidism, as well as his later opinion, submitted in 1824. For unknown reasons, among the three documents missing from the complete documentation of the case are the two

Having questioned their hasidic witnesses, re-examined the documents, and held extensive discussions, the committee set about preparing its final report. Its contents follow:[72]

On the present day, that is to say, 10 August, the committee presided over by the Honourable Minister of State Staszic and comprised of the following members: the Honourable Senator Castellan Oebschelewitz, the Right Honourable Councillors of the Government Committee for Religious Denominations and Public Enlightenment Lipiński and Surowiecki as well as the Honourable Müller, Councillor of His Majesty's Imperial Court, implementing the recommendations of the Government Committee for Religious Denominations and Public Enlightenment, after an extensive exposition by the Presiding Minister as to the importance and necessity of measures with regard to Jews in our country, and after considerable discussion, reached the final verdict of the Government Committee for Religious Denominations and Public Enlightenment's report and opinion. Accord was thus reached on the following points:

1. That there is no true, significant difference on the grounds of faith between the hasidim and ordinary Jews.

2. That this more contemplative sect requires four or more hours daily in order to raise themselves to the heavens, whereas other Jews need only from half to one hour.

3. That they know more than ordinary Jews of the ways of mystical exultation and are stubborn with regard to their maintaining all principles which are in conflict with Christian morality and the civilized societies of Europe.

4. That the hasidim adhere in total to both the early and the later Talmuds with all their books, namely the Mishnah and Gemara, the sole exception to this being that the word *goy* is not extended to Christians, but only to idolaters.

5. That they have a greater adherence to mysticism and kabbalah.

6. That they do not have permanent rabbis and no obligation in this manner, but that they place their trust in certain leaders appointed by them, of whose sanctity and piety they are convinced; likewise they are convinced of their inspiration by divine spirit and communion with the angels.

7. That the hasidim themselves admit that dancing, shouting, drinking, and nocturnal gatherings are not necessary to their worship, that they are a violation and may be forbidden by the Government.

Therefore it is the opinion of the committee:

reports by Hoge. This might suggest the deliberate erasure of traces of his involvement in the matter. See *11.61; AGAD, CWW 1871, p. 130.

[72] See *11.73, *11.74; AGAD, CWW 1871, pp. 187–90; see also Wodziński, 'Sprawa chasydymów', 240–1.

1. That there is not the least need to persecute them nor for the Government to issue any resolution sanctioning their faith; on the contrary, in this matter an attitude of indifference should be maintained.

2. That they may retain the freedom they have had to date to worship God, but under the condition that it be recommended that all municipal authorities beware that there be no shouts, noises, drunkenness, nor nocturnal gatherings, inasmuch as they themselves call those things a violation.

3. The Government should not intervene in any recognition of the differences between Jews because this could restrict the Government in the formulation of any further plans in the overall scheme of their reforms.

4. After the steps already initiated in the reform of the Jews, such as the establishing of elementary schools, the abolition of the Jewish communities, the establishing of synagogues, prayer rooms, and their community boards, it is absolutely necessary to embark upon the plan which the Government Commission has already been carrying out for some years, which is the founding of a rabbinical school. Only then can the boundaries of Jewish communities be established and the designation of synagogues, or Jewish parishes, occur. In addition, regulations will be issued that in the event of a vacancy for a rabbi, two or three candidates be put forward from those trained and examined in the aforementioned school. These are the suggestions and recommendations that the committee has the honour to present in the matter of the hasidim as well as in the matter of the general reform of the Jews in our country.

Staszic, Oebschelwitz, and Surowiecki were thus agreed that hasidim were basically no different from other Jews, so they were thus not a separate sect. They were also neither better nor worse than other Jews. The fundamental differences were the greater inclination to mysticism and interest in kabbalah; a persistence 'in maintaining all principles which are in conflict with Christian morality and the civilized societies of Europe' (the committee apparently did not have much faith in the tsadikim's assertion that hasidic morality conformed more closely to Christian values than did the morality of Jews in general); the lack of permanent rabbis; and, compared with other Jews, a greater willingness to maintain neighbourly relations with Christians. Moreover, the committee reported that the hasidim had admitted that 'dancing, shouting, drinking, and nocturnal gatherings are not necessary to their worship', so these practices could be banned. The conclusions state that 'there is not the least need to persecute them', but that they should not be officially legalized either. Rather, the group should be treated with complete indifference, in order not to limit the opportunity to initiate a more general reform of Jewish society, which was recognized as the most urgent need. The committee's fundamental conclusion was the need to establish a state rabbinical school, which would facilitate the placement of enlightened rabbis in Jewish communities, and a campaign against Jewish backwardness, including that of the hasidim. Lipiński added a separate note that 'the separation they demand cannot be allowed, or, if so, only under such exact and severe conditions as to stimulate greater affinity to civilizing processes'.

De Müller submitted a separate opinion that confirmed most of the conclusions and recommendations of the report; in further stages of the investigation, however, it was completely ignored.[73] It was interesting, though, because it expressed very clearly the fundamental themes and hopes associated with this issue that were either concealed or omitted by many of the other members of the committee. Above all, De Müller was adamant that anti-hasidic charges did not merit credence because they came from Jews motivated 'only by [self-]protection, jealousy, and the particular interests of rabbinism'. As we remember, Radomiński had expressed similar scepticism at an earlier stage of the investigation; the same attitude was exhibited by a majority of the officials, with Staszic in the forefront. This general distrust of the leaders of traditional Jewish society and their opposition to the hasidim was a significant factor in determining the course of the investigation; thus, paradoxically, the antisemitic prejudices of the officials investigating the issue served to benefit the hasidim. De Müller also warned that persecution of the hasidim 'would only mean the recognition of the faith of the other Jews', and so would make Judaism a religion protected by law, when at this time it was only a tolerated belief. Clearly, then, the support for hasidism did not stem from recognition of the merit of hasidic demands or any kind of sympathy for their position, but rather from fear of strengthening the non-hasidic majority, their society, and their religion. Along with this went the conviction that the hasidim might turn out to be a positive force for destabilizing the unity of Jewish society and thus might be used in the future in 'civilizing' actions directed towards this community (though De Müller suspected that the hasidim would strongly resist this process). His only really interesting contribution was the idea of 'triggering a debate on hasidism among Jews', since 'the press publications appearing then, thanks to mutual recriminations, would throw light on this material and also on all of rabbinism'. The Polish authorities never took up this interesting suggestion.

In the name of the Government Commission for Religious Denominations and Public Enlightenment, Grabowski basically accepted the committee's recommendations; however, in accordance with Lipiński's advice, he recommended strict control of the *shtiblekh*. His report to the viceroy stressed three points: (*a*) hasidim were no worse or better than other Jews, so they could be allowed to organize separate services; (*b*) there should be put in place 'such exact and severe conditions as to stimulate greater affinity to

[73] See *11.75; AGAD, CWW 1871, pp. 191–8.

civilizing processes between the two sides' (once again in accordance with Lipiński's idea); (*c*) the most urgent need was the establishment of a state rabbinical school. On this basis, on 30 September 1824 the viceroy issued the following decree to the Government Commission for Internal Affairs and Police:

Understanding from the decision of the Government Commission for Religious Denominations and Public Enlightenment of the 16th of this month, No. 10.099/1.818, that the Jewish sect of hasidim or *kitajowcy* has nothing in principle against decency and distinguishes itself from other Jews only by the desire to have separate synagogues, we therefore do not wish to create any obstacle to the practice of common services in private homes.[74]

Zajączek allowed the hasidim to hold services in private homes, but he ignored the Government Commission's demand to introduce certain limitations and instead returned to the committee's original version. The demand to establish a rabbinical school also disappeared; there was, however, nothing odd about this, as such a school could not be brought into being through a ruling of the viceroy so the issue would in any case have to be discussed again at a meeting of the government. This happened shortly afterwards, and the Warsaw Rabbinical School opened in 1826. The decision of the viceroy was again unequivocally positive for hasidism. One should not necessarily see Jewish pressures here. The decision is in line with Zajączek's more general political approach to Jewish issues, which avoided the excessive restrictions of the anti-Jewish political line and the obsession with regulation. In addition, the ruling of the viceroy returned to the original tone recommended by Staszic, Oebschelwitz, and Surowiecki in the committee's final report; the departure from regulations proposed by Grabowski may have been the result of intervention by these members of the committee and the conflicts between Zajączek and Grabowski. The tone in which Staszic informed Grabowski of the viceroy's final decision seems to confirm this supposition.[75]

The Government Commission for Internal Affairs and Police soon informed the Government Commission for Religious Denominations and Public Enlightenment and the voivodeship commissions of the viceroy's decision, and the ban on organizing hasidic *shtiblekh* was withdrawn throughout the entire country. In this way, the most extensive investigation into hasidism in the Kingdom of Poland ended with a decision entirely favourable to hasidism.

[74] See *11.78, *11.80; AGAD, KRSW 6635, fo. 6; see also AGAD, CWW 1871, p. 213; Mahler, *Haḥasidut vehahaskalah*, 491; Wodziński, 'Sprawa chasydymów', 241.
[75] See *11.81; AGAD, CWW 1871, p. 212; see also AGAD, KRSW 6635, fos. 7ᵛ–8ʳ.

5. Hasidism Delivered: Conclusions

The first, most important, and most directly felt result of the investigation of 1823–4 was the full legalization of hasidic *shtiblekh* for prayer and hasidic gatherings for other purposes. The accepted, though not unanimous, more general political attitude towards hasidism was also considered unequivocally positive. In an effort to gain the support of the hasidic leaders, the government recommended a policy of non-intervention in conflicts internal to Jewish society. For the non-hasidic majority, this meant the loss of the last potential source of political authority that the community board could exploit in its fight with the breakaway hasidic group. Though official efforts to limit the range of these decisions appeared almost immediately (as discussed in the next chapter), the regulations introduced in 1824 had immense significance for the future of hasidism in the Kingdom of Poland. Not only did they open the way to further hasidic expansion, they also created a situation in which hasidim were in essence the only group in Polish Jewish society for which the state guaranteed the freedom of assembly. Contrary to the intentions of the committee and of Minister Grabowski, the decision was so favourable to the hasidim as to almost give them the status of a denomination protected by the state. Thus in the continuing fight regarding private prayer rooms in Płock, the president of the Voivodeship Commission, Florian Kobyliński, instructed his subordinates, following the ruling of September 1824, to make sure that 'they [Jews] do not gather for services in the room of any home, other than the homes of the *kitajowcy* Jews'.[76] Hasidim were then the only ones to whom the ban on Jewish prayer rooms did not apply. We might think that the hasidim realized the importance of this result of the investigation and fully exploited this opportunity. We know that at least some hasidic groups were given a copy of the September 1824 decision, to which they gladly referred in their defence at the request of authorities or during any kind of controversy regarding their legality. When in 1844 in Pabianice, an important industrial centre in the central part of the Kingdom, the mayor uncovered a hasidic group, he reported:

When the undersigned was convinced of the existence of this sect, he went to the meeting place of the Hussites that day, and, upon telling them that it was not allowed to meet in any other place besides the synagogue, the Hussites gave me a letter (which I enclose); I ask if I may presume upon the kindness of the honourable commissioner of the district to explain for me the subject of the copy of this letter, as the copy is not confirmed in any way and I do not know if it should be believed.[77]

---

[76] APP, AmP 325, fo. 28.
[77] APŁ, Akta miasta Pabianic 31 [11/23 Mar. 1844, mayor of Pabianice to the district office].

The hasidic groups thus knew the law relating to their movement better than the representatives of the state administration, and they were able to take full advantage of that fact.

However, at the same time other changes took place in the relations between the hasidim and the state. Most importantly, hasidism came out of the shadows. Awareness of the existence of the hasidim had become increasingly common, at least from 1818 on, but the 1823–4 investigation was still a turning-point because of the large number of reports and opinions of many officials, from the highest level to mayors and town councillors, gathered for the investigation. Many officials were engaged in the preparation of these materials, so awareness of the movement would have increased radically. Moreover, the reports and opinions provided a foundation for a thorough understanding of the movement. Equally important was the fact that for the first time a decision regarding hasidim was sent to all the voivodeship commissions and from there to all district commissions and mayors in the country, so the entire state administration was informed about the decisions related to hasidism. This was not only one decision but an entire series of legal acts: first, the Government Commission for Religious Denominations and Public Enlightenment issued a ban on gathering for prayer in private homes (together with a copy of Stern's very important report); then the Government Commission for Internal Affairs and the viceroy confirmed this decree; next, these decrees were temporarily withdrawn; finally, the last decision legalized the *shtiblekh* and the hasidic movement. Such a large number of rulings actually introduced more confusion than order into the relationship between the government and hasidism; still, officials could hope that they had learned what hasidism was and how to deal with it. This was a fundamental change; in subsequent official investigations, hasidim could no longer deny that they constituted a separate entity. Thus concluded the investigation of 1823–4, the first stage in the relations between the government and hasidism.

The investigation also showed that hasidism could potentially become an important element in the government's more general political programme for the Jewish population. Once state officials began to connect hasidism to the broader issue of the Jewish Question, their interest in the movement greatly increased. Also, the investigation of 1823–4 was more significantly influenced by the Enlightenment approach to the reform of Jewish society than earlier investigations had been. A major factor here was the active participation of Staszic, who constantly returned to the continuing debate on the Jewish Question. This was true of other participants in the investigation as well, for example Jan A. Radomiński and Wawrzyniec Surowiecki. Thus, after 1824, hasidism was seen as having a direct bearing on one of the most sensitive areas of contemporary social politics. Moreover, as we have seen, an awareness of the existence of hasidism led in 1824 to changes in how the government saw the entire Jewish Question, and also in its relation to the non-hasidic Jewish majority. The first result of this was the renewal of the project regulating the status of the rabbis and the state rabbinical school. While the establishment of that institution in 1826 was not solely the result of the 1823–4 investigation, there must have been a connection. More generally, the growth of internal Jewish conflicts, information about which now reached the government more often (usually through anti-hasidic letters from the boards of *kahals* and, later, Jewish community boards, but also sometimes through the requests of hasidim for help from state authorities), clearly revived government interest in regulating the status of the Jews and in their reform. The direction and development of this interest is the subject of the next chapter.

However, at the same time, the investigation revealed the government's structural inability to exploit the information it had acquired to effect the planned social transformation. Significantly, anti-Jewish prejudice again turned out to be one of the main factors determining the attitude of Polish officials towards the Jewish population. In spite of the sober, critical opinion expressed by officials and politicians favourably inclined to Jewish society, it was the voices of politicians operating from fear and xenophobic stereotypes, not rational calculation, that dominated. The continuation of this typical dilemma of the so-called Jewish Question, present in Polish discourse from the 1780s, is evident here too. In effect, all projects (and even information on Jewish society, particularly if it came from Jews themselves) were treated very critically; the basic concern of officials was that any decision made would turn out to be accidentally beneficial for the Jews themselves, because, as they believed, such decisions would be immediately exploited by Jews against the Christian population. In spite of the richness of the information gathered, the government did not develop a consistent, sensible view of the hasidic movement. With difficulty, it accepted a fragile political line that was based on a strange combination of unarticulated fears and phobias and a rational and far-sighted political vision. Moreover, even when the government intended to exploit the internal divisions of Jewish society and take a decision meant to gain the favour of the hasidim, it turned out to be incapable of such positive action. A number of the politicians engaged in the investigation, with Staszic leading the way, could not overcome their attitudes of paternalism, contempt, or feelings of superiority in relation to Jews, a result of which was to convince the hasidic leaders of the hostility of the government towards their movement, just the opposite of the government's intentions. The language of symbolic violence, then, turned out to be a trap to an equal degree for those subject to power and those in power, who were not able to free themselves from the habitus limiting their thinking and their customary actions. This enduring confusion of ideological antisemitism and personal prejudice among many representatives of the political class turned out, paradoxically, to be one of the most important factors forming the political attitude of the Polish government towards hasidism. The influence of these factors on the government's views regarding hasidism will be discussed in the next chapter.

CHAPTER FOUR

Between Words and Actions

THE INVESTIGATION IN 1823–4 revealed the discrepancies between the government's official policy towards hasidim, which was generally positive, and the somewhat negative personal attitudes of the bureaucrats who had formulated the policy and were supposed to implement it. A subsequent investigation that started at the end of 1824 and continued into 1825 was to fully reveal the nature and destructive consequences of these unresolved contradictions.

In November 1824 the tsadik Meir of Opatów complained to the Government Commission for Internal Affairs and Police that local police harassment was impeding the assembly of hasidim for prayer and demanded the immediate enforcement of the ruling of the previous investigation that had legalized hasidic *shtiblekh* in full.[1] On behalf of the commission, Staszic sent Rabbi Meir's complaint to the Government Commission for Religious Denominations and Public Enlightenment so that the issue could be examined more closely. That august body dismissed the complaint on the grounds that it did not concern religious freedom but rather police order, and that it therefore came under the jurisdiction of the Commission for Internal Affairs. The Commission for Internal Affairs duly agreed to investigate.[2]

Rabbi Meir, questioned in Opatów, denied authorship of the petition. He claimed that he had never accused the local police, had not submitted a complaint to anyone, and had not consulted anyone about this issue. But, he said, disturbed by the fact that the decision of the viceroy to allow hasidim to hold separate services had still not reached Opatów, he had written to the Bereksohn family in Warsaw, 'asking that a ruling be sent quickly and that they try to remove all possible obstacles'.[3] In accordance with this wish, Jakub

---

[1] Rabbi Meir's petition has not been preserved, but its contents are known through the official correspondence to which it gave rise. See *12.01; AGAD, CWW 1871, pp. 214–15; see also AGAD, KRSW 6635, fo. 9. Some documents related to Rabbi Meir's intervention are published in Mahler, *Haḥasidut vehahaskalah*, 492–501. Unfortunately, Mahler's version is incomplete and biased; see Mahler, *Hasidism and the Jewish Enlightenment*, 329–32.

[2] See *12.01–*12.03; AGAD, CWW 1871, pp. 214–15, 218; see also AGAD, KRSW 6635, fos. 9–10; Mahler, *Haḥasidut vehahaskalah*, 492–3.

[3] See *12.05; AGAD, KRSW 6635, fo. 18–22; see also Mahler, *Haḥasidut vehahaskalah*, 498–501.

Bereksohn Sonnenberg had submitted a note to the Government Commission for Internal Affairs, but, in consequence of a misunderstanding, according to Rabbi Meir, the note had included a complaint about the behaviour of the Opatów police. Since an unsubstantiated charge could have led to police harassment of Rabbi Meir, and even to legal action against him, Rabbi Meir consistently denied any connection with the accusation and even stressed that during searches the police had not committed 'any indecency or impropriety; they behaved quietly, calmly, and respectfully'. The investigation, however, revealed that the charge was not entirely unfounded. The police had often interrupted meetings between Rabbi Meir and groups of hasidim visiting him, demanding to see identification on the pretext that they were looking for smugglers and contraband, and had even banned large religious gatherings of this type. Rabbi Meir assumed that this was simply due to their lack of knowledge about the new regulations legalizing hasidic gatherings. However, the government correspondence shows unequivocally that this assumption was mistaken. The police regarded the gatherings of Jews as subject to general law and order, so the law guaranteeing hasidim freedom of assembly did not apply. Astonishingly, this interpretation was supported by senior state officials, including those who had been involved in creating the law sympathetic to hasidim that had been passed only a few months earlier, thereby nullifying the essence of the royal decree from 1824. Jan A. Radomiński wrote: 'the travelling of the *kitajowcy* Jews from different places to the private home of the rabbi, an act not entirely consistent with the permission granted to hold services in appropriate locations, can be abused in many ways and should not be tolerated'.[4] Minister Grabowski agreed.[5] Fortunately for the hasidim, however, this restrictive interpretation was rejected. We do not know the deciding factors, but in the end a different interpretation won the day, and Rabbi Meir achieved a moderate victory. His explanation in the matter of the unsubstantiated accusation of the police was accepted, and the police denied any kind of harassment of or even interest in hasidim.[6] At the same time, however, neither the Government Commission nor any other body or individual confirmed that hasidim had the right to assemble freely; it merely confirmed that hasidim 'had not experienced' any disturbance by police during gatherings, and that only by mistake was a complaint

---

[4] See *12.02; AGAD, CWW 1871, pp. 214–15.

[5] In a draft letter to the Government Commission for Internal Affairs and Police, dated 23 Dec. 1823, the minister of the Government Commission for Religious Denominations and Public Enlightenment, Stanisław Grabowski, outlined his intention to reject Rabbi Meir's appeal: see AGAD, CWW 1871, pp. 216–17. Eventually, however, the appeal was transferred to the Government Commission for Internal Affairs and Police for further processing: see *12.03; AGAD, KRSW 6635, fo. 10; also Mahler, *Haḥasidut vehahaskalah*, 493.

[6] See *12.06; AGAD, KRSW 6635, fos. 16–17; see also Mahler, *Haḥasidut vehahaskalah*, 493–4.

to that effect sent to the Government Commission'.[7] With this, the Government Commission considered the issue closed. In reality, however, the question of freedom of assembly remained unanswered; the Government Commission had simply avoided the issue. Its response resulted neither from the logic of the political position adopted several months earlier nor from rational analysis of the situation. Local police and officials of the Voivodeship Commission, senior government figures, and even the authors of the 1824 ruling favourable to hasidim simply did not accept in practice that hasidim—or any other Jews—could enjoy full freedom of assembly and activity without government restriction. This was due to a combination of factors: ideological motivations, personal fears and prejudices, and, above all, a bureaucratic mentality. One must also remember that around this time (1825) the government viewed all assemblies, for any purpose and whether Christian or Jewish, with hostility, because (as elsewhere in Europe at the time) everyone was potentially suspected of subversive activity. This was, after all, a time of revolutionary upheaval and harsh anti-liberal repression throughout the states of the Holy Alliance. It seems, however, that an even more important factor was aversion to the Jewish community as such: as indicated in earlier chapters, unarticulated and irrational antisemitic stereotypes, prejudices, and fears were rife.

The petty harassments described here were the consequence of an attitude typical of a demoralized state bureaucracy alienated from the society under its governance. This attitude manifested itself in three basic types of behaviour. The first was a reluctance to do anything at all, an inertia that led to hostile arrogance and sometimes open aggression towards those who were demanding action, especially any unusual action. The second type of behaviour, related to the first, was an aversion to anything that did not conform to standard procedures and government regulations. This also often led to obstructiveness towards anything perceived as a problem. The third type of behaviour was hostility to anything that tried to limit the power of the government by placing something beyond its control. The arrogant attitude of the organs of power and the various obstructive measures they employed were thus an expression of dissatisfaction, feelings of superiority towards Jews, and an attempt to restore the correct hierarchical order between 'the authorities' and 'the Jews'. To be sure, such phenomena are present in almost all bureaucracies. Here, however, they had special significance because, since these attitudes towards Jews were evident from the very beginning of the Kingdom of Poland's policy on hasidim, they set the tone of the government's approach and shaped it definitively. It should be noted, moreover, that the government's attitude towards hasidim did not differ substantially from its attitude towards other parts of Jewish society; all Jews experienced the

---

[7] See *12.08; AGAD, KRSW 6635, fo. 23; see also Mahler, *Haḥasidut vehahaskalah*, 501–2.

hostility and demeaning attitude of the administration to some degree. The aversion towards hasidim was particularly evident since it was they who most frequently came into contact with the bureaucracy as they tried to establish their rights; their contact was mostly with lower-level bureaucrats who were often poorly educated, always badly remunerated, and generally disgruntled about having to grapple daily with the implementation of state policy towards Jews.[8] But it was not just hasidim who had to suffer such indignities: the Warsaw maskil Jan Glücksberg rightly complained of 'arbitrary conduct and harassment for even the least amount of profit from officials, even from high officials, who are not worthy of being called citizens'.[9] Thus, similar attitudes towards Jews could be found both in the highest echelons of the political elite determining the policies towards Jews and among the local officials responsible for their implementation; any difference was only one of degree.

The relationship of the authorities to hasidim and hasidism was determined above all by such factors; the policy formulated after the investigation in 1824 was soon almost completely forgotten, and other factors, often articulated only obliquely if at all, soon revealed themselves to be equally influential. Thus to the anti-Jewish stereotypes, fears, and prejudices already mentioned one must add the private interests of the numerous officials involved; the inertia and laissez-faire tendencies of the local administration; and the government's alarming ignorance of Jewish matters. Moreover, in the dozens of issues that appeared to have a hasidic connection, each of these factors might occur in a different combination, and each individual configuration was not always easily decipherable even by the people involved. In other words, the government's approach to hasidism gave rise to a chaotic complex of intertwining and mutually disruptive tendencies that could be supplemented by any number of less substantive factors, to which completely accidental factors, or even individual circumstances, might also contribute. Though this political situation barely resembles 'policy' in its classic sense (or at least our understanding of what that might mean), this is what I call here the politics of the authorities concerning the hasidic movement. Later sections of this chapter are concerned with the reappearance of the influence of these factors on the political approach adopted in 1824 and the reconstruction of these structural, though less substantive, irregularities.

1. Big Politics, Small Politicians

As we saw in the Opatów incident, the political stance towards hasidism was characterized from the very beginning by bureaucratic inconsistency and acts

---

[8] An interesting analysis of the social profile of the state administration officials in the Voivodeship of Mazovia can be found in Rostocki, *Korpus w gęsie pióra uzbrojony*, and id., *Pochodzenie społeczne, kwalifikacje i przebieg kariery urzędników Komisji Województwa Mazowieckiego*.   [9] [Glücksberg], *Rzut oka na stan Izraelitów w Polsce*, 1–2.

in contravention of the formal findings of the 1824 investigation. Indeed, it rapidly became apparent that the findings of the 1824 investigation were largely disregarded even by the most senior state officials, and that basically no agency, including the Government Commission for Religious Denominations and Public Enlightenment that had been responsible for the investigation, was able to implement its findings and recommendations. Given that conflicts involving hasidim came increasingly to the attention of the authorities in dozens of communities after 1824, it is striking that the government never tried to exploit such conflicts so as to gain greater influence over Jewish society or to realize the reforms proposed following the 1824 investigation. Moreover it failed to do so even when proposals in this regard were actually formulated by local officials or by others interested in the modernization of Jewish society. The conflict surrounding the hasidic rabbi in Płock in 1829, in which the state authorities played a not insignificant role, offers an excellent illustration of these attitudes and of the mechanisms that determined the shape of the policies towards hasidim.[10]

After the death of Rabbi Ozyel Rubinstein of Płock in 1825, there was no one in the town sufficiently qualified to act as expert witness for Jews presenting divorce cases in the local civil court. The task of the expert witness was to confirm that the divorce had been conducted in accordance with Jewish religious law, and this function was traditionally performed by the rabbi. Given the lack of a qualified rabbi after Rubinstein's death, the civic authorities called on Daniel Landau, one of the wealthiest members of the local Jewish community and an unusually influential member of the Jewish community board, to take on this role. In 1828, for reasons unknown, the two other members of the Jewish community board, Manes Jakub Torner and Michał Goldberg, attempted to remove Landau from this position. The attempt was only partly successful as the candidate proposed to replace him was disqualified by the government, who suggested instead the possibility of dismissing Landau and presenting another candidate who could also act as expert witness.[11] The board then proposed the candidature of Alexander Zusya Kahana, the Przysucha hasid involved in the political interventions described earlier, offering him the post of rabbi and expert witness at a salary of 2,000 złotys yearly. Landau meanwhile proposed appointing as rabbi his son-in-law, Abraham Raphael Landau, then rabbi in Ciechanów, with himself as expert witness, at a salary of 1,500 złotys each. In the event, 218 members of the Jewish community in Płock, a very significant number,[12] signed the

---

[10] The investigation in Płock has been analysed in Wodziński, *Haskalah and Hasidism*, 105–7. The hasidic point of view can be found in T. Y. Michelson, 'Kuntres mareh kohen vehu toledot rabenu hameḥaber', 5 [separately paginated].   [11] See *13.01; AGAD, CWW 1666, p. 250.

[12] In 1827 there were 3,412 Jews in Płock, which makes about 700 'fathers of families', but only a few of them had actual voting rights. In 1839 the number eligible to vote was as low as 178. See APP, AmP 31, fos. 200–6.

Figure 4.1 Płock, one of the oldest Polish towns, a provincial capital during the Kingdom of Poland, and one of the most important towns of the Kingdom. Lithograph by Maksymilian Fajans, from the original by K. Beyer, 1854. Biblioteka Narodowa w Warszawie, Zbiory Ikonograficzne, A.5542/ G.XIX/ II-73, pl. 3

rabbinical contract of Abraham Landau; 88 signed the contract appointing Daniel Landau as expert witness.[13] Strangely, however, the Voivodeship Commission did not consider the candidature of either Landau at all but simply rejected the community's decision, and shortly afterwards, without offering any explanation, appointed Alexander Kahana as rabbi.

Procedurally this was clearly out of order, but no one appeared to be bothered. The incident seems quite mysterious; Kahana's nomination took place behind the backs of the Jewish community—in the sense that although two of the three members of the community board supported the nomination, they sent their proposal straight to the Voivodeship Commission without consulting the community, while Daniel Landau—the third member of the community board—collected many signatures for contracts for himself and his son-in-law and likewise submitted his proposal to the Voivodeship Commission. The proposal submitted by Manes Jakub Tomer and Michał Nota Goldberg was reviewed positively, while Landau's was rejected with no reason given. Moreover, both proposals were submitted directly to the

[13] Both contracts have very early dates. The rabbinical one is dated 25 Jan. 1829, the expert witnesses's 12 May 1829. Thus it seems reasonable to assume that both contracts were antedated and actually issued only as a response to the nomination of Alexander Kahana. See *13.02, *13.03; AGAD, CWW 1666, pp. 230–3, 240–2.

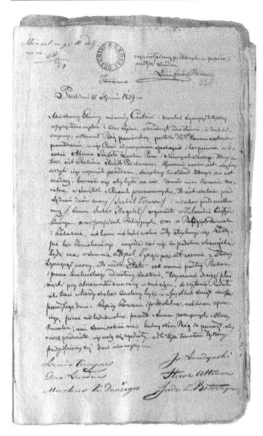

Figure 4.2 The contract of
Abraham b. Raphael Landau of
Ciechanów for his rabbinical post
in Płock, 1829. AGAD, CWW
1666, p. 230

Voivodeship Commission rather than through the city authorities, as the
statutory procedure required; yet the Voivodeship Commission not only
accepted this procedure, but also the candidate proposed. This was in fla-
grant contravention of the regulations, especially as legally the appointment
of a rabbi required the summoning of a general assembly of all male heads
of household and the following of a specific procedure, with minutes of
the proceedings being recorded by an official of the magistrate's court.[14]
Apparently as the result of an informal understanding, a faction of the Jewish community board and officials of the Voivodeship Commission, acting
against the majority of the Jewish community and the city council, decided to
push through their own candidate as rabbi. Not surprisingly, the decision
elicited a counter-action from others within the community. Daniel Landau,
along with a group of influential Płock residents associated with him,
registered their protest formally, and their complaints about the decision of

[14] This was based on the statutes of the rabbinical school in Warsaw, issued in 1826, which
regulated all the laws on rabbinical nominations in the Kingdom; see *Z dziejów gminy
starozakonnych w Warszawie w XIX stuleciu*, i: *Szkolnictwo*, 49–56.

the voivodeship was sent directly to the Government Commission for Religious Denominations and Public Enlightenment.[15]

The Government Commission was shocked by the voivodeship's decision, undertaken without any prior consultation or report on the ongoing issue, and demanded an immediate explanation.[16] The report submitted in response cited two fundamental arguments, as formulated earlier in a petition of the Jewish community board and derived from correspondence from the camp opposed to Landau.[17] First, Abraham Landau did not know Polish and was therefore not qualified for the post. Secondly, appointing Kahana would result in significant savings: his total salary for both posts would be only 2,000 złotys yearly, whereas appointing the Landaus would mean paying 3,000 złotys in total.

The Government Commission accepted the logic and confirmed Kahana's nomination as rabbi; almost at the same time, however, the Jewish Committee (the government body responsible for Jewish issues, as discussed in Chapter 1, §5) sent the Government Commission a report, composed in response to a petition of the residents of Płock, that presented new arguments, and new accusations against Kahana. The issue could thus not yet be considered closed.

In their petition, the residents of Płock requested 'that Alexander Kohn [Kahana], chosen as rabbi of this community and former rabbi in the voivodeship town of Siedlce, should not be appointed to this post because he belongs to the sect of hasidim and is suspected of usury'.[18] The members of the Jewish Committee were not particularly conversant with the issues raised, but they showed goodwill in exploring the facts of the case. The main point on which they were unclear was why there should be a problem in appointing a hasid as a rabbi, so on this issue they turned to the Advisory Board, the official body of experts established by the committee, which was dominated by acculturated Jews.

The Advisory Board's report was very much opposed to Kahana's appointment. The first point was that Kahana was a hasid. While admitting that 'religious regulations do not clearly forbid a hasid from being a rabbi', the board justified its decision on the grounds that 'hasidism [was] formed later than the period in which the religious regulations, i.e. the *Shulḥan arukh*, were compiled and published, so, as an unforeseen case, it is natural that this issue is not mentioned'.[19] It also offered the quite logical argument that 'it is improper for a hasid to be named rabbi in a city where the majority

---

[15] See *13.04, *13.05; AGAD, CWW 1666, pp. 219–29, APP, AmP 568, fo. 64.
[16] See *13.07; AGAD, CWW 1666, pp. 251–2.
[17] See *13.06, *13.08; AGAD, CWW 1666, pp. 246–9, 259–61.
[18] See *13.12; AGAD, CWW 1666, pp. 265–7.
[19] See *13.11; AGAD, CWW 1666, pp. 268–9.

of the community do not belong to hasidism. It would be ridiculous if in the performance of certain religious rituals the community acted differently from their own rabbi.' It went on to enumerate the negative social consequences of the appointment of a hasidic rabbi in a community dominated by people indifferent or hostile towards the hasidic movement. As to the accusation of usury, the Advisory Board knew nothing more than the rumours, but acknowledged that the very suspicion threw bad light on the candidate, and that as a result he should not be appointed.

The committee basically accepted the demands of the Advisory Board. At the same time, however, it linked the issue to the wider issue of the reform of Jewish society and recommended that the government should not confirm Kahana's appointment in order that 'the vacant post of rabbi in Płock be reserved for a graduate of the rabbinical school'. The Jewish Committee intended, then, to exploit the conflict for the purpose of reform by appointing a candidate from the Warsaw Rabbinical School with a progressive outlook. It thought that the community would be willing to accept this since the last rabbi, Ozyel Rubinstein, had himself been an active supporter of modernization. It clearly intended to implement the policy outlined in 1824 and to link its position on hasidism with the more general plans for the reform of Jewish society.

On receiving the Jewish Committee's report, the Government Commission ordered the Voivodeship Commission to investigate whether Kahana really was a hasid and a usurer, and whether hasidim really were a minority in Płock,[20] and the Voivodeship Commission conveyed this demand to the local authorities in Płock. The results of the investigation were unclear. Seventeen people testified that the charges against Kahana were false; but on the very same day the mayor received a letter signed by three influential Płock Jews that confirmed the charges against Kahana, so it was decided to investigate further. During the second investigation, ten of those questioned said the charge of usury was unfounded, but they were divided on his affiliation with hasidism.[21] The mayor sent both protocols to the Voivodeship Commission without expressing an opinion in the matter, except to confirm that the hasidim were decidedly a minority in Płock.[22]

The Voivodeship Commission took a different approach. Its president, Florian Kobyliński, presented a report to the government that stated that 'the accusations could not be substantiated',[23] and that the government should distance itself from them. This positive attitude to Kahana was based neither on the records of the investigations nor on the mayor's letter, but

[20] See *13.14; APP, AmP 568, fo. 68; see also AGAD, CWW 1666, p. 271.
[21] See *13.16–*13.18; AGAD, CWW 1666, pp. 281–92.
[22] See *13.20; APP, AmP 568, fos. 69–70; see also AGAD, CWW 1666, pp. 278–80.
[23] See *13.20; AGAD, CWW 1666, pp. 276–7.

rather was a consequence of the earlier decision of the voivodeship authorities that had been unequivocally favourable to Kahana's candidature. The Voivodeship Commission also ignored entirely the question of Kahana's allegiance to hasidism, focusing instead on the claim of Kahana's supporters that the charge of usury had been trumped up by Daniel Landau in an effort to ensure the salary of expert witness for himself and the position of rabbi for his son-in-law.[24]

The Government Commission accepted this explanation. It was persuasive above all because it was true, at least in part, and accurately suggested the actual mechanism of the Płock conflict. The argument that Kahana was a hasid was only a pretext, not because Kahana was not a hasid (that was not in doubt), but rather because the candidate of the opposing camp, Abraham Landau, was also a known hasidic leader. In actuality, Landau was to become one of the most famous Polish tsadikim; among his most active supporters was one Lejzer Kohn, possibly identical with the hasidic leader and rabbi Eleazar ben Ze'ev Wolf Hakohen, who had been involved in communal matters in Płock from his youth and was a vociferous supporter of Abraham Landau.[25] Thus, the conflict was not between hasidim and their opponents. Abraham Landau was the candidate of part of the Płock *kahal* oligarchy and the rabbinical elite surrounding Daniel Landau (Abraham's father-in-law), one of the richest and most influential of Płock's Jews;[26] Kahana was the candidate of the less well-known faction concentrated around part of the Jewish community board (Manes Jakub Torner and Michał Nota Goldberg) and supported by the Voivodeship Commission. The explanation proposed by the Voivodeship Commission, then, was only half-true; it concealed that Kahana had also not been selected properly, but rather as the result of a deal with a pressure group representing one faction within the Jewish community board. The fact that Kahana's nomination had not been conducted properly, and was therefore actually illicit, had not been communicated to the higher authorities, suggesting that the Voivodeship Commission was not a non-partisan observer in the conflict. What we are talking about was a conflict between two interest groups, in which the Voivodeship Commission favoured one side. The question of hasidism was treated purely instrumentally by all sides in the conflict, as a pretext covering up a completely different but

[24] See *13.06, *13.13; AGAD, CWW 1666, pp. 246–9, 270–1.

[25] See AGAD, CWW 1666, pp. 226–9. Interestingly enough, neither hasidic nor local tradition preserves any trace of the conflict between Alexander Zusya Kahana's supporters and those of Abraham Landau, only an enigmatic hint about contacts between Abraham Landau and Eleazar Hakohen regarding the candidacy of the latter for the rabbinical post in Płock. For more on Eleazar Hakohen and his contacts with Płock and with Abraham Landau, see Grynszpan, 'Rabanim: kovets masot al rabanei plotsk', 101–4.

[26] See 'Plotsk/Płock', in *Pinkas hakehilot: polin*, iv: *Varshah vehagalil*, 358–72; Grynszpan, 'Rabanim: kovets masot al rabanei plotsk'.

clear divide. Landau's supporters accused Kahana of being a hasid, while Kahana's supporters used typical anti-hasidic rhetoric against Abraham Landau. For example, one of the petitions put forward by the Jewish community board accused Daniel Landau of proposing a candidate (in fact, his son-in-law) 'full of old superstitions and old wives' tales';[27] three of Kahana's supporters endorsed his candidacy on the grounds that with his open-minded approach he aspired to 'real enlightenment . . . in accordance with the will of the government', while if Abraham Landau were to be appointed, 'the youth of our community will be threatened with further darkness through the teaching of their superior, who himself does not possess any acquaintance with secular knowledge'.[28] This confirms once again that in nineteenth-century conflicts in Jewish society, anti-hasidic rhetoric was the standard way of criticizing opponents; in practice, such accusations certainly indicated the existence of a conflict, but the conflict might be over another matter entirely. The best evidence of this is cases in which one hasidic group charged another with hasidism, as for example in Węgrów in 1851, when hasidic supporters of the tsadik of Izbica, Mordecai Josef Leiner, requested the dismissal of the hasid Mendel Safir from the function of rabbi because he was selected 'by Hussites and fifth-class residents', when in reality they opposed Safir because he was the candidate of a competing group of hasidim from Kock.[29] As we have seen, a somewhat similar incident occurred in Płock.

Notwithstanding the instrumental character of the anti-hasidic rhetoric, however, it is worth considering the broader significance of the actions of the Voivodeship Commission in the implementation of state policy concerning hasidism. In lending its support to one of the candidates and participating in this game of pretexts and instrumental rhetoric, the commission was in violation of the law. It is difficult to determine if the usual bribe or some other kind of service or relationship was behind this. There is no doubt that officials everywhere had numerous connections with the local economic elite, including Jews, which created considerable opportunities for the informal influence of bureaucratic procedures (though these were not unlimited, as discussed in Chapter 5, §5). Moreover, this is only a technical question; the real point is that the Voivodeship Commission was not influenced to any significant degree by the government's official policy towards the hasidic movement. Far more decisive, at least in this instance, were the informal arrangements, private interests, and behind-the-scenes connections of the bureaucrats concerned.

[27] See *13.06; AGAD, CWW 1666, pp. 246–9.
[28] See *13.09; AGAD, CWW 1666, pp. 256–8.
[29] AGAD, CWW 1789, p. 206. On anti-hasidic rhetoric as a medium for various messages and social conflicts unconnected with actual anti-hasidic conflicts, see Gertner, 'Rabanut vedayanut begalitsiyah bamaḥatsit harishonah shel hame'ah hatesha-esreh', 74–83.

The final decision of the Government Commission is also interesting, and instructive for understanding the implementation of government policy concerning hasidism. The commission had received not only the reports of the Voivodeship Commission and the documents from Płock, but also the opinions of the Advisory Board and the Jewish Committee. The conclusions of the Jewish Committee contradicted the demands of the Voivodeship Commission and the arguments it raised, and did so sensibly and rationally. Moreover, its objectivity was less in doubt, and the measures it proposed were consistent with the official policy on Jewish society in general and hasidism in particular. It would seem natural, then, that the Government Commission would agree with the opinion of the Jewish Committee. However, the opposite happened. In a one-sentence note, Minister Grabowski stated simply: 'If the charges against the rabbi of Płock turn out to be false, then there is no reason to prevent him from carrying out his obligations.'[30] The Government Commission completely ignored the formal irregularity in the selection procedure, the clear bias of the Voivodeship Commission, the significant arguments of the Jewish Committee and the Advisory Board, and, above all, the hasidic context of the issue. Having been through the formalities of conducting an investigation, it approved the appointment and simply rejected the Jewish Committee's proposal to take advantage of the conflict to introduce reforms. In other words, it took the path of least resistance.

In practice, then, the government's policy on hasidism turned out to be the sum of the bias and interests of the voivodeship officials, on the one hand, and the legalistic formalism motivated by the inertia of government authorities on the other. At the end of the 1820s similar factors and mechanisms played an ever greater role not only in government policy on hasidism but also, and more significantly, in every aspect of government.[31] The first signs of this administrative atrophy were evident in this failure of policy implementation and in the deteriorating relations between Tsar Alexander I and the Polish political elite, particularly after 1820 when the former underwent a personal transformation, abandoned his liberalism, and became increasingly reactionary. Although on becoming the constitutional king of Poland in 1815 he had granted the country a very liberal constitution, he came to believe that the Poles were taking too much advantage of their political rights; the increasing conflict with part of the Polish political elite on this matter, and especially with the parliamentary opposition, led the tsar to harden his political stance. The infamous personification of this politics was his official

[30] See *13.20; AGAD, CWW 1666, pp. 276–7.
[31] The progressive atrophy of the administration of the Kingdom of Poland before 1832 has not yet been properly described. I am grateful to Maciej Mycielski for his interesting remarks on this issue.

plenipotentiary, Senator Nikolai Novosiltseff, but also—and to an equal degree—his own brother, Grand Duke Constantine, commander of the Polish army, who was responsible for the secret police, the institution of the censor, and other repressive institutions. Both Novosiltseff and Grand Duke Constantine, who had been appointed to their positions by the tsar acting as Polish king, fulfilled their functions legally and officially, but the manner in which they did so and the extent of their powers meant that they caused numerous controversies and that the political system became less and less transparent. The confusing system of relationships, and sometimes extra-legal arrangements, naturally did not favour effective administration, though the Kingdom of Poland in its first decade was no more unlawful than any other European state of that era.

However, the effectiveness of the administration suffered greatly in 1826 from the death of Viceroy Zajączek. Though Zajączek was rightly criticized for lack of strategic vision and political weakness, he was a surprisingly efficient administrator. Thanks to him, the Kingdom of Poland in the first decade of its existence had a relatively skilful and dynamic administration capable of realizing its goals. After Zajączek's death the king did not name a successor, and the authority of the viceroy was transferred to the government. The jurisdictional chaos, the confusing relations between the highest institutions of state (the government committee with some prerogatives of the viceroy, the Council of State, and the secretary of state) and unofficial centres of power meant that the government administration was soon in no position to propose even the simplest legislation or even to co-ordinate interdepartmental activities, let alone to implement any long-term policy. In addition, conflicts between the political coteries of Grand Duke Constantine (supported by Novosiltseff and Grabowski) and the equally influential Treasury minister, Franciszek Ksawery Drucki-Lubecki, further complicated the situation. Moreover, after the death of Tsar Alexander I in 1825, his successor Nicholas I consciously encouraged this conflict with the goal of weakening the position of his brother Constantine and increasing his own sphere of influence. As a result, state activity was limited to 'managing' rather than governing, and real political debate and activities of a strategic nature disappeared. Under the exceptionally strong and skilful administration of Drucki-Lubecki this atrophy did not affect the Government Commission for Income and Assets, but the latter had relatively little connection with government policy on Jews.

The death of Stanisław Staszic, also in 1826, was similarly an important factor in the progressive atrophy of the political activity of the authorities of the Kingdom, and this time especially regarding Jews. Staszic personified not only the symbolic but also the real continuity of the Enlightenment vision of the state, including the reform of the Jewish population (together with all its limitations and discontents). Indeed, he was not only the author of government policy towards Jewish society and, to a great degree, concerning hasidism, he was also one of the great, though controversial, authorities of the Enlightenment faction, which consistently developed the Kingdom's strategic goals. His death meant a final departure from this kind of political practice, which was reflected almost immediately in policies regarding hasidism, among other things. While the change only became evident in 1832, following the collapse of the anti-tsarist uprising of 1830–1 and as a result of the withdrawal of the constitution and the Kingdom of Poland's loss of sovereignty, the first indications of the crisis to come and the increasing degeneration of the state administration were evident several years earlier. The 1829 conflict about the rabbi in Płock is just one example.

2. Silent Turning-Point: Hasidism in the Politics of the Kingdom after 1831

By the end of the 1820s, rabbinical appointments had become one of the two major reasons for conflict between hasidim and others in the Jewish community; the other was the continuing controversy surrounding the establishment of *shtiblekh*. Sometimes the courses of the conflicts were strikingly similar, allowing for a very instructive comparison illustrating the nature of the turning-point in 1831. A conflict almost identical with that of 1829 in Płock occurred in 1835–6 in Pilica, a small town in the Kraków voivodeship, which in 1827 had had a population of 2,861, of whom 1,096, or 38.3 per cent (though a more likely estimate put the figure at 1,500), were Jews.[32] This time the cause of the conflict was not the hasidic orientation of the rabbi—Shaul Spira—but rather his opposition to the hasidic movement, which was well documented. It had led to his dismissal from the post of rabbi in Wodzisław in 1830, and was also possibly the background to the loss of his rabbinical post in Nowy Sącz (in Galicia) several years earlier.[33] The conflict between Spira and the hasidim thus had a long history. In 1835, a group of hasidim led by Lejbuś (Aryeh Leib) Hirszberg, a wealthy merchant and close follower of the tsadik Menahem Mendel of Kock, tried to replace Spira with a hasidic candidate Meier Eibeszyc (I have not been able to establish a connection to the well-known Eybeschütz family). The balance of influence in Pilica was similar to that in Płock six years earlier. Two out of three members of the Jewish community board favoured the appointment of a hasidic rabbi, and the Voivodeship Commission supported them; but the majority, who favoured Spira, were supported by the District Commission, and eventually the Government Commission, which found the attitude of the voivodeship in-

---

[32] See AGAD, CWW 1472, pp. 28–102.
[33] On Spira in Wodzisław see Dynner, '*Men of Silk*', 65–6.

explicable. In August 1835, at the request of part of the Jewish community board, the Voivodeship Commission removed Spira from the position of rabbi and nominated Eibeszyc in his place. Spira appealed to the District Commission (under the Voivodeship Commission), which ruled that the decision of the Voivodeship Commission was mistaken; it therefore initiated an investigation and delayed the implementation of the Voivodeship Commission's decision until the investigation was finished. Soon, however, Spira was again removed from his post, most probably under pressure from the voivodeship. This situation did not last for long either, because the previous community board had been dismissed at the same time and the new board members turned to the Government Commission for Internal Affairs, Religions, and Public Enlightenment (a new body that combined the earlier Government Commission for Internal Affairs and Police and the Government Commission for Religious Denominations and Public Enlightenment) to request Spira's reinstatement. Once again the issue was reopened, and once again the Voivodeship Commission rejected all the arguments for Spira and against Eibeszyc and sent the issue back to the local authorities for further investigation. The unresolved conflict continued over several months despite overwhelming arguments against Eibeszyc; the dismissal of the pro-hasidic board of the community; pressure from the Government Commission for Internal Affairs; and even the results of the repeated election for rabbi, which Spira won, ninety-three votes to eighteen. The whole affair was an excellent example of conflict between two interest groups, in which (legitimate) accusations of hasidic sympathy raised by the Jewish participants in the conflict were entirely ignored by the authorities and did not influence the course of the conflict to any degree.

Despite the striking similarities, however, the incidents in Płock and Pilica were not identical. The seven years separating them had seen a quiet, slow, but very distinct evolution in the policy of dealing with hasidism. This was a consequence of more general changes in Poland—that were not entirely quiet or slow—as a result of which the authorities occupied themselves less and less with governing and more and more with managing. The rapid collapse of the anti-tsarist uprising in 1830–1 ended the formal sovereignty of the Kingdom and led to a significant limitation of civil liberties. Immediately afterwards the old pro-Enlightenment group lost its position (the movement of eminent politicians away from this group was already evident before 1830), and as a result broader projects of social reform, including those related to Jews, were abandoned. This dramatic change naturally affected the relationship between the government and the hasidic movement. The details of the two conflicts in Płock and Pilica allow us to grasp quite precisely the nature of these changes, though on a smaller scale.

In the 1829 Płock investigation, the Jewish Committee, the Advisory

Board, the Voivodeship Commission, and the Government Commission all thought it necessary to raise the hasidic issue in their reports, to the dissatisfaction of part of the Jewish community. It is true that in the case of the last two institutions this move was more symbolic than an expression of a real attempt to resolve the issue, but it is none the less instructive that the government recognized that such engagement on its part was necessary. In other words, even if there was lack of real intention of resolving the hasidic issue it was recognized as correct to raise the issue; even if doing so was thus somewhat disingenuous, it did reaffirm the government's notional policy concerning the hasidic movement.

By the time of the Pilica incident of 1835–6, this convenient hypocrisy was absent. Reports from the Jewish community made it clear that it was the hasidic group that was the source of dissent, and the District Commission report on the investigation similarly stated that 'disagreements, outbursts, and damages due to the loss of income' from the kosher tax were 'caused primarily by the appointment of Meier Eibeszyc from the Hussite sect as assistant rabbi, though he does not have the basic qualifications'.[34] However, this did not induce the commissioner to draw the obvious conclusions regarding the role of the hasidic issue in the conflict in Pilica, and both the Voivodeship Commission and the Government Commission completely ignored the information about Eibeszyc's hasidic affiliation. The silence here was clearly no accident; one might conclude that it did not result from the usual bureaucratic laziness, as did the final decision of the government in Płock in 1829. If we conclude that the lack of interest in hasidism was due to administrative inertia, we must also add that after 1831 this inertia became the official policy in all incidents relating to Jewish society. With the collapse of the uprising and the dissolution of the government, the new authorities consciously abandoned many previously proposed policies, including those or reforming Jewish society, and aimed instead, above all, at preserving the political and social status quo. All new initiatives were considered potentially dangerous to the existing order and so were treated as possible social threats.[35] Even the projected reforms in legal status intended to facilitate the integration of the Kingdom of Poland with the Russian empire were realized either only partly and with great reluctance or not implemented at all because they went beyond routine 'management'. Inertia was thus elevated to the level of a leading political principle. The 'moral reform' of the Jews was regarded less and less as a priority. All that remained of the earlier Enlightenment debates about 'reform' and 'civilization' was rhetoric.

[34] AGAD, CWW 1472, p. 57.
[35] On the 'Jewish policy' of the Kingdom of Poland in the 1840s see Eisenbach, *Emancypacja Żydów*, 316–22.

This change naturally had further implications. Abandoning the call for 'moral reform' made it easier to articulate attitudes that had not been compatible with the discourse of the Enlightenment. The first of these was the belief that there was no need at all for any intervention with regard to the spread of hasidism. In 1829, when supporters of Kahana had written to the government that even if 'Alexander Kohen [Kahana] were essentially a Hussite, we would not have anything against him, as in this regard this has no implications for us, as long as he fulfils the obligations of his calling',[36] and further stated that hasidism should not be of concern to the government because it had no influence on the sphere of collective life that might interest state authorities, the government did not respond. In the 1836 investigation, however, it was the Voivodeship Commission itself that formulated a similar opinion. From then on this idea became one of the arguments most frequently used to justify government passivity in matters relating to hasidism. For example, the authorities made several such declarations during the conflicts in Włocławek over hasidism between 1835 and 1839, on which more below.[37] In many other incidents the government either ignored the existence of issues relating to hasidism or simply claimed that they were of no significance. When, for example, in 1860 in Płock the conflict concerning the local rabbi and hasidic leader Eleazar Hakohen again worsened, one of the central arguments brought against him was the fact that 'he is a Hussite and denigrates everything not belonging to this sect'.[38] The provincial authorities (in 1837 the voivodeships had been replaced by provinces—*gubernias*—and the voivodeship commissions by provincial governments—*rządy gubernialne*) conducted an investigation that was unremittingly hostile to the rabbi and upheld most of the charges against him. In a report to the Government Commission, however, they did express doubt that the charges could have any legal effect: 'Lejzer Wolf Kohn (Eleazar Hakohen) himself admitted that he is a Hussite; whether this is appropriate for his position as rabbi is difficult to determine; it is known only that Hussites conduct prayer in homes and not in synagogues, which may interfere with the rabbi carrying out his obligations with respect to the community.'[39] The government authorities had no such dilemmas and recognized the complaint as groundless, since 'whether or not the Jew Lejzer Kohn belongs to the so-called sect of Hussites has no influence on the dissolution of the contract between him and the community, in the light of the agreement endorsed by the Provincial Government'.[40] For the government, a rabbi's hasidic affiliation had no significance if he held a contract that had been signed by the community and had

---

[36] See *13.17; AGAD, CWW 1666, pp. 284–8.
[37] See e.g. *18.04, *18.09; AGAD, CWW 1734, pp. 39–41, 50.
[38] AGAD, CWW 1667, pp. 181–2.   [39] Ibid. 186.   [40] Ibid. 245–6.

been confirmed in that position by the state authorities: its concerns, in other words, were purely legalistic.

Declarations of this type are especially telling because they not only reflect the inertia of the government but are also public confirmation of that attitude. Moreover, there were many more cases in which even though no such formal declaration was issued, the government persistently refused to recognize any kind of hasidic context to situations of conflict. For example, the dispute that divided the Jewish community of the small town of Rypin in the province of Płock from 1849 to 1851 was very similar to the situations in Płock in 1829 and Pilica in 1836. A group of hasidim attempted, with the support of the regional authorities, to dismiss Rabbi Nuchym (Nahum) Gutentag from his post and replace him with a hasidic candidate: originally Icek (Isaac) Bytenfeld from Warsaw and then, when this did not happen, Wolf Kronenbach, the rabbi of Żuromin. Their efforts were unsuccessful as the majority of the community supported Gutentag, but an investigation ensued. Strikingly, throughout the entire investigation neither the central nor the provincial authorities referred even once to the strongly worded argument that appeared in almost all the petitions: that the incident resulted from the intrigue 'of an opposing sect with only a few hasidim'.[41] Similarly, the petition of Manes Zylber of Łęczna in the province of Lublin, which demanded in the name of a larger group the dismissal of the local rabbi and known hasidic leader, the tsadik Joshua ben Solomon Leib, was seen in the same way. Zylber described Leib as 'a rabbi of the Hussites, including some of our residents, and others who come to him from various cities for the Jewish festivals', and claimed that as Leib wanted to gain certain privileges associated with the position of communal rabbi, especially being allowed to wear traditional Jewish dress (something that after 1850 was permitted only to rabbis and elders), he tried to enlist the support of the town's residents for that position, 'even though in no way was he fit to perform the duties' of a communal rabbi.[42]

As before, the government authorities paid no attention at all to the anti-hasidic arguments, preferring to take at face value the declaration of the Jewish community board that a majority of the community simply wished the present rabbi to stay in post.[43] In 1860, when a conflict arose regarding Berek Dauer, the rabbi of Nasielsk, government officials at all levels—from the Government Commission to the mayor of Nasielsk, Wodziński—consistently ignored the fact that all the calls to dismiss the rabbi came from hasidim and had no real substance.[44] Similarly, the government consistently paid no attention to information regarding the hasidic nature of the conflict sur-

[41] AGAD, CWW 1684, pp. 117–18; for more on the opposition to Gutentag see pp. 48–126.
[42] AGAD, CWW 1613, p. 210.   [43] Ibid. 213–20.
[44] AGAD, CWW 1663, pp. 236–627.

rounding rabbinical posts in Hrubieszów (1852), Ostrowiec Świętokrzyski (1856), Piątek (1860), and in many other communities.[45] In fact it can be said that, from the 1830s on, the role of hasidism in communal conflicts was generally ignored; exceptions became increasingly rare.

3. The Last Investigation

The last major investigation of the hasidic movement undertaken at state level—an investigation in which the state attempted to examine the nature of the movement with a view to adopting a more general policy on hasidism—provides an interesting illustration of what I am calling the 'quiet turning-point' in government policy in the Kingdom of Poland.

In 1833 a teacher of geometry at the Volhynia Lyceum in Krzemieniec in the Russian empire, Aleksander I. Sawicki, asked the well-known maskil Isaac Ber Levinsohn for an opinion concerning illegal hasidic printing in Russia. Sawicki and two Jewish printers from Krzemieniec, Leib Michel and Jakob Borenstein, used Levinsohn's opinion as the basis of a petition to the Minister of Internal Affairs in Russia, Prince Dmitri Nikolaievich Bludov.[46] The petition stated that illegal hasidic publications were flooding the western provinces of the empire; some were illegal because they were smuggled in from abroad, others because they were printed as supplements to classical rabbinic writings, which meant they gained wider currency than they might otherwise have had. The proposal was that the government should inspect all books owned by Jews: non-hasidic writings should be physically stamped as authorized, hasidic writings should be destroyed. From then on, possession of unstamped books would be illegal and subject to a substantial fine. They further proposed that all Jewish printing presses in Poland and Russia should be closed, and three licensed printing houses established in their place—in Brześć Litewski (Brest Litovsk), Żytomierz (Zhitomir), and Szkłów (Shklov) —under the strict control of the censor and with a monopoly for fifteen years.

---

[45] On Hrubieszów, see AGAD, CWW 1602, pp. 237–89; on Ostrowiec Świętokrzyski, see AGAD, CWW 1446, pp. 23–105, and AGAD, CWW 1513, pp. 120–6; on Piątek, see AGAD, CWW 1716, pp. 131–287.

[46] There is a rich literature on the issue, e.g. 'Tsenzura evreiskikh knig v tsarstvovanie imperatora Nikolaia I', 131–2; Beilin, 'Iz istoricheskikh zhurnalov', 417–18; Zinberg, *A History of Jewish Literature*, xi: *The Haskalah Movement in Russia*, 61–3; Stanislawski, *Tsar Nicholas I and the Jews*, 41–2; and Lederhendler, *The Road to Modern Jewish Politics*, 95–6. The best study so far is Elyashevich, *Pravitel'stvennaya politika i evreyskaya pechat v Rasiyi*, 166–78. Wolf Tugendhold's report was published in Ia. I[zraelson], 'Bor'ba pravitel'stva s khasidizmom', 91–5. For more on Jewish censorship in imperial Russia see Elyashevich, *Pravitel'stvennaya politika i evreyskaya pechat v Rasiyi*; on the censorship of Jewish prints in the Kingdom of Poland see Gąsiorowska, 'Cenzura żydowska w Królestwie Kongresowym'; ead., *Wolność druku w Królestwie Kongresowym 1815–1830*, 256–63.

Minister Bludov asked the minister of public enlightenment in Russia, Sergei Uvarov, for an opinion, and the latter confirmed the existence of abuses in the printing and distribution of Jewish books. He recognized, however, that the methods proposed in the petition were 'so harsh that making them effective will be extraordinarily difficult, even impossible, inasmuch as the actions of the censor cannot go beyond the legislative boundary confirmed and defined by His Majesty'.[47] Bludov decided, however, to consult the new viceroy of the Kingdom of Poland, General Ivan Paskevich, who had recently been responsible for crushing the Polish uprising, and so began the Polish phase of the investigation. The 1834 investigation was thus not only the last investigation of hasidism to be undertaken on a state-wide scale, but also the only one instigated directly from Russia.[48] This surely symbolizes the nature of the 'quiet turning-point' in the Kingdom of Poland's attitude towards its Jewish population: increasingly, it saw its role as being to implement imperial policy rather than to chart its own. What is more, the conflicts of interest between Tsar Nicholas I, who wanted to integrate the Kingdom more closely with the empire, and Viceroy Paskevich, who wanted to preserve as much autonomy as possible (so as to maximize his own powers), meant that the government of the Kingdom became to an increasing degree the pawn in a contest of foreign interests.

Bludov's letter was sent to Warsaw in March 1834. More than a month later the viceroy commissioned the Government Commission for Internal Affairs, Religions, and Public Enlightenment to conduct a proper investigation, to examine the results of the inspection of Jewish books in Poland, and to prepare information 'about the present state of affairs in the Kingdom of Poland, with special reference to the Jewish project'.[49] The Government Commission relayed the order to the Jewish Committee and to the Committee for the Censorship of Hebrew Books and Periodicals. The response of the latter committee has not been preserved, but its content is known from a summary in a report of the Government Commission for Internal Affairs, Religions, and Public Enlightenment.[50] Fortunately, though, we have the original letter of the Jewish Committee.[51] In response to the five questions the committee was asked, it stated that: (*a*) hasidism existed exclusively in Polish lands, including the Kingdom of Poland; (*b*) the basic religious prin-

---

[47] See *16.01; AGAD, CWW 1871, pp. 233–6.

[48] There had been earlier enquiries from Russia to the Polish authorities, but they had never produced any significant reaction from the Kingdom, even when they were supported by Senator Novosiltseff. See e.g. AGAD, Kancelaria Senatora Nowosilcowa 626, pp. 308–10.

[49] See *16.02; AGAD, CWW 1871, pp. 230–2, 237–9.

[50] See *16.06; AGAD, CWW 1871, pp. 251–1.

[51] See *16.05; AGAD, CWW 1871, pp. 245–50; Mahler, *Haḥasidut vehahaskalah*, 506–8. See also an analysis of the document in Mahler, *Hasidism and the Jewish Enlightenment*, 334–7. Mahler, however, did not realize that there was a connection between the Polish and Russian investigations in the matter of the hasidic publications.

ciples of hasidism did not differ fundamentally from those of the 'sect of the rabbinical Jews', the only significant difference being that hasidim abided not only by 'talmudic knowledge, which the sect of the Rabbanites relies on, but also on talmudic commentaries, known under the general name of kabbalah'; (*c*) the number of hasidim in the Kingdom of Poland amounted to no more than 5 per cent of the local population, with Menahem Mendel of Kock (Kotsk) and Yerahmiel of Przysucha currently the most important leaders; (*d*) the books used by hasidim were primarily talmudic commentaries printed in Lithuania and distributed in Poland with the permission of police authorities; (*e*) possibly illegal hasidic presses could be closed by proper use of available police, but that more generally the committee regarded fighting hasidism as 'extremely difficult, even impossible, since such preventative actions would affect matters of conscience, and the sect of hasidim is a religious denomination; freedom of religious denominations is protected by the Organic Statute, and the sect of hasidim can rely on this statute as an invincible shield and put in place insurmountable barriers to any action if they wanted to take forceful action'. The Organic Statute (Statut Organiczny) mentioned here is the legal code granted to the Kingdom by Tsar Nicholas I after he rescinded the constitution in 1832. One of its regulations did indeed concern freedom for religious denominations.

The committee did not identify the source of the information presented, but it seems that it came from one of the Warsaw maskilim. This is suggested by the statement that the government could find out more about hasidism 'from being in close contact with enlightened Israelites, who never refuse to offer explanations when demanded from them in this regard', as well as by the statement that the only possible way to influence the further development of hasidism was to bring about a reconciliation with the non-hasidic majority, a development for which 'more enlightened men of the Israelite people work continuously'. Most likely the author was Jakub Tugendhold, who was known at this time as an advocate for Jewish interests, but also for defending hasidism against accusations of corruption and for supporting the reconciliation of all Jewish groups. This conjecture finds confirmation in the fact that the conclusions of the report are similar to suggestions mentioned in the report of the Committee for the Censorship of Hebrew Books and Periodicals, a committee in which Tugendhold participated and whose report he co-authored.[52]

[52] His conciliatory attitude may be reflected in the report of the Jewish Committee, for example the observation that 'regarding the content of their teachings about Moses, hasidim agree with Rabbanites and consider the advice of rabbis or rabbinical fathers in matters of conscience, just as Rabbanites also consult rabbinical leaders or hasidic rabbis in these matters'. Numerous other sources from the period confirm that hasidic leaders frequently offered advice to non-hasidim and vice versa, which shatters the traditional view that an impassable wall separated the hasidim from their opponents. See more on this in Wodziński, 'How Should We Count *Hasidim* in Congress Poland?'.

After receiving the reports of the Jewish Committee and the Committee for Censorship, the Government Commission for Internal Affairs, Religions, and Public Enlightenment assembled with exceptional diligence to prepare its own opinion. It studied not only the two reports that had been sent to it but also the entire documentation of the investigation of 1823–4. On the basis of these materials, the Commission prepared a special report in which it repeated almost word for word the characteristics of hasidism as formulated by the commission headed by Stanisław Staszic in 1824, along with his observation that 'there is not the least need to persecute them'.[53] It recognized the decision of the previous government as the only possible one and agreed with the Jewish Committee that any anti-hasidic campaign was doomed to failure because 'this is a religious denomination involving matters of conscience and protected by Organic Statute'. The commission also noted that the practical recommendations of the 1824 commission had already been implemented (the creation of the rabbinical school and the abolition of the *kahal*), although the desired results were still awaited: 'whether the methods initiated recently will bring about the expected reform of Jewish customs through the constant effort and ministrations of the government, only time will tell'. The report therefore marked the formal abandonment of all political activity directed against hasidism, in itself another sign of the 'quiet turning-point'.

The most important part of the report, however, was formulated on the basis of the opinion of the Committee for Censorship. Relying on this report, the Government Commission presented information about the mechanism of controlling books. According to the report, the import of Jewish books was banned, with the exception of a few titles that could be brought in from Russia with special government permission. All Jewish books allowed into circulation from 1828 on were marked with a special stamp; within the Kingdom there were only two Jewish presses, both operating only under the strict control of the censor and police authorities. On this basis, the Committee for Censorship and the Government Commission also recognized that 'the statement of the Jews under discussion, that already there are almost no old Hebrew works into which hasidic principles have not been added, does not agree entirely with the truth'. As the censors stated, the vast majority of works printed in Hebrew had no hasidic content, and those few that did propagate the teachings of hasidism 'did not interest the average hasid and were less harmful [than] their leaders' oral talks at their meetings, which ignite their imaginations to exultation and are the real life of the sect, and so the method suggested by the Jews from Krzemieniec would not work'. The Committee for Censorship, along with the Government Commission,

---

[53] See *16.06; see also *11.73, *11.74; AGAD, CWW 1871, pp. 251–79.

rejected Sawicki's proposal in its entirety, on the grounds that the charges were groundless and that the proposed measures would be unduly oppressive.

Moreover, the authors of the report suspected Sawicki, Michel, and Borenstein of bias and self-interest; in their view, 'their statements against the sect of hasidim should instead be regarded as a pretext thought up to appropriate and take direct or indirect advantage of the entire printing industry'. This analysis seems accurate. As has already been mentioned, Sawicki was a teacher of geometry in the Volhynia Lyceum in Krzemieniec. From 1831 on, that is, following the active engagement of numerous students from this school in the anti-tsarist uprising of 1830–1 (which for a short time occupied not only the Kingdom of Poland but also the lands of the Russian empire proper, i.e. Lithuania, Volhynia, and Podolia), the lyceum itself was under threat, and teachers' salaries were paid only irregularly. It was finally and officially closed in October 1833. We do not know the extent of Sawicki's personal loss, but we can assume that he was aware that his post was at risk and that he sought a new place of employment.[54] The same can certainly be said of Leib Michel and Jakob Borenstein. The only printing house in Krzemieniec had been based at the Volhynia Lyceum and operated by the well-known Warsaw printer Natan Glücksberg, represented in Krzemieniec by his sons Teofil and Gustaw Leon,[55] but after Natan Glücksberg's death in 1831 the printing house was sold to pay the debts of the deceased. Both Michel and Borenstein were thus most probably unemployed from 1831 or soon after. The concurrence of the date with the report regarding hasidic printing suggests that the report was essentially motivated by the desire to find employment.

Regardless of the accuracy of the assessment put forward by the Committee for Censorship as to the intentions of the petitioners, attention should be paid to the unequivocal defence of hasidism that the committee presented. The report not only rejected the charge as groundless, but even suggested that any action directed against hasidim would be a violation of religious freedom. The members of the committee at this time included the maskilim Jakub Tugendhold and Abraham Stern (and also Krystian Czerskier, who had converted to Christianity but was less of a public figure), and since it was Tugendhold and Stern who wrote the majority of reports on issues related to

[54] The Volhynia Lyceum's faculty, collections, and even its garden were transferred to Kiev, where a decree of the tsar made it the basis for St Vladimir's University, established in 1834. The transfer did not involve all employees of the lyceum, however, and especially not the teachers at its affiliated institutions, such as the school of geometry. For more on the circumstances surrounding the dissolution of the lyceum see Przybylski, *Krzemieniec*, 176–96. On Sawicki, see Słowikowski, 'Wspomnienia szkoły krzemienieckiej', 472, 480.

[55] For more on the failure of the printing industry in Krzemieniec and legal suits against the successors of Natan Glücksberg, see Peczenik, *Glücksbergowie*.

the Jewish community,[56] it seems reasonable to assume that they were also the authors of the report on hasidism. If this supposition is correct, the report is all the more surprising since Stern, who appears here as a defender of hasidism, had become known as the movement's harshest critic in the Kingdom of Poland (as discussed in Chapter 2, §3, and Chapter 3).[57] Perhaps his change in attitude was connected to the increasing disappointment of the maskilim with the government from the beginning of the 1830s and their consequent distancing themselves from fighting for the reform of traditional Jewish society (on which more in Chapter 7, §1).

Equally striking was the conclusion of the Government Commission, which was decidedly positive for the hasidim. The ministerial authorities accepted the recommendation of the Committee for Censorship that Sawicki's proposals were not appropriate for the Kingdom of Poland, and also the recommendation of the Jewish Committee that the current policy of absolute tolerance towards hasidism was the only feasible approach and should be continued. However, this had nothing to do with any change of heart regarding the need for reform or the need to challenge the unity of traditional Jewry as explained in 1824, but rather the total abandonment of any policy of reform. The new policy was one of capitulation.

We do not know whether, in the end, the viceroy accepted the conclusions of the Government Commission. Very likely the issue was dropped. Moreover, the opinion of the commission most clearly took into consideration Paskevich's concern not to subjugate his political approach to hasidism in the Kingdom (or indeed, any other aspect of his prerogatives), to the Russian authorities. Since any curtailment of the Kingdom's autonomy diminished the viceroy's own powers, he jealously defended his authority even in areas as seemingly insignificant (from his point of view) as Jewish printing. This became most obvious several years later, when all Jewish printing houses in Russia except two had been closed, probably as a result of the 1834 investigation,[58] but the printing of Hebrew books, including hasidic works, still faced no significant obstacles in the Kingdom of Poland. Instigated from St Petersburg, the final investigation into hasidism proved that the politics of Russia and the politics of the Kingdom were still not identical on this issue:

[56] See e.g. AGAD, CWW 1420, pp. 104–13; CWW 1455, pp. 298–337, CWW 1709, pp. 8–12.

[57] See Mahler, *Hasidism and the Jewish Enlightenment*, 318–22 (note again that Mahler wrongly attributes this report to Abraham Buchner instead of Stern). See also Shatzky, 'Avraham Yakov Shtern (1768–1842)', and Wodziński, *Haskalah and Hasidism*, 86–94.

[58] Despite the lack of hard evidence, it is commonly assumed that the closure of all Hebrew printing shops in Russia in 1836 was a result of the investigation initiated three years earlier by Sawicki. See e.g. Stanislawski, *Tsar Nicholas I and the Jews*, 41–2; Lederhendler, *The Road to Modern Jewish Politics*, 96; Elyashevich, *Pravitel'stvennaya politika i evreyskaya pechat v Rasiyi*, 166–78.

the clearest characteristic of 'hasidic politics' in the Kingdom was the total abandonment of any policy at all.

4. Ignorance, Inertia, Frustration

The total abandonment of any kind of active policy, on this and on many other issues, was certainly often convenient for the government, but not always. Although the decision to refrain from any action was a conscious policy decision, it was not the only decisive factor of this or any other political position. Between the beginning of the nineteenth century and the 1830s or 1840s, the hasidic movement in the Kingdom of Poland had transformed itself from a small pietistic group into a well-organized mass movement. As it grew, it became increasingly difficult to control it by administrative measures or to exert any effective influence over it. Seen in this light, the government's passivity was the result not only of a conscious decision but also of a realization that effective action was no longer possible. The situation was compounded by increasing ignorance of conditions on the ground, something that in the 1840s was characteristic of every aspect of the administration of the Kingdom and not only on Jewish matters. However, in the case of the Jews and their religious life the ignorance was especially great, as Jewish polemicists had long noticed. Even during the Four Year Sejm, Herszel Jozefowicz, the rabbi of Chełm, had stated that all the projects of the reformers who were of noble origin were 'dilettantish and vain' because they knew very little about the society they wanted to reform. As he put it, prejudice and megalomania prevented even the most noble reformer from understanding the Jewish community properly; but even if this prejudice could be overcome, a reformer would not be able to understand the essential problems of the Jewish community, just as the healthy cannot understand the sick. Jozefowicz added, with some irony, that 'such small things should not worry the nobles; we are the least in their eyes . . . not worthy of consideration'.[59]

After 1831 this ignorance not only grew but, to a certain degree, became institutionalized. The gradual disintegration of the functioning of the state meant that in the 1840s and 1850s officials at all levels were increasingly ignorant of even the fundamental legal regulations regarding the Jewish community. Accordingly, they made decisions that contravened the law or implemented policies that were mutually contradictory. A striking example of this is a question posed by the Government Commission for Internal and Religious Affairs, which in 1852 tried to find out 'if the so-called German Israelites are a sect like the Hussites, talmudists, and others, or if their reli-

[59] Jozefowicz, 'Myśli stosowne do sposobu uformowania Żydów polskich', 100–1.

gious principles and rituals are completely or only in part different and separate'.[60] The question makes it clear that the Government Commission with responsibility for matters concerning the religious affairs of the Jewish people knew nothing about any of these groups, given that it was unable to differentiate between them in any meaningful way. The commission's ignorance is even more apparent in its attempt in 1840 to implement an anti-hasidic initiative through reference to legal regulations: when Izrael Rozenblum of Lublin pledged 3,000 złotys for synagogues in Lublin, the commission asked whether 'those gathering for prayer in these synagogues belong to the sect known as hasidim, or the so-called *kitajowcy*, for whom, according to the ruling of 26 March 1824 No. 3226/677, prayer in private homes is forbidden'.[61] It was left to the authorities responsible for dealing with the problem at the lowest level to point out that the ruling of March 1824 had been withdrawn long before, and that the assembly of hasidim in private *shtiblekh* had been legalized by the viceroy in a ruling of 30 August 1824. In a similar case already mentioned in an earlier chapter, the mayor of Pabianice only became aware that hasidic *shtiblekh* were legal when the hasidim themselves gave him a copy of the 1824 decree.[62] These examples are only a few of many; the bureaucratic documentation reflects this situation particularly well. The phenomenon of ignorance was universal and reached to the highest levels.

Even in the few cases where the administration considered taking action on matters relating to hasidism, this ignorance made effective intervention impossible. Government officials did not know how to differentiate hasidim from other Jews, or what the consequences of such differentiation might be. In 1844 the governor of Suwałki wrote to the Government Commission that numerous officials under him had reported that hasidim were holding services in private homes and that they did not know how to respond to such gatherings.[63] He knew of the 1824 law legalizing hasidic *shtiblekh* but asked if there had perhaps been changes in this area in the twenty years that had elapsed or if the government had changed its opinion on the matter. If the law still applied, he said, the officials wanted to know what kinds of proof of belonging to hasidic groups they could demand from those praying in *shtiblekh* and how they could recognize hasidim. They argued that since the privilege of gathering for prayer in private homes applied only to hasidim and not to other Jews, they needed to ensure that others were not impersonating hasidim in order to take advantage of this privilege as this would lead to a decline in the income of the Jewish community from collection boxes and from fees for the provision of various religious services. The question reveals

---

[60] AGAD, CWW 1728, pp. 189.   [61] AGAD, CWW 1608, pp. 436–7.
[62] APŁ, Akta miasta Pabianic 31 [11/23 Mar. 1844, mayor of Pabianice to the district office]. See Ch. 3, §5.   [63] See *26.01; AGAD, CWW 1871, pp. 280–1.

that provincial authorities in Suwałki (and doubtless in many other centres) were not able to recognize hasidim and were completely ignorant of how to apply the laws affecting them. Astonishingly, however, and more importantly, the government authorities turned out to be equally clueless. The Government Commission, through municipal authorities in Warsaw, immediately asked the the local Jewish community board to respond urgently on whether 'Jews belonging to the sect of hasidim cannot pray in common with other Jews holding services in synagogues, and, if so, what external signs of the believers of this sect can be used to recognize them or if some other sort of proof should be demanded from the group's followers'.[64] It took the Jewish community board a whole month to respond (and not with complete veracity) that 'Jews of this sect do not show any external signs of belonging and they do not have any other kind of proof that they belong to it'.[65] The Government Commission accepted this explanation as clear evidence that hasidim could not be recognized as such and that it was therefore impossible to develop any kind of policy regarding the group. In the relevant ruling, the minister ordered that hasidim be allowed to pray separately only under the condition that they reach an understanding with the Jewish community board to recompense the board for its losses from their joining the hasidim and separating themselves from the community. But at the same time, he admitted that hasidim 'do not distinguish themselves from other Jews with any external signs and may also not have any other kind of proof of their belonging';[66] government action in this area was therefore impossible precisely because hasidim could not be identified as such. The government thereby admitted its complete lack of knowledge and agreed by default that legal regulations introducing any kind of limitations on hasidim remain unenforceable; if they did not know how to identify hasidim, they could not force them to abide by the law ordering them to reach a financial understanding with the Jewish community board. Moreover, the impossibility of enforcing this law had already been revealed when it was first entered into the statute books in 1835 in connection with the conflict in Włocławek, to be discussed further below.

As already mentioned, total inertia was convenient for officials, though sometimes it turned out that this enforced passivity could touch sensitive areas of professional pride and lead to resentment. Indeed, in many of the incidents known to us, the perceived ineffectiveness in matters concerning hasidism caused deep frustration. A very telling example of this is an incident in Lublin, one of the largest cities in the Kingdom of Poland and the capital

[64] See *26.02; AGAD, CWW 1871, pp. 283–4.
[65] See *26.03; AGAD, CWW 1871, pp. 285–6.
[66] See *26.04; AGAD, CWW 1871, pp. 287–8.

of an important province with numerous official bodies. On 26 October 1853 the provincial governor was walking along a street when he happened upon a drunken hasid in traditional Jewish dress, that is, with hair cut very short but with long *peyes* (sidelocks) around his ears, and wearing a silk coat—that is, dressed in a way that was forbidden by law.[67] When arrested, the hasid not only showed no remorse but openly mocked the authorities. In the presence of the mayor of the city, and most probably the governor too, he simply said that in his joy as celebrating a religious festival he had drunk too much alcohol (the incident occurred on the day after Simhat Torah), so that he did not know what he was wearing; and whether the hair around his ears was longer than allowed he did not know because he couldn't see his ears. This was a ludicrous situation: a drunken hasid openly mocked the highest officials of a large provincial city, and there was little they could do about it. The man was 'compelled to shave his beard and cut his *peyes*' and taken back to Końskowola, where he came from, but otherwise the authorities were helpless in the face of his arrogance and ostentatious lack of respect for state regulations. The written report offers clear proof of the official's frustration at being faced with a situation that did not conform to official regulations and standard procedures and that thereby challenged the administration's authority and forced it to adopt irregular measures. It was this kind of situation that made government officials so unsympathetic to hasidism.

Moreover, the post-Enlightenment idea of 'civilizing' the Jewish population, though no longer official policy in practice after 1831, still remained the official rhetoric. There was no sympathy for dark or fanatic elements of any sort, not only hasidism. The influence of this post-Enlightenment rhetoric was very clear, when, for example, candidates for the Jewish community board were disqualified by the governor of Warsaw on the basis of a report identifying them as hasidim.[68] Similarly, when the St Petersburg Committee for the Organization of Jews in the Empire asked the authorities of the Kingdom of Poland in 1858 to prepare a report on the state of Polish Jewry, the most negative section was that on the hasidim. The committee set up in Warsaw to write the report stated that 'among the Jewish sects practising the most hideous religious deviations and customs' was the sect known as hasidim, 'having the largest number of believers in this country and distinguishing themselves by the indignity of their type, with their fanatical propaganda of all kinds and their activity paralysing the government'.[69] Accordingly, the committee suggested that 'members of this sect should not be admitted to any positions of honour, such as community elections, mem-

[67] See *33.01; APL, AmL 2258, p. 217.
[68] See AGAD, CWW 1727, p. 944. On the context of the 1851 elections to the Jewish community board in Warsaw, see Guesnet, *Polnische Juden im 19. Jahrhundert*, 403–10.
[69] AGAD, KRSW 6600, fo. 333.

bers of Jewish community boards, or rabbis, and that they should not be allowed to maintain separate prayer rooms or to gain any kind of prerogative intended for Jews making progress on the road to civilization'.[70] In fact this never happened; the attempt to standardize the rights of Jews in Russia and the Kingdom stalled because it would have demanded a degree of discipline and determination that the authorities were unable to attain.

5. Who Profited? On the Ostensible Equality of Hasidism

As we have seen, the government's lack of action on the question was a consequence of ignorance and inertia rather than an affirmation of hasidism and hasidim. The government disliked the hasidim, though even in this it lacked real conviction. Occasionally, there were policies directed against them, as, for example, in Piotrków Trybunalski, when the Government Commission for Internal and Religious Affairs grew tired of the constant conflicts between hasidim and their opponents and decided to ban them from standing for election to the Jewish community board: the commission simply decreed that, when the current three-year term of office ended, 'a new selection of members for the next term of office shall not include any believers from this sect'.[71]

Government inertia was not always beneficial to the hasidic movement. As described earlier in this chapter, in 1829 in Płock the insistence of the Voivodeship Commission and the party it supported had led to a hasidic candidate remaining in the position of rabbi, but a similar incident in 1836 in Pilica did not lead to the removal of a non-hasidic rabbi. The reason for the opposite outcomes in these cases was identical: the determination of the government to avoid conflict. More effectively than in Płock, organized pressure from the Jewish community of Pilica led the government to withdraw its support for the hasidic candidate. This happened in many other cases too—for example, in the incident in Rypin mentioned earlier in which government inertia worked in favour of the non-hasidic majority who wanted a non-hasidic rabbi. In spite of these and many similar cases and the government's generally negative attitude towards hasidim, its politics regarding them after 1831 actually had positive consequences, in that it allowed the movement to grow even without any special organizational efforts or political strategies on the part of the hasidim.

To illustrate how the hasidim benefited from the political line taken by the government, and, more generally, from the political situation in the Kingdom of Poland after the defeat of the anti-tsarist uprising in 1830–1, I offer as evidence a series of conflicts surrounding hasidim in Włocławek from 1835

[70] AGAD, KRSW 6632, fo. 31.   [71] AGAD, CWW 1560, p. 197.

to 1839. The circumstances of the uprising and the first years of the development of the local hasidic community are exceptionally well documented, allowing for a relatively precise understanding of the interdependence of different factors in the growth of the hasidic community.

Until the beginning of the nineteenth century Włocławek was a bishop's town, and Jews were not allowed to live there (though the city never formally acquired the privilege *de non tolerandis Judaeis*).[72] The first four Jewish families settled in Włocławek between 1803 and 1805. In the following years the Jewish community developed quickly: by 1812 there were 99 Jews living in the city; by 1827, in the period of interest to us, there were 343 Jews, comprising 8.1 per cent of the city's population. The occupational structure of the Jewish population was dominated at this time by tailors, cabinet-makers, and retail traders, but most influential was a group of wholesale traders and factory owners. Representatives of this last group, very often strongly acculturated and integrated into Polish society, maintained their dominant position in the community right up to the beginning of the twentieth century, but the community was deeply divided over numerous issues. Particularly drastic was the conflict between two wealthy families, the Giełdzińskis and the Rypińskis, which lasted from the 1820s to the 1850s. Civil suits related to this conflict reached the state authorities at least as early as 1827, when Majer Rypiński informed the government of alleged embezzlement by the Giełdzińskis, who dominated the Jewish community board. In this same year, the Jewish community board refused Rypiński permission to set up a prayer room in his home for the purpose of holding a service on the anniversary of his mother's death so that the standard memorial prayer could be recited. News of the controversy spread throughout Poland and ended with a victory for Rypiński, who procured a government decision confirming the right to prayer in private homes.[73]

In 1835 a hasidic element was added to the controversy. Rypiński's relative, Heyman (Hayim) Lowenstam, tried to remove the community's ritual slaughterer, Hersz Aron Lewy, on the grounds that he was not fit to fulfil the function and that he was committing fraud.[74] The community board rejected

---

[72] On the beginnings of the Jewish settlement in Włocławek see Gruszczyńska, 'Początki osadnictwa żydowskiego we Włocławku'; see also Thursh and Korzen (eds.), *Vlotslavek vehasevivah*; 'Vlotslavek/Włocławek', in *Pinkas hakehilot: polin*, iv. 202–9.

[73] See AGAD, CWW 1411, pp. 66–74; CWW 1734, pp. 4–20; KWK 702, pp. 171–4; Archiwum Państwowe w Częstochowie, Akta miasta Częstochowy 200, pp. 19–21; APK, RGR 4405, pp. 4–8; APL, AmL 2419, pp. 84–90; Archiwum Państwowe w Radomiu, Rząd Gubernialny Radomski I 4338, pp. 231–50.

[74] A comprehensive collection of documents on this conflict has been preserved in the State Archives in Włocławek. See Archiwum Państwowe w Toruniu, Oddział we Włocławku, Akta miasta Włocławka 313.

Figure 4.3 Włocławek, 1875. This late nineteenth-century image of the main entrance to the town and its cathedral clearly shows the town's ecclesiastical heritage. Until the beginning of the nineteenth century Jews were forbidden to settle in Włocławek. From *Tygodnik Ilustrowany*, no. 372 (1875), p. 97. Biblioteka Narodowa w Warszawie

Lowenstam's claim and presented an opinion maintaining that Lowenstam was a leader of the hasidim and was merely trying to install a hasid as ritual slaughterer. The controversy is reminiscent of earlier conflicts in many other places during which the hasidim aimed simultaneously to consolidate their group identity and to strengthen their position in the community by filling the post of ritual slaughterer or controlling kosher meat distribution.[75] This latest confrontation with the community board made Rypiński and his circle cut their links with the community synagogue, and join Lowenstam in setting up an independent hasidic *shtibl*.[76] The community board saw this as a serious threat to community finances because at least three of the nineteen hasidim known to the board belonged to the town's financial elite. On the whole, the

[75] The earliest conflict of this kind known to us took place in Połaniec, then in Western Galicia, and later in the Kingdom of Poland. On the conflict in Połaniec, see Kuperstein, 'Inquiry at Polaniec', and some remarks in Ch. 2, §1. On the social significance of ritual slaughter (*sheḥitah*), see Shmeruk, 'Mashma'utah haḥevratit shel hasheḥitah haḥasidit', and Stampfer, 'The Controversy over *Sheḥitah*', 342–55.

[76] See *18.01; *18.02; AGAD, CWW 1734, pp. 25–7, 29–31.

hasidim of Włocławek were richer than the other Jewish residents of the town, despite the relative wealth of the latter and the presence of one beggar and several lower-paid craftsmen among the hasidim.[77] This new development potentially meant a dangerous decrease in synagogue income, which traditionally came from the sale of seats, the sale of honours such as being called up to the Torah, and the sale of *etrogim* for the holiday of Sukkot. As mentioned earlier (Ch. 2, §2), similar situations had developed elsewhere in the Kingdom of Poland following the establishment of hasidic *shtiblekh*, so it did not take great foresight on the part of the Jewish community board to predict such consequences. Indications of a financial component in the conflict between hasidim and their opponents had first appeared in 1798 in the records of the Vilna Jewish community board and were to recur many times throughout the nineteenth century. In the name of the community board in Włocławek, therefore, Samuel Izbicki sought the help of the authorities in closing down the hasidic *shtibl* and collecting all the funds owed to the community by the hasidim.[78]

Izbicki also claimed that Rypiński's group were really posing as hasidim so as to create financial difficulties for the community and as a way of getting back at his rivals: 'By falsely calling themselves hasidim and by creating the second synagogue, and not just a prayer room (which would upset the order maintained until this time), they aim at nothing less than making this small community so impoverished as to eventually put an end to any religious services at all, and only because they are concerned for their own glory.'[79] Izbicki then tried to show that Rypiński's group was not eligible for the privileges given to hasidim in accordance with the law of the Kingdom of Poland, meaning not only the right to assemble freely for prayer in private homes but, in practice, many other freedoms as well. The evidence presented in this connection is indeed interesting. Izbicki maintained that the people in Rypiński's group who claimed to be hasidim actually lived outside the Jewish district (*rewir*) on streets not permitted to Jews, did not dress in the Jewish manner (some even shaved their beards), and that women frequented their *shtibl* whereas in real hasidic *shtiblekh* 'women have no place'.[80] The

[77] This is based on my so far unpublished research and archival findings in AGAD, CWW 1734, p. 224; Archiwum Państwowe w Toruniu, Oddział we Włocławku, Naczelnik Powiatu Włocławskiego 438, pp. 178–9; Archiwum Państwowe w Toruniu, Oddział we Włocławku, Akta miasta Włocławka 319.   [78] See *18.01; *18.02; AGAD, CWW 1734, pp. 25–7, 29–31.

[79] See *18.02; AGAD, CWW 1734, pp. 29–31.

[80] This last argument is both unusually interesting and troublesome, because we know so little about how women associated with the hasidic movement prayed. If we can trust the source (and there is no reason to doubt this part of the letter), women were not able to enter hasidic *shtiblekh*, at least in central Poland around the mid-19th c. According to contemporary hasidic tradition, separate sections for women were universal in Galician *shtiblekh* (especially the Nowy Sącz (Sanz) and Bełz dynasties), but did not exist in the *shtiblekh* of hasidim from Przysucha,

Figure 4.4 This synagogue in Włocławek, built in 1850–4, was dominated by the polonizing and modernizing sector of the Jewish community. Postcard, probably 1920s. Private collection of the author

information seems reliable, at least the part that we can check regarding the places of residence outside the Jewish district. A comparison of the names of the people claiming to be hasidim with those of the Jews registered as living outside the Jewish quarter shows that at least six of the nineteen hasidic families lived in the Christian part of town.[81] Moreover since the information on dress and the absence of beards was easy enough to verify, it is unlikely that Izbicki would have lied openly about this. Were the members of Rypiński's group in fact only pretending to belong to the hasidic community? Many sources describing contemporary and later events unequivocally identify the people mentioned here, Majer Rypiński and Heyman Lowenstam, as hasidim. It seems, then, that Izbicki's testimony was only true in part, at the level of facts that could be verified by the naked eye, but not in its interpretation. The available sources suggest that Rypiński and his supporters were indeed in some respects 'progressive' Jews who had abandoned some of the customs of traditional Jews and thus looked very different from the

Kock, and Góra Kalwaria (Ger). I thank David Singer (Boro Park) and Efraym Grossberger (New York) for this information.

[81] See *19.07; AGAD, CWW 1734, pp. 221–4; Archiwum Państwowe w Toruniu, Oddział we Włocławku, Naczelnik Powiatu Włocławskiego 438, pp. 178–9; Gruszczyńska, 'Początki osadnictwa żydowskiego we Włocławku'.

Figure 4.5 One of the important occupations of the inhabitants of Włocławek, including a significant number of wealthy modernizing Jews, was the grain trade on the Vistula river. Lithograph by Maksymilian Fajans, from the original by Alfons Matuszkiewicz (1854). Biblioteka Narodowa w Warszawie, Zbiory Ikonograficzne, A.5542/ G.XIX/ II-73, pl. 7

accepted image of hasidim, but at the same time they in other respects followed hasidic practices and created a hasidic community in 1835 that continued in existence in the following decades. Perhaps the apparent contradictions can be more easily explained if we treat seriously the other information provided by Izbicki, namely, that the reasons why Rypiński's group embraced hasidism were not strictly religious in character. Izbicki's contention that they were motivated solely by a desire for revenge and to cripple the community financially may not have been wholly true, but it seems reasonable to assume that at this time in the first half of the nineteenth century, when the hasidic movement in Poland was becoming a significant social force, groups and individuals identifying with hasidism did not have to be motivated solely by religious reasons. Sometimes it was simply a question of taking sides with a rival interest group within the community, as in Włocławek. If one group became dominant in the community board, the other would naturally try to free itself from the control of the institutions dominated by its opponents. One of the easiest ways to contest the domination of the community board was by forming a hasidic community, since from 1824 hasidim were guaranteed the right to pray in private *shtiblekh* and, as we saw earlier, were given a privileged position in the community. It seems that this was the situation in Włocławek.[82] Moreover, accusing people of being 'fake hasidim' was not unusual in the nineteenth-century Kingdom of Poland or in other territories of eastern Europe.[83]

If the above interpretation is correct, it explains not only one of the possible reasons for the increasing popularity of the hasidic movement in Poland, but also, and more importantly for us, the way in which the legislation of the Kingdom of Poland and its administrative practices relating to hasidism unintentionally supported this movement by encouraging rebellious factions in the community to adopt a hasidic identity. I am not trying to diminish the significance of strictly religious arguments in the choice of hasidism by the numerous adherents of this movement. However, as this was a time when both the membership of the group and its influence were increasing in broad swathes of society, we need to be aware of other factors that may have contributed to its growth—as one would for any other movement.[84] One of these factors was certainly the ease with which individuals could free themselves from community ties, especially when the community board became the instrument of only one faction. Hasidism offered the competing side a convenient, legal, and protected form of organization and, certainly, a collective identity.

The Government Commission for Internal and Religious Affairs took Izbicki's complaint seriously. It requested a report from the Voivodeship Commission in this matter, and, after receiving it, almost immediately asked the Jewish Committee to explain the circumstances. When the latter gave a rather noncommittal response referring only to the formal aspects of the question, the Government Commission ordered it to review the matter further.[85] When the committee finally delivered a full response it supported Izbicki. To be sure, the committee recognized that hasidim were entitled to freedom of belief; however, it stated that this did not excuse them from complying with the rules and regulations of the Jewish community, including

[82] It should be noted here that some hasidim did wear the usual dress of the time, as some wear modern dress today. A good example is the well-known hasidic leader Israel of Różyn (Ruzhin) and his descendants: see Assaf, *The Regal Way*, 72, 195. Moreover, following talmudic tradition (BT *BK* 83*a*; JT *Shab*. 34*a*), wealthy men who had close economic relations with the non-Jewish world were allowed to compromise on outward signs of Jewishness, such as Jewish dress, *peyes*, or beard. The modern dress worn by Rypiński and his closely shaved beard are therefore not necessarily evidence of his not being a hasid. I am grateful to David Assaf for bringing to my attention the talmudic provenance of this tradition.

[83] See a fascinating account in Kotik, *A Journey to a Nineteenth-Century Shtetl*, 295. See also APŁ, APRG 2558, pp. 224–5, 230, 279–81.

[84] Discussing the complicated nature of the tie between the developing ideology of early hasidism and the accompanying social conditions in the Polish–Lithuanian Commonwealth, Adam Teller aptly points out arguments that speak against interpreting hasidism as a purely religious category. See Teller, 'Hasidism and the Challenge of Geography', 6–8.

[85] See *18.06; AGAD, CWW 1734, p. 42.

those relating to money. It also did not authorize one group 'to separate from a second and, under cover of establishing or creating a new religious sect, to take away funds intended for the maintenance of Jewish community and its board'. In conclusion, the Jewish Committee's opinion was that Rypiński's *shtibl* should either be closed down or that the people praying there should be obliged to pay contributions to the community's official synagogue.[86]

The Government Commission accepted the findings of the Jewish Committee without any amendments and wrote to Izbicki and the Voivodeship Commission that in the Kingdom of Poland all residents, including hasidim, had freedom of belief, but that this did not mean that those who considered themselves hasidim could establish their own synagogue and completely sever ties with the community. If hasidim did not want to attend the community synagogue they could pray in private homes; but in such a case they were obliged to contribute to the maintenance of the synagogue. Therefore, the Voivodeship Commission saw its role as 'to forbid most forcefully the establishment of a second synagogue for hasidim'.[87]

It seems, then, that Izbicki's intervention was a complete success. According to the Government Commission, hasidim were not allowed to establish a public *shtibl* but they could pray in private homes. But it seems that the authorities still did not understand what hasidic *shtiblekh* were and how they functioned, for what did this ruling mean in practice? What were its real consequences? A few words of explanation are perhaps in order. Usually, one of the first steps of the emergent hasidic groups within communities was to establish, or at least attempt to establish, a separate *shtibl*. In Włocławek, however, the situation was a bit more complicated, because the Włocławek community itself was very small and young—so much so that it did not have the *beit midrash* (communal house of study) typical of well-established traditional communities. According to Izbicki, the hasidim attempted to set up a *beit midrash*; but since it was exclusively under their control it was a communal institution in name only.[88] Such a facility could be limited in its status by the government's decision, but not closed. The government could prevent the operation of a *beit midrash* but could not close a hasidic *shtibl* because of the law of 1824. The *shtibl*, then, still existed and functioned, but could not claim to be the communal *beit midrash*, or a 'second synagogue', as the government called it. Izbicki's success was, at best, partial.

Significantly more important was the requirement that hasidim must contribute to the maintenance of the community board, because this potentially had long-lasting, painful consequences for hasidic autonomy. If mem-

[86] See *18.08; AGAD, CWW 1734, pp. 47–9.
[87] See *18.09; AGAD, CWW 1734, pp. 50.
[88] Similar events were recorded in other communities, too, for example in 1822 in Płock. See AGAD, CWW 1666, pp. 6–10.

bers of hasidic groups were not excused from paying the levies set by the community board for the benefit of the general community, they would lose the important financial incentive that they had been able to offer potential members—an incentive that, according to some polemicists, was what had attracted wealthy people to the hasidic movement in the first place. Moreover, it is easy to imagine that the community's right to extract levies from unwilling hasidim could easily become an instrument of repression, giving the board a convenient and legally valid instrument to burden hasidim with additional payments. The history of the conflict in Włocławek over the next four years illustrates that this threat was real; it also shows how the law was impractical, and how hasidim profited from the atrophy of government administration.

At almost the same time as the decision of the Government Commission in the matter mentioned above, a subsequent conflict in Włocławek engulfed the local hasidic community. This time the issue was income from synagogue honours. Traditionally the right to be called up to the Torah was auctioned, such that the person offering the largest donation secured this privilege. However, considering both the desire to ensure a guaranteed income from this practice and the ongoing critique of the custom by maskilim as undignified, many communities abandoned the traditional bidding system in favour of selling leaseholds. The person purchasing the lease paid the community a predetermined sum for a fixed period (most often three years) and then collected the income for the honours according to principles established in a contract, sometimes by auction in the synagogue and sometimes for a set fee (though this in itself could be dependent on the income of the person purchasing the honour).

In 1836 the leaseholder in Włocławek, Hersz Kowalski, brought a charge against the Rypiński family and their hasidic supporters for refusing to pay part of the fees they had been assessed. He claimed that the solidarity of the hasidim not only made it impossible to auction synagogue honours in the traditional way but that the hasidim also refused to pay the sums that he proposed. He claimed that this was unequivocal evidence that Rypiński's group, under the guise of being hasidim, was trying to reduce the fees due to the Jewish community, a charge that was supported by testimonies from Szmul Płocki, Zelik Lubrański, Icek Poznański, and Jakub Kruszyński, all of whom had left the hasidic group.[89]

Investigating the course of this conflict, however, we find out that the fault did not lie exclusively with the hasidim. Rypiński's supporters had refused to pay because Kowalski was asking very high fees: 150, 200, or even 260 złotys per year. If the hasidim had accepted this, the amount they would have paid

---

[89] See *19.03; AGAD, CWW 1734, pp. 80–2.

would have represented 28.6 per cent or even 50 per cent of the entire income of the Jewish community in Włocławek from this source.[90] This was in stark contrast to their proportion in the community: if we can believe the list drawn up by the hasidic group a year later, there were only nineteen hasidim (meaning adult males) in Włocławek at this time,[91] but since these men should be taken as representing families, this would have meant that there were nineteen hasidic families—but still barely 12 per cent of the Jewish population of Włocławek.[92] Even if the list is incomplete (and there is nothing to indicate that it is), and even if the hasidim were on average wealthier than the remaining part of the community (which we can determine from a comparison of the list of the hasidim and the list of taxpayers), Kowalski's calculation was evidently skewed to the disadvantage of the hasidim: around 12 per cent of the population was supposed to cover between 28 per cent and 50 per cent of the total fee. This calculation confirms the presumption that the government decree that hasidim should participate in community funding served community boards as a convenient instrument of anti-hasidic repression and was employed as such in Włocławek. One also finds additional confirmation in the fact that, during the entire conflict, Kowalski acted with the full support of the community board.[93]

None the less, Kowalski's accusation had immediate effect. The state authorities, sensitive to any instances of tax evasion, gave him police support, thanks to which Kowalski 'took the Torah scrolls belonging to the hasidic sect, without which prayer could not be practised', until such time as the hasidim paid what was due.[94] Soon, however, Heyman Lowenstam, on behalf of the hasidic community, convinced the voivodeship authorities that Kowalski was demanding 'a payment that was exceedingly high and arbitrarily determined by the leaseholder'. The Voivodeship Commission ordered district authorities to see to it that the Torah scrolls be returned to the hasidim, and 'that both the leaseholder and sect testify that, regarding the fees from Torah scrolls, both sides come to an understanding in good will and

[90] Kowalski claimed that the hasidim had paid 150 złoty yearly to his predecessor, but that seems very doubtful. The hasidic *shtibl* did not start to operate until 1835, and Kowalski began his term of office as a tax leaser on 1 Jan. 1836, so there was not much time for the hasidim to have paid these fees. See *19.03, *19.14, *19.16; AGAD, CWW 1734, pp. 80–2, 148–50, 152–4.

[91] The list seems very reliable, because during a conflict such as this one in Włocławek any significant misrepresentations would certainly have sparked animated protests from the opposite side. It should thus be stressed that neither the Jewish community board nor Kowalski himself questioned the completeness of the list. The only issue was the amount to be paid by those listed.

[92] In 1837 there were 612 Jews living in Włocławek: see Gruszczyńska, 'Początki osadnictwa żydowskiego we Włocławku'. My calculations are comprehensively explained in 'How Many *Hasidim* Were There in Congress Poland?'.

[93] See *19.09, *19.16; AGAD, CWW 1734, pp. 148–50, 225.

[94] See *19.02; AGAD, CWW 1734, pp. 83–4.

establish the leaseholder's charge for reading from the Torah scrolls'. If such an understanding could not be reached because the hasidim offered too little and the leaseholder demanded too much, 'the [reading from the] Torah scrolls would be auctioned off during the time of each service as in synagogues and the leaseholder would be obligated to be content with the payment gathered in this way'. This decree of the voivodeship authorities, which was soon confirmed by the Government Commission, limited the anti-hasidic bias of the 1835 law regarding the contribution of hasidim to community funds. Nevertheless, the community board still theoretically maintained a certain degree of control over the hasidic *shtibl* and local worship by controlling the payments for reading from the Torah. A further hasidic campaign, however, revealed this control to be illusory.

The understanding ordered by the Voivodeship Commission was not reached. Kowalski demanded a lump-sum payment of 150 złotys per year; the hasidim rejected this demand. After a further round, which included a petition, police intervention, and a ministerial decree, in July 1837 the mayor of Włocławek summoned the local hasidim to a hearing.[95] During the hearing, the mayor presented the demand of the leaseholder, who continued to ask the hasidim to pay 150 złotys per year. The hasidim refused, but agreed to 'pay the leaseholder income gathered by bidding in their house of prayer from 10 January 1836 onward'. They also accepted the presence of the leaseholder or his representative in the *shtibl* to conduct the auction, but only on condition that 'the reading of the Torah scrolls . . . cannot in any way be granted to anyone not belonging to their sect'. Three days later the hasidim gave the mayor details of the payments that had been collected for being called up to the Torah during the period of Kowalski's lease, which was more than a year and a half. The total was 66 złotys and 20 groszy, and not the 225 złotys (or, according to another version, the 300 złotys) that Kowalski had expected. This amount was evidently lower than any reasonable estimate: even if we assume that Kowalski was due only the amount pledged, i.e. without any margin whatsoever as income for himself, the average per person on the list of hasidim would have amounted to around 2 złotys 10 groszy per year, compared to the 3 złotys 20 groszy paid by the non-hasidic Jews during the same period. (The arithmetic here is complicated: 19 hasidim × 1.5 year × 2 złotys 10 groszy = 66 złotys, since before metrification there were 30 groszy to the złoty.) Since this meant that the non-hasidim each paid around 50 per cent more than the hasidim, it suggests that the claims that Rypiński's group intended to harm the community finances were not unfounded. It also suggests that the condition they had insisted on placing on the leaseholder in auctioning honours, viz. that only members of the hasidic group could be

---

[95] See *19.07; AGAD, CWW 1734, pp. 221–4, 237–8.

called to the Torah, was merely a ploy to ensure that they could continue to fix the auction: ostensibly, the honour would go to the highest bidder, but in reality the amount would have been fixed in advance, according to the internal needs of their group. By banning outsiders from being called to the Torah the hasidim also excluded them from the bidding, and thereby avoided the risk that the fees paid would be significantly higher.

Kowalski did not accept Rypiński's conditions, on the grounds that the amount the hasidim were proposing was too low.[96] The Jewish community board again supported Kowalski, but the local authorities found that the 150 złotys annual fee that he wanted from the hasidim had no real basis. Moreover, although the hasidim had agreed to supervised bidding, the local authorities thought that this would restrict their religious freedom. The provincial government (as noted earlier, the voivodeships had changed into provinces—*gubernias*—and the voivodeship commissions into provincial governments) did not respond to this conclusion, so Kowalski appealed to the provincial government for police help in collecting the money due to him. The provincial government again did not react, offering Kowalski only a flimsy pretext for its failure to do so. The deliberations of state authorities at all levels lasted almost continuously for the next two years but did not produce any new arguments or any fresh breakthroughs. Responses were typically superficial, supposed to create the impression that the administration was working on the issue with a view to developing its own regulations, while in truth nothing was happening; nobody (besides, of course, Kowalski) sought a clear and quick resolution. The only action actually taken by the local authorities was, paradoxically, to enforce the law by sending the military, in the form of a single soldier, to Kowalski because of his failure to make his own payments to the community.

Impatient with the lack of a clear response and ever more in debt, Kowalski submitted a complaint in February 1838 to the Government Commission for Internal and Religious Affairs, arguing that the government had broken the conditions of its contract with him by failing to provide him with police assistance in collecting dues when necessary. By this time the hasidim had not paid their dues for three years; the local authorities had refused to send in the police; and the provincial government had not responded to his petitions for two years. Moreover, the administrative costs Kowalski had incurred in the course of this long-drawn-out situation, including sending around thirty petitions to authorities at all levels, had reached the sum of 360 złotys, a loss almost equal to the amount that he had hoped to collect from the hasidim for the three-year lease. Kowalski's charge was not unjustified; the leaseholder was guaranteed state help in enforcing the collection of dues, so

[96] See *19.08; AGAD, CWW 1734, pp. 234–6.

even if the state questioned the dues demanded it was formally required to offer him support. The reality was that the provincial government was so frustrated with the situation that it even proposed that in the future no income should be raised from the sale of Torah-related honours, the selling of *etrogim*, or burial fees, since this led to conflict between hasidim and lease-holders in many communities.[97] According to the governor, such conflicts had taken place in Włocławek, Radzymin, Łęczyca, and in many other locations. The proposal was completely unrealistic as these fees provided the financial basis of most of the Jewish communities, but it demonstrated the degree of helplessness and frustration felt by the state administration, and also its incompetence.

As Kowalski's lease approached its end, his determination grew ever greater. He addressed two further petitions to Sergei Pavlovich Shipov, the minister of internal affairs, demanding help in collecting 600 złotys (or even just 450 złotys) for the three years of the lease. Failing that, he demanded to be freed from the terms of the lease since the government was not fulfilling its own obligations. To be sure, the Government Commission did correspond with the provincial government on this issue, but both issued purely formal responses and no decision was reached. Finally, in November 1838, shortly before the expiry of the lease, Kowalski sent a complaint to the Administrative Council, and a month later to General Ivan Paskevich, the viceroy of the Kingdom. The viceroy ordered the Government Commission for Internal and Religious Affairs to investigate. After a year of further correspondence, the Government Commission finally recommended that the legal section should prepare an expert opinion. The expert opinion definitively established that Kowalski's demands had substance, as income from the reading of the Torah had fallen after the emergence of a group of hasidim; he therefore had the right to demand a lump sum from the hasidim or to offer the community board a discount as negotiated in a contract. On this basis, the Government Commission issued a final decision in December 1839 recognizing the validity of Kowalski's argument. At the same time, however, instead of offering Kowalski administrative support in collecting the monies owed by the hasidim, the government authorized him to decrease by 450 złotys the amount he owed to the community board on the basis of the contract.[98]

The decision was curious in many respects. Above all, it entirely rejected the 1835 law which obliged the hasidim to contribute to community expenses. In the light of the conditions then prevailing in the Kingdom,

[97] See *19.13; AGAD, CWW 1734, pp. 210–13.
[98] See *19.16, *19.19, *19.20, *19.22, *19.27; AGAD, CWW 1734, pp. 148–50, 157–9, 162–4, 241–2, 245–7.

however, it was the only possible decision. The 1835 law had no clear enforcement mechanism so was effectively dead. Moreover, the community board and, by extension, the non-hasidic majority had been burdened with costs from which the hasidim had been excused. The hasidim had to pay neither the 450 złotys for which they had been assessed, nor the lower amount (66 złotys 20 groszy) that they themselves had declared reasonable. To be sure, the Government Commission formally left the community board the freedom to collect this amount from Rypiński's group, but this would entail embarking upon a costly and risky legal journey, since the government had not provided any administrative support for these claims.

In the end, the government recognized that Kowalski was right, but it made no real attempt to resolve the conflict equitably as the hasidim remained free of any obligations towards the community. The striking contradiction and illogicality of the decision did not bother the ministry at all. The government failed to come up with a just or even a consistent legal solution to the problem, not to mention its failure to realize any kind of far-reaching policy. Its only goal was ending the conflict at the lowest possible cost. Rather than engage in a time-consuming, costly, and painfully unpleasant fight with a breakaway group, the government ignored the real source of the conflict and simply passed all costs on to the Jewish community. This was the easiest solution for it since the decision did not touch the state finances, the Jewish community had limited alternatives, and the population that would suffer from the decision was one for which the state administration had little sympathy in any case.

The main beneficiary of the decision, in fact, was the hasidic movement. Interestingly, the hasidic community achieved this success without any kind of engagement on its part. Besides the one petition of Heyman Lowenstam (and probably bribes to the clerks of the district commissioner), there is no trace of any kind of hasidic activity; the only instrument employed by them in this struggle was the consistent refusal to pay the dues levied on them. They achieved their victory because, as we have seen, the government did not have the least desire (and certainly no real opportunity) to engage in arduous interpretations of the law, investigations, police enforcement, appeals for legal and judicial solutions, or, finally, the possible pacification of social unrest or provision of support for the Jewish community board. Under these circumstances, the hasidic tactic of abrogating contractual obligations, community obligations, and state law worked to their advantage. The hasidic community in Włocławek managed to achieve full financial autonomy and to free itself of the obligation of at least certain community fees. This was a springboard for subsequent success in strengthening the movement institutionally, not only in Włocławek but throughout the Kingdom of Poland. As Kowalski wrote, the impunity granted to hasidim in respect of their failure to pay dues and taxes meant that support for the group in Włocławek increased daily: 'their number is greater, daily they [i.e. many Jews] are leaving the synagogue to join them'.[99] Though this example from Włocławek is particularly glaring, it illustrates the more general benefits accruing to the hasidic movement from the weakening of state influence on Jewish society throughout the Kingdom of Poland. The hasidim could rely on the state administration growing tired of examining accusations levelled against them and therefore preferring to allow the movement freedom of action, as long as this freedom did not conflict with more important goals of the state and as long as it did not assume a subversive character. The various investigations in which bureaucrats at all levels ignored the hasidic context demonstrate that this phenomenon was universal. The Jewish community board, deprived of real authority as long as the state administration was not behind it (and it usually wasn't), remained a powerless witness to the success of the hasidim.

6. Epilogue: In the 1860s

The final attempt of the Kingdom of Poland to implement an active policy concerning hasidism was in the 1860s. The revolutionary upheaval of 1861–3 and the uprising and defeat that followed in 1863–4 radically changed the political situation: the anti-tsarist uprising led to a violent deterioration of the political situation, the loss of the Kingdom's remaining autonomy, and the introduction of an aggressive and restrictive policy of Russification intended to crush Polish national ambitions once and for all. The new anti-Polish political stance necessitated, of course, a reformulation of all political relationships in the country, including the relationships with the Jewish population. The rapid growth of pro-Polish attitudes evident among the Jewish intelligentsia from the beginning of the 1860s—a phenomenon known as Polish–Jewish brotherhood—led to their increasing integration into Polish society. For the tsarist authorities, this was a politically delicate situation bordering on the suspicious.[100] And though real support for Polish independence, or simply participation in revolutionary organizations, never became universal among Jews (because, after all, such support and participation were not universal among the ethnic Polish population either—peasants, for example), the tsarist authorities looked with increasing suspicion on the relatively rapid progress of integration and its pro-Polish direction. This

[99] See *19.16; AGAD, CWW 1734, pp. 148–50.
[100] On Polish–Jewish brotherhood, see Opalski and Bartal, *Poles and Jews: A Failed Brotherhood*. For more on the emergence of the integrationist camp, see Gelber, *Die Juden und der Polnische Aufstand 1863*; Eisenbach, *Kwestia równouprawnienia Żydów w Królestwie Polskim*, 241 ff.; id., *Emancypacja Żydów*, 468–513; see also Weeks, *From Assimilation to Antisemitism*, 33–50.

inclined the government not only to make a complete break from the post-Enlightenment rhetoric of 'civilizing' the Jewish population but also to search realistically for new relationships and political alliances. By the 1860s, government plans to civilize the Jews had been replaced by a desire to win enough social support to block or at least hinder the increasing Jewish identification with Polish nationalist attitudes. One possible political strategy for accomplishing this seemed to be to reach out to those traditional groups within the community that had hitherto been defined as fanatical but were now regarded in a much more positive light because they were those least attracted by Polish nationalist ideas. Thus, the attention of the state administration now focused on the hasidim, among other traditional groups.

The opportunity to formulate a new policy that was positive in its attitude to hasidism came with the reform of Jewish community board regulations concerning elections, in line with the planned standardization of electoral regulations in the entire country. In this context the governor of Lublin, General-Major Mikhail Butskovskiy, circulated a ruling of the Government Commission for Internal and Religious Affairs that stated, among other things:[101]

The Jewish population is divided into two parties, one more wealthy and civilized, inclined to innovation and showing in recent times a sympathy for unrest, the other less progressive Hussites more inclined to support the legal government. Given that these parties are divided into still smaller sects, members of the Jewish community board and the rabbi cannot belong to one and the people to a second party; at the same time the religious freedom of these groups should not be limited: progressive Jews should not be favoured by the government and the hasidim should not be harassed.

The ruling unequivocally identified the 'wealthy and civilized party' with unreliable political elements, and the 'less progressive Hussites' with loyalists and supporters of the monarchy. On this basis, the government forbade further support for 'progressive Jews' and ordered that support be given to hasidim. Later in the ruling, the governor also ordered municipal authorities to adopt election procedures that would ensure the representation on Jewish community boards of the hasidim, the group considered to be better disposed to the authorities.

We do not know how these or similar orders were realized in practice in the country as a whole, but if the case of Lublin is representative we can conclude that the municipal authorities actually took steps to ensure that hasidim had a privileged position in the community. The mayor of Lublin gathered over two hundred representatives of the Jewish community, recounted the current electoral regulations, and suggested they be changed

[101] See *42.01; APL, AmL 2419, pp. 236–7, 244; see also APL, RGL adm 1725, pp. 419–21.

in line with the government recommendations so as to ensure that within the community there would be 'preservation of complete balance so that the religious principles of all tolerated sects are respected and that the less wealthy Hussites will not be harassed'.[102] As he said, in Lublin there had been no cases of limitations on religious liberty, but in order to ensure the liberty of hasidim in smaller localities belonging to the Lublin community too, care should be taken to ensure that 'one or more members of the Hussites belong to the Jewish community board'. Special regulations meant to support this guarantee focused on ensuring that voting (and indeed standing for election) was not just a privilege of the rich who had supported the anti-tsarist uprising of 1863–4. Hasidim were thus the only group to be guaranteed representation on the community board as well as government protection.

Of course, the strategy of alliance with anti-modernist groups was not entirely new. Similar suggestions had been made as early as the 1820s by the hasidim themselves, to whom the idea seemed almost natural. As early as 1824, Alexander Zusya Kahana had written to government authorities as follows: 'Our opponents say that we are fanatics and superstitious, but if superstition makes a person moral and good, we do not know any reason why the government should eradicate superstition.'[103] And again in 1855, the idea of the 'subservient fanaticism' of hasidim was the key argument in the hasidic campaign against the liberal Jewish community board in Warsaw. Local hasidim there under the leadership of Chil Erlich wrote that though their opponents considered them fanatics, this 'fanaticism' deserved government support since as a pure religion its hallmark was 'subservience to the throne, the general public, and to order'.[104]

Declarations of this type began to appear with increasing frequency, and moreover accurately reflected the current political mood. Similar alliances between the ruling powers and conservative religious groups were not unusual in eastern and central Europe after the beginning of the nineteenth century. For example, the Habsburg monarchy, especially in Galicia, struck a similar political alliance with the leaders of the traditional Jewish community in the first decade of the 1800s. Likewise in the Kingdom of Poland, at least from the 1830s on, an alliance developed between the state administration and the leaders of the hasidic movement (a topic addressed in the next chapter) for purely pragmatic reasons, along with a growth in the political significance of the hasidic movement. After the aforementioned successful campaign of the Warsaw hasidim to gain control of the local community board, the mayor of Warsaw, Teodor Andrault, acknowledged that the new community board had fewer enlightened Jews among its members, but that it

---

[102] See *42.02; APL, AmL 2419, pp. 252–5, 270–1; see also APL, RGL adm 1725, pp. 567–74.
[103] See *11.52; AGAD, CWW 1871, pp. 88–90.   [104] AGAD, CWW 1730, pp. 94–111.

therefore caused fewer problems and was therefore preferable from the point of view of the state.[105] Raphael Mahler has even expressed the opinion that 'the government preferred hasidism to the Haskalah'[106] earlier than this, i.e. in the constitutional period (1815–31). While it is difficult to agree with Mahler's assessment, the mayor's statement clearly shows that government attitudes to liberal modernization and to 'fanatical' hasidism were ambivalent even in the period of Enlightenment reform.

As the incidents described above show, the political reality was more complex than Mahler recognized. The 'need to fight against fanaticism and darkness' was still the official rhetoric of the state administration, but the philosophy that had given birth to that language was slowly dying. The rhetoric continued, but along with acceptance of the continued development of the hasidic movement—as long as this development did not require any involvement on the part of the authorities. The official stance on hasidism, then, was one of resignation and toleration from a position of powerlessness, rather than a policy adopted with a view to achieving the objectives of a political strategy. Tellingly, until the 1860s no government body had formulated a programme benefiting the hasidic movement as an instrument in the political fight against liberal tendencies.

In this sense, the 1860s were a real turning-point. For the first time, the government adopted a strategy that saw the hasidim as a potential counterbalance to the liberal Jews aligned with the Polish insurrectionist camp. Moreover, the declared objective of reforming the electoral regulations of the Jewish community boards in 1866 was actually achieved in several instances. When, for example, there was conflict over a rabbi for Hrubieszów in 1865, both the provincial and the central government consistently supported the hasidic candidate against Kisel Gelernter, presented by his supporters as the candidate of the 'civilized' party. This is an example of the new political approach that was to find expression in the 1866 regulations.[107] Similarly, the response of the Government Commission for Internal Affairs and the Provincial Government to a request of hasidim from Sokołów for permission to establish another *shtibl* there in 1868[108] was unequivocally positive, and there were several other blatantly pro-hasidic decisions too.

At the same time, however, one should note that the policy was not consistent, and government at all levels frequently adopted contrary positions, favouring modernizing Jews over hasidic groups. Administrative practice was still shaped by the factors that had hampered the political strategy of previous decades: above all, paternalism, frequently coupled with disdain for the

[105] AGAD, CWW 1730, pp. 168–74.
[106] Mahler, *Hasidism and the Jewish Enlightenment*, 316.
[107] See AGAD, CWW 1602, pp. 400–522.   [108] See AGAD, CWW 1871, pp. 313–15.

Jewish population (especially its more traditional element); bureaucratic arrogance; a reluctance to intervene in the internal affairs of the Jewish community; self-interest; and a continuing ignorance about Jews. The ignorance was seemingly even greater in the 1860s than it had been earlier, possibly due to the involvement of new personnel (including numerous officials from Russia), meaning that the bureaucrats themselves were not knowledgeable about either the laws or the social situation of the Kingdom of Poland. This is suggested by the increasing frequency with which provincial governments asked for basic information regarding the legal status of hasidim and their *shtiblekh*.[109] The situation was not better at the level of the government of the Kingdom of Poland, which was essentially liquidated after the complete loss of its autonomy as a result of the anti-tsarist uprising of 1863–4; it was replaced with institutions that performed more or less the same functions but were totally subjugated to the Russian authorities and, above all, were staffed by personnel unfamiliar with the situation in the Kingdom of Poland. Thus in 1871, when Alexander Sergeievich Muchanov, a tsarist official in Warsaw overseeing the Kingdom's denominational affairs, planned to make the laws relating to hasidim and their *shtiblekh* in the Kingdom of Poland the same as those in Russia, the authorities in St Petersburg thought it appropriate to issue a delicate reprimand and to demand '[better] consideration of the above-mentioned issue and an account of the local circumstances and conditions of Jewish life in the Kingdom'.[110] The incompetence was all too evident.

It was not easy to implement a policy of supporting hasidim rather than acculturated Jews, especially at the local level. If tsarist officials made contact with representatives of the Jewish community, it was more often with Jewish doctors, pharmacists, or teachers than with the Orthodox Jews, whom the bureaucrats universally disdained. This does not mean, of course, that rich and influential representatives of the Jewish community from the hasidic milieu did not have access to high state officials. Such contacts stemmed especially from common economic interests, and even from covert partnerships or other financial ties. Still, contacts with acculturated Jews were both more frequent and much closer because of their growing participation in the cultural and social elites of Polish cities and towns. The influence of this type of social contact was sometimes quite striking, as for example when the Russian military and civil authorities in Piotrków closed the *shtibl* of the tsadik Moses Brukman at the suggestion of local Jewish doctors and consistently fought against the tsadik's influence to the extent of putting him on trial for

[109] Good examples of the ignorance of the state administration at the provincial and central level can be found in AGAD, CWW 1871, pp. 313, 316–19.

[110] AGAD, CWW 1871, pp. 325–7.

quackery.[111] Even after Brukman was cleared of the charges against him the provincial authorities remained under the influence of the opinion of the doctors and did not allow the *shtibl* to reopen. Perhaps the strongest evidence of the influence of the acculturated Jewish intelligentsia, however, is that when hasidim reported to the tsarist authorities that there were Jewish doctors who had pro-Polish sympathies and were actively engaged in insurrectionary activity, the authorities blatantly ignored the accusations, even though, since the participation of Jewish doctors from Piotrków in the uprising of 1863–4 was quite significant, the accusation was quite probably correct.[112]

The overall effect of the factors discussed here—prejudice, ignorance, inertia, personal interests, and social ties—was similar to that observed in earlier decades: inconsistency, to the degree that senior officials came out with contradictory decisions at almost the same time and so had no real influence on the hasidic community and relations with the entire Jewish population. Thus the provincial government of Lublin, which in 1866 ordered the support of hasidic representation on Jewish community boards, almost simultaneously blocked the nomination of hasidim as board members, closed down hasidic *shtiblekh*, and carried out minor acts of harassment against 'hasidic fanatics'. In 1868, barely two years after introducing pro-hasidic changes in the electoral regulations for Jewish community boards, General Butskovskiy, who had been personally responsible for the previous policy in support of the hasidim, refused to ratify the nomination of a hasid to the Jewish community board on the grounds that the 'sect of hasidim' was an enemy of the empire.[113] Government policy concerning the hasidic movement in the 1860s was as chaotic and ineffective as the policy of its predecessors in decades past.

7. Conclusions

As we have seen in previous chapters, the seeds of the failure of the government's policy concerning hasidism were present from the beginning: anti-Jewish fears and prejudices, and disdain and paternalism regarding

[111] See AGAD, CWW 1411, pp. 550–9, 591–4. Brukman's conflict with local maskilim and Russian investigation into the matter have been analysed in detail in Wodziński, *Haskalah and Hasidism*, 194–6, 289–95.

[112] On this see Fijałek, 'Do zagadnienia szpitalnictwa żydowskiego w Piotrkowie Trybunalskim', 54; Feinkind, *Dzieje Żydów w Piotrkowie*, 24. For more on the participation of the Jewish doctors in the January Uprising, see Ringelblum, 'Yidishe doktoyrim un mediker in oyfshtand fun yor 1863', and id., 'Reshime fun yidishe doktoyrim, mediker un farmatsevtn'.

[113] Kuwałek, 'Pomiędzy tradycją a asymilacją', 233–4. Other examples of the inconsistency in the governmental policy in relation to hasidism can be found in id., 'Chasydzkie domy modlitwy w Lublinie w XIX–XX wieku', 61–2.

Jewish society as a whole and 'fanatical hasidim' in particular. These features were evident as early as 1824, at the high point of the great investigation, and they were ultimately to contribute to the complete disintegration of this political strategy. The fundamental reasons for this were significantly more general than the issue of hasidism, which was a secondary concern from the state's point of view, and related to the overall deterioration of the state administration after 1826 and the radical changes in state organization after the 1830–1 uprising. Less visible factors that also played a part in shaping the policy towards hasidism included growing ignorance on the part of the bureaucrats involved, coupled with incompetence, a natural inertia, and their own self-interest. In effect, any attempt at instituting a cohesive political approach to the hasidic movement was abandoned in the 1830s. This was all the more striking since at the same time the number of anti-hasidic reports to authorities at all levels increased dramatically and conflicts surrounding hasidic groups (primarily concerning *shtiblekh* and hasidic rabbis) increasingly became the concern of local authorities. It may also seem surprising that the government officially withdrew from any kind of consistent political stance towards hasidism just at the time when the movement was enjoying its greatest triumphs in Poland. This, however, is only an apparent paradox. In actuality, it was an expression of a very deliberate ploy on behalf of the government, which was abandoning the attempt to institute any long-term policy in the interests of maintaining social peace and civil order. Simply put, the rapid increase in the number of incidents involving hasidim from the 1820s on was paralleled by the equally rapid atrophying of government policy on the issue, to the point that it quickly ceased to exist.

Numerous investigations, intermittent activity, and sporadic legal action did not change this fact. The final investigation, in 1834, not only failed to provide new impetus to government policy concerning hasidism but also revealed the official abandonment of any active engagement in the social conflict increasingly connected to this movement. Moreover, even when government officials, frustrated with hasidic arrogance and the conflicts surrounding the movement, sporadically did try to initiate anti-hasidic activity, it turned out that their determination, level of knowledge regarding hasidism, and even their understanding of the legal situation were insufficient to achieve even the most modest results. These same factors meant that the last effort to link hasidism to the broader political strategies of the government in the 1860s was equally ineffective. From time to time the government managed to formulate strategic policy objectives towards Jews (including hasidim), but each time it turned out that it was not in a position to realize them.

For the hasidic movement, this situation was beneficial in all respects. Even if the querulous, chaotic, and at times corrupt actions of the state institutions were frequently onerous for the hasidim, the general situation of paralysis in the state administration carried with it decidedly more advantages than disadvantages. The Jewish community boards, now unable to count on consistent state support, were not in a position effectively to oppose hasidic expansion, their evasions of community taxes, establishment of new *shtiblekh*, or avoidance of communal jurisdiction in increasingly greater areas of social life. The hasidic movement did not encounter significant institutional opposition from either the Jewish community or the state administration; the latter gladly avoided taking any definite action in any matter, especially in conflicts seen as insignificant from the administrative point of view—such as those between two 'Jewish sects'. As we saw in Włocławek, the hasidim were in a position to gain significant concessions even without special political engagement on their part. Their consistent refusal to pay the dues levied on them sufficed. In the end, the state administration grew tired of the prolonged conflict and simply passed on the costs to the institution that was the easiest target, the Jewish community. With time, the hasidic community became increasingly adept at benefiting from the political situation, and was able to do so systematically on a larger and larger scale. The involvement of representatives of the hasidic movement in political activity and the evolution of their political competence will be treated in the next chapter.

CHAPTER FIVE

The Hasidim Strike Back: The Development of Hasidic Political Involvement

HASIDIM were not simply dispassionate observers of policies implemented by the central and regional organs of the state. One would hardly expect them to be, given that they were the party most interested in the favourable outcome of government investigations into hasidism. After all, an issue that was for the government only one of many social problems (and a marginal one at that), and for the maskilim an important but not a key concern, was for them something absolutely fundamental. From the beginning of government interest in them, we see petitions written by hasidim to all levels of the state administration, attempts to gain powerful allies, and various public and behind-the-scenes efforts to attain decisions favourable to their interests. As already demonstrated, a relatively large number of hasidic leaders, including such figures as Alexander Zusya Kahana, Meir Rotenberg of Opatów, and Abraham Kamienicer, were engaged in this type of hasidic *shtadlanut*, as representation of the Jewish community or communities before the state and local authorities was known. Hasidic literature is full of stories of tsadikim interceding in defence of the Jewish people. Several cases have been discussed in earlier chapters. The aim of this chapter is to give a more general account of those cases, and especially of the nature and mechanisms of hasidic political activism. If we set aside traditional hasidic stories—such as how the tsadik Elimelekh of Leżajsk (Lyzhansk) spilled soup so that Emperor Joseph II would spill ink at the same time and be prevented from signing an anti-Jewish decree[1]—surprisingly little is known about the nature of hasidic political activism and how that activism was perceived within the hasidic world.

The most important questions in this context are as follows. Why, and under what circumstances, did hasidic political activism develop? How did hasidic activists react to political challenges? Did their reactions evolve over time? How did they differ from those of non-hasidic traditional Jews? And the most important: how, and in what way, did political involvement change the hasidic movement—organizationally, ideologically, and in terms of its

---

[1] See Langer, *Nine Gates to the Chassidic Mysteries*, ch. 5.

self-perception? Another set of important questions relates to the technical characteristics of hasidic political activism, and the relationship between that and the forms of Jewish political involvement in the pre-modern Polish–Lithuanian Commonwealth. How much did modern hasidic politics inherit from earlier forms of *shtadlanut* and other traditional Jewish politics? How did it adapt them to modern circumstances? What new forms did it adopt?[2]

The term *shtadlan* has been used to cover both formal intercessors employed by Jewish institutions and approved by the non-Jewish authorities (a pattern typical of the Polish–Lithuanian Commonwealth) and informal intercessors who used their own privileged position for the benefit of their fellow Jews.[3] This second category of *shtadlan*, which includes 'court Jews' and religious leaders, has aroused considerable scholarly interest.[4] However, although the literature dealing with these and other *shtadlanim* is quantitatively impressive, the vast majority of studies have until recently paid frustratingly little attention to their methods (or operational techniques, or simply means) and their effectiveness. Possibly the thinking was that since these activities were carried on informally, and therefore in a way that was not fully transparent (and may perhaps even have been to some degree illicit), they have been regarded as shrouded in mystery and therefore unavailable for investigation.[5]

More recently a pioneering study by Scott Ury has suggested that the fundamental operational techniques of the *shtadlanim* in early modern Poland were not secretive machinations carried on behind the scenes but rather formal requests or even appeals for help, petitions containing legal arguments, or bribes. Ury assigns the most important role to bribery (which was anything but 'illegal and behind the scenes' in the old Polish–Lithuanian Commonwealth).[6] Even if we accept the pertinence of this assertion in relation to the seventeenth or eighteenth centuries (and it is possible to have

[2] The most ambitious attempt to tackle these issues so far is a study by David Assaf and Israel Bartal, who formulated the thesis that the Polish tsadikim in the 19th c. tried to take over the function of *shtadlanut*, which in the early modern period had been subjugated to the *kahal* when it was still autonomous. But even if we accept this claim, most of the central questions about the relationship between traditional *shtadlanut* and hasidic political activism remain unanswered. See Assaf and Bartal, 'Shetadlanut ve'ortodoksiyah'.

[3] Essential reading on *shtadlanut* is Leszczyński, *Sejm Żydów Korony, 1623–1764*, 117–21, and Biale, *Power and Powerlessness in Jewish History*, chs. 3 and 4. For an analysis of *shtadlanut* as a form of political activism, see Goldberg, 'Pierwszy ruch polityczny wśród Żydów polskich'; Ury, 'The *Shtadlan* of the Polish–Lithuanian Commonwealth'; Guesnet, 'Politik der Vormoderne'; id., 'Die Politik der "Fürsprache"'.

[4] For a general account of the 'court Jews' as political representatives, see Lederhendler, *The Road to Modern Jewish Politics*, 19–21; see also Stern, *The Court Jew*. On Josel Rosheim, the most famous 'court Jew', see Stern, *Josel of Rosheim*. On other 'court Jews', see e.g. Kaufmann, *Samson Wertheim*; Mevorach, 'The Imperial Court-Jew Wolf Wertheimer'.

[5] See e.g. Horowitz, 'A Portrait of a Russian-Jewish Shtadlan', 1–2.

[6] Ury, 'The *Shtadlan* of the Polish–Lithuanian Commonwealth', 284–7 (Ury applies the

doubts, given our virtual ignorance of decision-making processes in the areas of interest to us), a number of questions arise with regard to the nineteenth century. Did those methods change, and if so how? What was the effect of the abolition of the official Jewish *shtadlanut* in the nineteenth century as part of wider changes in the political and legal system consequent on the increased adoption of universalist principles?

In our context it is important of course to ask how the development of hasidism fitted into this process. Were the intercessionary activities of nineteenth-century tsadikim different from those of the early Polish *shtadlanim* and their counterparts elsewhere in central Europe? This seems highly likely, as the whole political and legal system of the state changed during the turbulent years of the Polish partitions (1772–95) and subsequent Napoleonic Wars. The state machinery itself had changed, and a new legal system, 'universal' at least in theory, had taken the place of individual and group privileges. In addition, a professional and relatively effective administrative system, something totally unknown in the old Polish–Lithuanian Commonwealth, had brought profound changes to all strata of society, including the Jews. This change was augmented by the continuous efforts to reform Jewish society undertaken by the regime of the Kingdom of Poland from its beginning in 1815 up to the shift in policy after the collapse of the anti-tsarist uprising in 1831, after which the government became increasingly conservative.[7] This political transformation and its subsequent phases must also have had a fundamental influence on Jewish political activism in the first half of the nineteenth century.

One should note here that the political world of nineteenth-century Europe, even in its eastern reaches, differed fundamentally from pre-modern politics as practised in the early modern Polish–Lithuanian Commonwealth. Political mechanisms came to be subordinated to criteria that Max Weber called the fundamental factors of state modernization: bureaucratization; the universalization of law and administrative procedures; the professionalization of administrative services; the written nature of all procedures; depersonalization; the increased role of the state in regulating and co-ordinating relations between groups and individuals; and the broadening of the categories of citizenship and civil rights (though under east European conditions this last area was limited).[8] In these circumstances, those interested in politics

term *shtadlanim* only to the first category of official intercessors). On the 'clientele' system and the corruption of the political system in Old Poland, see esp. Mączak, *Klientela*.

[7] The 'Jewish policy' of the government of the Kingdom of Poland has best been summarized in Eisenbach, *Emancypacja Żydów*, 164–223.

[8] Weber, *On Law, Economy and Society*, 354. A broad discussion of the political parameters of modernity, including the influential opinions of Max Weber on the subject, can be found in Sztompka, *The Sociology of Social Change*, ch. 5.

had to adopt contemporary political methods; this in itself indicated a certain form of modernization.[9] But modernization in the sense of adopting modern political methods did not necessarily imply modernization across the board. Thus, anti-modernist social groups sometimes embraced some elements of modernity so as better to preserve other elements of their anti-modernist character, a process that has been termed 'defensive modernization'.[10] What did this process look like for hasidim?

Although the literature on Jewish political activism in the nineteenth century has recently been enriched by several valuable studies, we are still far from answering these questions. Equally, hasidic literature cannot provide us with answers; the tsadik is presented as having supernatural qualities, so the effectiveness of any intervention is attributed to this. Such stories are very common in the hasidic literary corpus, but they do not bring us any closer to understanding the phenomenon that is of interest to us.

Events reconstructed and carefully described in the foregoing chapters will be used here as a starting point for investigating the questions posed above. Although all the examples come from the Kingdom of Poland, I believe that they are of more general importance. I am not claiming that the Kingdom of Poland can provide a universal model for the development of hasidic political activism in all the regions of eastern Europe; certainly this process played out somewhat differently, perhaps even entirely differently, in Galicia, in Ukraine, or in Lithuania. However, precisely for that reason it seems to me that focusing on a single political region and its local social, political, and legal context can help identify pointers that can be applied elsewhere. This seems to me more useful than trying to draw conclusions from a generalized picture based on hagiographical hasidic literature. It is true that archival sources are less compelling than hasidic tales and can present only a fragmentary picture, especially for the earlier periods, but they do offer some important advantages: because they are contemporary with the events under investigation and were generated without thought to a narrative, their analysis is less likely to be affected by the distortions and anachronisms present in other types of account, especially those composed retrospectively.

The vast majority of the cases discussed and analysed in this chapter will focus on instances of high politics, i.e. political machinations at the state level, rather than low-level communal politics. This is so not because I attribute less importance to low-level politics, but rather because the focus here is the interaction between state politics relating to hasidism and the develop-

---

[9] On this see an innovative article by Moshe Rosman, 'Hasidism as a Modern Phenomenon'.

[10] The term was introduced by Hans Ulrich Wehler in *Deutsche Gesellschaft*, i: *1700–1815*, though with a somewhat different context and meaning.

ment of hasidic political activism. As I shall try to demonstrate, the growth of hasidic political activism, both high and low, as well as the development of its goals, methods, and more technical characteristics, was a direct result of continuous interaction with state institutions. The link between high politics and low-level hasidic political activism will be discussed in Chapter 6.

1. Beginnings: Berek Sonnenberg and his Circle

Until the beginning of the nineteenth century the politics initiated by hasidic leaders had an episodic character, and the reliability of the testimonies describing their activity in this sphere is often questionable. Such is the case with stories of the appearance of Levi Isaac of Berdyczów (Berdichev) during the Four Year Sejm in Warsaw (1788–92) and the political meetings and rallies held by hasidic leaders during this time.[11] Even if we accept that hasidic tradition has preserved a trace of the reality of the times (and this does not seem unreasonable), we may surmise that a story told fifty years after an event occurred will incorporate an anachronistic projection of its meaning—a general problem in considering the credibility of any traditional genre.[12] This does not mean, of course, that accounts of political activity of an earlier period are not credible at all. For example, the political aspects of the famous conflict between hasidim and their opponents in Vilna at the start of the nineteenth century are well documented by independent sources and described in the literature on the subject.[13] It also seems that certain of the leading figures of the period, hasidic and non-hasidic, had a natural talent for politics, and their political activity was ahead of their times. Certainly this was the case with Shneur Zalman of Lady (Lyady) and, among the tsadikim active in central Poland, Levi Isaac of Żelechów, better known as the tsadik of Berdyczów .

Characteristically, though, even in the case of these most engaged hasidic political leaders, the nature of their political activity shows that they viewed

[11] The information about the visit of Levi Isaac of Berdichev to Warsaw in 1791 is supported by hasidic oral sources, but can also be inferred from a remark by Menahem Mendel Lefin, who mentions a hasidic leader who arrived in Warsaw from Ukraine: see [Lefin], 'Essai d'un plan de réforme', 419–20. For more see Halperin, 'Rabi levi-yitshak miberditshev', 67–9. Emanuel Ringelblum, however, doubts whether the person mentioned by Lefin was indeed Levi Isaac: see Ringelblum, 'Khsides un haskole in varshe', 125–6.

[12] Methodological discussion of how to use hasidic stories as historical evidence has been revitalized by a pioneering publication: Rosman, *Founder of Hasidism*. For the most articulate reactions to Rosman's arguments, see Etkes, 'The Historical Besht'; id., *Ba'al hashem* (English edn.: *The Besht*) and Haviva Pedaya's reviews of Rosman and Etkes: 'Bikoret al m. rosman Habesht' and 'Bikoret al e. etkes Ba'al hashem'. See also the exchange between Rosman, 'Lemeḥkar bikorti al habesht hahistori', and Pedaya, 'Teguvah liteguvato shel moshe rosman'.

[13] On the conflict in Vilna see esp. Klausner, *Vilna bitekufat haga'on*, 30–6; see also Lederhendler, *The Road to Modern Jewish Politics*, 43–4; Dubnow, 'Vmeshatelstvo russkogo pravitelstva v antichasidskuyu borbu'.

Figure 5.1 Title page of *Kedushat levi alhatorah* [Sanctity of Levi] (Munkach, 1905), a collection of teachings on the Torah attributed to Levi Isaac of Berdyczów (Berdichev), here described as the rabbi of Żelechów, where he held a rabbinical post in the years *c.* 1765–75. Private collection of the author

politics in a strictly theological sense, in the way that normative Jewish culture had viewed politics since the early medieval period. In other words, they saw it as a means of achieving spiritual or religious objectives, such as protecting the chosen people, carrying out the will of God or the public sanctification of God, and even as hastening the coming of the messiah. The clearest examples of this are the pronouncements of tsadik Pinhas of Korzec

(Korets) on political topics and the theological role of the Polish–Lithuanian Commonwealth in the Jewish history of the diaspora, and the later conflict among tsadikim on the role and meaning of the Napoleonic Wars, including the pronouncements of the leading politician among tsadikim of this period, Shneur Zalman of Lady.[14] Of course, neither a lack of originality nor theological views of politics ever stymied practical work in the political arena. However, in early hasidism the issue is not only the lack of originality in a more general philosophy of politics but also a lack of clear goals, and even elementary vision, concerning the significance of politics, and a rather limited understanding of what politics is and how it can be used. It is understandable that until hasidism had grown to become a real social force, the political involvement of its representatives would be incidental and have only inconsequential impact; serious political reflection and activism would have been unlikely before hasidism had transformed itself from an elite pietistic grouping to a mass social movement.

Material from Polish archives shows that this transformation did not take place until the second decade of the nineteenth century, and it is indeed during this same period that we find the first clear traces of hasidic political activism. Beginning from the first investigation in 1817, provincial government administrations (and soon central government ones too) took an interest in the conflicts that accompanied the emergence of hasidic groups in numerous cities of central Poland. A rapidly growing number of reports of different types of conflicts concerning the 'Michałki', *kitajowcy*, or 'Hussites' (the different names applied to hasidim further deepened the chaos and confusion) reached local and provincial state authorities. An important turning-point was the investigation of 1818 instigated by the Government Commission for Religious Denominations and Public Enlightenment in an attempt to learn more about hasidism and to regulate it on a national level. This prompted the first organized political activism by representatives of hasidic groups in central Poland: three days later, ten hasidim appealed to the Voivodeship Commission 'in everyone's name' to protest against the decision to close the hasidic *shtiblekh* in Płock (see Ch. 2, §3). This in turn prompted the Government Commission for Religious Denominations and Public Enlightenment, and subsequently Viceroy Józef Zajączek, to take an interest in the matter. Their involvement was sparked by the petition to the Voivodeship Commission, and, it seems, by mass bribery (the information we have is not very precise, but it seems that there were many bribes, most of them quite small), a typical instrument of politics, Jewish and non-Jewish, in eastern Europe. As Florian Kobyliński, president of the Voivodeship Commission,

---

[14] On Pinhas of Korzec (Korets) and his ideas on the role of the Polish–Lithuanian Commonwealth, see Heschel, *The Circle of the Baal Shem Tov*, 40–3. On political manifestations of hasidism during the Napoleonic period, see Levine, '"Should Napoleon Be Victorious . . ."'.

wrote, 'in spite of all kinds of government bans', the *kitajowcy* were able to maintain an active *shtibl* in many locations throughout the province 'by paying off lower police officials'.[15] In the end, after obtaining numerous opinions, Zajączek and the government recognized the right of hasidim throughout the country to assemble for prayer, and banned the persecution of the hasidim. The investigation ended in complete victory for the hasidim.

The hasidic response to subsequent investigations in 1820, 1822, and 1823–4 was very similar. A typical example was the series of formal petitions, signed by Abraham Kamienicer and Alexander Zusya Kahana, seeking to overturn a decision of 1824 banning hasidic *shtiblekh* and a successful attempt to influence Viceroy Zajączek in the same matter. This is discussed in more detail below.

In spite of these undoubted successes, hasidic political activism was of an exclusively defensive character, both at the level of state politics and at the community or provincial level. The only known instance during this time of proactive political behaviour on the part of hasidim was their partly successful attempt to compel the municipal authorities of Częstochowa to force concessions on the non-hasidic majority. In general, however (as is clear from the fact that this was the only known case), the hasidim were hesitant to involve government authorities in what they perceived as an internal Jewish conflict. In fact, it was only an extreme and atypical situation that led them to involve the mayor and the president of the Provincial Commission: the refusal of a Jewish burial society, which was controlled by the Jewish community board, to bury a hasidic child.[16] Thus even this seemingly proactive move was really defensive, imposed by circumstances rather than freely undertaken. This does not mean that hasidic political activity was ill prepared or ineffective, rather that it offers no evidence of co-ordination or long-term strategy.

Interestingly, if the archival sources are to be believed, the individuals involved in this activity were not the spiritual leaders of hasidic groups, though many of the latter were certainly worldly enough (the tsadik Simhah Bunem of Przysucha, for example, was a grain merchant and pharmacist) and thus seemed perfect candidates for political leadership.[17] Rather, they were people with political experience resulting from their professional contacts with the Polish government and legal system. Most prominent was a group

[15] AGAD, CWW 1869, p. 9.

[16] AGAD, KWK 702, pp. 15–87, AGAD, CWW 1542, pp. 4–10. See also Wodziński, 'Chasydzi w Częstochowie'.

[17] For example as previously noted (Ch. 3 n. 66), Bunem did not show up when summoned for interrogation during one of the most important anti-hasidic investigations in Poland in 1824. See *11.66; AGAD, CWW 1871, pp. 168–9; see also AGAD, CWW 1871, pp. 181–6; Wodziński, 'Sprawa chasydymów', 235–9.

concentrated around Berek Sonnenberg, the richest Polish Jew and a known supporter of hasidism. The group included his wife Temerl; their son Jakub Bereksohn Sonnenberg; Alexander Zusya Kahana, a follower of the Przysucha school of hasidism; and Abraham Kamienicer and Hersz Sztamm, wealthy collaborators in Sonnenberg's business endeavours.[18] Because they had been involved in numerous negotiations with the government during the period of Prussian rule and under the Duchy of Warsaw (1795–1815) they had developed useful contacts with representatives of the Polish authorities and had also learned to deal effectively with a bureaucratic administrative system. Evidence of this is Berek Sonnenberg's astonishing success in persuading the government to accept his terms for the supply of salt, and the fascinating conflict between his children and the government surrounding inheritance tax on their father's estate.[19] The latter conflict, which reached its peak around the end of 1822, i.e. nearly contemporary with the events under investigation here, demonstrated the effective and very close cooperation between the members of the group, their sound legal preparation, and their mastery of the political tools available in a conflict with an apparently stronger opponent. A particularly interesting figure in this circle was Alexander Zusya Kahana, then relatively little known. His first attested intervention in politics was in 1824, when he was only 29 years old and had no formal position. It is not clear if he acted then on behalf of Rabbi Simhah Bunem, his spiritual patron; his ties with the Sonnenberg family suggest that his political interests could have developed independently. For the next ten years he was the most active hasidic *shtadlan* in the Kingdom of Poland. His reputation grew quickly: by 1829 the superior quality of his intercessions had been recognized by no less an individual than Rabbi Isaac of Warka, later an iconic figure of hasidic political activity, who asked him to intercede on behalf of the imprisoned Jews of Zambrów.[20]

The fact that hasidic political activism was merely defensive at this stage and that the individuals engaged in it were not key figures in the hasidic movement led to it being perceived as something divorced from 'real' hasidism, thereby maintaining the image of hasidism as a conservative and antimodern phenomenon. However, the reality was that although hasidic leaders did not engage in political activism partly because they did not have the proper preparation, it was principally because they viewed themselves, and

---

[18] For more on Berek Sonnenberg and his support for the hasidic movement, see Dynner, '*Men of Silk*', 99–104, and id., 'Merchant Princes and Tsadikim'; see also Schiper, *Przyczynki do dziejów chasydyzmu w Polsce*, 86–8.

[19] On Berek Sonnenberg's negotiations on the salt monopoly, see AGAD, *Protokoły posiedzeń Rady Administracyjnej Królestwa Polskiego*, i. 156–61, 181–4; vii. 501–6; viii. 8; ix. 2–3, 54–7, 72–7; x. 254, 257; on Sonnenberg's last will see Wodziński, 'Tsavato shel berek zonenberg'.

[20] See *Mikhtavim ve'igerot kodesh*, ed. Mandelbaum, 215. I should like to thank Shaul Stampfer for bringing this collection to my attention.

Figure 5.2 Berek Sonnenberg (1764–1822) and his wife Temerl, the
best-known patrons of hasidism in central Poland in the nineteenth century;
Berek was the only traditionally dressed, bearded Jew allowed to live in
Warsaw outside the Jewish district. From Ignacy Schiper, Arie Tartakower,
and A. Haftka (eds.), *Żydzi w Polsce Odrodzonej* [Jews in Reborn Poland]
(Warsaw, 1933), i. 427. Private collection of Jan Paweł Woronczak

were viewed by others, as spiritual rather than political leaders. Put simply,
nobody expected them to be involved in politics. In turn, the fact that the
political activists who acted on their behalf were not universally recognized
representatives of the hasidic community allowed them to operate outside
the sphere of activity that was recognized as normative for hasidism. This was
the case with Berek Sonnenberg, whose identification with hasidism was only
partial and who was considered by some hasidim to be an outsider precisely
because of his involvement in such worldly activities. Hasidim experienced
politics as an external phenomenon, foreign to their world, and categorized it
as such.[21]

All this meant that the political involvement of hasidim at this period
was minimal, and largely restricted to the community level. They defended
themselves against accusations brought against them by community boards,
and sometimes appealed to non-Jewish authorities for help in such conflicts,
but did not appear to be interested in politics at the state level. Even with
the key investigation that took place in Warsaw in 1818, the traces of hasidic
involvement that have come down to us are modest enough: appeals to

[21] For an interesting testimony revealing the lack of awareness among hasidim of the nature
of their leaders' political activities, see *Sefer me'ir einei hagolah*, i. 100, no. 206.

voivodeship commissions for permission to open *shtiblekh*; petitionary actions; and evidence of bribes. Hasidism had not yet matured enough to undertake political initiatives on a larger scale independently, even in matters related exclusively to hasidic society.

2. Offensive: Meir Rotenberg of Opatów

Around the mid-1820s we begin to see qualitative changes in hasidic political activism in the Kingdom of Poland, a consequence both of the growing government interest in hasidism as evidenced by the numerous investigations of 1823 and 1824 and of the spectacular political gains that the hasidim had achieved in these investigations. The significance of these successes, as described in Chapter 3, is difficult to overestimate. After a series of formal petitions from Alexander Zusya Kahana and Abraham Kamienicer against the restrictions imposed on hasidim, the viceroy ordered a further inquiry into the potential dangers of the movement. The committee established for this purpose summoned five hasidic figures for questioning, of whom only one, tsadik Meir Rotenberg of Opatów, deigned to appear. Accompanying him, however, were several rich and influential supporters of hasidism: Abraham Kamienicer, Hersz Sztamm (connected to the Bereksohn Sonnenberg family), and Jakub Bereksohn Sonnenberg, the son of Berek Sonnenberg. Their testimonies convinced the committee that there was not 'the least need'[22] to persecute hasidim, and Viceroy Zajączek decided that since 'the Jewish sect of hasidim, or *kitajowców*, did not hold any principles that were against good custom, and only wished to have their own separate synagogues, to distinguish themselves from other Jews',[23] they should be tolerated. This ruling not only removed the threat of illegality and persecution but gave hasidim full liberty of assembly, and essentially put them in a better position than other Jews. This achievement, due entirely to the aforementioned individuals creating a climate of opinion in the committee that was favourable towards hasidim, would doubtless have encouraged them to further and more sophisticated political involvement, and this indeed soon happened.

Their next initiative was so different from the tactics employed in the investigation of 1823–4 that it is fair to describe it as a new model of hasidic politics. Our source here is a letter sent by Meir Rotenberg of Opatów to the Government Commission for Internal Affairs and Police, as described in Chapter 4, accusing the local police of harassing hasidim and obstructing their peaceful religious assembly, and also demanding immediate implementation of the above-mentioned decision to legalize the hasidic *shtiblekh* in full. Several details here are noteworthy. Above all, this was the first time that hasidim had gone on the political offensive, in that a hasidic leader had him-

<hr />

[22] AGAD, CWW 1871, pp. 187–90.   [23] Ibid. 213; AGAD, KRSW 6635, fo. 6.

self initiated contact with the authorities in an attempt to get them to change legal regulations and bureaucratic policy. To be sure, political activity of a defensive character did not disappear entirely (and moreover the difference between defence and offence was not always clear). However, the essential difference was that, from the mid-1820s on, the hasidim themselves increasingly encouraged the government to get involved in their disputes with the community; this was a major development since until then they had avoided contact with the government. A good example of this is the collective action of hasidim in Będzin from 1835 to 1843, which resulted in the dismissal of the rabbi and informer Abraham Hersz Rozynes despite the support he enjoyed from the secret police and the military authorities; another example is the somewhat later hasidic campaign to change the regulations for elections to the board of the Jewish community in Warsaw.[24]

A second characteristic feature of this new phase of hasidic politics was better co-ordination and a better long-term plan of action, introducing strategic actions and the conscious use of all available political means to reach specific goals. The details of the intervention of Meir of Opatów are not fully known, largely because he and Jakub Bereksohn Sonnenberg attempted to cover their tracks. Nonetheless, their success in avoiding responsibility for falsely charging local police and their effective manipulation of ministers and of bureaucrats used tactics later masterfully employed by Isaac of Warka, a topic to which I shall return shortly.

A third striking characteristic of Rabbi Meir's intervention in 1824–5 is that he himself, rather than merely one of his representatives, appeared officially in the role of *shtadlan*, though he certainly benefited from the advice of Jakub Bereksohn Sonnenberg. The testimonies of Rabbi Meir suggest that Bereksohn even used the latter's name without previous consultation, though, given their close co-operation, it is somewhat difficult to believe this.[25] It is noteworthy too that during this same period petitions continued to be submitted in the name of tsadikim, which further supports the idea that the name of Rabbi Meir on a letter to the Government Commission was not a mistake.[26] It would seem that the tsadik's direct intercession in this manner

[24] On the Rozynes affair and subsequent attempts by the hasidim in Będzin to dismiss him from the rabbinical office see AGAD, CWW 1481, pp. 6–307, 347–418; AGAD, CWW 1474, pp. 40–326; AGAD, CWW 1445, pp. 223–32; see also more in the next chapter. On the campaign concerning the electoral law in Warsaw, see AGAD, CWW 1727–9; see also Guesnet, *Polnische Juden im 19. Jahrhundert*, 403–10.

[25] Also during an interrogation run by Stanisław Staszic in 1824, Jakub Bereksohn served as an interpreter to Meir of Opatów, who 'because of lack of knowledge of Polish or even understandable German, was assisted by Jakub Bereksohn Sonnenberg, a businessman of the local factories'. See AGAD, CWW 1871, pp. 168–79.

[26] See AGAD, CWW 1871, pp. 114–17, 119–21; see also Boim, *Harabi rebe bunem mipeshisha*, ii. 633–40 (copy and the Hebrew translation). Alexander Zusya Kahana was also a hasidic

signalled a more general change in the hasidic attitude to political activism. The first half of the nineteenth century saw an increasing tendency to rabbinical involvement in political matters throughout eastern Europe, to the extent of creating what Eli Lederhendler has termed a 'rabbinical shadow government'.[27] Among the politically engaged 'rabbis' (Lederhendler places all religious authorities in this category) were, of course, hasidic leaders such as Israel of Różyn (Ruzhin), Menahem Mendel Schneersohn of Lubawicze (Lubavitch), and Isaac of Warka. Meir of Opatów, asked by the district commissar from Olkusz, Stefan Pomianowski, about the basis for his title of 'superior among the hasidim', responded that 'being of this sect and by its principles honoured, I am universally regarded by it as superior'.[28] For hasidim as for the rest of the Jewish community, the appearance of politically engaged religious leaders marked an essential ideological change. By signing a petition to a government commission, a tsadik changed from being just a spiritual leader to being the earthly political protector of his hasidim. In some ways, this was perfectly in line with the more general doctrine of hasidism, as developed by Rabbi Meir's teacher, Jacob Isaac Horowitz of Lublin, who stressed the responsibility of a hasidic master for the earthly well-being and everyday life of his followers. The change to accepting the new role of political protector might, then, have seemed to Rabbi Meir and his followers as minor and self-evident. However, when analysed retrospectively, it can be considered a symbolic turning-point that led to far-reaching changes in the image of Polish hasidism. Rabbi Meir accepted the concept of the tsadik as political leader and the image of hasidism as a movement with distinct political aims, and so, in certain aspects, a modern phenomenon. Of course this does not mean that after 1825 the rank-and-file hasidim began to understand contemporary politics and to see themselves as activists in a process of modernization. On the contrary, hasidic literature suggests that the understanding of political mechanisms was limited to ensuring protection and taking advantage of opportunities to exert influence through bribery, and that—far from considering itself as a modernizing movement—the self-perception of hasidism as anti-modernist actually increased in the latter half of the nineteenth century. At the same time, the image of hasidism as interested not only in the spiritual but also the material well-being of its followers was undoubtedly significantly strengthened in Poland by the political involvement of its leading representatives.

---

religious leader, in the broad sense; he was not a tsadik, only a communal rabbi in Siedlce and Płock, but he was an intimate associate of Simhah Bunem of Przysucha.

[27] Lederhendler, *The Road to Modern Jewish Politics*, 74; for more, see ibid. 68–83.
[28] AGAD, KRSW 6635, fos. 18–22; Mahler, *Haḥasidut vehahaskalah*, 498–501.

3. Triumph: Isaac Kalisz of Warka

The political activism of hasidic leaders in central Poland in what I have identified as its second phase reached a peak in the 1840s, after which further qualitative changes marked the beginning of a third phase. This third phase was personified in the political activity of the tsadik Rabbi Isaac Kalisz of Warka, communal rabbi and founder of the hasidic dynasty there, who was probably the best-known figure in the fledgling Jewish politics of the Kingdom of Poland in the mid-nineteenth century.[29] A disciple of David of Lelów, Jacob Isaac Horowitz of Lublin, and Simhah Bunem of Przysucha, he was one of the most influential Polish tsadikim in the nineteenth century. His most important trait, emphasized in both the hagiographical and the scholarly literature, was his 'love of Israel', a trait that also expressed itself in his numerous appearances before the state authorities in defence of Jewish interests in Poland and Russia. Active from the mid-1830s onwards, the range of his intercessions soon exceeded by far that of his predecessors.

Rabbi Isaac and his political activism are especially instructive because the available source materials allow us to reconstruct precisely how he worked. The surviving documentation enables us to understand not only the changes that took place in the realm of Jewish political activity during the nineteenth century but also the specific position that hasidism occupied in this process. In particular, we are able to trace the methods employed in hasidic political representation in the crucial period between the demise of the traditional *shtadlanut* of the old Polish–Lithuanian Commonwealth and the beginnings of a new Jewish politics in the last decades of the nineteenth century. The historiography of this period unfortunately displays very little interest in this subject, and the depiction of Rabbi Isaac's political activity and that of other *shtadlanim* of the time has not brought us any closer to understanding these issues as the accounts lack detail and a real comprehension of what was going on.[30]

The rabbi's best-known attempt at mediation is perhaps the instance when his contact with the great British philanthropist Moses Montefiore resulted in the latter presenting Tsar Nicholas I in 1846 with a request to improve the lot of Jews in the Russian empire and the Kingdom of Poland.[31]

[29] For critical historiographical writings, see Assaf and Bartal, 'Shetadlanut ve'ortodoksiyah'; for hasidic historiography see Bromberg, *Migedolei hahasidut*. Of the hagiographic works on Rabbi Isaac, the most important are Walden, *Ohel yitshak*, and [Zalmanov], *Sefer shemu'at yitshak*, 28–38, 369–85.

[30] For studies of the 19th-c. *shtadlanim*, mainly in the Russian empire, see Shochat, 'Ligezerot hagiyusim shel nikolai harishon'; Klier, 'Krug Ginzburgov i politika shtadlanuta v imperatorskoi Rossii'; Khiterer, 'Iosif Galperin'; and Horowitz, 'A Portrait of a Russian-Jewish Shtadlan'. For a more general account see Bartal, 'Moses Montefiore'.

[31] See Kandel, 'Montefiore w Warszawie', 74–94; Shatzky, *Geshikhte fun yidn in varshe*,

Figure 5.3 Putative portrait of Isaac Kalisz of Warka (1779–1848), communal rabbi and founder of the hasidic dynasty in Warka, and the best-known hasidic political activist in the Kingdom of Poland in the mid-nineteenth century; like the portrait of his teacher Simhah Bunem of Przysucha (Figure 3.2), this portrait's unskilled execution is typical of early hasidic iconography. Itschak Alfasi, *Haḥasidut midor ledor* [Hasidism from Generation to Generation] (Jerusalem, 1998), ii. 392

Hasidic accounts record Rabbi Isaac's contacts with the well-known Warsaw maskil and industrialist Jakub Epstein, with the equally well-known *mitnaged* Solomon Zalman Posner, and with several other influential figures of the Jewish bourgeoisie.[32] However, the surviving accounts tell us nothing of the methods or outcome of these contacts, though we know that the incident involving Montefiore ended in spectacular defeat.[33] There is only one hasidic story that correctly names the participants and circumstances of an attempt at mediation. This is the history of an intercession by Mordecai Motele Michelson of Kałuszyn, representing Rabbi Isaac, to prevent a planned burning of all copies of *Ḥoshen mishpat*, part of the *Shulḥan arukh*. The story is interesting as the key figure appears to have been Michelson rather than Rabbi Isaac; we know that he was a wealthy merchant with a good understanding of non-Jewish society who was the rabbi's follower and helper, and in many cases he even appears to have initiated a campaign and provided expertise on how to conduct it; possibly he also organized the wider circle of followers supporting

ii. 86–9; H. M. Rabinowicz, 'Sir Moses Montefiore and Chasidism'; Assaf and Bartal, 'Shetadlanut ve'ortodoksiyah'; Walden, *Ohel yitsḥak*, 14–16, nos. 27–8; Unger, 'Der sar montefiore un der vurker rebe'.

[32] Walden, *Ohel yitsḥak*, 7–8, no. 6; 25, no. 59 (on Posner); 53–4, no. 128 (on Epstein). See also M. M. Michelson, *Ma'amar mordekhai*, 16 (on Posner).

[33] David Assaf and Israel Bartal even suggested that the hasidic *shtadlanut* was, as a rule, ineffective: see Assaf and Bartal, 'Shetadlanut ve'ortodoksiyah', 89–90.

the rabbi's cause. The truth is that Rabbi Isaac was not always involved
directly in all the campaigns that bore his name, but he was certainly the
point of moral reference for those involved behind the scenes. This is
confirmed by hasidic and non-Jewish sources alike. If we are to believe
hasidic literature, Michelson, who was both wealthy and had good connections in Warsaw, was the most important member of the rabbi's circle.[34]
Independent sources confirm that Rabbi Isaac also had other wealthy friends
in Warsaw who were eager to give support, both in preparing legal petitions
and in his dealings with the government (this use of a 'support team' is the
first of a number of modern features of his activity that I discuss below).[35]
Paradoxically, however, other elements of the description of the *Ḥoshen
mishpat* affair seem to conflict with available and reliable archival data, and
are therefore probably inaccurate.[36] Fortunately, this is not always the case
where the activities of Rabbi Isaac and his circle are concerned. Government papers of the time allow us to reconstruct his intercessions in several
instances and to examine the methods he employed in his public activities.
Above all, however, they enable us to investigate the complex links between
the Jewish politics of the Kingdom of Poland and Polish hasidism. How did
hasidic intercession actually work? What resources and whose assistance
did the *shtadlan* draw on? How effective were his efforts? And, finally, what
consequences did they have for Jewish society in Poland, for the shape of
Jewish politics, and for hasidism itself?

Below I examine a number of cases in which Rabbi Isaac and his circle
were involved in negotiations with the authorities: the demarcation of Jewish
districts by *eruvin*; the inspection of Jewish butcher stalls; inconsistencies in

[34] See Walden, *Ohel yitsḥak*, 6–8; 64, nos. 2–6; 64, no. 163; T. M. Rabinowicz, *Bein peshisḥa
lelublin*, 521; M. M. Michelson, *Ma'amar mordekhai*, 9, 16–17. For more on Michelson see
Shamri, 'Rabonim, rabeim un parneysim in der kehile kalushin', 85–90. Evidence of
Michelson's positive relationship with the provincial authorities can be found in archival
documentation as well. See AGAD, CWW 1706, pp. 32–4; Central Archives for the History of
the Jewish People in Jerusalem, PL/82: Archives of Jakub Tugendhold [no pagination]: 8/20
Jan. 1844: *Do współwyznawców naszych*.   [35] AGAD, CWW 1481, p. 405.
[36] The hasidic version of the story is found in Walden, *Ohel yitsḥak*, 7, no. 5; M. M.
Michelson, *Ma'amar mordekhai*, 16. The essential archival sources covering the investigation of
Ḥoshen mishpat appear in AGAD, KRSW 6630, fos. 47–80; 6636, fos. 135–49; CWW 1435, pp.
445–997. For a brief and imprecise description of the events, see Mahler, *Hasidism and the
Jewish Enlightenment*, 198. However, the possibility that Isaac influenced the committee
investigating *Ḥoshen mishpat* cannot be ruled out. The chairman, Jan A. Radomiński, suggested
in his final report that the government should order a list of errata to be printed for all 2,380
copies of the book remaining in the Kingdom of Poland. Radomiński wanted the list to explain
that the rules of *Ḥoshen mishpat* were not relevant to Christians, and that it should be signed
by the rabbis of the large cities of Lublin and Kalisz as well as of the far smaller town Warka,
i.e. Rabbi Isaac. The government did not accept this suggestion. See AGAD, KRSW 6630,
fos. 46–80.

the divorce laws; and the rights of Jewish prisoners. All of these were of singular concern to the Jewish community of the time. By analysing the rabbi's work in addressing these concerns in the context of the local background I aim to present a vivid picture of this self-appointed leader and his role in developing hasidic politics in the Kingdom of Poland.

3.1 *Eruvin*

Jewish law forbids the carrying of objects between private and public domains, or between two private domains, on the sabbath. To circumvent this, however, individual private domains or private and public domains may be united as a single domain by establishing an *eruv* (pl. *eruvin*) around the area. This is done by demarcating a halakhic boundary using string, rope, or wires to supplement existing boundary markers and permitted natural features to create a continuous area; once the area is halakhically a single domain, objects can be carried within the designated area without violation of the sabbath laws. In practice there have been many centuries when *eruvin* were rarely encountered; cities were usually surrounded by walls or moats, which rendered *eruvin* unnecessary. (Walls and moats were recognized as naturally demarcating an intercommunal domain.) It was only in the nineteenth century, when many east European cities disposed of their previous forms of fortification, that the situation changed.

The question of the existence of *eruvin* attracted the attention of the government of the Kingdom of Poland as early as 1818.[37] Having consulted the maskil Ezekiel Hoge, the Government Commission for Religious Denominations and Public Enlightenment ruled that *eruvin* were an expression of Jewish superstition and instructed the voivodeship commissions that they should be dismantled.[38] However, it appears that the law was not actually enacted until 1834, when, for reasons unknown, the Jewish community board of Kowal in the voivodeship of Mazovia applied for confirmation of the existing right to erect *eruvin* in that city. The Voivodeship Commission of Mazovia passed the question on to the ministry, which, quoting police regulations for the removal of all elements disfiguring the city, recommended the dismantling of the *eruvin*. The government decision was announced in the official gazette of the Mazovian voivodeship (*Dziennik Województwa Mazowieckiego*) on 9 December 1834, prompting a wide-ranging campaign on the part of Rabbi Isaac of Warka (or, in reality, of his team). In the two-week period from 7 to 23 March 1835, requests to lift the ban on *eruvin* reached the Voivodeship Commission of Mazovia not only

[37] The most recent work on *eruvin* in the Kingdom of Poland is Bergman, 'The *Rewir* or Jewish District and the *Eyruv*'.

[38] See the report by Hoge in AGAD, CWW 1410, pp. 4–5; an English translation of some passages can be found in Bergman, 'The *Rewir* or Jewish District and the *Eyruv*', 92–3.

from Warka itself but from six other Jewish community boards in the vicinity: Brześć Mazowiecki, Grójec, Kałuszyn, Mszczonów (Amshinov), Rawa, and Sochaczew. The petitions were almost identical in format, and some were even in the hand of the same scribe—evidence of an organized undertaking.[39] That Rabbi Isaac and his circle were responsible is confirmed by a letter accompanying the petitions signed by 'Icyk Kalisz, rabbi of the town of Warka'.[40] In the letter, he presented precisely the same arguments as those put forward by the community boards: since 'by his calling' he 'maintained vigilance over the whole of the religion', he claimed that he had the right to represent Jewish interests more widely. Specifically, his argument was that the construction of *eruvin* was based not on superstition but on an important religious law; as such they should be permitted, given that the constitutional Organic Statute guaranteed tolerance and legal protection for all religions. He added that the construction of *eruvin* in the main streets would not be necessary if the law requiring the enclosure of vacant properties were to be properly enforced since the fences would perform the same halakhic function; *eruvin* would then be needed only on side streets, where they could be constructed less obtrusively—for example, with wires replacing strings (it isn't obvious why this would have been less obtrusive, but that is what he wrote). Halakhically it is not clear that fences would always have been a feasible solution, but it is certain that implementing the requirement of fencing vacant properties certainly was not. Thus Rabbi Isaac was on safe ground in shifting the blame to the authorities and claiming that official inaction gave the Jews no alternative.

We do not know which of the arguments proved effective, but the Voivodeship Commission passed Rabbi Isaac's petition on to the government authorities, and they in turn requested an opinion from the Jewish Committee.[41] On the recommendation of the Advisory Board to which it referred the matter (a common practice), the latter concurred with Rabbi Isaac's opinion and declared that the construction of *eruvin* was obligatory for Jews living in cities not surrounded by a wall or moat. It also added that the reason for the ban was misleading, as

> to date, there has never been a case, or at least no case is known to this committee, in which the hanging out of partitioning strings and chains on holy days, in accordance with the religious rules incumbent upon the Israelites, has occasioned popular disorder or turmoil, or where the existence of the aforesaid chains and strings, which are barely visible to the naked eye (they are, after all, thin and hung at a height), would disfigure the city.[42]

---

[39] See AGAD, CWW 1410, pp. 7–31.   [40] See *21.01; AGAD, CWW 1410, pp. 42–4.
[41] The one (outdated) study of the Jewish Committee and its Advisory Board is Kandel, 'Komitet Starozakonnych'. See also Eisenbach, *Emancypacja Żydów*, 193–6, 258–60.
[42] AGAD, CWW 1410, pp. 49–51.

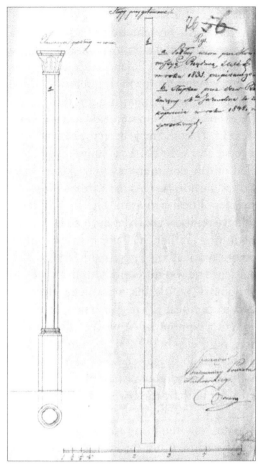

Figure 5.4 An official blueprint of the supports for *eruvin* to be erected in towns in the Kingdom of Poland, 1848. AGAD, CWW 1809, p. 76

On this basis the Government Commission permitted *eruvin* to be constructed in cities and towns which were not surrounded by a wall or moat.[43]

The decision did not end the controversy, and complaints about the 'Jewish chains' continued to be voiced in the 1840s, 1850s, and 1860s. However, the well-organized intercession by Rabbi Isaac, involving the participation of seven Jewish communities and using irrefutable constitutional arguments, was at least temporarily effective. Even if the right to set up *eruvin* was later questioned on a number of occasions, the ordinance of 8 July 1835 legitimizing their existence was always referred to as the basis for future government decisions.[44] Rabbi Isaac's intercession had been effective.

This is the earliest public action by Rabbi Isaac of which we are aware. Although it does not seem to differ significantly from the old style of

[43] Ibid. 52–3.
[44] More on this can be found in Kirszrot, *Prawa Żydów w Królestwie Polskim*, 13–14.

shtadlanut in the way that his later campaigns did, it does in essence give a
hint of the characteristics that would mark his subsequent activities. Thus,
although the basic method employed was the presentation of a petition—a
traditional method of classic *shtadlanut*—the radical innovation was that he
claimed to represent the entire Jewish population of Poland. Although in this
case (but not subsequently) he galvanized support for his intercession in the
form of petitions from Jewish communities, what is significant is that he was
acting not because a community (or even several communities) had commissioned him to intervene for their benefit, as would have been the case with an
old-style *shtadlan*, but quite the reverse: it was Rabbi Isaac himself who, as a
self-appointed representative, called on the communities to back his intervention and in so doing established his authority. This has cardinal implications for the very concept of Jewish political activism. The new style of
shtadlan was no longer aiming to achieve political goals determined by a community or a supra-community institution; rather, his 'authority' stemmed
from his self-perception as a representative of all the Jews. In other words, his
authority was self-bestowed. In that sense he was different both from the old
style of *shtadlan* and from contemporary politicians, who need electoral
authorization before they are able to act politically. This was a new situation:
the new style of *shtadlan* was no longer a communal employee but an independent political figure (if not quite a politician in the contemporary sense as
he was self-appointed). As we shall see, Rabbi Isaac's success lay not only in
what he achieved as regards the issue in question but also in that he came to
be accepted as a significant political actor both by the government and by the
Jews themselves.

Rabbi Isaac's reference to an obscure law requiring vacant properties in
cities to be fenced is also noteworthy because it put the enforcement of the
law relating to *eruvin* on a par with the enforcement of a law that applied to
the population more widely, and in this way he transferred part of the responsibility for the existence of *eruvin* to the municipal authorities. This marked a
significant change in the *shtadlan*'s use of legal argumentation because the
main objective was no longer to prove whether or not Jews had a right to
construct *eruvin*, but rather to show inconsistencies in the application of
the law of the land. This would be evident in later intercessions in a much
clearer form. However, the most important argument was that the existence
of *eruvin* was not a question of superstition but one of religious law, the
upholding of which was guaranteed by the constitutional Organic Statute.[45]
As it would have been difficult for the ministry to reject an opinion related to
constitutional religious rights expressed by a rabbi representing seven Jewish

[45] The 1815 Constitution guaranteed the freedom of all the faiths 'with no exceptions'. The
Organic Statute of 1832 (which supplemented and partially replaced the Constitution) reinforced these laws of religious freedom.

communities, it was forced to consult with the Jewish Committee. Rabbi Isaac would have foreseen this, as such consultation was common practice. It may well have been his intention to achieve this outcome, since a positive ruling was more or less guaranteed; notwithstanding the dubious reputation of the Jewish Committee in traditional historiography, the committee and its Advisory Board usually acted in the defence of traditional Jewish society and religious laws, particularly in the 1830s after the government had withdrawn from its radical plans to reform the Jews.[46] This was another characteristic of the new approach: the skilful manipulation of government procedures. In this case it allowed Rabbi Isaac to direct the case to the desired decision-making body. It should be noted that all these methods resulted from a very thorough understanding on the part of Rabbi Isaac's circle of the mechanisms of government.

We do not know whether the petition was the sole form of pressure brought to bear and we can neither confirm nor deny whether it was backed up, for example by the intervention of people with influence in government circles or simply by bribes. Nevertheless, Rabbi Isaac's petition created the conditions for a positive decision based only on the arguments he put forward and for administrative procedures to be put in place to review previous negative decisions. In both senses his intervention must therefore be considered a success.

3.2 Inspectors at Butcher Stalls (1839–1845)

Because the achievements of the *eruvin* campaign were gained with relatively little effort, hasidic leaders were encouraged to become involved in political activism in other areas. One of the most important of these was a campaign waged against provincial and central government authorities in the matter of the appointment of inspectors (Heb. *ne'emanim*; Pol. *wiernicy*) at Jewish kosher butcher stalls.[47]

In 1839 Rabbi Isaac and several other rabbis from the province (or in Polish *gubernia*, the administrative unit that had replaced the earlier voivodeships) of Mazovia petitioned the Government Commission for Income and Assets (in contemporary terms, the Ministry of Finance and the Treasury Department) to introduce ordinances to prevent the sale of non-kosher meat as kosher. The proposal was connected with a problem that had

---

[46] Some good examples of the Advisory Board's reports defending traditional Jewish society and its religious laws can be found in AGAD, CWW 1409, pp. 82 ff.; 1411, pp. 66–74, 81–90, 98–125; 1416, pp. 19–24; 1417, pp. 100 ff.; 1504, pp. 63–75; 1508, pp. 41–53; 1708, pp. 4–27; 1779, pp. 5–17; 1784, pp. 52–65.

[47] See AGAD, CWW 1412, pp. 6–512. The regulations issued by Rabbi Isaac regarding the inspection of kosher meat have also been noted in hasidic literature; see Walden, *Ohel yitshak*, 96, no. 13.

arisen in Warsaw: the right to collect the tax on kosher meat was held by a Christian called Karol Kurtz, who refused to submit to the control of the Jewish community,[48] meaning that the community lost its control over its butchers and over the *kashrut* of the meat being sold as kosher. The response of the Government Commission was that 'the establishment of separate butcher stalls for the sale of kosher meat, as well as the appointment of inspectors to ensure that non-kosher meat is not sold as kosher meat, is a matter for the police authorities in the city concerned'.[49] Accordingly, Rabbi Isaac submitted his petition to the provincial government together with the opinion of the Government Commission, but the latter was ignored, and his demand that inspectors be appointed was rejected. Rabbi Isaac then asked the provincial government of Mazovia to explain its decision, but as it had no reasonable explanation it applied to the Government Commission for Internal and Religious Affairs for a ruling on the matter. After a correspondence lasting some eighteen months, the Government Commission for Internal and Religious Affairs admitted that it was taking no action in the matter as the grievances had come only from a handful of rabbis in the province of Mazovia; that it knew of nothing similar in other provinces; and that the complaint presented was only that of an insignificant minority. This shunting between the provincial government and central government institutions while trying at all costs to avoid taking a stand on the issue was typical of the time. It was not only symptomatic of a general lack of willingness on the part of the bureaucracy at the end of the 1830s to take any kind of action, but also reflected the politics of expediency of a state that had withdrawn from its plans to 'reform the Jews' after the 1831 uprising and was aiming, above all, at maintaining the political and social status quo.

Rabbi Isaac was undeterred by the official evasion and continued to press his case. A year or so later (1841) he sent the Government Commission letters from the rabbis and community boards of nearly all the provincial capitals, i.e. Siedlce, Chęciny (there was no Jewish community in nearby Kielce), Radom, Płock, Kalisz, Łomża, and Lublin, confirming that he acted in their name and that they had long since granted him power of attorney in dealings with the authorities regarding the sale of kosher meat.[50] This confirmation that he had been granted power of attorney was particularly significant not only because he was the very first rabbi to be recognized as representing all Polish Jews, but because he attained this status despite being a hasidic leader.

One should remember at this juncture that from the time that the Kingdom of Poland had been established its most prominent politicians, and

[48] AGAD, CWW 1409, pp. 221–41; 1412, pp. 228 ff.
[49] Ibid.   [50] See *21.07; AGAD, CWW 1412, pp. 198–9.

Stanisław Staszic in particular, had consistently aspired to abolish all supra-communal Jewish institutions on the grounds that they strengthened the cause of Jewish separatism and threatened their own plans for reform. This was one of the most characteristic traits of the politics of the Kingdom of Poland regarding the Jews, significantly distinguishing it from the political line of virtually all the other states of central and eastern Europe: Jewish attempts to establish regional rabbinical offices, central or provincial Jewish assemblies, or any other form of political representation were consistently rejected.[51] It was only in the 1840s, when the government backed down from its plans to 'civilize' the Jewish people, that this policy changed. Rabbi Isaac saw the opportunity and availed himself of it, which brought him a twofold advantage. First, he forced the government to revisit its decision concerning the appointment of inspectors as a decision of a general nature. Second, he became the recognized representative of all Polish Jews; this status initially derived from a power of attorney granted by the communal rabbis of provincial capitals, but as will be explained later, he unilaterally extended this one-off authorization as granting him the right to represent all Jews—a status he claimed despite having no formal authority to do so. The recognition he achieved in being granted the power of attorney was his personal success but came to be regarded as an achievement for the hasidic movement—even if the power of attorney granted him was both limited and conditional (it was explicitly to deal with this matter only), nor was there a specific connection with his hasidic beliefs and practices. However, the fact that a tsadik had become the representative of Polish Jewry for the first time in nearly half a century (let us not forget that there had been hasidic emissaries during the Four Year Sejm of 1788–92, and similar plenipotentiaries in the early years of the Duchy of Warsaw *c*.1807) undoubtedly enhanced the prestige of the movement and increased its appeal to potential adherents. In later letters, Rabbi Isaac emphasized that he had the mandate of all Polish Jewry 'as a rabbi in whom the Jews place their trust'. It appears that all this was not lost on the authorities, in that, rather than communicating their decisions to Jewish community boards via regional institutions as in the past, they actually began to treat him as the representative of the Jewish community and corresponded with him directly.

Interestingly, the government even ignored the fact that Rabbi Isaac demanded recognition of his power of attorney on the basis of the letters of rabbis of provincial capitals, who were, after all, in the eyes of that same government not entitled to represent the Jews of their province or even of their own Jewish communities. (Legally, the rabbi of a provincial town was not a 'provincial rabbi' as no such position existed.) Rabbis were merely

---

[51] See for example the fascinating debate on the project of calling a Jewish 'synod' and the hostile voices of Jan Lipiński and Julian Ursyn Niemcewicz: AGAD, CWW 1431, pp. 72–97.

functionaries, not political figures; they did not represent their communities, even in religious matters: that was the role of the community board. In fact, in 1840 the government was still categorically refusing to recognize the right of rabbis to represent their Jewish communities. This was revealed in response to a petition submitted jointly by Rabbi Isaac and Warsaw's chief rabbi, Solomon Lipschitz, regarding the law *de non tolerandis Judaeis* that prohibited Jews from settling in a town granted this privilege.[52] A year later the situation changed completely, and Rabbi Isaac was officially permitted to have audiences even with the viceroy of the Kingdom, General Ivan Paskevich: on 30 December 1843 he headed a delegation of nine rabbis and community leaders to discuss the rural settlement of the Jews.[53] In the same month he was one of the eight rabbis who visited the viceroy to request the abolition of Jewish conscription.[54] One can conjecture that Rabbi Isaac's rapid success in becoming the recognized representative of the Jewish community in Poland was partly due to the convenience this offered the Polish authorities. Among other things it allowed them to regard such a representative as responsible for maintaining social order among the Jews—a basic aim of politics in the 1840s—thereby relieving them of their own responsibilities in this regard.

One may well ask why the rabbis and representatives of the various Jewish communities entrusted Rabbi Isaac with such prerogatives, especially as it is clear that not all of them were keen on the idea of having a politically involved representative, and a hasidic one at that.[55] For example, one of the signatories, Moses Hirsh Weingarten, a communal rabbi of Siedlce from 1833, was known for his opposition to the movement and his continual clashes with the local hasidic community in Siedlce.[56] Similarly another signatory, Meshulam Solomon Zalman Ashkenazy, a communal rabbi of Lublin, was an active *mitnaged*. Two other signatories seem to have belonged to the non-hasidic camp, even if they were not active opponents of hasidism.[57] What motivated them to accept Rabbi Isaac's involvement? It would appear that he made them a generous offer: in return for helping them to regain control of the supply of kosher meat, he asked only for the temporary and limited right of

[52] See AGAD, Sekretariat Stanu Królestwa Polskiego 199, fo. 534.

[53] See the Central Archives for the History of the Jewish People in Jerusalem, PL/82: Archives of Jakub Tugendhold [unpaginated]: 8/20 Jan. 1844: *Do współwyznawców naszych*. The delegation included Rabbi Isaac of Warka; Judah Bachrach, rabbi of Sejny (*mitnaged*); Mendel Lipmanowicz, rabbi of Zduńska Wola (a hasidic *rebbe*); Raphael Lewenthal, rabbi of Zakroczym; Moses Teitelbaum; Mordekhai Motele Michelson (the most important of Isaac's aides); S. S. Ehrlich; M. E. Morgenstern of Lublin; and Józef Safir.

[54] See T. M. Rabinowicz, *Bein peshisḥa lelublin*, 523, although this could be a corrupted version of the former event.

[55] For more on rabbinical opposition to political involvement, see Bacon, 'Prolonged Erosion, Organisation and Reinforcement'.   [56] See AGAD, CWW 1784, pp. 41–67, 190 ff.

[57] On Eliyahu b. Josef Sorozon, rabbi of Łomża until 1842, see AGAD, CWW 1561, pp. 38–76; on Hayim Tsevi Jakubowicz, deputy rabbi in Kalisz, see AGAD, KWK 710.

Figure 5.5 Ivan Paskevich (1782–1856), who conquered insurrectionist Warsaw in 1831 and subsequently became the viceroy of the Kingdom of Poland, was a popular figure in the political tales of Polish hasidim. Lithograph, second quarter of the nineteenth century, signed '[Nicolas-Eustache] Maurin, Lith[ographie] de Thierry frères succ[esseu]rs de [Godefroy] Engelmann à Paris'. Biblioteka Narodowa w Warszawie, Zbiory Ikonograficzne sygn G. 424

representation. As already mentioned, the letters of support signed by the provincial rabbis did not give him any long-term authority. For the government, however, the limits on his power of attorney were of no importance: this was merely another case in which Rabbi Isaac represented Jewish society in matters of general interest, only this time he had the additional support of the provincial rabbis. Each such case must have strengthened his position in the eyes of the government such that ultimately he was acknowledged as representing *de facto* the entire Jewish community.

Equipped with his power of attorney, Rabbi Isaac submitted a proposal to the Government Commission recommending that kosher meat be sold separately from non-kosher meat and that an inspector be appointed to ensure this, 'in accordance with the way it already is in the Warsaw District on the basis of the recommendation of the provincial government of Mazovia'.[58] He

---

[58] *21.06; AGAD, CWW 1412, pp. 192–3. This recommendation by the provincial government has not been preserved, so its connection with the above-mentioned report, in which the provincial government refused to take any action, is unclear.

emphasized that this would help Jews keep the laws of their faith, and would thereby help maintain the constitutional right to religious tolerance. It would also increase the income from the tax on kosher meat, while at the same time the rabbi and the inspector would be able to ensure that the sale of giblets (which were legally not considered meat) did not incur this kosher tax, which would be beneficial to poorer sections of society and could consequently relieve some social tensions. Thus this time Rabbi Isaac's approach highlighted the benefits to the government of accepting his recommendation: an increase in tax income, improved social order, and consistency with constitutional law.

The renewed proposal was dealt with by the Department of Religious Affairs, the Department of General Administration, and the Legal Section of the Government Commission for Internal and Religious Affairs. Ultimately, on 2 May 1843, the commission adopted Rabbi Isaac's postulates, with the stipulation that inspectors could only be brought in where meat was being sold by Christians; if the meat was being sold by a Jew, that in itself should authenticate it as kosher. If he betrayed the trust of his co-religionists, the Jewish community board could withdraw his licence. A further provision was that separate stalls for the sale of kosher meat could be constructed only in Jewish districts, and only in those areas in which there were no public butcher stalls built from municipal funds as that would reduce the city's income. (This was because revenue from the tax on kosher meat went to the state, while payment for the use of municipal butcher stalls went to the city.)

However, that was not the end of the matter. Because the ruling allowed for inspectors to be brought in only where kosher meat was sold by Christians, Rabbi Isaac soon applied to have the decision overturned. His argument was that the price of kosher meat was so much higher than that of non-kosher meat that it was not possible to trust the honesty of the butchers and allow them to be judges in their own affairs. Also, he added, 'on more than one occasion the Jewish butchers, for the most part of the low and ignorant classes, have exploited the community'.[59] This time, the Government Commission took into account a number of opinions (including those of a magistrate and the Jewish community board of Warsaw) and, a year later, responded favourably to the request.

In 1844 and 1845 Rabbi Isaac had cause to intercede again in this matter because of difficulties encountered in carrying out the government edicts. His complaint was that in the province of Podlasie (later renamed Siedlce after its capital) the authorities had decided to permit inspectors to be brought in only after the discovery by the Jewish community board of an irregularity concerning a Jewish vendor. Rabbi Isaac argued that the board

[59] AGAD, CWW 1412, p. 436.

would never investigate butchers itself as that would arouse hostility which would in turn impede investigation. In justifying his request he once again emphasized that the introduction of inspectors would increase the revenue from taxation since without proper inspection people were reluctant to eat meat, suspecting it might be not kosher: when the consumption of meat fell, so did the income generated by the tax on meat.[60] This time too, the government acknowledged the logic of the proposal and even accepted its claim that the interpretation of the provincial government was erroneous.

Rabbi Isaac had thus succeeded not only in protecting Jewish interests but also in being seen as contributing to law and order. Overcoming the official torpor of provincial governments and of three central government commissions, he had persuaded them to recognize him as the true representative of the entire Jewish population of the Kingdom of Poland; to make rulings in his favour; and, on three occasions, to overturn previous rulings—all this despite the lack of any document confirming his status. His outstanding success was due, above all, to his consistently competent application of official procedures, to his accurate understanding of the changes in Jewish politics in the 1840s, and to his ability to turn these changes to his advantage. At the same time, his emergence as a self-appointed leader was itself undoubtedly a catalyst in changing the shape of Jewish politics, even if only because the government authorities were relieved to be able to delegate to him responsibility (even if only partially and unofficially, which is why it was never proclaimed as such) for the internal affairs of the Jewish population.

3.3 Divorce Law (1840–1842)

In 1836 a new law was introduced in the Kingdom of Poland. Henceforth, marriages were to be authorized and conducted by the appropriate religious authorities, and merely registered by the state authorities. However, divorce now came under the jurisdiction of the civil courts rather than the religious authorities. This created an impossible situation, whereby a person granted a divorce by a civil court could not remarry because the religious authorities required a religious divorce.[61]

Rabbi Isaac recognized the potential for influencing the state regulations to the benefit of the Jewish people as he saw it, and decided to take advantage of it. In March 1840 he made a submission to the provincial government that pointed out the inherent inconsistency, noting that the new law did not state whether the parties were required to obtain a religious divorce before or after the civil formalities. This situation, he claimed, would cause many diffi-

---

[60] See *21.08; AGAD, CWW 1412, pp. 508–9.

[61] See Kirszrot, *Prawa Żydów w Królestwie Polskim*, 242–7. For a more general examination of Jewish marriage and divorce in the politics of imperial Russia, see Freeze, *Jewish Marriage and Divorce in Imperial Russia*.

culties,[62] whereas requiring the parties to obtain a religious divorce prior to approaching the civil authorities would have benefits for the state and the Jewish community alike. The problem was that without evidence of a religious divorce having been granted, a rabbi could not authorize a second marriage, even if a civil divorce had been obtained, which inevitably created problems for the community, for the state, and for the individuals involved.

The provincial government did not respond immediately but sought a ruling from the Government Commission for Justice. The commission, consistent with its usual practices, refrained from giving a proper answer; it merely pronounced that it was of no import to the law when, or even whether, a religious divorce had been granted. The provincial government did not accept this answer, fearing (and justifiably so) that the absence of regulation could lead to the parties neglecting to obtain a civil divorce and only obtaining a religious one. It therefore ruled that a religious divorce could take place only after a civil divorce had been granted and applied to the Government Commission for Internal and Religious Affairs for a confirmation of the ruling. That commission gave a similarly evasive answer, claiming that the submission had no legal basis because the resolution of the provincial government clearly stated that a religious divorce could only take place after the civil divorce. This was an odd response because it took the very decree questioned by Rabbi Isaac as the legal basis for a decision in the matter. In the words of the provincial government, 'only when the divorce proceeding has been legally adjudicated by the court will Jews be able to perform the religious divorce ritual'.[63]

Undeterred, Rabbi Isaac appealed to the government, which in turn consulted both the appropriate government commissions. Both responded that Rabbi Isaac had a rightful grievance: the provincial government's decision was illegal, and its response was contrary to the decision of the ministries. Both similarly emphasized that the law did not specify that a religious divorce could be given only after a secular one, and since a religious divorce was so important to Jews, the law should be interpreted in such a way that a religious divorce should be an indispensable condition for granting a civil divorce. However, the government chose in this instance to exercise its prerogative and ignore the recommendations of the commissions, and the provincial government therefore informed Rabbi Isaac of a new ruling, viz. that the order in which the civil and religious divorces were granted was simply not an issue to be regulated by the state.

Ostensibly Rabbi Isaac had this time achieved only partial success, in that he had been unable to force the authorities to change the law so as to require

---

[62] AGAD, CWW 1446, pp. 198–211; CWW 1450, pp. 85–122, 233–41, 286–97.
[63] AGAD, CWW 1446, pp. 202–3.

a civil divorce to be granted only after a religious divorce had been secured. But had that actually been his intention, and was he really seeking a legal settlement of the situation? From his point of view, it was not critically important whether a civil divorce could be obtained without a religious one, or how matters of state were to be regulated. What was of far greater importance for him was that the Jews should be freed from the troublesome obligation of having to have a civil divorce before they could obtain a religious one. The lifting of this restriction would mean, as the authorities rightly surmised, that Jews would not have to apply for a civil divorce at all. It would relieve them of a costly legal obligation and, above all, remove the threat of penalty for non-compliance. This latter situation burdened numerous members of the community, as well as the rabbis responsible for the proceedings. With the new ruling Rabbi Isaac thus achieved what had in truth been his fundamental aim, and his satisfaction with it is confirmed by the fact that he wanted to have the resolution disseminated among all the rabbis in the Kingdom.[64]

Here too his success was due to adroit use of the law: his grasp of the inconsistencies in the marriage and divorce laws in force; his skilful use of all avenues of the official administration; and his familiarity with government regulations, to which he effectively referred in his proposals and counter-proposals. By using the legal system to the Jews' advantage, he forced the government to take a decision that conflicted with the original intentions of the lawmakers. Jews thenceforth ceased to apply for civil divorces, and although the local authorities alerted the central government to this and pointed out that this weakened government authority, the regulation was not reversed until 1858, sixteen years after Rabbi Isaac's victory.[65] This case is possibly the best example of the influence brought to bear by a hasidic leader on a law promulgated in the Kingdom of Poland.

3.4 Jewish Prisoners (1840–1841)

Rabbi Isaac was equally prepared to intervene in more minor matters. As early as 1829 he had interceded in the case of Jews of Zambrów imprisoned in Łomża on the basis of a false accusation,[66] and there was a further case involving Jewish prisoners in 1840–1.

There were two major problems. The first was that, by law, all prisoners could be conscripted to the Russian army on completing their sentence. The second problem was the impossibility of observing Jewish ritual law in prison. Where enforced conscription was concerned, Jews in the Kingdom of Poland

[64] See AGAD, CWW 1450, pp. 286–97.
[65] See AGAD, CWW 1451, pp. 432–3 (grievances of the provincial government); CWW 1453, p. 40 (decree of the Government Commission for Justice).
[66] See *Mikhtavim*, ed. Mandelbaum, 215.

were generally exempt from compulsory military service because they could instead pay a recruitment tax, and this privilege also extended to criminals of the first and second degree (i.e. those with a sentence of no more than a year). However, the law did not clarify the position of embezzlers and debtors whose sentences exceeded a year. In 1840 Rabbi Isaac and Hersz Birnbaum, a wealthy deputy to the Jewish community board of Góra Kalwaria (Ger),[67] referring specifically to Order No. 12067 of the Administrative Council of 1 December 1837, applied directly to the viceroy, General Ivan Paskevich, with a proposal that embezzlers, who could not be considered more dangerous than persons sentenced for crimes of violence, should also be included in the exemption. The viceroy accepted Rabbi Isaac's argument and ruled that only repeat offenders who received a second term of imprisonment lasting more than a year would be subject to obligatory military service. Hence the threat of conscription was limited to major recidivist embezzlers and did not apply to those convicted for a first time.[68] The important point here is that Rabbi Isaac went straight to the viceroy, who recognized his right to represent the entire Jewish population in Poland and was prepared to issue an order of a general nature despite the fact that since the petition had come from an individual it was not clear whether it represented the position of a wider group. This situation again provides confirmation that Rabbi Isaac was in practice the *shtadlan* of the Polish Jews, recognized as such by the authorities even though he had no official appointment. In this capacity, he and his circle could monitor the functioning of state law regarding the Jews on an ongoing basis, identifying contradictions in the different provisions and intervening in such matters at the highest levels. His long-term strategy of establishing himself as the representative of Polish Jewry in matters of both general and specific importance was proving fruitful.

Rabbi Isaac's next campaign concerned the transportation of Jewish prisoners on sabbaths and Jewish festivals. In July 1841 he wrote to the Government Commission for Internal and Religious Affairs to protest against the practice of transporting Jewish prisoners on Jewish holidays and of forcing them to shave their beards and *peyes*.[69] The letter is particularly interesting for its ineptitude—in this respect it was glaringly different from previous letters. It is addressed to the Government Commission 'for Internal Affairs and Police', though this name was ten years out of date at the time; there are errors of grammar and spelling; the line of argument is loose and lacking in logic and, most importantly, it is not supported by legal citations, apart from a general citation of the freedom of religion guaranteed by the constitution (already revoked by Tsar Nicholas I in 1832 after the defeat of

---

[67] On Birnbaum's activities see *Sefer me'ir einei hagolah*, 305.
[68] See *21.09; AGAD, CWW 1435, pp. 424–5.
[69] See *21.10; AGAD, CWW 1435, p. 435.

the 1830–1 uprising) and an unspecified ukase, or edict of the tsarist government. The only clearly articulated statement is the assertion that the transportation of Jews on the sabbath and the shaving of their beards and *peyes* was
contrary to Jewish law and should be forbidden. As one might have guessed,
this poorly prepared proposal was rejected out of hand. The commission
responded that the objections were too generalized and that without
information about actual cases of violation of religious freedoms there was
nothing to investigate. It appears that Rabbi Isaac did not pursue the matter
any further.[70]

Despite its faults, or indeed because of them, the letter is interesting
because it provides evidence of Rabbi Isaac's knowledge of Polish. More
broadly, it also shows something of his dealings with the Polish authorities.
Although we cannot prove that the petition is in Rabbi Isaac's hand, it is clear
that his linguistic ability can have been no better than that of the author, as
otherwise he would have corrected the mistakes. This leads us to suspect
that statements in hasidic sources concerning Rabbi Isaac's knowledge of
'Polnisch' are erroneous or exaggerated, and thus possibly other information
is too. We learn, for example, that Rabbi Isaac was a manager of Temerl Sonnenberg's properties in Ruda; but as a manager he would have had to have
known Polish in order to communicate successfully with the peasants.[71] We
can therefore assume that even if he was officially the manager of Temerl's
properties, his duties were not really of a managerial nature, but perhaps
merely formal supervision; perhaps the position was even a concealed form of
patronage by Temerl? The clumsiness of the letter also strongly suggests that
the highly successful letters already mentioned concerning the divorce law or
the appointment of inspectors for butcher stalls cannot have come directly
from Rabbi Isaac's hand; rather, he was lending his authority and the weight
of his reputation to legal and editorial work done by others at his behest.
Presumably it was the temporary absence of these experts that resulted in the
failure of Rabbi Isaac's intervention in this instance. As far as I am aware, this
is the only one of his interventions to have ended in such a fiasco, which in
itself underscores the overwhelming effectiveness of his efforts and political
activities (or those of the people on whose skills he relied).

It is worth mentioning that many hasidic leaders engaged in political
activity had a limited knowledge of Polish, at least in the first half of the
nineteenth century. Although hasidic sources may claim that a particular
tsadik had mastered Polish, the level of mastery was often relative; they may

[70] See *21.11; AGAD, CWW 1435, p. 435.
[71] On Rabbi Isaac's linguistic abilities, see Walden, *Ohel yitshak*, 63, no. 161; 17, no. 23; 19,
no. 43. On the Polish-language ability of Jewish administrators in 18th-c. Poland–Lithuania,
see Rosman, *The Lords' Jews*, 174–9. On the administration of Temerl's properties by Rabbi
Isaac see Walden, *Ohel yitshak*, 54, no. 131; Dynner, *'Men of Silk'*, 107–8.

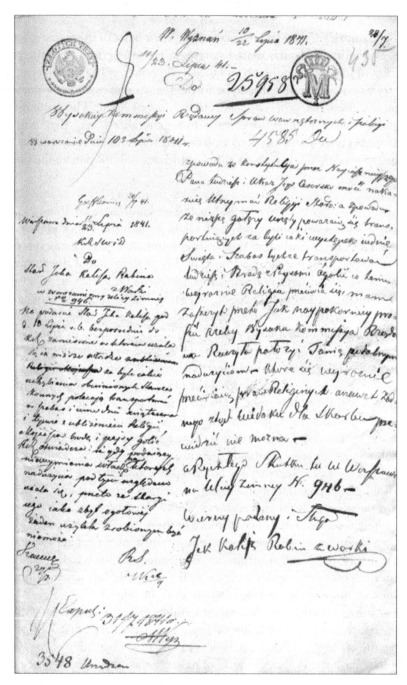

Figure 5.6 Letter issued by Isaac of Warka (1841) to the non-existent Government Commission for Internal Affairs and Police. Possibly in his own handwriting, it supplies an interesting example of the scribe's incompetence in cursive script, grammar, and style. AGAD, CWW 1435, p. 435

have known more than some of their followers, but still not have been able to use the language freely in speech or writing. The document discussed above as probably having been written by Rabbi Isaac is an example of this. Similarly, it seems that even the Maggid of Kozienice, Israel ben Shabbetai Hapstein, known in hasidic tradition for weaving Polish sayings into his Hebrew prayers, was not actually able to communicate in the language;[72] certainly, the citations of his Polish sayings in hasidic literature are stylistically and grammatically incorrect.[73] The one exception among Polish tsadikim appears to have been Solomon Rabinowicz of Radomsko, who conducted a lively correspondence in Polish and is known to have written his own curriculum vitae in the language.[74] As he himself remarked: 'Besides Hebrew I also have adequate German and Polish.'[75] This fact was exceptional enough to have been noted by the authorities of the Jewish community in Radomsko when he was a candidate to become the communal rabbi there.[76] There is also no doubt that Simhah Bunem of Przysucha knew non-Jewish languages, as his handwriting displays a stylish German calligraphy (see Figure 3.7 above). The tsadik Henokh Lewin of Aleksandrów (Alexander) also wrote Polish well.[77] Interestingly, neither Solomon of Radomsko nor Simhah Bunem of Przysucha belonged to the group of hasidic leaders who were especially engaged in politics (as we have seen, Rabbi Simhah Bunem actively avoided politics). Among the tsadikim who emerged as politically active and who could neither speak nor write Polish was Meir of Opatów. In 1824 when he was summoned before Staszic and the committee investigating the legality of hasidism, he was accompanied by Jakub Bereksohn Sonnenberg as translator because he had neither fluent Polish nor even 'comprehensible German'.[78] The Polish of Abraham Landau of Ciechanów was of a similar level: his opponents often described him as 'lacking ability in the Polish language'.[79] The charge was certainly apt: it is true that he was able to sign his name in Polish, but his handwriting was extremely clumsy.[80]

[72] This can be inferred from the memoirs of Leon Dembowski, who described a visit to Israel of Kozienice by Prince Adam Jerzy Czartoryski. According to Dembowski's eyewitness account, the prince asked Israel questions in Polish, German, and even in Hebrew, but Israel did not answer any of them. See Dembowski, *Moje wspomnienia*, 55.
[73] See e.g. T. M. Rabinowicz, *Bein peshisḥa lelublin*, 184.
[74] See AGAD, KWK 710, pp. 292–3, 295; APŁ, APRG 2559, pp. 692–5, 904–7.
[75] AGAD, KWK 710, p. 292.   [76] Ibid. 293.   [77] See APŁ, APRG 2491, pp. 122–3.
[78] See *11.66; AGAD, CWW 1871, pp. 168–79; see also AGAD, CWW 1871, pp. 181–6; Wodziński, 'Sprawa chasydymów', 235–9; see also above Ch. 3, §5. The comment about the lack of 'comprehensible German' refers, of course, to Yiddish as 'corrupted German'. The well-known Polish novelist and journalist Józef Ignacy Kraszewski described the linguistic abilities of the tsadik from Stepan in Volhynia, Israel Dov Ber, very similarly: he could 'speak neither Polish, nor Ruthenian, but only Hebrew and corrupted German': Kraszewski, *Wspomnienia Wołynia, Polesia i Litwy*, 49–50.   [79] See *13.06,*13.11; AGAD, CWW 1666, pp. 246–9, 268–9.
[80] See APP, Komisja Województwa Płockiego / Rząd Gubernialny Płocki 17, fo. 165ʳ.

Moreover, although his followers defended his candidature, saying that he was a 'man of honour and a strong talmudist',[81] they never sought to deny his linguistic incompetence (this too was the reason his father-in-law Daniel Landau had to act as expert witness before the civil tribunal; see Chapter 4, §1 above). Interestingly enough his opponent, Alexander Zusya Kahana, knew Polish well. This was, however, the exception not the rule among Polish hasidic leaders, and his supporters triumphantly stressed this fact in promoting his case.[82]

This almost universal lack of knowledge of Polish among politically engaged tsadikim allows us to make the judgement that their *shtadlanut* did not go beyond recruiting aides among influential circles of Jewish society, who then had to represent the interests of the tsadik before the state authorities. The circle of influential advisers supporting Rabbi Isaac was thus typical of other hasidic *shtadlanim* too. This is of great importance for our understanding of the nature of hasidic politics in the Kingdom of Poland. It suggests that the political successes of several well-known hasidic *shtadlanim*, as revealed in the surviving archival material I have discussed, were due to the efforts of broad circles of hasidic supporters and sympathizers rather than simply to isolated individuals. Even if the political activism described here was limited to the elite of the hasidic movement and was not the mass politics it would become half a century later, it seems unquestionable that it was an enterprise shared by a relatively wide circle of that elite and by economic and spiritual leaders alike. Hasidic political activism depended on the combined efforts of a significant number of first-rank religious leaders, such as Meir of Opatów, Isaac of Warka, and Alexander Zusya Kahana (but also many others, as we will see), interacting with a large group of wealthy and influential figures sympathetic to the hasidic movement, such as Berek Sonnenberg, his wife Temerl and their son Jakub, the Warsaw businessmen Fayvel Kamienicer and Hersz Sztamm, Juda Leib, a wealthy merchant from Chełm, and Hersz Birnbaum, a wealthy deputy to the Jewish community board of Góra Kalwaria (Ger). The range of these connections suggests that the political activism described here was central to hasidic life in Poland rather than something separate from, or at best marginal to, it.

4. The Third Phase

Consideration of these interventions by Rabbi Isaac allows us to make a reasonably accurate analysis of the specific characteristics of the new phase of hasidic political activity that they represented. A key feature is that he was

---

[81] See *19.25; AGAD, CWW 1734, p. 206.
[82] Proof of Alexander Zusya Kahana's linguistic competence can be found in APP, AmP 568, p. 72.

acting not on behalf of the hasidic community but rather on behalf of Polish Jewish society as a whole. Moreover, in dealing with the Polish authorities Rabbi Isaac did not present himself as a hasidic leader, but rather as 'a rabbi in whom the entire Jewish nation places its trust' and 'whose true vocation is to oversee the religion as a whole'.[83] This was a revolutionary change in hasidic politics and a characteristic feature of this new phase. Hasidic political activity was no longer limited to fighting a rearguard action to defend narrow hasidic interests but had developed into full-scale, active engagement with the government on a range of issues. An excellent example is Rabbi Isaac's approach to Moses Montefiore, visiting Poland and Russia in 1846, to ask him to intercede with Tsar Nicholas I concerning the obligation to perform military service and the ban on traditional Jewish dress (or more precisely its external elements: hats, caps, coats, stockings, and shoes)—a task that Montefiore indeed took on.[84] A number of the details relating to the meeting between the two men are unclear (the various sources even give different locations for example), but unquestionably the topics at issue were of importance to Jewish society as a whole, not just the hasidic community. One might think that the ban on traditional dress concerned hasidim more than other Jews, and so in a sense was 'hasidic',[85] but in reality this was not so. As Agnieszka Jagodzińska has demonstrated in an excellent study, although the law of 1846 banned Jewish dress, exceptions were made for religious functionaries (defined as rabbis and 'spiritual leaders', a term which apparently included *dayanim*); elders (meaning all people over the age of 60); and those who chose to pay for an exemption.[86] For most Jews, then, the problem was one of finance rather than the degree of religious observance; there is no reason to assume either that hasidim were poorer than others or that they were keener than others to purchase exemptions.[87] The regulations were tightened in 1850, in that there were no longer any exemptions except for religious leaders; at this point the

---

[83] AGAD, CWW 1409, pp. 221–41; 1412, p. 228.

[84] Assaf and Bartal, 'Shetadlanut ve'ortodoksiyah'; H. M. Rabinowicz, 'Sir Moses Montefiore and Chasidism'.

[85] This is, in fact, a dominant view in the hasidic tradition (see e.g. *Sefer me'ir einei hagolah*, 304–5), as well as in traditional Jewish historiography.

[86] AGAD, KRSW 6643, fos. 1–102. See further Jagodzińska, *Pomiędzy: Akulturacja Żydów Warszawy w drugiej połowie XIX wieku*, 86–102; see also Klausner, 'Hagezerah al tilboshet hayehudim'.

[87] The issue of the socio-economic standing of hasidism in the 19th c. remains to be investigated, but the once dominant claim by Raphael Mahler (*Hasidism and the Jewish Enlightenment*, 7–10) that 19th-c. hasidism was a movement of the oppressed masses is often challenged today. My claim is based on my as yet unpublished sample analysis of prosopographic materials from Aleksandrów (Alexander), Częstochowa, Koniecpol, and Włocławek between 1820 and 1837. See AGAD, CWW 1734, p. 224; Archiwum Państwowe w Toruniu, Oddział we Włocławku, Naczelnik Powiatu Włocławskiego 438, pp. 178–9; APŁ, APRG 2512, pp. 117–20; Archiwum Państwowe w Toruniu, Oddział we Włocławku, Akta miasta Włocławka 319.

hasidim who were better organized than other members of the Jewish community, took the lead in fighting the ban. But Rabbi Isaac could not have known that the matter would develop in this way at the time of Montefiore's intercession in 1846.

Rabbi Isaac's concern for the community as a whole rather than just for the hasidic community with which he personally identified is clear from the archival sources documenting his activity from 1835: his representations concerning the right of local Jewish communities to establish *eruvin*; his interventions regarding the establishment of special kosher controls for kosher butchers; his efforts to relieve Jews of having to obtain a civil divorce before a religious one; and his attempt to improve the rights of Jewish prisoners. In all these matters the beneficiary was Jewish society in the broadest sense, not just hasidim. It is not my intention here to question or guess at Rabbi Isaac's motives; I readily accept that his goal was essentially the defence of 'the people of Israel' as he saw their interests and defined them in his representations on their behalf. However, independent of these external goals and his sincerity in pursuing them he probably had another motive, and from our point of view a more important one: he wanted Jews to take a more positive attitude to hasidism.

Political activity in the state arena gained, then, an additional dimension, becoming in a certain sense the instrument of an internal Jewish struggle concerning the position of hasidism within Jewish society. Rabbi Isaac certainly had sound religious motives for his campaign to establish the legal right to construct *eruvin* in all Jewish neighbourhoods and ensure that the sale of kosher meat was adequately supervised; his success in doing so, however, also established his own credentials as a saviour of the Jewish people in Poland and, by implication, the credentials of the hasidic movement with which he identified. The involvement of many people in the various campaigns, including numerous rabbis and community elders, suggests that his activities must have been widely known. People would have been well aware of who was protecting their interests in such matters as oppressive divorce laws, the prohibition on *eruvin*, or the enforced conscription of prisoners. Thus it seems reasonable to assume that the successful lobbying by Rabbi Isaac and other hasidic leaders would have influenced the standing of the hasidic movement among the Jewish population. Well-known examples of other hasidic 'defenders of Israel', such as Levi Isaac of Berdyczów, unequivocally confirm this claim.[88] This must surely have influenced the movement's self-image and nascent ideology, and even more so the dynamics of its development, though I have not found strong evidence to support such a

---

[88] See for example an interesting analysis of the communal activity of Levi Isaac of Berdichev in Petrovsky-Shtern, 'The Drama of Berdichev'.

claim. Nevertheless there is much circumstantial evidence that suggests that there was a connection between the success of hasidic political initiatives and the movement's growth. Thus, between the late 1820s and the 1840s—that is, precisely when the hasidic *shtadlanim* were having their most spectacular successes—hasidism grew at an unprecedented rate and extended its sphere of influence; available numbers suggest a threefold growth rate, from around one-tenth of the Jewish population in the late 1820s to around one-third of the total in the 1840s.[89] Second, and even more significant, in the late 1830s and 1840s, hasidim for the first time aspired to take over positions of power in a number of Jewish communities throughout the country.[90] This was certainly a result of the growth in their numbers, but it was also because of their increasing confidence in their political strength and communal standing— a self-assurance doubtless stemming from the growing success of hasidic political representation. Moreover, as I shall demonstrate in the next chapter, the fact that the political interventions undertaken by Rabbi Isaac and other hasidic *shtadlanim* were visible both at the state level and at the level of individual communities meant that rank-and-file hasidim would have had confidence that their leaders could safeguard their political interests—a factor that undoubtedly lent further impetus to the movement's growth.

Finally, the career of Rabbi Isaac itself suggests that his political success was of major importance for his emergence as a successful hasidic leader. Although hasidic tradition suggests that the circle of his followers was moderate, if not meagre, in size, contemporary sources suggest quite the opposite. According to testimonies gathered in 1846 by missionaries from the London Society for Promoting Christianity amongst the Jews, it was due to his influence in Warka that the town was almost entirely hasidic—so much so that it was popularly known as the 'hasidic capital' of Poland.[91] This is corroborated by evidence from other communities in the mid-nineteenth century in which Warka hasidim were dominant among local hasidic groups.[92] Other testimony from the same source suggests that Warka was one of the most popular sites of hasidic pilgrimage in Poland: more than 4,000 hasidim are said to have spent Rosh Hashanah at Rabbi Isaac's court there in 1846. This compares with about 1,000 hasidim who gathered at the court of Israel of Różyn in 1826; about 3,000 who gathered around Rabbi Meir in Przemyślany; and a similar number who gathered at the court of Israel of Różyn in Sadagóra (then in Bukovina) on Yom Kippur of 1844, a time when he was at the peak of his popularity and widely regarded as the most venerable leader of his generation.[93] In 1852 it was expected that up to 5,000 pilgrims

[89] See more on this in Wodziński, 'How Many *Hasidim* Were There in Congress Poland?'.
[90] For extensive evidence and further discussion, see Wodziński, *Haskalah and Hasidism*, 126–35.   [91] AGAD, CWW 1457, p. 575.   [92] See e.g. APŁ, Akta miasta Pabianic 31, n.p.
[93] Assaf, *The Regal Way*, 157, 352, regards these figures as inflated.

might arrive for Rosh Hashanah at the court of Menahem Mendel of Kock, the most popular of the Polish tsadikim.[94] Even if the figures for Warka were inflated (and the other figures probably were too), the fact that they were inflated by contemporaries would suggest the existence of a popular perception of massive support for Rabbi Isaac and his approach to hasidism. To conclude, none of these arguments is strong enough to demonstrate unequivocally the impact of hasidic political activism on the development of Polish hasidism. Taken together, however, they make a plausible case.

The second characteristic feature distinguishing Rabbi Isaac from earlier *shtadlanim* is the increased professionalization of his campaigns and his use of more modern and accurately targeted mechanisms of political activity. The highly competent circle he gathered round him maintained excellent personal contact with representatives of the government. Its members understood the process of petitions and the relative importance of the decisions of the various government bodies so could skilfully take advantage of all administrative options: they oriented themselves skilfully in the legal regulations; they demanded formal decisions, and appealed against them as necessary to higher authorities; they demanded explanations of the legal basis for the decrees enacted; and they agitated to ensure that decrees were implemented. Rabbi Isaac's political activity further suggests excellent knowledge of changes in the political climate and their consequences. In his most successful campaign—concerning the question of inspectors of kosher butcher stalls—he succeeded in overcoming the bureaucratic inertia of the provincial government and three departments of the Government Commission and persuaded provincial authorities and ministers to recognize him as the *de facto* representative of all of Jewish society in the Kingdom of Poland; to hand down decisions in accordance with his own positions; and to overturn previous decisions. It was the professionalism that underlay these achievements, unknown in earlier hasidic *shtadlanim*, that established Rabbi Isaac's position as the unchallenged political representative of traditional Jewish society in Poland, accepted as such by the government.

Achieving such spectacular success, however, demanded that Rabbi Isaac and his team of assistants should immerse themselves in the mechanisms of contemporary politics. The success they achieved in turn encouraged further participation in politics, and further 'modernization' of the parameters of their political involvement. In the 1840s and 1850s, we therefore see the apogee of intense hasidic involvement in contemporary politics, in a process that I described earlier as 'defensive modernization'. This intensity manifested itself both in the number of tsadikim who were politically active and the number of effective interventions. Rabbi Isaac was by no means the

---

[94] APP, AmP 883, p. 109.

only tsadik to be politically engaged: both hasidic tradition and archival sources confirm the similar, though not so spectacular, involvement of other hasidic leaders, such as Menahem Mendel of Kock, Abraham Landau of Ciechanów, Henokh Henikh Lewin of Aleksandrów (Alexander), and, above all, Isaac Meir Alter of Góra Kalwaria (Ger), known as the Gerer Rebbe. The last of these became famous for his political involvement in 1831, when he actively supported the anti-tsarist uprising in central Poland. In the early 1840s he played an active role in the committee for the agricultural colonization of the Jews.[95] His later co-operation with the conservative wing of the Polish Haskalah—maskilim unhappy with the radicalism of young integrationists—in intervening to limit the reform of traditional Jewish education at the end of the 1850s was also an essential part of his political activity.[96] This intervention, like the analogous action conducted jointly with the maskil Abraham Winawer, ended with complete success. The Gerer Rebbe's effectiveness, based on his ability to employ unusual methods and create unexpected alliances, suggests that he was a loyal student of the methods of his friend and close collaborator Rabbi Isaac. In fact, hasidic tradition stresses that he was Rabbi Isaac's closest aide in his political interventions, and after the latter's death he indeed became his political successor.

Although Rabbi Isaac and the Gerer Rebbe were by no means the only hasidic leaders who were politically active in the mid-nineteenth century or who used the most up-to-date political methods, it does not mean that hasidism became a modern movement. On the contrary: while it accepted that its representatives in the political arena would use modern methods in their political activities, in general terms it rejected the values of the modernizing world and clung to its anti-modernist self-perception. This ambivalent approach can also be seen in the interventions of Rabbi Isaac.

I have not yet mentioned that one of the characteristic features of hasidic political activity was the tendency to present the tsadik as the prime mover. Stories about political interventions thus constitute an important part of the hagiography of many nineteenth-century tsadikim, not only in Poland.[97] In all these stories, the tsadik appears as the sole representative of Jewish society before the government, a leadership position paralleling his position within hasidic society as also represented in hasidic hagiography.[98] Of course, con-

[95] A well-known appeal for Jewish agricultural settlement was signed, among others, by Isaac of Warka and Isaac Meir Alter of Góra Kalwaria (Ger). See Frenk and Zagorodski, *Di familye dawidsohn*, pp. xii–xx; Gelber, *Hayehudim vehamered hapolani*, 38–9.

[96] See Jastrow, 'Bär Meisels, Oberrabbiner zu Warschau', *Hebrew Leader*, 15/25: 2; American Jewish Archives in Cincinnati, Marcus Jastrow letter to Jacob Raisin, n.d.

[97] On Isaac Meir of Góra Kalwaria (Ger) see e.g. Alfasi, *Gur: hameyased ḥidushei harim*, 84–99; Walden, *Ohel yitsḥak*, 36, no. 86; 73–4, no. 182; 121–2, no. 282; *Sefer me'ir einei hagolah*. On Menahem Mendel Scheersohn, see e.g. Schneersohn, *The 'Tzemach Tzedek'*.

[98] See *Sefer me'ir einei hagolah*, 100–3, no. 206–12; 304–6; Walden, *Ohel yitsḥak*, *passim*, but

temporaries would have known that the tsadik did not act alone but usually relied on his circle of highly capable people. Numerous, though subtle, mentions of this can be found in the hasidic literature on Rabbi Isaac to which I have already referred. But essentially, all political activity was undertaken in the tsadik's name, authorized by him, and attributed to him in its entirety. It might even be said that the tsadik acted through his followers. Moreover, in hasidic tradition, this activity acquired supernatural dimensions, and its mythologization followed.

Another typical way of legitimizing the adoption of modern political methods was by presenting them as being in the tradition of the archetypical *shtadlan*, the biblical Mordecai, interceding for the Jews in the court of King Ahasuerus.[99] Interestingly, the hasidic literature on Rabbi Isaac, and indeed his own writings, exploited this analogy extensively.[100] The use of the figure of Mordecai went beyond a simple parallel with his ancient predecessor, however. In an exegetical comment on the book of Esther (Esther 3: 6), Rabbi Isaac equated the biblical Mordecai with the people of Israel, and by implication the political intentions of Mordecai (and of any other *shtadlan*) with the deepest will of the people of Israel.[101] Here one can see an attempt to legitimize the authority of the tsadik theologically and politically by identifying it with the will of the people of Israel.

The simplest way to mythologize the political activity of hasidic leaders was to blur the border between real activities and miraculous interventions.[102] This is a feature of numerous hasidic stories, especially those relating to Rabbi Isaac. For example, one story tells of a time in the reign of Viceroy Paskevich when various (unspecified) anti-Jewish decrees were enacted in Warsaw that normal methods of intercession were powerless against. One night, Rabbi Isaac approached the palace of the viceroy (of course in disguise, so the viceroy's guards would not recognize him). Suddenly, he vanished from sight, all the gates opened before him, and he entered the palace and simply destroyed the decrees.[103] Other hasidic sources add that Rabbi Isaac usually employed natural methods, for that was how his great predecessor, the biblical Mordecai, acted; however, when these methods turned out to be insufficient, like Mordecai he achieved his objectives through miracles.[104] The very structure of the story applies an analogy that

also texts of the hasidic hagiographical historiography, e.g. Bromberg, *Migedolei haḥasidut*, 40–7.

[99] On the motif of Esther and Mordecai as a traditional metaphor for *shtadlanut* see Walfish, *Esther in Medieval Garb*; Guesnet, 'Die Politik der "Fürsprache"', 69–72.

[100] See e.g. Walden, *Ohel yitsḥak*, 7, no. 6; Zalmanov, *Sefer shemu'at yitsḥak*, 193–5.

[101] See Zalmanov, *Sefer shemu'at yitsḥak*, 193.

[102] See e.g. Walden, *Ohel yitsḥak*, 36, no. 76; 83, no. 96.

[103] Bromberg, *Migedolei haḥasidut*, 46–7.   [104] Walden, *Ohel yitsḥak*, 36, no. 76.

blends reality and miracle. The actual circumstances (the reign of Paskevich), the time, and the precise location (Warsaw, the palace of the viceroy) appear here alongside unclear elements (undefined decrees) and a completely miraculous event. The nature of the intervention is sanctioned by biblical tradition (Mordecai too behaved in this way). We observe, then, a kind of cycle: from the image of the tsadik as an apolitical religious leader, to his appearance in the world of politics, to the introduction of politics into the religious sphere through the mythologization of this politics. In this way, the apparently contradictory images of the tsadik as a political player participating in the complexities of contemporary politics and the tsadik as a leader of a conservative community, loyal to the traditions of its fathers, are reconciled. The hasidic movement received the full benefit of the skill of its representatives at operating in the sphere of contemporary politics but remained ideologically an anti-modern movement and, in its own view, non-political.

The effort to create a doctrinal link between hasidic engagement in modern political activity and the traditional image of hasidism is also clear in the teachings of Rabbi Isaac, or at least in the sayings attributed to him. To be sure, none of the sources attributed to him was published during or even close to his lifetime, so one can reasonably suspect that they are at best anachronistic. But this does not weaken the value of these sayings for our analysis. Like any folk proverb, the sayings transmitted in the name of Rabbi Isaac can be regarded as having the collective authority of the broader hasidic community of the time. This is because, regardless of their origin, it is only those sayings that gain the acceptance of the collective and are recognized as important that survive in oral transition and are thereby transmitted to later generations. In this sense, regardless of whether they originated with Rabbi Isaac or not, the sayings attributed to him reflect the mentality of the hasidic collective of his time and thus offer an insight into broader features of the political culture and issues of concern to that collective.

Like many other hasidic leaders, Rabbi Isaac devoted much attention in his teachings to belief and trust in God as necessary attributes of piety.[105] A particularly important issue for him, however, was the question of reconciling this teaching with rational activity and so with natural solutions in the realm of human activity to solve political problems. The conflict between reason and belief finds its most complete expression in the midrashic interpretation of the story about the alleged lack of trust shown by the biblical Joseph, who instead of trusting God sought to escape from slavery by intercession, and for this sin was punished with an extension of his slavery for another two years.[106] Does the attempt to solve problems by normal means,

---

[105] Zalmanov, *Sefer shemu'at yitshak*, 80–4, 225, 268–70. For more on *bitahon* in hasidic doctrine, see Werblowsky, 'Faith, Hope and Trust', and Schatz-Uffenheimer, *Hasidism as Mysticism*, 85–9.   [106] Zalmanov, *Sefer shemu'at yitshak*, 80–4.

as opposed to divine intervention, constitute a sin? Rabbi Isaac's efforts to address this apparent contradiction theologically took several forms. First, he developed the concept that 'each instance of divine salvation occurs naturally, and the individual is obligated to search for naturally occurring methods of intervention'.[107] Second, he distinguished between intervention in individual instances, where problems could be solved through prayer and belief, and concerns of the general community (*kelal yisra'el*), which demanded intervention in the form of political activity.[108] Most interesting, however, and at the same time most characteristic, is his interpretation of the analysis of the case of Joseph: he suggested that there exist two levels of trust. Ordinary people should actively seek ways to solve their problems because action is an expression of the belief that God will respond by providing a solution.[109] A true tsadik such as Joseph, however, has the obligation to trust God completely, and so in his case looking for natural ways out of difficulties is a sin—even though such intercession would normally be the fulfilment of God's commandment and thus not sinful. This explanation only ostensibly solves the contradiction regarding the kinds of activity associated with belief, however, since it forces us to question the status of Rabbi Isaac's political activity in his own view. Did Rabbi Isaac see himself as belonging to the first category or to the second? In my opinion the evidence does not justify ascribing to him the view that he was not a true tsadik. Rather, his arguments should probably be understood as proof that, despite various attempts at resolving the contradictions between reason and belief, ambivalence in the hasidic world towards political activity was never eliminated in nineteenth-century Poland, even in the teachings of the most political tsadikim; in reality, the hasidim experienced great difficulty in coming to terms with the new forms of political activity. Their later successes, then, are even more worthy of admiration.

5. Digression: Corruption

In analysing the political strategies employed by Rabbi Isaac (and indeed other representatives of Jewish interest groups), one cannot ignore the method known in the Polish of early modern times as 'Jewish swords'—that is, bribery. Bribery had always been one of the more effective tools of the *shtadlanim* and their nineteenth-century successors, and must have assumed major significance in imperial Russia and its satellites, i.e. those states in which the bribe was an established and sanctioned institution.[110] In Poland

[107] Zalmanov, *Sefer shemu'at yitshak*, 80–4.
[108] Ibid. 194–5; Walden, *Ohel yitshak*, 7, no. 6.   [109] Zalmanov, *Sefer shemu'at yitshak*, 81–4.
[110] On bribes distributed by the *shtadlanim*, see Ury, 'The *Shtadlan* of the Polish–Lithuanian Commonwealth', 285–7, and also Lederhendler, *The Road to Modern Jewish Politics*, 33. On corruption in imperial Russia and the Kingdom of Poland, see the innovative study by Andrzej

this was not an import from tsarist Russia: the tradition reached back to the Polish–Lithuanian Commonwealth, in which taking bribes from representatives of Jewish society was so common that it led to the conviction that 'Whoever speaks in support of a Jew has obviously taken a bribe; whoever speaks against a Jew obviously wants to take a bribe.'[111] Jews also commonly bribed judges (as indeed did others), as an anonymous author of a satire from the period of the Four Year Sejm wrote: 'I'm not naming names, but I'm saying that Jews / Have their way with the courts, so we mock them / He who has a solid case fears the court / Knowing that his opponent can be bought off.'[112]

There appears to be little doubt that Rabbi Isaac and his aides would have practised bribery, particularly given the universality of corruption in imperial Russia. For example, in the campaign that he and other hasidic leaders waged against Abraham Hersz Rozynes (see Ch. 6, §5.2), he is alleged to have said, 'My loss cost them 40,000 złotys; they can pay even more and destroy me completely.'[113] Incidents mentioned earlier were similar; for example, in Płock in 1818, thanks to small bribes to local police authorities, the hasidim were able to keep their *shtibl* going despite the formal decree closing all prayer rooms. Corruption in some form characterized the *modus operandi* of many officials at different levels, as in the aforementioned incident in Płock in 1829, when hasidim managed to corrupt the Voivodeship Commission, and in the very similar affair in Pilica in 1835, when the voivodeship authorities were exceptionally supportive of the hasidic candidate for rabbi. In Kazimierz Dolny in 1862 the provincial government's bias towards the hasidic candidate for rabbi, Jacob ben Moses Goldman, was so explicit that the ministerial authorities were forced to admonish it formally and to demand an explanation for its incomprehensible position.[114]

The Jews themselves, and not only hasidim, were convinced of the universality and power of bribes. Thus, when Alexander Zusya Kahana tried to demonstrate the legitimacy of his own position when he stated in 1824 in his petition to the Government Commission: 'Each of the dignified men sitting on the Government Commission may be convinced of our righteousness since we did not try to find ways to influence them to support our wishes, as Jews usually do',[115] he unwittingly also demonstrated the widespread belief in

Chwalba, *Imperium korupcji w Rosji i Królestwie Polskim*. See also some interesting cases described in Chimiak, *Gubernatorzy rosyjscy w Królestwie Polskim*, 141–9. Of the older literature on the subject, see especially Torte, 'Das russische Beamtentum'; Zaionchkovsky, *Pravitel' stvennyi apparat samoderzhavnoy Rossii*; Christian, 'Vodka and Corruption in Russia'.

[111] *Diariusze sejmowe z wieku XVIII*, ed. Konopczyński, ii: *Diariusz z r. 1746*, 175.
[112] 'Zwierciadło polskie dla publiczności', 249.
[113] AGAD, CWW 1481, p. 404.   [114] AGAD, CWW 1632, pp. 95–245.
[115] AGAD, CWW 1871, p. 89. See also numerous denouncements of hasidic bribes in AGAD, CWW 1731, mainly from the years 1858–9.

the efficacy of bribes. However, even taking bribery for granted and considering its possible contribution to the efficacy of hasidic activism, we should not overrate it, for a number of reasons.

First of all, after putting aside the Western myth of a 'Byzantine bureaucracy' in eastern Europe, we must distinguish between the practice of bribery and its influence on the ultimate decision. Administrative practices in the Russian state (which were also in force in Poland, though to a lesser degree) were such that a bribe was needed to set a matter in motion; it was not necessarily a guarantee of a successful outcome.[116] Without a bribe, the issue would languish at the lowest level and never reach the desk of anyone responsible for taking a decision. Bribery was thus not an exceptional method of guaranteeing a favourable decision, but rather a 'tax' required to set a procedure in motion. Of course, this does not mean that bribes as such did not exist as a means of influencing an official's decision. The history of the Russian empire is filled with them: 'down payments' intended to facilitate acceptance into a school, or to obtain a concession for building railroads, or to gain a position (including a ministerial one). But one cannot conclude from the fact of a bribe being given that it necessarily had any influence on the outcome. More probably, it was simply an incentive to make an official take care of the case.

Secondly, we must remember that not all spheres of public life were affected by corruption in the same way. Andrzej Chwalba, in his innovative study of corruption in late imperial Russia, came to the conclusion that offering and accepting bribes was most commonly encountered with reference to the following 'services' and 'products': positions in the administration, passports, school examinations, police and court 'protection', censorship, recruitment, licences, and government concessions. Payments varied from 3 roubles for crossing a border to 100,000 roubles for a ministerial position. What is worth noting is that all of these involved individual matters. A second category of bureaucratic situations to which a bribe might have applied was the payment required to set a procedure in motion, but without any guarantee of a positive outcome (as discussed above). A third situation, generally impervious to bribery, mainly concerned decisions of a political nature, or general, as opposed to individual, rulings.[117] Most of Rabbi Isaac's interventions belonged to this 'political' category. Bribery in such situations was very difficult, if not close to impossible, because decisions were made collectively and cases could easily be transferred between decision-making bodies; a bribe to just one party would be ineffective. Furthermore, such cases were subject to strict supervision from higher political authorities (as the cases discussed above show), so decisions made on flimsy grounds could be overruled. As a

---

[116] See Chwalba, *Imperium korupcji w Rosji i Królestwie Polskim*, 136–8.   [117] Ibid. 217.

result, an unofficial rule concerning bribery came into being, requiring that an official should not accept bribes for cases he could not settle. Thus, even if an official accepted a bribe in connection with one of the matters mentioned above, the case had to have strong legal arguments on its side so that the official would be able to explain his behaviour convincingly to his superiors; in other words, the bribe only worked with cases that could anyway be won. Paradoxically, an awareness of the nature of corruption in nineteenth-century Russia prompts us to see the influence of a bribe on the final shape of a decision as being of less significance, while simultaneously acknowledging the universality of corruption and the important role bribes played in setting a decision-making process in motion.

In this context, one needs to consider critically the frequent references to bribery in traditional Jewish literature (hasidic and non-hasidic) and in historical works on Jewish politics and social life in eastern Europe. I would say that for many historians, 'corruption' became the mythologized explanation for any phenomenon that seemed too complex to comprehend. For example, according to the well-known Israeli historian Shmuel Ettinger, large bribes were the only reason (or at least the only reason mentioned) for the horrendous debts of the Jewish communities in the eighteenth-century Polish–Lithuanian Commonwealth.[118] I would suggest, on the contrary, that the repeated references to bribes in traditional sources simply suggest a lack of awareness of other methods of intervention, rather than their non-existence. We have seen from the above examples that *shtadlanim* certainly used other means of achieving their objectives, but ordinary people may not have been aware of them. 'Bribery' was a category that people could understand, a shorthand way of characterizing their representatives' political activism—even when no bribe was involved. The masses simply did not, and could not, have any idea of the actual nature of their leaders' activities. Bribes were the most obvious explanation, in particular because they constituted the only form of intervention in which a broad section of the population participated, that is, in public collections for funding for the *shtadlanut*.[119] Since bribery involved all sectors of the population in imperial Russia (even the very poor), and since coercion of the Jewish population was a frequent occurrence, knowledge of it would have been very common among Jews.

One should also not forget that in hasidic literature bribery was presented in the context of a moralizing tale in which the stereotyped adversary—corrupt civil officials—was ethically inferior to the representatives of Jewish society. In large part, these tales were heuristic devices to show that the

---

[118] Ettinger, 'The Modern Period', 764.

[119] See Walden, *Ohel yitshak*, 53–4, no. 128, on public collections for the 'prevention of evil decrees [*gezerot*]'. This work also provides an interesting rationalization for them: see p. 83, no. 196.

Jewish world was superior to non-Jewish society, and they should be understood as such, rather than as credible historical sources.

What is most important is that, in the four cases discussed above, archival
records show no evidence of external factors unrelated to the merits of the
case itself influencing the decisions made by regional or central state authorities. Quite the contrary: the surviving materials often allow us fully to reconstruct the rational decision-making mechanism (such as in the regulation of
divorce laws or the presence of inspectors in butcher stalls) and show it to be
completely in order. Besides, the interventions by Rabbi Isaac often passed
through multiple administrative levels—from the local municipal office and
city police department, through the provincial government and government
commissions, right up to the Administrative Council. It is true that the
petitioner did not have to bribe all the officials involved in the case. It was
sufficient to bribe just one of them, who would then distribute the payment
among all those involved. In cases such as those discussed above, however, it
seems unlikely that Rabbi Isaac would have had the means to do so: the sum
of money required to bribe the viceroy, several ministers, and many other
officials was far too high to make this enterprise worthwhile, especially given
that the issue did not touch on the existence of the hasidic movement, but
merely on matters of amelioration. This was particularly true in matters as
delicate as general legal regulations of a political nature that involved a large
number of high-ranking bodies.

In considering the significance of corruption, its influence on decision-
making processes, and the social perception of this phenomenon, we must
also recall one other issue. The Jewish people were generally perceived as
defenceless and so particularly susceptible to any kind of extortion. Collecting bribes from a Jewish individual or group was, then, a common and easy
procedure and, it seems, socially sanctioned. One of the Warsaw maskilim,
Jan Glücksberg, complained in 1831 that 'Israelites, whose hearts have grown
hard and whose feelings of dignity have been trampled on by this behaviour,
have thus far been exposed to arbitrary behaviour and abuse so that officials,
even high officials not worthy of the name of citizens, might make even
the smallest profit; the officials have used Jews as a way to increase their
incomes'.[120] The affair of Mojżesz (Mateusz) Józef Birnbaum, a convert and
collaborator with the secret police in Warsaw in the 1820s who specialized in
extortion from Jews, illustrates the universality and motives of this administrative procedure. As Birnbaum himself stated, his zeal in extorting money
from Jews was not so much a result of his dislike of his former co-religionists,
but rather of the fact that they were particularly easy targets and gladly paid
up because they wanted to avoid becoming embroiled in scandal.[121]

---

[120] [Glücksberg], *Rzut oka na stan Izraelitów*, 1–2.
[121] See a detailed description of this once well-known case in Mochnacki, *Sprawa Birnbauma*.

The frequency of attempts at extortion should not obscure the fact that the connection between such attempts, and even actual extortion, and official progress in the matter under consideration might be uncertain or even non-existent. A well-known story concerning Birnbaum's activity in this regard is indicative. One of his most infamous actions regarding hasidim took place on the margins of a well-known investigation in 1823–4. In February 1824 the Government Commission for Religious Denominations and Public Enlight-enment published a decree which, we recall, banned all hasidic *shtiblekh* and pilgrimages to tsadikim but did not institute administrative measures to implement this and forbade the use of force (see Ch. 3, §2).[122] This decree was quickly handed down to the provincial administration, and in March 1824 Viceroy Zajączek confirmed it, repeating again the ban on using force.[123] Soon, however, Birnbaum and his collaborators spread a rumour in Warsaw that St Petersburg had issued a decree ordering the arrest of all hasidim; they were to be kept in custody, and their beards and *peyes* were to be shaved. Of course, the content of the decree was quite different, but persecution and (illegal) arrests began immediately, with the goal of extorting bribes.[124] This appeared to the witnessing Jews to be an example of an attempt to extort money from Jews to ease the execution of the ruling or, in the longer term, to overturn the ruling. In reality, however, this campaign was the independent initiative of officials who had no ties with the investigation, so the bribes handed over by the hasidim were completely useless as they did not even reach the officials investigating the matter, either before the ruling or later (as we remember, the matter did not end with this decree). Thus, despite the universality of corrupt procedures, the link between the bribe and the matter to which it related could be, and often was, illusory.

All of the above allows us to assume that bribes, even if they did play a certain (and even at times significant) role, were not the most important element in the decision-making process, but, at most, worked together with other methods important to the overall success of the undertaking. These were (*a*) organized petitions, which showed Rabbi Isaac to be the acknow-ledged representative of the whole Jewish community; (*b*) legal arguments; (*c*) arguments pointing to the fiscal and social benefits for the government; (*d*) proposals that were superficially legal and which reduced the govern-ment's responsibility for resolving social tensions within Jewish society; (*e*) the exploitation of administrative procedures, such that through skilful use of the law and administrative procedures Rabbi Isaac forced the administra-tion to do things that were contrary to its own objectives. Above all, it was the

[122] See *11.29; AGAD, KWK 702, p. 136; see also AGAD, CWW 1871, p. 49.
[123] See *11.35; AGAD, KRSW 6634, fo. 249; see also AGAD, CWW 1871, fos. 52–3; Mahler, *Haḥasidut vehahaskalah*, 484–5. This has been described in detail in Ch. 3.
[124] Mochnacki, *Sprawa Birnbauma*, 64–6.

petitions and legal arguments that were ultimately of key importance to favourable decisions being made by the government bodies. And as we have seen, in the one instance when Rabbi Isaac's petition was poorly written, it did not achieve the desired result.

6. The Local Context: Conclusions

The schema introduced above as a means of characterizing the evolution of hasidic political activism is typological rather than strictly chronological. The fragmentary nature of the sources does not allow for much more; only for the intensive activity of Rabbi Isaac's times are the sources somewhat more extensive. One should remember, too, the natural limitations of any attempt at systematization. The events described here took place between the second half of the 1810s and the mid-1840s, and so encompass no more than thirty years—a relatively short period in considering the evolution of political activity since many of the people involved were active for all or almost all of this period, and their attitudes certainly did not all evolve in accordance with the schema I have presented. Especially in activities such as those described here, the influence of individual, and even incidental, factors (as for example the talents of leaders such as Rabbi Isaac, or the degree of corruption among individual officials) were also essential. The point of the schema, then, is to reconstruct the evolution of the collective political consciousness (though 'collective' does not cogently describe the actions of a relatively small group of activist politicians), rather than that of individuals. As always, this type of generalization carries a significant risk of error, but I think the risk is worth taking. My understanding is that the political activism undertaken at this time by hasidic leaders derived from a common consciousness and can thus be termed political culture, with all the ambiguity of the term. I would not dare to call this hasidic political culture; it must be said that there is not enough to distinguish it from other traditional forms of political culture in Jewish eastern Europe. But exclusive to hasidism in the Kingdom of Poland was the direction of its evolution from 1815 to 1848. As the result of factors both external (numerous attempts to reform Jewish society undertaken by the government from 1815 to 1830, the interest of the government in hasidism, and investigations into this issue) and internal (the rapid rate of hasidic expansion in central Poland), hasidic leaders turned during this period to the political tools of a modernizing state. The successes and often surprising advantages they achieved in the early phase of their involvement led to an intensification of activity. As their political skills developed, their achievements increased and they were encouraged to broaden the scope of their efforts. In this sense one can say that the new political categories mentioned at the beginning of this chapter—the concept of people being subject to the law as individuals rather than with reference to an estate; citizens' rights guaranteed by law; the universalization of law and administrative procedures, the depersonification and professionalization of the state administration, and so forth—all played their part. But other factors were at work too: the move away from Enlightenment ideas of reform and amelioration to the policy of maintaining the status quo and the anti-liberal conservative shift of post-Napoleonic Europe all influenced Polish hasidism, or perhaps more precisely, influenced the political consciousness of hasidic leaders, both lay and religious. Notwithstanding this development in their political thinking, however, these leaders managed to preserve the distinctively anti-modernist character of the hasidic community, which continued to see itself as upholding the traditional world of its forefathers. Incredibly, this amalgam of a traditional self-image and modern political behaviour turned out to be functionally efficient and even exceptionally lively.

The question that emerges here is whether the development of the activities of the Polish tsadikim was unique or simply an example of the more general political processes under way in eastern Europe in the middle of nineteenth century. It is possible that they were neither.

The analysis by David Assaf and Israel Bartal[125] accurately points to the fact that the emergence of the hasidic *shtadlanim* was part of a more general tendency in nineteenth-century hasidism to take on the different functions of the Jewish community boards, now weakened or even disbanded; hence it was a reaction to the politics of virtually all the states of central and eastern Europe with regard to Jews. Many tsadikim undertook political activity at this time, and many were surprisingly successful. According to an anti-hasidic report of 1853, the tsadik Menahem Mendel Schneersohn of Lubawicze (Lubavitch) developed such an excellent 'spy network' that information about anti-Jewish laws reached him faster than it did local state officials.[126] Recent archival research confirms, moreover, that Schneersohn certainly was an aware and effective political player, exerting influence on numerous state projects; he was engaged, for example, in a project for a state Jewish school in Lubawicze and, using methods very similar to those of Rabbi Isaac, influenced the school's educational profile.[127] The similarities between political activity in the Kingdom of Poland and in the empire were, of course, significantly greater.

However, it would appear that, along with this generalized east European factor, we should take account of another, possibly more important, local factor encouraging Polish tsadikim to become involved in intensive political

[125] See n. 2 above.
[126] Ia. I., 'Bor'ba pravitel'stva s khasidizmom', 100.   [127] Lurie, *Edah umedinah*, 62–93.

activism. This was the specific nature of the Kingdom of Poland and the form
of its 'Jewish politics' from the second decade of the nineteenth century.

As with any country in nineteenth-century Europe, it is difficult to call
the Kingdom of Poland a genuinely legally governed state as we understand
the term now. Civil and constitutional rights were limited almost from the
very beginning. After 1831, many constitutional freedoms were permanently
withdrawn and huge areas of social life came under the autocratic rule of
the tsar of Russia, now also king of Poland. However, compared with many
European states it was relatively modern and legally governed. Because of
the heritage of the Napoleonic Duchy of Warsaw and its constitutional
foundations, it enjoyed a legal and administrative system based on relatively
modern premises, in which laws and civil obligations were defined by the
constitution and a universal civil code (the so-called Napoleonic Code). The
tradition of the Napoleonic Duchy of Warsaw and the influence of the liberal
sympathies of Alexander I at the time the Kingdom was created meant that its
state apparatus and administration reflected universal and secular ideals. This
had, of course, a lasting influence on the structure and functioning of the
state apparatus even many decades later, when the liberal period had been
long forgotten. Even if bureaucrats allowed numerous abuses to be committed, the fact that official procedures and legal formalities were generally
observed was a significant factor in how matters concerning representatives
of hasidic society were handled, and also in the shaping of Jewish politics.
A number of Polish tsadikim, and especially Rabbi Isaac, managed to exploit
the potential of an administrative system that made possible an effective
defence of Jewish interests (as hasidic leaders perceived them), based on
formalized bureaucratic procedures and codified legal rules. Of course, sending petitions to the authorities and resorting to legal arguments were not
methods originated by Rabbi Isaac and the Polish tsadikim—they had been in
existence from the beginnings of *shtadlanut*[128]—but in the nineteenth century
this type of activity assumed new meaning. Thus, pre-modern *shtadlanim*
functioned in a legal system that allowed for the existence of parallel and
quite contradictory legal regulations; for example, wide settlement privileges
were granted to the Jewish community, while privileges granted to Christian
burghers effectively limited Jewish rights of settlement. The basic precept of
this legal system was tradition, which in itself was subject to interpretation. In
addition, medieval or early modern legislators were not obsessed with a sense
of omnipotence: they did not endeavour to interfere in all spheres of social
life. This 'moderation' created even broader spheres of application for extra-
judicial regulations. In this sense, the law was subject to personal contacts and

[128] See e.g. Stern, *Josel of Rosheim*, 48–50, 66–71, and Ury, 'The *Shtadlan* of the Polish–
Lithuanian Commonwealth', 280–7.

negotiations. In the nineteenth century the situation changed, as decisions were not dependent (at least officially) on the will of members of the state administration, but on a formalized and depersonalized set of laws. This affected all European states, including the Russian empire, over the course of the nineteenth century, though at different rates and to varying extents. This depersonalization of the law circumscribed, though it did not eliminate, the importance of the humiliating and frequently ineffective personal intercessions with representatives of the government elite and the politically influential 'Deutsche', as the maskilim were sometimes termed by the hasidim (traditional historiography contains much information about this).[129] Instead, the circumstances demanded professional legal action, of which the effectiveness was foreseeable and the associated risk inconsiderable. These, then, were purely rational and 'modern' activities and their effectiveness (as we have seen) was such as to encourage an intensification of activity in this area. Changes in the legal system did not necessarily bring about profound political and social transformation, but even if they only reshaped the discourse rather than actual bureaucratic mechanisms and political relations, they nevertheless contributed significantly to the effectiveness of Jewish intercession, as is evident in the cases presented. Thus the rules of the game between the government and the representatives of the Jewish community did change, even if from the perspective of the Jewish masses the change was mostly cosmetic.

The accounts discussed above, and especially those of the campaigns of Rabbi Isaac, show that the tsadikim successfully responded to this change. From an ostensible neglect of political issues at the beginning of the nineteenth century, over the course of thirty years the hasidic leaders became significantly involved in political issues and developed considerable political skill. Inadequate responses to government initiatives gave way to more proactive involvement that developed in turn into a highly complex, instrumental approach to politics, such that the activism of Rabbi Isaac and his legal advisers achieved unparalleled proficiency and effectiveness. Based on legal reasoning, their interventions sometimes even forced the administration to make decisions that were at variance with avowed government objectives.

We are of course unable to compare Rabbi Isaac's methods with those of early modern *shtadlanim* as we do not have access to detailed information on the earlier period. However, we can assume that even if earlier petitions also employed a legal line of argument, the new circumstances were very different. First, Rabbi Isaac and the other *shtadlanim* operating in this period were not employees of a community or supra-community institution, but rather self-appointed representatives not subject to the control of a higher

---

[129] See Walden, *Ohel yitsḥak*, 36, no. 86; 53–4, no. 128; 121–2, no. 282; *Sefer me'ir einei hagolah*, 102, no. 211.

echelon. An act of *shtadlanut*, especially if it was successful, reinforced the status of the hasidic *shtadlan* in the community and in effect established him as a political authority. Furthermore, there were differences on a more technical plane that, even if they were ostensibly trivial, were of paramount importance for the new shape of hasidic political involvement: for a legal argument to be used effectively and administrative procedures exploited advantageously, a proper legal system and effective public administration system had to be in place. These features did not exist in eighteenth-century Poland; a universal legal system was the creation of Napoleonic France. So even if Rabbi Isaac's petitions, like the majority of those in a tsarist state, were backed up by various kinds of 'presents' and bribes, our knowledge from archival materials of the official channels through which the petitions passed leads us to believe that the bribe was of minor or secondary importance in these matters. For Rabbi Isaac's petitions to be effective, well-prepared legal arguments were a basic requirement, as was a thorough knowledge of the state's official machinery and its weaknesses (above all, the inertia and the unwillingness of officials to take on any work or take decisions), and a proper understanding of the political situation and the range of possibilities associated with it.

However, it was the pronounced changes in the Kingdom of Poland's politics regarding the Jews in the 1830s that was most conducive to the political activism by prominent representatives of the Jewish community. After the failure of the 1830–1 revolution, the people who had held power in the Kingdom of Poland until that time either emigrated or were dismissed from the government (the dissolution in 1837 of the Jewish Committee was a reflection of this); the government withdrew its plans to 'reform' the Jews and adopted instead a new political line in relation to the Jewish community. Anyone who could be useful in supporting the new direction of the government's politics (which were aimed at reducing social problems and conflicts and simultaneously maximizing taxation) was a potential ally. Rabbi Isaac and his circle understood the opportunity this offered. Thanks to a series of successful intercessions, he came to be seen as speaking on behalf of the entire Jewish population of the Kingdom, and his petitions were considered favourably by the highest authorities in the land.

Thus it seems that 'administrative law and order' had double significance for the hasidim of Poland. Not only did it afford their leaders an effective means of protecting Jewish interests (thereby bringing about a modification of Jewish political strategy) but it also encouraged broader activism of a political/legal nature and expanded its social frame of reference, meaning that more and more people were involved. In these new circumstances, the tsadikim achieved quite spectacular success. Although they were perceived by their contemporaries (and by later historiography as well) as merely continuing the tradition of *shtadlanut*, they actually evolved as highly successful political activists, able to manipulate the Polish legal system to their own ends. Moreover, they were remarkably successful at maintaining an image of being the embodiment of traditionalism while simultaneously adopting modern forms of political activism that fully corresponded with the new conditions of the Kingdom of Poland in the nineteenth century. This became, in fact, the most characteristic feature of Polish hasidic leadership in the following decades. It also seems possible—though it is, to be sure, difficult to prove—that the very success of the political involvement of the hasidic *shtadlanim* contributed to the attractiveness and further successful development of the hasidic movement in Poland in the middle of the nineteenth century.

CHAPTER SIX

Communal Dimensions of Hasidic Politics

WHEN ANALYSING hasidic political activity it is important to consider its scale, and particularly the relationship between activities on the macro and micro historical levels. The political activism of Alexander Zusya Kahana, Rabbi Meir of Opatów, and Rabbi Isaac of Warka discussed in Chapter 5 consisted for the most part of interventions at the level of the highest state authorities and involved attempts to solve problems pertaining to the Jewish community as a whole. This applies to nearly all the best-known initiatives of hasidic *shtadlanim*, such as Rabbi Isaac's successful efforts to legalize *eruvin*, to allow rabbis to monitor kosher meat butchers, to argue for changes in divorce laws, or even, as an example of an unsuccessful intervention, to deal with the problems of Jewish prisoners. This portrayal of hasidic politics as being chiefly engaged in problems at the macro level is what has come down to us in the literature; I am thinking particularly of Raphael Mahler's evocative narration of the hasidic leadership of the passive resistance of the Jewish masses,[1] or the martyrological historiography of the Lubavitch dynasty, focusing on the sufferings of the holy men of the Schneersohn family at the hands of the central government.[2]

Nevertheless, it is not unreasonable to suppose that a significant proportion of hasidic political activism, at least in terms of the number of matters dealt with, was concerned with local issues. Such cases include the campaign in Częstochowa in 1820 in defence of the right to use the *mikveh* (see Ch. 2, §4), the campaigns to obtain the support of the Voivodeship Commission for a hasidic rabbinical candidate in Płock in 1829 and Pilica in 1835 (Ch. 4, §§1–2), and even Meir Rotenberg's intervention in Opatów in 1824–5 in defence of the right to freedom of assembly (Ch. 5, §2). There were countless similar political initiatives in virtually every Jewish community in eastern Europe. The vast majority had a purely local, communal character, and many of them involved hasidim.[3] Thus in considering the nature of hasidic political activism it is important to examine the communal level too.

---

[1] e.g. Mahler, *Hasidism and the Jewish Enlightenment*, 200–1.

[2] Rapoport-Albert, 'Hagiography with Footnotes'.

[3] An interesting analysis of Menahem Mendel Schneersohn's involvement in the creation of the Jewish state school in Lubawicz in 1851 can be found in Lurie, *Edah umedinah*, 78–83.

A full discussion of this topic—including the power structure in the extended hasidic family, inside the hasidic group, and between hasidic groups existing in the same community, and relations between hasidic groups and different segments of the non-hasidic members of the community—is beyond the scope of this book. These wide-ranging issues demand separate and comprehensive studies, to which I hope to return one day. For example, a thorough description of the chronology and evolution of the different stages of communal hasidic politics, which is surely one of the central issues of hasidic historiography, has hardly been touched at all, and it is difficult to regard those studies that do exist as satisfactory.[4] They tend to simplify the issues and make unsubstantiated generalizations; most often mistakenly attributing to hasidic activity at the communal level a meta-awareness of political goals realized in conflicts with the Jewish community board and other communal institutions.[5] I am convinced that politics, and perhaps especially communal politics, is not a result of the consistent realization of strategic goals or a master plan established in advance; rather, politics is the result of the complex and usually accidental outcome of individual negotiations of power, changing conditions, the availability of means (including knowledge), and of constantly shifting political goals—shifting because in the real world goals change as situations develop. This means that interpretations of political actions in terms of a historical goal may misrepresent reality. To my mind, to attribute political meta-awareness to actors in a historical narrative is to distort the historical process; in the discussion that follows I therefore focus on the fundamental questions at the communal level that transpire from the cases discussed in previous chapters. My conclusions, such as they are, do not represent the culmination of research on the place of hasidim within the Jewish community, but rather an introduction to the topic. I describe in turn the hasidim engaged in politics (Who?), the competitors with whom the hasidim struggled (Whom?), the fundamental goals of hasidic communal political activity (Why?), and the means the hasidim used to try to achieve their goals (How?). Cogent answers to these fundamental questions are a necessary prerequisite for a successful theoretical model of the chronology and political typology of the growth of the hasidic movement.

The second fundamental issue treated in this chapter is directly linked to the cases discussed in Chapter 5: we need to ask whether there were structural similarities between local activities and wider national politics. If there

---

[4] The most important studies of the communal aspect of hasidic expansion are Ettinger, 'Hasidism and the *Kahal* in Eastern Europe'; Shmeruk, 'Chasydyzm i kahał'; id., 'Hasidism and the Kehilla'; and Dynner, '*Men of Silk*', 5 5–88.

[5] For example the tendency to claim that the hasidim 'sought chiefly to appropriate the existing socioreligious infrastructure, not to undermine or supplant it' (Dynner, '*Men of Silk*', 56).

were, what was their source? Were these activities in any way connected or dependent on each other? What implications did this have for the relations between the leaders and the community in a non-democratic political system? What was the Kingdom of Poland like, in terms of its political structure, and what was the implication of this for engaging in politics there? Similarly, what was the political structure of the hasidic community? More broadly, what were the relationships that influenced political life? How were representatives selected, what authority did they have, and what was the structure of the constituency? We are concerned here with the fundamental question of the legitimacy of political activities in non-democratic systems, an issue that has remained outside the sphere of interest of political history because it is essentially dominated by a Western perspective that absolutizes electoral politics. Meanwhile, making the obvious assumption that any authority, even a self-appointed one, needs legitimizing, one needs to ask how hasidic representation was to be legitimized at the level of rank-and-file representatives of the Jewish community, who did not participate in high politics and, as we have seen, had only a very foggy notion of what it was. Were the local campaigns by great *shtadlanim* in some way connected, and if so, how?

In the following pages I shall briefly summarize the forms of hasidic political activism at the communal level as they transpired from the cases discussed in earlier chapters and then analyse two cases that appear to shed some light on the relationship between state and communal politics: a conflict in Czyżew surrounding the appointment of a communal rabbi, and a campaign to dismiss the rabbi of Będzin on the grounds that he was an informer. In both these cases the strategy employed at the communal level was essentially similar to that used in state-level campaigns, and I shall try to demonstrate that this was because the nature of government administration in the Kingdom of Poland required interaction with the modernizing state at all levels.

1. Who? Agents of Hasidic Communal Politics

The most obvious answer to the question of who the agents of hasidic communal politics were is, simply, hasidim. This assertion, however, is only partly accurate, because the participants in political activism, even at the lowest level, were not all representatives of the community involved. Instead of trying to define the social profile of the entire hasidic community in an attempt to answer this question, it would therefore seem more reliable to describe those representatives of hasidic society who appear as more or less active participants in political life and how they are defined in the sources themselves. The answer to the question may, of course, sometimes be identical with the response to the more general question regarding the social composition of the entire hasidic community, but while the social composition of hasidism (a fascinating issue) still remains outside the range of contemporary historiography, I shall try here to define the social profile of hasidic groups engaged in social and political activity, at least in fundamental outline, on the basis of available archival sources. This undertaking may help explain one aspect of the social composition and institutional development of hasidism, namely the hierarchy and power structure within the grass-roots hasidic group at the level of a Jewish community. Contrary to the prevalent assumption of the radically egalitarian nature of the hasidic movement and apparent equality of all the followers of the tsadik, the available sources suggest clear hierarchies of social involvement and social influence within these groups.

To begin, one should note that more than 51 per cent of Jewish society habitually and permanently had no involvement in activities of a political nature, whether active or passive. This percentage, of course, indicates the position of women,[6] the exclusion of whom is clearly revealed, for example, in the elections to the board of the Jewish community, when all widows, even those paying relatively high communal fees, were included in the fifth tax class, in accordance with the electoral law depriving this class of the right to vote. This practice remained almost unchanged in all electoral protocols of the Jewish community boards throughout the Kingdom of Poland in the period under discussion. The election of the rabbi was similar. In accordance with the law, all 'fathers of families' were supposed to participate in the election of a rabbi, without regard to the taxes paid, thereby giving electoral rights to taxpayers in the fifth class, which formally included women registered as heads of families, such as widows. However, the term 'fathers of families' was interpreted literally, meaning that in cases where the household was managed by a woman (a widow), she was excluded from the electoral list, as she did not meet the strict definition of 'father of the family'.

The exclusion of women pertained not only to formal political activities such as elections but also to informal ones, such as requests, reports, and petitions, and even to entirely spontaneous events such as street disturbances, public arguments, or minor domestic disputes. While women were quite possibly not involved in communal petitions or reports to city officials, it is difficult to believe that they were completely absent from communal conflicts of a spontaneous nature, and in fact traces in the sources allow us to discern

[6] The literature on the place of women in Jewish society is already immense, but while many attempts have been made to define the gender boundaries of social roles and to analyse the limitations of earlier Jewish historiography, the question of political participation has not yet been of particular interest. A solid discussion of the literature on Jewish women in eastern Europe can be found in Freeze, 'Introduction: A Historiographical Survey'; see also Rosman, 'The History of Jewish Women in Early Modern Poland'.

their occasional participation in them, as some examples below illustrate. The extant sources offer only a very narrow—I should add, deliberately narrow—window through which to observe women's activity, and the picture we get from them was probably quite different to the reality. Characteristically, the voices of women are consistently excluded from accounts of events, and their participation was simply erased. This was not deliberate falsification, but merely adherence to socially accepted convention. It is important to realize that the accounts that have come down to us not only depict the ideal social norms according to the representatives of society authorized by that society to make normative judgements, but in a certain sense also reveal how those who were interested and involved perceived those events. An exception to the exclusion of women from the record is an 1840 account from Bełchatów, which states that a certain woman, identified only as 'Rothszyldowa' (that is, of the Rothszyld family), dared to shout out during the service in the synagogue that the local Jewish community board members 'shaved their beards and cut their hair'—a public accusation of liberal tendencies at odds with community norms.[7] The situation was so unusual that witnesses felt bound to record it. A significantly more typical situation concerned a certain Naftali Flomenbaum from Kazimierz Dolny, who testified: 'I went to the rabbi to ask him for certification for a marriage, but he did not give it to me, because he wanted from me 5 złoty and 6 groszy, though I am poor and in the fifth [i.e. lowest fiscal] class.'[8] In his last sworn testimony, however, Flomenbaum stated: 'I can swear to this, because my wife told me all this, as she went to the rabbi',[9] which contradicts what he has just said— that he, not his wife, went to the rabbi. This did not prevent Flomenbaum from presenting events in the first person, attributing his wife's actions to himself and even offering sworn testimony on her behalf (it may be, of course, that he was simply influenced by the traditional halakhic concept of *ishto kegufo*—that husband and wife are essentially one unit, and the actions of one are binding on the other). Though this incident may seem trivial in itself, I think it is a good illustration of the mechanisms by which women were excluded from the arena of political activity even in those situations where they did in fact participate in events of a political nature. Their participation was seen as not being in accordance with the normative public and political view of the life of the community, so the authors of the narratives used men as symbolic substitutes. The source of the societal norm was, on the one hand, the general principle of excluding women from political life found throughout eastern Europe, and on the other the halakhic principle of the incapacity of women to take legal action, even as witnesses, and the practices of Jewish society that stemmed from this idea.

[7] APŁ, APRG 2496, p. 586.   [8] *40.02; AGAD, CWW 1632, pp. 145–80.   [9] Ibid.

This double exclusion, real and symbolic, affected women of hasidic and non-hasidic families alike. Within the hasidic community, the question of women's political participation is additionally complicated because of a fundamental doubt about whether women are really part of the hasidic world. This question has repeatedly been, and still is, the subject of study. This is not the place for a detailed analysis;[10] however, I would briefly state that I am inclined to agree with the tsadik Meir of Opatów when he said during the 1824 investigation that 'women generally are not hasidim' (see Ch. 3, §4). This statement stems directly from the nature of the hasidic community, which, despite the prevailing terminology, was not a sect but rather a religious brotherhood on the model of other *ḥevrot*, membership of which was usually limited to men. I shall leave this question for further exploration elsewhere.[11]

Though women were not 'members' of the hasidic community in the full sense of the word, this does not exclude the possibility of their having emotional and even institutional ties with both the community and the court of the tsadik. The fact that numerous women made pilgrimages to the tsadik's court to ask his advice is a clear expression of these ties. We know, too, of women who identified themselves with hasidic values: a good example is the wife of Yekhezkel Kotik, who 'leaned towards hasidism' and was deeply disenchanted when her husband rejected it.[12] So in spite of women's lack of formal ties with hasidism and their general absence from communal politics, we can legitimately expect to find women who sympathized with hasidism to appear occasionally in this arena. In reality, however, women typically appear in only one social role, as patronesses or benefactors of the hasidic community or an individual tsadik. The best-known example of such a woman is Temerl Sonnenberg, the wife of Berek Sonnenberg and wealthy patroness of numerous Polish tsadikim. Significantly less wealthy and less influential women, however, also appear in similar roles; for example, in 1819 the daughter of Melekh Liwerant offered hospitality in the Warsaw suburbs to the tsadik Moses of Kozienice, and in 1860s Lublin a certain Krajndel

[10] The most important historical studies so far on the relation between women and hasidism are Horodezky, *Haḥasidut vehaḥasidim*, iv. 65–71; Rapoport-Albert, 'On Women in Hasidism'; ead., 'The Emergence of a Female Constituency in Twentieth-Century Habad Hasidism'; Polen, 'Miriam's Dance'; Loewenthal, '"Daughter/Wife of Hasid" or "Hasidic Woman"?'; id., 'Women and the Dialectic of Spirituality in Hasidism'; Deutsch, *The Maiden of Ludmir*; Lewis, '"Eydele, the Rebbe"'; Wodziński, 'Women and Hasidism'; and Rosman, 'Al nashim vaḥasidut: he'arot lediyun'. This topic is currently being researched by several scholars, including Moshe Rosman, Ada Rapoport-Albert, and David Assaf.

[11] The question of hasidism as a brotherhood (*ḥevrah*) will be discussed in my essay on the nature of hasidic relationships and the components of hasidic identity, still in preparation, though for some preliminary thoughts on the subject see my 'Chasydzkie konwersje?', 135–56.

[12] Kotik, *A Journey to a Nineteenth-Century Shtetl*, 361.

Sejdenwajsowa offered 'half of her home, a part of the ground floor, at
No. 620 in the city of Lublin in perpetuity as a new synagogue for hasidim
in Lublin belonging to the company of the rabbi from Kozienice'.[13] The
role of patroness and benefactor was not only a source of prestige for these
women but also gave them a certain political influence. Temerl Sonnenberg
certainly took advantage of this, as did other women. The influence women
had in this way on public life was socially acceptable because it could be
substantiated in the traditional system of values of their public charitable
activity, but it was very limited because they could only act in the arena of
communal politics under the veil of this kind of charity work. To be visible
and socially effective, the charity had to be substantial, and so by definition
was limited to a very small number of rich women possessing their own
property. Those whose generosity was limited to giving their local hasidic
leader a few pennies and a bottle of schnapps for the sabbath—as Hinde
Bergner (1870–1942), a memoirist from Galicia, recalls her mother did—
certainly did not gain any social influence from their generosity.[14] Thus the
presence of women in the incidents of interest to us is entirely marginal; the
activists in communal politics were almost exclusively men.

In considering the structure of the social organization of these politically
active men, a distinction has to be made between communities in which a
tsadik resided and those (significantly more numerous) communities where
a tsadik was not in residence. In places where tsadikim lived, the focus of
politics and the structure of the hasidic community naturally concentrated
around his person. Interestingly, however, the personal engagement of
tsadikim in politics at the communal level and in resolving ongoing communal conflicts was surprisingly limited, at least as far as can be determined
from the extant archival sources. The tsadik's involvement was somewhat
greater in those rare instances when he was also the communal rabbi and his
position or activity was contested by part of the local community. Such was
the case in Radomsko from 1850 to 1852, when a new Jewish community
board tried to reduce the remuneration of tsadik Solomon Rabinowicz as
rabbi and, in essence, to withdraw his guaranteed rabbinical contract.[15] In the
copious official correspondence concerning the case, the Jewish community
board argued that Rabbi Solomon was the leader of the hasidim and not the
rabbi of the entire community; however, he did not appear here as the tsadik

[13] AGAD, CWW 1610, p. 549; for more on Moses Bria of Kozienice in Warsaw in 1819, see
*6.01; AGAD, CWW 1424, pp. 11–12. On Sejdenwajsowa and her donation see AGAD,
CWW 1610, pp. 547–50, 596–606, 611–28; CWW 1611, pp. 47–63, 172–89, 200–5.

[14] Bergner, *On Long Winter Nights . . . Memoirs of a Jewish Family in a Galician Township*, 42.

[15] On the conflict between Solomon and the Jewish community board of Radomsko see
*30.01–*30.03; APŁ, APRG 2559, pp. 692–4, 900–1, 906–7, 913, 917–18. On Solomon
Rabinowicz of Radomsko's rabbinical contract, see *17.01; AGAD, KWK 710, pp. 290–1, 295;
see also APŁ, APRG 2559, pp. 909–11; T. M. Rabinowicz, 'Toledot radomsk', 47.

but as the communal rabbi, and there is no trace of involvement of the hasidim in the conflict. A similar situation occurred in Łęczna in 1852, when the anti-hasidic opposition tried to block the payment of a salary to the local rabbi and tsadik Joshua ben Solomon Leib.[16] These were, however, rare and atypical cases, because they were limited to places in which the tsadik was at the same time the communal rabbi and where his position was contested.

In centres where the tsadik did not fulfil the functions of the communal rabbi, including the largest and most established centres of hasidic influence such as Przysucha and Kozienice, his presence in ongoing communal politics is actually invisible. This does not mean, however, that he was not involved in this politics. Certainly his significant influence would have allowed him to realize political goals through groups and individuals representing him; he simply did not have to engage personally in the process, though there is no doubt that in many cases he pulled strings. But this influence should not be overestimated: even the highly reputed tsadik of Radomsko faced strong internal opposition in community politics and he was repeatedly unable to maintain the status quo.[17] Secondly, and more important, a tsadik who did not fulfil communal functions was in a certain sense independent of the community, meaning that conflict with the interests and activities of the Jewish community board was comparatively rare. Analysis of hundreds of files concerning Jewish communities in nineteenth-century Poland shows that political involvement on the part of tsadikim was strikingly rare; this is true not only of places where hasidim dominated (which is understandable), but also in places where they were not in the majority and where the tsadik had to struggle for social recognition. This might suggest that hasidism should be understood not as an alternative social structure to that of the Jewish community but rather as a supplementary form of social organization.

Not surprisingly, the social organization and political activity in hasidic communities far from a hasidic court was quite different from that in the major hasidic centres that developed where a tsadik took up residence. In the more remote hasidic communities we can generally identify three phases of development, starting from an unstructured group of individuals identifying as hasidim which evolved into a relatively united hasidic group and then eventually emerged as a distinct and cohesive group with its own internal hierarchy and social and political representation.

In the first of these phases, hasidim were thus unaffiliated individuals, at least in terms of public activity that can be recognized as political. Their only common characteristic was the evasion of certain communal obligations, and

---

[16] See *31.01–*31.03; AGAD, CWW 1613, pp. 210–20.

[17] The British missionaries visiting Radomsko in 1850 reported that 'the local rabbi, because of his exaggerated ideas and behaviour, fell into disfavour among the local population': see AGAD, CWW 1458, p. 402.

above all a preference for spending the religious festivals at the court of their tsadik. The extant sources show unequivocally that the exodus of hasidim from their native communities during important festivals was seen by the community elite as a serious threat to the social order (see for example the interventions in Łask and in the voivodeship of Kraków described in Chapter 2, §2); however, it is difficult to speak of any kind of co-ordinated political activity on the part of the hasidim since this exodus was entirely spontaneous, and the individuals concerned still prayed in the communal synagogue and participated in almost all public activities of the community after their return.

The turning-point was the creation of a private *shtibl*, a development which marked the presence of a distinct hasidic group because in accordance with Jewish law a group meeting for prayer requires a minimum of ten formally adult men (that is, males aged 13 or older).[18] The creation of a *shtibl* was usually the first catalyst of sharp confrontation with the non-hasidic majority and the board of the community, and the first occasion on which a politically active group of hasidim could be identified. The most typical structure of an early hasidic political group was therefore a number of men praying in one *shtibl*, often supporters of the same tsadik (which might suggest that 'general hasidic' *shtiblekh*, though very popular, were structurally less close-knit and politically less effective),[19] usually peers, and usually young. Thus, when in 1823 the Jewish community board and local authorities in Parczew complained about an emerging hasidic group, they unequivocally defined the group as a concentration of young people (see Ch. 3, §1).[20] Similarly, in 1840 when the Jewish community board in Międzyrzec Podlaski complained of hasidim smoking tobacco in the *beit midrash* against the rules, they mentioned that those doing this were primarily young men.[21] The high percentage of young men among hasidim is not surprising. *Mitnagedim* and maskilim alike often stressed that the hasidic movement attracted naive people, women, and especially young men[22]—or as the maskil Abraham Stern put it, hasidim tried 'to beguile and ensnare youth and less sensible

[18] However, we should note that there were at least some *shtiblekh* where it was usual for fewer than ten men to gather, for example in 1823 in Terespol, where there were only 'five men attending the hasidic prayer house regularly'. See *11.20; AGAD, CWW 1871, pp. 7–8.
[19] See for example: on the group from Parczew, the followers of Simhah Bunem of Przysucha, in 1823, *11.01; AGAD, CWW 1871, p. 4; on the group in Węgrów, the followers of Mordecai Joseph Leiner of Izbica, *29.04; AGAD, CWW 1789, pp. 209–17; on the group in Częstochowa, the followers of Issachar Ber of Radoszyce, B[ursztyński], 'Russland und Polen'.
[20] See e.g. *11.01; AGAD, CWW 1871, p. 4; Wodziński, 'Sprawa chasydymów', 229; *11.17; AGAD, CWW 1871, pp. 11–21; see also *11.25; AGAD, CWW 1871, p. 39; AGAD, KRSW 6634, fo. 233ᵛ.   [21] *23.01; AGAD, CWW 1780, pp. 34–5.
[22] See for example memorials by Eliasz Moszkowski in AGAD, CWW 1436, pp. 215–33. Menahem Mendel Lefin especially emphasized the attraction of hasidism for young men: see Sinkoff, *Out of the Shtetl*, 113–67.

Israelites, particularly the rich and women'.[23] Elsewhere he complained that hasidim exerted a 'deplorable influence' on Jewish youth. These comments may not accurately reflect the age structure of the hasidic community in its later stages, but the dominance of young men among politically active hasidim is certainly evident not only in the movement's formative phase but actually throughout the entire period I am discussing; it was not a transitory phenomenon. The publicly assertive nature of hasidic activity, in which (as we will see below) group pressure and even physical force played a considerable role, may partly be explained by the fact that hasidism attracted the young (as all new movements do), and young men tend to be violent. Of course, young people always and everywhere dominate in triggering street fights, so it should not be surprising that the same was true among hasidim. When Płock's anti-hasidic rabbi Isaac Auerbach was attacked in 1838,[24] the investigation showed that all the perpetrators belonged to a peer group in their twenties led by the 20-year-old Shmul Moses Szpiro.[25] Similarly, the hasidic group that initiated riots, disturbances, and public insults in Bełchatów in 1840 and extinguished the candles in the synagogue was unequivocally defined as consisting of 'only youth employed in nothing but idleness and drunken nights'.[26] This was not entirely unfair: the most consistent characteristic of the socially active part of hasidic circles was a peer group of young men.

An alternative structure to the peer group was the interest group. An excellent example of this is the hasidic community concentrated around Majer Rypiński in Włocławek (see Ch. 4, §5), but more or less distinct interest groups are also evident in many other cases, for example in the conflict regarding the position of the rabbi in Płock in 1829 mentioned earlier. I have discussed the emergence and workings of such groups more broadly in Chapter 4, §5, but here I would like to mention that from the outset the internal hierarchy and political leadership emerged more clearly within the interest group than within the peer group. This is because such interest groups usually reflected a client system, meaning an arrangement of informal dependency in which a wealthy patron gave his clients economic support in exchange for their political support. In such an arrangement, the rich patron, or his entire family, was naturally the leader.

---

[23] *4.07; AGAD, CWW 1871, pp. 43–6; AGAD, KWK 702, pp. 137–41; AGAD, KRSW 6634, fos. 239–42; Mahler, *Haḥasidut vehahaskalah*, 477–81; Wodziński, *Oświecenie żydowskie w Królestwie Polskim*, 268–71; id., *Haskalah and Hasidism*, 260–3.

[24] Isaac Auerbach was the son of Hayim Auerbach, the rabbi of Łęczyca and a descendant of a well-known rabbinical family. Auerbach was a *mitnaged*, the rabbi first in Dobrzyń, then in Dobre, and after 1838 in Płock, where he met with strong hasidic opposition. After the death of his father, he became rabbi in Łęczyca. He is the author of the halakhic tract *Divrei ḥayim* (Breslau, 1852).

[25] See *22.01–22.06; APP, AmP 568, fos. 142–8.   [26] APŁ, APRG 2496, p. 586.

Moreover, it seems that the influence of the client arrangement appears not only in the case of an interest group but also in hasidic groups for which economic dependency may not have been the main factor. In other words, even if the group was not concerned primarily with economic issues, the political and economical factors typical of a client system did play a central role in the election of a leader and in establishing the social hierarchy. The co-dependency of economic and political roles was probably universal in hasidic communities. We find examples in many of the incidents described earlier in this volume. For example, Józef Gayfler and Joachym Lerner, both very wealthy, were representatives and leaders of the hasidim in Częstochowa (see Ch. 2, §4).[27] The situation was similar in the incident in Włocławek (see Ch. 4, §5) and the almost identical conflict in Koniecpol in 1836–7.[28] The leaders of the local hasidim, the Wargoń brothers and their relative Jakub Hejszek, were not only former members of the Jewish community board who had been dismissed in an atmosphere of scandal but were also members of the financial elite of the community.[29] In Pilica, the dominant figures in the local hasidic group were Aryeh Leib Hirszberg, a wealthy merchant and a learned talmudist, and his brother Moses, the richest Jew in town, a leadership structure that clearly reflected economic, social, and political influence.[30] In Piątek, the initiator and unquestioned leader of the hasidim was Chuna Ungier, a grain merchant and the richest Jew in the city, and his brother, who was also a follower of hasidism, was the communal rabbi.[31] We may conclude, then, that economic dominance was almost always an important factor, and sometimes even the most important one, in the emergence of the leadership of the hasidic group and its political influence. At the same time, the incidents in Pilica and Piątek show that at least sometimes economic influence alone was insufficient to assure a dominant position: real leadership required religious scholarship too. If, as in Pilica and Piątek, both factors were concentrated in the hands of one family, the family easily acquired a dominant position.

To sum up, the development of the essential hasidic structure at the communal level can be traced through several stages. The earliest stage was a loose group of individuals whose identification as hasidim derived primarily from negative considerations, i.e. through the forms of communal activity in which they did not participate. The turning-point was the creation of the most important communal institution of hasidism, the *shtibl*, which would typically be done either by a peer group or an interest group. It seems that the

---

[27] See AGAD, KWK 702, pp. 17, 26, 29, 31. See also Wodziński, 'Chasydzi w Częstochowie'.
[28] See *20.01–20.06; APŁ, APRG 2512, pp. 109–11, 260, 304–14.
[29] See tax lists in APŁ, APRG 2512, pp. 117–20, 319–20.
[30] See AGAD, CWW 1472, pp. 355–60.   [31] See AGAD, CWW 1716, pp. 131–243.

latter was the key to the development of more sophisticated hierarchies within the group, as in Włocławek and Koniecpol, and elsewhere too.

All this has further implications for our understanding of the hasidic movement. First, it reintroduces the old argument that one of the factors in the creation and development of the hasidic movement was financial interest. Though I do not wish to over-emphasize the economic aspect, I certainly think it is worth re-evaluating its place as one of several potential factors in the development of the movement. Second, it makes us reconsider the nature of social relations within the hasidic group: if local hasidic groupings were, even if only to a very limited extent, based on a client system with a complex structure of social and cultural interdependencies, it suggests a situation very far from the radical egalitarianism so often suggested in the scholarly literature; this means, in turn, that the map of economic, social, and cultural relations within the hasidic group must be radically redrawn. Third, the combination of economic strength and scholarship within a single family, as in the cases of Pilica and Piątek, possibly brings us closer to understanding the nature of leadership in the hasidic groups at the communal level.

2. Whom? Protagonists

The political opponents of hasidism at the communal level can be divided in a general way into five fundamental groups. The first is the local and provincial government administration. The hasidic community, like any other, encountered legal constraints on its daily activities; conversely, the existence of the rule of law enabled it to gain various concessions and privileges. Reference had to be made to state laws even when breaking them, when filing petitions in the local offices, participating in numerous activities of the municipality, responding to questions from the mayor, looking for ways to evade anti-hasidic activities of the municipal bureaucracy, and so forth. More importantly, though, the confrontation with the state administration emerged from the conflict brought on by the general change in political direction in the nine-teenth century. In its early decades, the government of the Kingdom of Poland tried consistently to limit the powers of the Jewish community boards by taking upon itself all their traditional functions other than the strictly religious, a strategy understood by majority of Jews as an attempt to deprive them of their most important form of communal life. This made the Jews antagonistic not only towards the government, but also towards the state itself. This may have been an important factor in facilitating the acceptance of the factional activity of hasidim in the first half of the nineteenth century. The *shtiblekh* that the hasidim established were seen by many not as something contrary to the interests of the Jewish community (though the Jewish community boards saw them in that way because of the consequent loss of income), but rather as an attempt to put at least some of the activities of the community beyond the control of the state. One aspect of state interference to which all elements of the Jewish community were vehemently opposed was the attempt to gain control of communal budgets. The local authorities were fully aware of Jewish opposition to this. For example, a report prepared by the municipal authorities in Pyzdry in 1827 specifically linked the establishment of *shtiblekh* with this development: 'Jews are driven by the fact that synagogue income is now handled by municipal authorities' and were therefore attempting to create breakaway institutions, 'understanding that in this way they are able to force the government to give them exclusive control of the communal income'.[32] Certainly the government's meddling in communal affairs and finances made a large segment of Jewish society less willing to be associated with the official Jewish community; this in turn helped legitimize the divisive actions of the hasidim and contributed to the movement's development, and perhaps even eased the way for hasidim to take on leadership of the incapacitated Jewish community boards.

The second political opponent of local hasidim, equally entrenched, was the Jewish community board, known until 1822 as the *kahal* and then as the *dozór bóżniczy*. At times it simply defended its own prerogatives, its right to control public life and to establish and supervise communal institutions—in other words, the functions it was appointed to perform. However, it frequently also acted in the name of a completely informal and spontaneous majority of the residents of the community, as in Częstochowa in 1820 when it spoke out in support of angry non-hasidic members of the community who had armed themselves with sticks to chase off hasidim trying to force their way into the local *mikveh* under police protection (see Ch. 2, §4). However, the *kahal* was by no means always anti-hasidic—for example in Parczew (see Ch. 3, §1), where it accepted the existence of hasidic groups but did not go along with the radicalism of a new group of Przysucha hasidim whose activity it deemed deleterious to the social order in the town. Naturally, relations with the community board changed radically as the hasidic movement developed and hasidim were able to gain significant representation on the boards of certain Jewish communities, and even dominate them.

A third group of political opponents of hasidism were various communal institutions, such as burial fraternities (which in Częstochowa refused to bury a hasidic child) or the boards of hospitals, usually dominated by Jewish doctors too progressive for hasidism. But the institution with which hasidim were most often in conflict was the office of the rabbi. There is no need here to rehearse examples of this type of conflict, mentioned many times in previous chapters, though I will return to this question shortly.

[32] *14.01; AGAD, KWK 724, p. 211.

Opposition to hasidim also frequently came from informal interest groups, usually concentrated around one family. The structure and methods of activity of such interest groups were essentially identical with those of the analogous hasidic groups discussed above. For example, in Bełchatów in 1840 a group opposing the hasidic rabbi and the hasidic youth supporting him was frequently described as 'the troubled Wajs family employed only in destroying others'.[33] Similarly, we recall that in Włocławek a hasidic group emerged around Rypiński as the result of an unsuccessful confrontation with the rival Giełdziński family (see Ch. 4, §5). The pattern was the same in other examples mentioned earlier.

Finally, hasidic groups could be opposed by other hasidic groups. The earliest example we have of this kind of conflict occurred in Parczew in 1823, when an aggressively proselytizing group of hasidim from Przysucha met with opposition from an older hasidic group that supported Jacob Simon Deutsch (see Ch. 3, §1). Similar internal hasidic conflicts are better documented, for example, in Płock in 1829 between the supporters of the two hasidic leaders Alexander Zusya Kahana and Abraham Landau of Ciechanów, or the 1851 conflict in Węgrów, when Izbica hasidim tried to have the rabbi dismissed because he was a supporter of the tsadik of Kock.[34]

Another interesting example comes from Warsaw. After the death of Menahem Mendel of Kock in January 1859, thousands of his supporters chose as their new leader Isaac Meir Alter, later the tsadik of Góra Kalwaria (Ger) but then still living in Warsaw. In April and May 1859 three anonymous letters were sent to the government authorities in the name of 'Jewish residents of the city of Warsaw' to demand that hasidim be forbidden from entering Warsaw on the grounds that they caused disruption and inflation and that increasingly they entered the city without paying the appropriate fee (until the 1860s Jews had to pay a daily tax, known as the *Tagzettel*, on entering Warsaw). Police authorities initiated an investigation, but it soon turned out that the source of the reports was not Jews from Warsaw but most likely hasidic Jews from the city of Kock 'who, because of the recent changes, lost income, primarily from the sale of alcohol, up to several thousand silver roubles annually', because hasidim stopped coming to Kock. In order to reverse this trend, they denounced Rabbi Isaac Meir so that the hasidim would not go to Warsaw but would instead return to Kock.[35] The police investigation found that the accusation that Rabbi Isaac Meir attracted large numbers of hasidim to Warsaw and that they did not pay the tax was untrue; interestingly, though, Rabbi Isaac Meir felt threatened by this result and

[33] APŁ, APRG 2496, pp. 562–75, 581–98, 606–19, 623–4.
[34] AGAD, CWW 1789, p. 206.
[35] *36.06; AGAD, CWW 1871, pp. 304–5; Borzymińska, 'Sprawa Rabiego Icchaka Meira Altera', 374–5.

decided to leave Warsaw and settle in Góra Kalwaria: 'feeling that he could not fend off the secret investigators, for his own peace he considered several places in the provinces, namely [probably meaning 'especially'] Góra Kalwaria, which for a certain time he had visited often'.[36] Certainly, internal hasidic conflicts were nothing unusual. Though they may shock those who believe in a theory of strong hasidic solidarity, they simply show the existence of conflicts of interest and competing goals within hasidic groups, a natural phenomenon in any large and internally differentiated social movement.

The political opponents of hasidism also changed over time. In the early phase, the opposition almost always came from the *kahal*—understandably so, since the first public acts of hasidic individuals, and then of hasidic groups, were aimed directly and indirectly at placing themselves beyond the authority of the *kahal*. Such acts included leaving their home town during major festivals so as to be close to the tsadik; establishing *shtiblekh*; refusing to pay their part of community obligations; and so forth. Even if these early actions sometimes had repercussions for the non-hasidic Jews in the town, the latter had neither the means nor the inclination to protest and merely left it to the *kahal* to do so. It was not until hasidim tried not only to gain their independence from the community but also to force it to make concessions, as in Częstochowa in 1820 over the right to use the community *mikveh*, that other players began to oppose them—normally a loose and ad hoc configuration of different institutions and interest groups. Only then did anti-hasidic political campaigns begin to be effective. This was the case in Kazimierz Dolny in 1861 when the non-hasidic majority resolved to dismiss the hasidic rabbi, Jacob ben Moses Goldman.[37] About 1,560 Jews lived in Kazimierz at this time, that is, about 380 adult men, of whom around 200 came to an understanding (Goldman called it a 'conspiracy') that, even at the risk of being placed under a *ḥerem*, they would not consult Goldman on halakhic matters but only the non-hasidic *dayan*, hoping through this boycott to force Goldman's dismissal. They were driven to such decisive action, they claimed, by Goldman's arrogance and his refusal to perform his official rabbinical duties, such as the registration of births, marriages, and deaths, unless he was paid high fees. Normally such loose coalitions against hasidim did not last because the objectives of those involved were ultimately incompatible, which made it easier for the hasidim to gain the upper hand and realize their political goals. In reality, hasidic groups seem to have been the only relatively large, cohesive, and stable groupings in Jewish communities; even when they were relatively small, they rarely found themselves confronting effective opposition in their political activities.

[36] *36.06; AGAD, CWW 1871, pp. 304–5.
[37] *40.01–*40.02; AGAD, CWW 1632, pp. 133–4, 137–42, 145–80.

3. Why? Goals

The basic goal of hasidic communal politics, as with any kind of politics, was to strengthen their position so as to create optimal conditions for further expansion, but over time these goals were refined in important ways. This process can be roughly divided into the two periods already discussed, but given the absence of a satisfactory consensus in the historiography of the movement regarding the chronology and typology of political expansion at the communal level, the suggested periodization can only be very basic. Initially, the nascent hasidic community grappled above all with factors threatening its existence. The hasidim tried to free themselves from external control and fought for social acceptance and the right to separate themselves from the community without interference from the non-hasidic majority— and the *kahal* representing that majority—in their own internal affairs. In the second period the goal was power—though of course this did not necessarily lead to actual power in the community. In other words, hasidim fought to extend their influence in society and to take control of at least some communal institutions. Now that their existence as an independent faction was no longer threatened, it was they and not their opponents who defined the area of conflict. In a certain sense, this was fully analogous with the switch from a defensive to an offensive phase in politics at the state level, as described in the previous chapter. This does not mean that the political activities of the second phase were always offensive, but it was the hasidim, and not their opponents, who usually determined the scope of the conflict. The difference between the two phases is well illustrated by the difference between the defence of the right to establish a *shtibl* (when hasidim expected from the community only that it should refrain from taking action against them—a goal typical of the earlier phase) and the defence of the right to use the communal *mikveh* in Częstochowa in 1820 (when hasidim demanded concessions from the community in recognition of their status—a goal typical of the later phase).

Below I present a chronological catalogue of the most typical reasons for conflicts involving hasidim, though it should be stressed that the chronology is rather loose and should therefore be regarded more as a theoretical model than as an actual reconstruction of the evolution of intracommunal conflict.

One of the oldest and most frequent charges raised against hasidim in mitnagdic sources, and also one of the most discussed in the literature on the subject, concerns their right to practise their own *sheḥitah* (ritual slaughter), separate from that of the community.[38] For the slaughterer's knife to be fit for

---

[38] On the social significance of ritual slaughter (*sheḥitah*) see Shmeruk, 'Mashma'utah haḥevratit shel hasheḥitah haḥasidit', and Stampfer, 'The Controversy over *Sheḥitah*'. See

this purpose it had to be not only strong, straight, and sharp, but also absolutely smooth—a requirement that was not easy to meet using the traditional iron blades. When the hasidim introduced the use of very thin, polished blades, the community authorities opposed the practice partly because the blades were so thin that they could easily become jagged in use (with the result that the meat would be non-kosher), and partly because being so sharp they caused difficulties for the inspectors (since they had to run their fingers across the blade). These arguments obviously had no halakhic basis,[39] so the objections were made on economic and social grounds: the money wasted if the meat was rendered non-kosher as the result of damage to the blade; the arrogance of hasidim in rejecting their forebears' traditions, and in representing themselves to the masses as superior in piety; and, most importantly, their aspiration to separate themselves from the community.[40]

The question of hasidic *sheḥitah* was the cause of several instances of controversy in central Poland, beginning with the oldest known case in Połaniec in 1798,[41] and then in Olkusz in 1818 at the time of the conflict between Jakub Brüll and the local 'Michałki' (see Ch. 2, §4). The Jewish community board of Sokołów Podlaski also complained in 1824 about hasidic separatism on the question of *sheḥitah* and the hasidim's claim that cattle and poultry slaughtered by other Jews was not kosher.[42] Despite these episodes, *sheḥitah* and the attempt to appoint hasidim as ritual slaughterers (*shoḥetim*) were surprisingly infrequent as a cause of communal conflict. Shaul Stampfer has suggested that this is because the issue was resolved in the first half of the nineteenth century by the introduction of steel knives, which were both very sharp and suitably strong and therefore fulfilled the expectations of both sides.[43] Even though the basic problem was resolved, there were

---

Wilensky, 'Hassidic Mitnaggedic Polemics', 253–7, for the significance of *sheḥitah* in anti-hasidic polemics. See also Wertheim, *Law and Custom in Hasidism*, 302–15.

[39] The hasidic changes did not actually violate halakhic rules, which is why some critics of the hasidim, including the more famous ones such as Elijah b. Solomon Zalman, the Gaon of Vilna, and Hayim of Volozhin, were very careful about making this accusation.

[40] See Katz, *Tradition and Crisis*, 208, for a discussion of separation from non-hasidic society as the most important aspect of hasidic *sheḥitah*. Suspicions of sectarian Sabbatian tendencies (typically raised against any dissenting religious activity), or simply doubts as to the religious integrity of the hasidic butchers (understandable during a time of major conflict) also meant that the *mitnagedim* foresaw that their appointment would endanger the entire Jewish community. Ritually unclean meat sold by a butcher as kosher caused ritual uncleanliness in all those who ate it, potentially the whole community. The anti-hasidic critic David of Maków described an investigation into a butcher who, on the recommendation of a hasidic *magid* (preacher), represented a non-kosher animal as kosher, thus causing the entire community to sin. See David of Maków, *Shever poshe'im*, in Wilensky, *Ḥasidim umitnagedim*, ii. 138–9; see also Wilensky, 'Hassidic Mitnaggedic Polemics', 256.

[41] On a case study in Połaniec see Kuperstein, 'Inquiry at Połaniec'.

[42] AGAD, CWW 1871, p. 106.   [43] Stampfer, 'The Controversy over *Sheḥitah*'.

sporadic conflicts until the end of the 1840s in which hasidim tried to push for the appointment of a supplementary slaughterer from their own community,[44] and even later over attempts to appoint a hasidic replacement for the post of ritual slaughterer (as in the Włocławek; see Ch. 4, §5).

Another source of conflict in the early stages of the formation of hasidic groups within a given Jewish community was the hasidic practice of visiting the courts of their tsadikim during religious festivals, causing an exodus of men from the town. This was especially marked during the most religiously intense part of the year, from Rosh Hashanah to Sukkot. This was a source of conflict not only because the hasidim thereby distanced themselves, quite literally, from the control of the rabbi and the elders of the Jewish community but also because it deprived the community of income—the major festivals were traditionally a time for making charitable donations to various communal institutions. The offerings were voluntary, but one should remember that social pressure in a small community means that the voluntary nature of giving is somewhat illusory. Be that as it may, the fact that hasidim absented themselves from the town had significant consequences for communal income.

One of the most frequent reasons for conflict was the creation of hasidic *shtiblekh*. This not only undermined the authority of the community but also had economic consequences because it meant a decline in the income raised by people bidding to be called to the reading of the Torah, from collection boxes, from payment for seats, and even from community taxes and additional contributions. In Kazimierz Dolny, where seventeen wealthy hasidic families had created their own *shtibl*, the Jewish community board complained that

this minority is wealthier and pays a significant part of auxiliary synagogue dues, but they only pay the dues; they do not carry any other part of the financial burden of the synagogue, such as paying to read from the Torah scrolls, so we can reliably claim with a clear conscience that this minority of families does not carry a greater financial burden for the synagogue but a lesser one. . . . In addition, these wealthy families do not go to the synagogue and so do not pay to read from the Torah scrolls, sit in the pews, or make offerings on Yom Kippur or pay to make repairs to the synagogue. The *mikveh* gets no income from these families because they have their own separate bath. In a word, they are a community within a community.[45]

This argument is found in the protocols of the Vilna *kahal* from 1798 and recurred frequently in the nineteenth century in complaints of the

---

[44] For example, in Wodzisław in 1845 the hasidim introduced an alternative slaughterer: see APK, Rewizor Skarbowy Okręgu Jędrzejowskiego 13, np.

[45] *40.02; AGAD, CWW 1632, pp. 145–80.

community boards against the hasidic *shtiblekh*,[46] but government officials showed little interest.[47] Moreover, by the mid-nineteenth century, the fight was less about the right to establish separate *shtiblekh* than about the community's concern about losing control.

The right of hasidim to assemble freely was a very similar source of conflict. The *kahal* disliked this type of gathering because it wanted to maintain control over all forms of organization of the community, including religious brotherhoods, prayer gatherings, and so on, but there was also concern about the particular nature of hasidic gatherings since the hasidim were generally young men, with young men's tendency to hooliganism and unseemly behaviour. Thus in Parczew in 1823 Przysucha hasidim were charged with carousing at night, incidents of drunkenness, and causing social disorder; night-time disturbances figure in other accounts too. All this naturally antagonized the community establishment. Conflicts concerning hasidic gatherings at night appear throughout the entire nineteenth century, even when hasidism had already become an important social force.

Other incidents reveal that the community was concerned about the loss of sources of revenue, such as the sale of *etrogim* or the income from morning prayer services on Mondays and Thursdays, when the reading of the Torah would have attracted a bigger crowd than on other weekdays, and therefore more charitable donations to synagogue funds.[48] Moreover, the example of hasidim encouraged others to stray from the principle of financial solidarity: 'The example of the hasidim leads to other religious gatherings in private, and these others, like the hasidim, hold services in their homes and do not pay all the appropriate fees.'[49] As I pointed out in the context of the conflict in Włocławek (see Ch. 4, §5), the financial autonomy of the hasidic community and its right not to contribute to the community purse was a very important factor in the growth of hasidism. Not surprisingly, finances were the cause of heated controversy, and at times even bloody conflict.

All the sources of communal conflict mentioned so far were characteristic of the early, formative phase of hasidic communal politics (though, as I pointed out, many of them also appeared later), when hasidim tried to gain at least relative institutional and financial autonomy and free themselves of obligations towards the community and the non-hasidic part of the population. The first type of conflict in the next phase, when the goal was power and

---

[46] See Wilensky, *Ḥasidim umitnagedim*, i. 208–9, for the Vilna protocol. For more on these conflicts see Ch. 2, §1. Several cases of communal strife over the creation of hasidic *shtiblekh* in Płock, Przysucha, Wodzisław, and Lublin are discussed in Dynner, '*Men of Silk*', 59–70.

[47] See for example such complaints from Chmielnik in APK, RGR 4405, pp. 2–3; for interrogation about the case in Chęciny see *3.01; APK, RGR 4409, pp. 4–7.

[48] See e.g. *7.09; *14.02; *18.01; AGAD, CWW 1734, pp. 25–7; AGAD, KWK 702, pp. 214–16; AGAD, CWW 1734, pp. 25–7.   [49] *14.02; AGAD, KWK 702, pp. 214–16.

dominance, concerned the right to influence the decisions of communal institutions. The earliest such conflict, mentioned in previous chapters, was the conflict in Częstochowa in 1820, when hasidim demanded separate hours for their use of the public *mikveh* (see Ch. 2, §4). Similar conflicts concerned the insistence by hasidim on the right to smoke in the *beit midrash* (see Ch. 7, §2.2), or indeed to take control of the *beit midrash* more generally. Efforts to gain influence over the functioning of the *mikveh*, the *beit midrash*, and other communal institutions did not necessarily come from a sense of political strength but rather from a conviction of entitlement as a result of their exceptional piety.

The situation concerning efforts to influence the appointment of rabbis was similar. Of course, hasidim had been appointed to rabbinical positions since the earliest stages of the existence of the movement—for example, Shmuel Shmelke Horowitz of Nikolsburg and Levi Isaac of Berdyczów (Berdichev). This does not mean, however, that they were appointed *as* hasidim. As I have attempted to show elsewhere, a hasidic affiliation was often not a criterion used in evaluating a candidate for the position of rabbi; significantly more important were talmudic knowledge, ties with influential families in town, or even the willingness to accept a position in a small town where the remuneration was very low.[50] Appointments to the rabbinate became a subject of political controversy only when a local hasidic community proposed its own candidate despite doubts regarding the candidate's suitability for the post, or when it opposed the non-hasidic candidate only because of his views on hasidism; in these cases, the basic criterion of evaluation was inevitably the candidate's hasidic or anti-hasidic affiliation. This type of conflict occurred only in situations when a local group of hasidim felt strong enough to influence the choice of rabbi despite the lack of broad community consensus.

The earliest conflicts arose not because hasidim were attempting to impose their own candidate but rather because they opposed an officiating rabbi with anti-hasidic views or objected to a proposed non-hasidic candidate.[51] As an embittered resident of Nasielsk complained to the state authorities in 1860, 'because of these subversive hasidim we may have no rabbi; for them, a rabbi is not necessary; His Excellency the Governor knows that hasidim have illegal rabbis [presumably, a reference to tsadikim] and [therefore] do not need a [communal] rabbi because they do not pray together with us in the synagogue but only go to the synagogue to make some kind of scene with the rabbi'.[52] Ignoring the polemical nature of this charge, it is fair to assume

---

[50] See Wodziński, *Haskalah and Hasidism*, 133–4.
[51] This is exactly what happened in Płock for example: hasidic opponents protested at the election of each new non-hasidic rabbi. See e.g. *22.01–*22.06; *43.01–*43.03.
[52] AGAD, CWW 1663, pp. 532–5.

that hasidim used the services of the communal rabbi significantly less than the non-hasidic community did; they therefore had little incentive to compromise over rabbinical candidates since they saw no urgency in making an appointment anyway. This naturally gave them the upper hand in the conflict with the rest of the community, which was significantly more concerned to resolve matters quickly and therefore more ready to compromise.[53]

Nevertheless, starting in the 1840s the hasidim became increasingly interested in the appointment of communal rabbis.[54] The reasons for this are complex, but from examining the writings and testimonies of representatives of different elements of Jewish society it seems there were three main factors. Perhaps the most basic was that appointment as a communal rabbi created the opportunity to spread hasidic values and thereby to influence community norms. A communal rabbi had the right and also the means to admonish people whose behaviour and attitudes he considered wrong and to support those whose behaviour he considered exemplary. When in 1850 a Jew from Pilica chose to follow the modern fashion and wear a short jacket in place of the long kaftan of traditional Jews, Rabbi Leibush Hirszberg issued a public reprimand: 'Why didn't he just pay the tax for Jewish dress? He is not so poor.'[55]

A second reason for seeking a rabbinical appointment was financial: rabbis received a salary from the communal budget, and even if this remuneration was modest it would be supplemented by extra income for performing marriages, circumcisions, and other ceremonies. In the mid-nineteenth century, many tsadikim found that their income from donations was dropping,[56] simply because the ever-growing number of tsadikim meant that the available resources were spread more thinly. Several hasidic leaders, such as Henokh Lewin of Aleksandrów (Alexander), became rabbis (and later tsadikim) only in the wake of bankruptcy following a business failure. The financial significance of a rabbinical position, however, also derived from the possibilities it offered of influencing the communal budget and benefiting from dealings in communal property. The financial activities of the rabbi and hasidic leader Eleazar Hakohen in Płock caused so much communal conflict that in the end he had to resign,[57] but many other rabbis seem to have profited from their position without getting embroiled in controversy.

A third reason for seeking a rabbinical appointment was that, after 1846,

[53] For a more general analysis of reasons for the diminishing role of the rabbis in 19th-c. eastern Europe, see Stampfer, 'The Missing Rabbis of Eastern Europe'.

[54] Some cases have been discussed in Ch. 4, §2. For an interesting case from Lublin from the 1860s see Kuwałek, 'Urzędowi rabini lubelskiego Okręgu Bożniczego', esp. 39.

[55] AGAD, CWW 1445, pp. 223–32.

[56] See Assaf, '"Money for Household Expenses"'; id., *The Regal Way*, 285–309, on *pidyonot*, *ma'amadot* (forms of financial contribution by the hasidim to their tsadik), and generally on the financial aspects of the hasidic courts.   [57] AGAD, CWW 1661, pp. 287–93.

the only way to avoid the tax imposed on wearing traditional Jewish attire was to occupy the post of rabbi or deputy rabbi; after 1850, only rabbis and deputy rabbis were allowed to wear such attire at all.[58] From the late 1840s to the 1860s, the most common accusation from non-hasidim against hasidic candidates seeking rabbinical appointments was that they were doing so only because it would enable them to wear traditional Jewish dress.[59] Thus opponents of the hasidic candidate for the post of rabbi in Łęczna, the tsadik Joshua ben Solomon Leib, wrote of him: 'Because he wanted to wear Jewish attire, he succeeded in gathering some support for the position of deputy rabbi from the lower classes as well as from a few individuals from the higher class thus he will be allowed to wear Jewish attire.'[60] It is hard to believe that this was the only reason to attempt to attain the position of rabbi or assistant rabbi, but it is also difficult to believe that it was not an important one in communities in which the number of assistant rabbis increased from one to seven in the year the law on Jewish dress was introduced.

The last major area of confrontation at the community level concerns the attempt to gain positions on the Jewish community board. Here too I am referring to situations in which the candidates were put forward *as* hasidim and not when they acted independently of their hasidic affiliation. The establishment of the Jewish community boards in the 1820s was originally regarded with indifference, but by the 1830s the advantages of taking control were clear, and hasidim were active in the struggle to gain ascendancy. In some cases they even managed to take over the Jewish community board completely, but such situations were rare and occurred only quite late in this period. The sources allow us to conclude that this occurred only in one of two circumstances: when two client interest groups, one of them hasidic, opposed each other; or when the non-hasidic group in power suddenly lost social support because of excesses of some kind or the misuse of authority. In such cases the hasidim gained complete power, but usually this situation did not last. Thus in Piotrków Trybunalski, according to Icek Bendermacher, 'the Jewish community board of the local community has in past years committed various abuses . . . they were removed from the board and penalized in court, and so the community has chosen from among themselves three new members of the board'; however, it soon turned out that the new board members, all hasidic, 'acted like their predecessors, leading to increased taxes and poverty for the impoverished residents'.[61]

The reasons why hasidim tried to gain influence over, or even take control

[58] See Kirszrot, *Prawa Żydów w Królestwie Polskim*, 271–2.
[59] See e.g. APL, AmL 2258; AGAD, CWW 1613, pp. 210–12.
[60] *31.01; AGAD, CWW 1613, pp. 210–12. In 1852 in Warsaw, Isaac Meir Alter of Góra Kalwaria (Ger) arranged for an unremunerated religious position; the reasons were apparently similar. See *36.5; AGAD, CWW 1871, pp. 301–3; Borzymińska, 'Sprawa Rabiego Icchaka Meira Altera', 373–4.   [61] *27.01; AGAD, CWW 1560, pp. 191–4.

of, a Jewish community board were the same as those of all other groups jockeying for power. The prime reason was perhaps the conviction that they would be better able to realize their own interests and the goals of the community. Attitudes like this, however, were expressed only rarely in the incidents discussed here; materialistic motivations appear significantly more often. These include the legalization of financial autonomy; influencing the schedule of communal taxes so as to minimize the financial burden for themselves; and assuming control over communal finances, including sources of income and even communal property. Icek Bendermacher of Piotrków Trybunalski described a quite typical scheme:

Several weeks ago the official auction of the lease of the *mikveh* [which conferred the right to charge for using it] was to have taken place in the office of the magistrate. The date of the auction was changed several times to confound those trying to obtain the lease. In the end, when the auction was taking place in the magistrate's office, they [i.e. the representatives of the hasidic-dominated community board] secluded themselves in the office and did not admit any of the competitors for the lease, which resulted in the *mikveh* being leased for a derisory sum, which will mean less income and hurt the community.[62]

Naturally this focus on money was not necessarily characteristic of all hasidim or of all their activities, but it seems to have become relatively significant in the nineteenth century and thus increasingly visible. Moreover, the effective incapacitation of the *kahal* (even if the community boards that replaced them were not completely devoid of all powers) led to a decline in identification with the Jewish community as a community of shared values for which individuals felt a sense of responsibility. This is not unusual for a community experiencing an identity crisis—or rather, a crisis of identification with incapacitated community institutions. In such cases, highly motivated individuals and groups can acquire power more easily even if their objectives are not in the communal interest because no one feels responsible for the common good and there is no credible alternative.

4. How? Means

Despite the existence and sporadic use of non-confrontational methods of political activity, the vast majority of the political encounters between hasidim and others had a confrontational character. We have seen this in the incidents already discussed and will see it even more clearly in what follows. In my opinion, confrontation was the prime feature of hasidic politics at the community level. Moreover, the level of aggression in some incidents suggests that conflicts were easily divorced from their original political context and took on a life of their own. Even so, a political agenda persisted as the

---

[62] *27.01; AGAD, CWW 1560, pp. 191–4.

ultimate objective was necessarily concerned with the distribution of power. The method of political action varied, depending on the context, but the key factor was the identity of the opponent: fighting government officials required different methods from fighting Jewish institutions and groups.

The political methods used in fighting the government were relatively few, and no different from those used by others. One method was the obstruction or boycott of services, causing a reduction in the government's income and therefore forcing a compromise. Thus, when the Jews of Wodzisław felt that the official taxes on kosher meat were excessive, 'they formed a group and swore together not to use kosher meat, and so the public income decreased; the treasury's income from this source declined'.[63] A more popular tool was appealing to higher authorities to overturn the decisions of a lower authority. However, the most universal method, and the most interesting, was subterfuge: the fabrication of a situation apparently conforming to government regulations while in fact business continued as normal. Thus for example in 1822 the state dissolved all Jewish religious societies such as those for reading psalms, for raising dowries for poor brides, and the *ḥevra kadisha* burial societies, as reformers perceived them not only as the embodiment of Jewish separatism but also as tools that enabled the *kahal* to maintain its control over ordinary Jews. Their dissolution was thus seen as making an important contribution to the reform of Jewish society. The Jewish communities did not protest and duly adopted appropriate protocols of dissolution—after which they were able to continue the *ḥevra* activities undisturbed so long as news of their existence and activities did not reach state authorities. (When, after twenty years, the illegality of such organizations had been completely forgotten by the Jews, news of the existence of a *ḥevra* would sometimes reach the authorities and spark a national investigation.[64]) Communal budgets, the position of rabbis, the jurisdiction of Jewish community boards, and ever larger spheres of official Jewish community life were simply fictitious: the scale of this virtual reality was immense. In 1850 the magistrate of Radomsko, a small town known mainly for being the seat of the influential tsadik Solomon Rabinowicz, reported to the authorities that the Jewish community board, which consisted mainly of hasidim, had access to significant funds intended to cover community expenses but not specifically itemized in the budget so that they were able to use some of these funds for their own benefit.[65] Hasidim were especially active in creating such fictitious situations, though there are also cases of hasidic denunciations revealing the scale of such fictions in communities dominated by non-hasidim. For example, in Międzyrzec in 1859 a hasidic

[63] AGAD, CWW 1432, pp. 197–200.
[64] For more on this see Guesnet, *Polnische Juden im 19. Jahrhundert*, 227–8.
[65] APŁ, APRG 2559, pp. 684–5.

informer revealed that the nominal communal budget of 1,433 roubles excluded at least 5,100 roubles of undeclared income, and that the true budget
was almost five times bigger than the official budget.[66]

The methods applied by hasidim in the internal politics of the Jewish
community were fundamentally the same as those used by their opponents;
in this sense, the groups were symmetrical. On the basis of the sources I have
analysed (primarily bureaucratic records), I estimate that the most widespread method in the entire period under discussion was denunciation to the
government with a request for intervention. Such denunciations were symptomatic of a more general change in the communal Jewish politics of the
nineteenth century. An illustrative case is a communal conflict in Chęciny,
a small and impoverished provincial town in the southern part of central
Poland, with 2,857 residents in 1827, of whom 60.9 per cent were Jews.
In 1818 the local *kahal* asked the provincial authorities for assistance in
preventing members of the community from spending religious festivals
outside the town.[67] As we have seen, this was a typical cause of conflict
between the *kahal* and the hasidim, and was indeed a cause of conflict with
other factions too; splinter groups had been creating their own *shtiblekh* since
the eighteenth century. All such factions wanted to conduct their affairs
independently, so it is quite understandable that the *kahal* tried at any cost to
oppose them. It was a sign of the times, however, that the way in which the
kahal tried to do so was to petition the government; it no longer had the
authority to control a dissident group. The incident mentioned occurred
before the formal dissolution of the *kahal*s in 1822, but even then the *kahal*
was no longer able to restrain breakaway groups (a situation quite unlike that
which would have prevailed a hundred years earlier, when state guarantees
of autonomy gave the *kahal* almost unlimited powers, including corporal
punishment). This degeneration, which was found not only in the Kingdom
of Poland but throughout central and eastern Europe, can be attributed both
to the institutional crisis of traditional Jewish society and to the reforms that
had been initiated by modernizing regimes since the end of the eighteenth
century. Above all, however, the weakening of the *kahal* was a consequence of
the general political ideal of the Enlightenment; henceforth the state denied
religious bodies the right to apply force in community conflicts and indeed to
exercise any jurisdiction over members of their community, now perceived
solely as a voluntary religious grouping.[68] This was of course a further factor
in facilitating the development of hasidism.

---

[66] See AGAD, CWW 1780, pp. 326–31.   [67] See *3.01; APK, RGR 4409, pp. 4–7.
[68] Of the general historical literature on the crisis of the Jewish communal structures in the
18th c. and beginning of the 19th c., see especially the classic study by Jacob Katz, *Tradition and
Crisis*; see also the iconoclastic opinion of Gershon Hundert in *Jews in Poland–Lithuania in the
Eighteenth Century*, 99–118. For more on the dissolution of the *kahal* in the Kingdom of Poland,

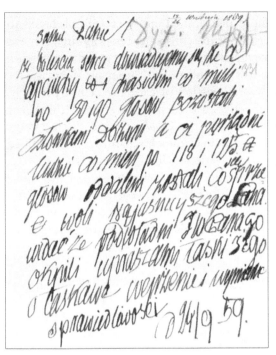

Figure 6.1 An example of an anti-hasidic denunciation from Warsaw submitted to the ministerial authorities, 1859. AGAD, CWW 1731, p. 331

Of course, it was not only the *kahal* that turned to the state for assistance in communal conflicts. Both parties could certainly do so, though undoubtedly it was more common for the *kahal* to seek the state's support in enforcing order than it was for the hasidim to seek protection. This was especially true while the hasidim were still only a small splinter group attempting to free themselves from the control of the *kahal* rather than in later years when they were trying to extract political concessions from the community. The disadvantage of this method, however, was that since the *kahal* could not control the process of state intervention it could have undesired results. In addition, despite the clear increase in Jewish denunciations and the equally clear inability of the *kahal* to halt the practice, many Jews still regarded informing against fellow Jews as unacceptable. As one aggrieved Jew from Sandomierz testified in 1816, none of his co-religionists was willing to support his testimony against the *kahal*, 'because they are afraid of the *kahal* and because this contradicts our religion'.[69] Certainly both these factors in combination—the uncertainty of the outcome and the traditional ban on turning to the intervention of non-Jewish authorities—were the main reasons why anti-hasidic accusers repeatedly refrained from testifying against the hasidim.

see Askenazy, 'Ze spraw żydowskich w dobie kongresowej', 1–14; Schiper, 'Samorząd żydowski'; Guesnet, *Polnische Juden im 19. Jahrhundert*, 223–9; see also Szternkranc, *Zniesienie kahałów*.

[69] APK, Oddział w Sandomierzu, Akta miasta Sandomierza 51, p. 59.

This, of course, weakened the effectiveness of the intervention. Of the two sides, the hasidim were the more determined and therefore prepared to escalate the conflict without regard for the consequences. The situation was typical enough: the conservative majority was not willing to fight in defence of its traditional values and so lost ground to the aggressive minority, for whom obtaining concessions was a question of existence. Unsurprisingly, then, the hasidim were more effective in their political strategy than their opponents. Time and again they forced the *kahal* either to reach a compromise that was beneficial for them (as in Częstochowa in 1820, as described in Ch. 2, §4), or to withdraw their opposition (as in Olkusz in 1818; see Ch. 2, §4) and agree to an unwanted innovation. One can surmise that this influenced the pace of the development of the hasidic movement in the following years. Other ways in which the government could be prompted to intervene was by burdening the other side with the obligation of billeting soldiers, or with taxes and fees.[70] Accusations of over-taxation appeared countless times in communal conflicts, suggesting both the relative popularity of this tactic and a widespread lack of confidence in how the community conducted its affairs.

The list of the remaining methods of political struggle in Jewish communities reads like an excerpt from the penal code, so it is worth stressing that the examples that follow are merely those that figured most often in the conflicts known to me from the Kingdom of Poland during this period. All were used more or less equally by both sides.

The most common weapon in the political arsenal was the simple threat. For example, in Łęczna during the investigation against the local tsadik Joshua ben Solomon Leib, 'Moszek Kliberg, the brother-in-law of Joshua ben Solomon Leib, the deputy rabbi, went daily to the treasury; when inhabitants were called to present testimony, Kliberg threatened them, saying his brother-in-law would be displeased with their actions and so they should withdraw their complaint'.[71] Complaints of threats from the Jewish community board were equally frequent.

The next most common method was the boycott, as in Kazimierz Dolny, when residents formed a 'conspiracy' against the hasidic rabbi Jacob Goldman. However, the opposite also often occurred, when hasidim formed a 'conspiracy' to apply pressure on non-hasidic individuals or groups.[72] An interesting variant of this method was to go on strike, as the hasidic rabbi in Bełchatów did. Under attack from non-hasidic residents, he decided to

[70] See e.g. AGAD, CWW 1602, pp. 237–57; AGAD, CWW 1780, pp. 326–30.

[71] AGAD, CWW 1613, pp. 210–12.

[72] An interesting example is a hasidic 'conspiracy' against a wealthy purveyor of flour suspected of denouncing the tsadik, described in Kotik, *A Journey to a Nineteenth-Century Shtetl*, 303–5.

Figure 6.2 A hasidic pasquinade (1867) accusing the communal rabbi of Płock, Leib Rakowski, of conversion and marrying a non-Jewish woman.
APP, AmP 569, p. 282

deny them religious services, which exposed them to additional costs and significant inconvenience because they had to travel outside Bełchatów to carry out obligations such as registering births, marriages, deaths, and so forth.[73]

Another method, applied equally often by hasidim and their opponents, was the ban (*ḥerem*), which could serve different goals, from 'punishing' opponents to attracting them to the hasidic camp ('by various methods they try to draw others to their group, persecuting those who are not inclined to join').[74] In accordance with local mitnagdic tradition, such a *ḥerem* by the anti-hasidic rabbi Yom Tov Lipman Heilpern[75] in Międzyrzec Podlaski is said

[73] See APŁ, APRG 2496, pp. 559–60.

[74] AGAD, CWW 1493, pp. 64–5. For an account of many bans investigated by the ministerial authorities of the Kingdom of Poland, see AGAD, CWW 1409; for examples of the bans involving hasidim see e.g. AGAD, CWW 1780, pp. 326–30; APŁ, APRG 2496, p. 592.

[75] Yom Tov Lipman Heilpern, also known as Lipele, was the son of Israel, rabbi and *mitnaged*, and a member of a well-known rabbinical family. He studied at a yeshiva in Mińsk. From 1836 he was rabbi in Kreve in Vilna province and from 1841 in Kajdanów, which he had to leave as the result of a conflict with the communal elite and his opposition to the practices of the so-called *khapers* (individuals employed by the Jewish communities to deliver recruits to the tsarist army). He was rabbi in Ciechanowiec until 1850, then in Międzyrzec Podlaski, where according to tradition he conflicted sharply with local hasidim; in 1859 he was appointed rabbi in Białystok. He is the author of the well-known halakhic work *Oneg yom tov*. See *Pinkas byalistok*, ed. Mark, i. 166–70.

to have been responsible for the death of tsadik Menahem Mendel of Kock; interestingly, hasidic complaints to the provincial government testify to the fact of a curse on hasidim at this time by Rabbi Heilpern.[76]

The ultimate level of communal conflict was direct aggression, which often and easily escalated to physical force. Verbal aggression, the prime tool, included public defamation, ridicule, insults, and the writing and distribution of libellous texts. Unfortunately few such texts have been preserved, so it is difficult to determine their content and form.[77] A text written in Płock in 1867, lampooning the local anti-hasidic rabbi Azriel Aryeh Leib ben Abraham Rakowski and distributed at night in sixteen places in different parts of the city by local hasidim, is therefore an especially valuable document:[78]

ליבל משומד ישו"ז [79]

עושה גזירות	ליבל עושה איסר
עובר עבירות	עובר איסור
יבואו עליו צרות	אוכל איסור
ועצמותיו נישברות	איסור א בונט
ועיניו מנוקרות	ליבל א הונט
יהיה לכפרות	ווער בלינט
	גאנץ געשוינד

פה פלאצק, העיר אשר בה
נקבר ליבל ראקרסקי ימח שמו
וזכרו שם רשעים ירקב

ער האט זיך גישמדט אונטער
יאגעסטאו אין האט חתונה גיהאט
מיט א גויה אונטר לאמזע
ליבל ליטואק מוחרם מנודה לפ"ק [80]

---

[76] See *37.01; AGAD, CWW 1780, pp. 326–30. Traces of R. Lipele Heilpern's curse on all those disturbing the peace of the community (referring above all to tsadik Menahem Mendel of Kock and his supporters in Międzyrzec) are preserved in the tradition: see *Pinkas byalistok*, ed. Mark, i. 167–8. Local legend ties R. Heilpern's *ḥerem* in Międzyrzec with the death of Mendel in Kock thirty days later (according to *Shulḥan arukh*, 'Yoreh de'ah', 334: 1, a period of thirty days is the usual and minimal term for a ban of the type called *nidui*; if during this time the penitent does not refrain from sin, the curse becomes stronger). Unfortunately, the date of the ban is not known, but it would have to have been several days before Ehenbalt's complaint of 7 Jan. 1859. Mendel of Kock died on 27 Jan. 1859.

[77] On the Jewish pasquinades, mainly from the Haredi Orthodox community in 20th-c. Israel, see Friedman, 'Pashkevilim umoda'ot kir baḥevrah haḥaredit'.

[78] APP, AmP 569, pp. 282–3. The event has also been preserved in the family tradition and recorded by R. Rakowski's granddaughter, Pua Rakovsky, in her autobiography, *My Life as a Radical Jewish Woman*, 32.

[79] ישו"ז—ימח שמו וזכרו 'let his name and memory be blotted out'. Possibly referring to the alleged conversion of R. Rakowski; the abbreviation makes an allusion to the name of Jesus—ישו.

[80] לפ"ק—לפרט קטן i.e. 'according to the minor reckoning', which omits indication of the thousands figure; thus, the numerical value of all the characters in the line is indeed 627, which in the full reckoning would be [5]627 of the Jewish calendar, or year 1866/7 CE. Interestingly,

The converted Leibel, may his name and memory be extinguished

Leibel did what was forbidden	A fatal sentence was proclaimed
going beyond what was forbidden	He who commits sin
eating what was banned	May he be met with plagues
Forbidden means rebellion	That his bones be crushed
Leibel is a dog	And eyes scratched out
and blind	May he be condemned
very soon	

May the city of Płock where Leibel Rakowski came and
stayed be the place of his burial

May his memory and name, the name of a sinner, die
Baptized near Augustów
And married to a heathen near Łomża

Leibel Litvak is cursed.

Reports of verbal abuse, insults, mockery, and so on are innumerable, allowing us to re-create the character and the dynamics of events with some accuracy. For example, in 1836 the Jewish community board of Koniecpol complained that hasidim 'gather for secret meetings and repeatedly verbally harass and actively insult the board'.[81] Similarly, in the attacks on Rabbi Isaac Auerbach in Płock in 1838 mentioned above, a group of hasidim 'offended him with the most insulting expressions' and shouted and challenged the rabbi saying, "*Rush* [probably *Rasha*, 'wicked'] you and your people are evil, you're not worthy to be here," along with other jibes.'[82] In contrast, in 1840 a hasidic rabbi in Bełchatów complained of members of an anti-hasidic group concentrated around the Wajs family:

First, one of them banged hard [on his *shtender*, or reading desk] and grabbed me . . . and tried to push me away. Herszke Kirszenbaum called out to catch me by the *peyes* and take me out of the synagogue. Mendel Layb called out to me in the synagogue *Poshie* [sic] *yisro'el*, meaning the entire Jewish nation is sinful, and to take me and lead me away. When I was standing in front of the *aron hakodesh*, Szlama Wajs grabbed me by my *kittel* and pulled me off the *aron hakodesh* and they extinguished the light . . . For no reason and without any justification, I was called a thief and he pulled my beard.[83]

the family name is misspelt 'Rakarski' instead of Rakowski (using *resh* instead of *vav*), no doubt alluding to the Polish term *rakarz* 'dog-catcher'. Note too that elements of the lampoon play on controversies between Polish and Lithuanian Jews. First, Leib is called a 'Litvak', a derogatory term for a Lithuanian Jew. Second, the places of supposed conversion and marriage listed in the lampoon, Augustów and Łomża, are among the best-known towns in the north of the Kingdom of Poland, in which Lithuanian tradition predominated and where hasidism was nearly non-existent.

[81] *20.01; APŁ, APRG 2512, pp. 310–12. See also *20.05; APŁ, APRG 2512, pp. 306–7, 313–14. [82] *22.03; APP, AmP 568, fos. 142–8. [83] APŁ, APRG 2496, pp. 566–7, 570.

This example demonstrates how easily verbal aggression could escalate into physical violence. This could take different forms; it could mean tearing the clothes of people who had abandoned traditional Jewish attire,[84] dragging them away from or pushing them out of the synagogue or *shtibl*,[85] extinguishing lights, banging windows, and throwing candles during services,[86] bundling people into sacks and taking them out of the city,[87] brutal beatings,[88] and, in exceptional cases, even murder.[89] For example, in Płock in 1867 Rabbi Leib Rakowski 'was at night at the wedding of the Jew Samuel Segał; suddenly hasidim tried to extinguish the light and beat the rabbi, but his Jewish companions at the wedding did not allow them to do this'. Unable to beat him, the hasidim distributed insulting notices about him in the town and smashed his windows.[90] Smashing windows seems to have been the preferred form of 'street' politics, since it is mentioned more often in the sources than any other type of physical force. Windows were broken in the cases of Rabbi Isaac Auerbach in Płock in 1838, Rabbi Leib Rakowski in 1867, and in Wolbrom in 1863 by people protesting against hasidic dominance of the community; in Bełchatów in 1840, when both sides smashed windows; and in Międzyrzec in 1859, when *mitnagedim* broke all the windows of the hasidic synagogue.[91] Hasidim smashed windows not only during street conflicts but also as an expression of high spirits, sometimes in both senses of the term. For example, in 1860 Franciszek Gwardyński, a Christian resident of Piątek, testified that 'Jews returning from synagogue had been drinking heavily and broke almost all of the panes in my windows, around twelve at night. I ran to the courtyard and recognized a few Jews who assured me that they would pay something for the broken windows; Icek Halpern came to me the next day and compensated me for the damage, so I have no complaints about any of them.'[92] An investigation revealed that those responsible were local hasidim 'celebrating' Rosh Hashanah.

A prime mode of conflict characteristic of hasidic communal politics was rapid antagonization, often escalating into violence on both sides. Sociologists call such a situation, in which each act of aggression generates further

[84] See examples from Łódź from 1848 in Wodziński, *Haskalah and Hasidism*, 138–40.
[85] See e.g. APŁ, APRG 2496, pp. 566–7.
[86] See e.g. *40.02; AGAD, CWW 1632, pp. 145–80.
[87] See e.g. *39.02; AGAD, CWW 1663, pp. 532–5.
[88] For example, in Nasielsk in central Poland the hasidim beat up the local cantor so violently that he 'was close to dying and because of this heavy beating got convulsions': see *39.02; AGAD, CWW 1663, pp. 532–5.
[89] On the murder of two Jewish informers, allegedly committed with the permission of the tsadik Israel of Różyn (Ruzhin), see Assaf, *The Regal Way*, 108–14.   [90] APP, AmP 569, fo. 271.
[91] See *41.02; AGAD, CWW 1493, pp. 68–9; *22.01; APP, AmP 568, fo. 141; APP, AmP 569, fo. 271; APŁ, APRG 2496, p. 592; *37.01; AGAD, CWW 1780, pp. 326–30.
[92] AGAD, CWW 1716, p. 223.

aggression by the other party, 'symmetrical differentiation'; although it heightens the tension it paradoxically decreases the effectiveness of the aggression since both sides invest increasingly great force with increasingly meagre results. As increasing physical force thus proved only minimally effective, the consequence was that exceptional social force was required even in relatively modest political negotiations. However, this vicious circle was eventually broken through the emergence of a new political actor: a hasidic *shtadlan* with supra-communal political competence.

5. Local or Universal?

The above examples show that local conflicts were frequently not resolved at the communal level; they escalated, became chronic, or became subject to the intervention of supra-communal political agents. This complex inter-relationship between communal politics and state politics was a key element of hasidic politics in nineteenth-century Europe, and indeed of many other political conflicts of that period. To better illustrate this and to demonstrate its consequences, I shall discuss two cases in which a hasidic *shtadlan* inter-vened at state level in a matter of local politics in order to protect wider communal interests.

5.1 A Rabbi for Czyżew?

In accordance with the law in the Kingdom of Poland, the election of a rabbi came under the control of the state authorities, and more precisely the Government Commission for Internal and Religious Affairs. In addition to being examined orally by the board of the Warsaw Rabbinical School (to establish his knowledge of Polish and of geography as well as his knowledge of the history of the Jewish people, of Hebrew, and of the Bible and the Talmud), the candidate had to win an election overseen by a magistrate, obtain a certificate from at least two rabbis and the local authorities attesting that he was a law-abiding and loyal citizen (this condition was introduced after the 1830–1 revolution), and also pay a licence fee (although this was a relatively minor burden).[93] The government was anxious to appoint a rabbi in every Jewish community to oversee the register of births, deaths, and mar-riages as well as the proper collection of the kosher meat tax. It wanted to be satisfied, however, that the appointment procedures were followed rigor-ously; whenever there were difficulties the government would threaten the community that it would simply appoint a graduate of the Warsaw Rabbinical School to the position. Although this never actually happened, it would appear that the threat was quite effective; once such an ultimatum had been issued, the conflicting parties would attempt to seek a solution quickly and

[93] See the general description in Kirszrot, *Prawa Żydów w Królestwie Polskim*, 27–38.

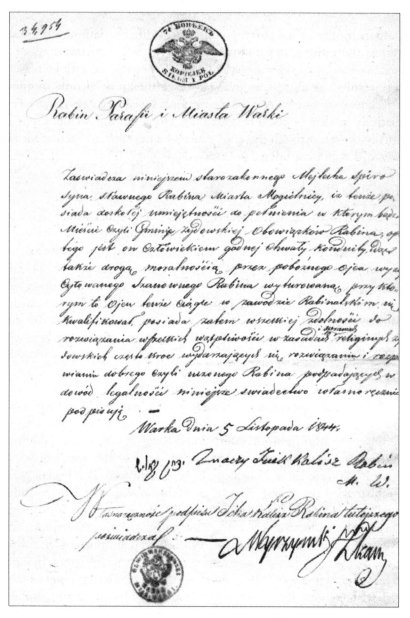

Figure 6.3 Letter of recommendation for Elimelekh Shapiro (1824–92), known as the tsadik of Grodzisk, or the Grodisker Rebbe, issued in 1844 by Rabbi Isaac of Warka. The letter is an example of the certificates issued to rabbinical candidates by rabbinical leaders, hasidic and non-hasidic alike, in order to prevent state intervention in nominations of communal rabbis in the Kingdom of Poland. AGAD, Komisja Województwa Mazowieckiego/Rząd Gubernialny Warszawski 6354, no page given

appoint a compromise candidate. This was not always easy to achieve because the compromise candidate not only had to be acceptable to both sides but also had to fulfil the official requirements, as explained above.[94] The major problem was usually the lack of knowledge of Polish.

Despite all these difficulties, the institution known in imperial Russia as 'crown rabbis' (i.e. rabbis appointed by the government, who worked alongside spiritual leaders who had the confidence of the local community but performed their duties unofficially) did not exist in the Kingdom of Poland.[95] This was attributable to the collective efforts of the rabbinical elite, hasidic and non-hasidic alike. Essentially, there were two ways in which the rabbis were able to minimize the risk of an unwanted or unqualified rabbi being imposed on the community. The first was by issuing certificates to rabbinical candidates so that they would formally qualify for the position of communal rabbi. This practice was of course widespread, and we find hundreds of such certificates issued for Polish rabbis, quite often issued by hasidic leaders for both hasidic and non-hasidic rabbis.[96] The second and more interesting way was the introduction of what I will call a quasi-crown rabbi, meaning a rabbinical figure nominated by the community who would fulfil a function similar to that of the crown rabbis of Russia, in the sense of meeting government requirements for the position while not actually performing the duties of a rabbi in the community. Curiously, the most successful of such quasi-crown rabbis—meaning the most successful in defending Jewish communities against the interventions of the state administration—was none other than Isaac of Warka.

The case in point was connected with a situation that developed in Czyżew (Płock province) in the years 1840–1.[97] The local Jewish community was divided on the question of a hasidic candidate for the rabbinate, as was often the case in the Kingdom of Poland in the mid-nineteenth century, for example in Płock (1829) and Pilica (1835). As stories of particularly heated controversy surrounding the Czyżew election reached the ministerial authorities, the provincial government proposed appointing a graduate of the

---

[94] Of course there were ways to overcome these difficulties. The candidate could send somebody else in his place to take the examination at the rabbinical school. The director of the school, Jakub Tugendhold, claimed that this was impossible, because 'nobody aspiring to spiritual leadership could undertake such a ruse', but he had to admit that the identity of people submitting themselves for examination was not verified. Denunciations suggest that such cases did happen. See AGAD, CWW 1827, pp. 242–52.

[95] On crown rabbis see Shochat, *Mosad 'harabanut mita'am' berusiyah*; Nathans, *Beyond the Pale*.

[96] See e.g. AGAD, KWK 710: the certificate for Szlamo Erdonast, the rabbi of Złoczew; AGAD, Komisja Województwa Mazowieckiego / Rząd Gubernialny Warszawski 6354: the certificate for Elimelekh b. Hayim Meir Yehiel Shapiro, the rabbi and tsadik of Mogielnica (known as the Rebbe of Grodzisk, where he moved in 1849).

[97] See AGAD, CWW 1677, pp. 29–132.

Warsaw Rabbinical School to the position. The candidates suggested by the
school's director were Jakub Szwajcer (the sole graduate of the school who
wanted to take on the duties of a rabbi)[98] and Michał Hertz (a young man
with traditional rabbinical training, but supported by the school's director).
Szwajcer declined, which solved one problem for the community; Hertz was
interested in the position, but even if he was not a graduate of the Warsaw
Rabbinical School he was not someone the community wanted as its rabbi.

At a loss for how to proceed, the community turned to Rabbi Isaac, who
indeed proposed a solution: he would sign a backdated contract in which he
agreed to serve as rabbi of Czyżew in addition to being the rabbi of Nadarzyn
and Warka. The community was thus able to inform the authorities that it
had itself appointed a rabbi, thereby forestalling the threat of a rabbi being
imposed by the authorities. The contract stipulated, however, that he would
not reside in Czyżew, and that his rabbinical duties would be performed on
his behalf by an unpaid honorary deputy rabbi or 'spiritual leader' (*duchowny*),
Hayim Joskowicz Indes. In subsequent years, up to 1865, there is no record of
a rabbi's wages in community budgets, which confirms that the agreement
reached with Rabbi Isaac remained in force even after his death—that is, the
rabbi's duties were carried out free of charge by an honorary deputy rabbi.[99]

How could the state authorities have accepted an agreement that was so
obviously fictitious, given that Czyżew was some 200 kilometres from Warka
and Rabbi Isaac would not live there?[100] He could not possibly have performed any rabbinical duties in Czyżew, nor even have overseen them. Yet
despite its obviously fictitious nature the agreement was formally in accordance with the law, and the Jewish community board in Czyżew had accurately gauged the government's desire to see the conflict resolved as quickly
as possible. The law required a community rabbi to meet certain requirements, but permanent residence in the community was not one of them; similar situations existed elsewhere too.[101] Moreover, the law did not stipulate
whether a rabbi could serve more than one community. Taking advantage of
these loopholes, the community board presented a candidate who, because

[98] For more on Szwajcer see Wodziński, *Haskalah and Hasidism*, 137.

[99] See AGAD, CWW 1446, pp. 327–8; see also ibid. 171–2.

[100] The ultimate proof of Rabbi Isaac's deep attachment to Warka was his generous will. He
bequeathed to the Jewish community there his house and all its furnishings and the sum of
1,000 złoty (together with annual interest), which he had received from Temerl and Berek
Sonnenberg, as well as 6 złoty weekly for the maintenance of the prayer house. See AGAD,
CWW 1741, pp. 10–67; AGAD, Komisja Województwa Mazowieckiego / Rząd Gubernialny
Mazowiecki 7149.

[101] See for example the interesting case of Dydia Landau, who became a communal rabbi in
Raków, a rather miserable small town in central Poland, but immediately after 'securing for
himself the rabbinical post, this in order to be exempted from the military draft, he settled in
Zawichost', some 80 km from Raków. Archiwum Państwowe w Radomiu, Rząd Gubernialny
Radomski I, 4374, p. 160.

of his authority, easily obtained the support of the entire community and fulfilled all the requirements expected of a rabbinical candidate in the eyes of the authorities since he already held the all-important certificate entitling him to work as a rabbi. The provincial government had no choice but to approve the candidate, especially as it was anxious not to prolong the conflict. The honorary deputy rabbi, who was mentioned in the contract, performed all the functions of importance to the government: he assumed responsibility for the register of births, deaths, and marriages; ensured that the meat was kosher (thereby increasing income from the tax on kosher meat); and since he would not be paid a salary (though of course he would still receive the customary *ex gratia* payments for performing specific services) he even reduced the burden on the community budget, the balancing of which was a persistent source of concern for the local government authorities because by law it was something they had to oversee. Significantly, the law placed no limitations on the honorary deputy rabbi, nor did it require him to have passed an examination. In this way the community was able to appoint as 'spiritual leader' a person who would not have been able to fulfil the official requirements for a rabbinical candidate, and the government had no grounds for objecting since the position was not officially remunerated and placed no burden on its budget. As long as the system of *ex gratia* payments did not create any conflict in the community the government turned a blind eye to it.

It is interesting that in this instance Rabbi Isaac did not petition the government to solve the problem but simply stepped in to fill the breach. This was a less confrontational mode of intervention than others discussed above, but it still reflected an effort to find an effective legal solution to a problem faced by a Jewish community, based on a sound understanding of the law, of bureaucratic procedures, and of the mindset of the individual bureaucrats. Rabbi Isaac's contract fulfilled the formal legal requirements and satisfied the authorities' desire for a rapid solution, but at the same time it also safeguarded the interests of the Jewish community. Both sides were perfectly satisfied with this outcome and ignored the fact that the settlement, while perfectly legal, was hardly in tune with the spirit of the law.

The Czyżew incident also illustrates how the two levels of hasidic politics were interdependent. First, it is noteworthy that Rabbi Isaac, the acclaimed political representative of the Jewish community in Poland, was as willing to apply himself to a small-scale communal problem as to large-scale political matters of state importance. Quite possibly he may not have made a distinction between communal and state politics but, rather, would have conceptualized a continuum of political activity extending from significant regulations in the state law, through all kinds of political practices at the state, provincial, and communal levels, down to small-scale cases of individuals, groups, and communities. In each case, he simply tried to achieve as much as possible

Figure 6.4 Wooden synagogue in Warka, built in the years 1811–17; as communal
rabbi of Warka from *c.* 1828 to 1848, Rabbi Isaac must have preached here.
Instytut Sztuki PAN sygn. nr 0000019179

without differentiating between what we consider low and high politics.
In this sense, and because he was not charged with representing a particular
institution but saw himself as acting in the general interest of all Jews, he
was the embodiment of the new type of *shtadlan*. As we shall see in the Będzin
case discussed in the next section, individual communal matters sometimes
required very extensive measures and complicated interventions.

Second, one should ask why the Jewish community of Czyżew turned
to Rabbi Isaac, a communal rabbi from the distant community of Warka
in another province. The Jews of Czyżew were not his hasidim, or indeed
hasidim at all. The conflict emerged from the opposition of the local non-
hasidic group, community elders included, to the hasidic candidate for the
rabbinical post put forward by the competing faction. Most likely it was
thanks to his well-known political activity at the state level that Rabbi Isaac
was known in Czyżew, as in virtually all other Jewish communities across the
Kingdom of Poland, and it was because of his fame as a successful political
activist that the representatives of the community of Czyżew decided to turn
to him for assistance. If this is so, it demonstrates an important aspect of
the interdependence of low and high politics: for the new *shtadlan*, fame
achieved during his state-level interventions paved the way to influence at the
communal level, while for the Jewish communities the same fame was an

Figure 6.5 Interior of the wooden synagogue in Warka.
Instytut Sztuki PAN sygn. nr 00019182

indispensable tool in finding someone truly qualified to help them solve their communal strife. The incident also suggests that the Jewish community turned to a professional political activist because it recognized its inability to solve its communal problems with the competencies and tools at its disposal. This was partly because what started as an apparently local conflict between hasidic and non-hasidic candidates for a rabbinical post was influenced by factors at the state level in the form of a law imposing certain regulations on the local Jewish community with a view to increasing government control. While the appointment of a rabbi was apparently a local problem, it could not be resolved without regard for the legal and political conditions imposed by the state.

5.2 The Rabbi-Informer in Będzin

Another interesting illustration of the link between the local and wider political dimensions is provided by an episode in Będzin, a medium-sized town in the south of the Kingdom where in 1825 the town's 1,196 Jews constituted 42.3 per cent of the total population. The affair was of a local nature—or at least it appeared to be—and had nothing at all to do with hasidim. After Rabbi Menahem Nahum Rozynes's death in 1835, his son Abraham Hersz Rozynes was appointed to the vacant post in somewhat unclear circumstances.[102] The appointment instantly provoked a negative reaction from the Jewish community board and a significant section of the Jewish community. Among the arguments against Rozynes was that 'he had a bad reputation, was unfit for the position, and that the community did not trust him',[103] but the real reason was that he was known to be an informer in the service of the tsarist army and secret police (he even boasted of this fact) and had been appointed only because of the active intervention of the commander of the army of the Kraków voivodeship, which was headquartered in Kielce.[104] He was also an abrasive and irritable person, driven by base impulses and low morals, 'dissolute in behaviour, stirring up quarrels, and launching attacks'. The Jewish community had good reason not to want him.

The presence of informers in a Jewish community was nothing unusual: they seem to have been one of the most common plagues afflicting nineteenth-century east European Jewish communities. Yehezkel Kotik, author of a well-known nineteenth-century memoir, reported that 'In those days there was almost no town without its informer.'[105] The source of the phenomenon is rather complex, but it seems to have arisen because the government's desire to extend its control over the affairs of the Jewish community was such that informers received a financial reward if their denunciations resulted in increased income to the state Treasury; at a time of a substantial increase in poverty, the incentive to inform against fellow Jews was considerable. In many more cases, the threat of denunciation served as a form of blackmail, allowing informers to earn quite a reasonable living. The weakening of social control within the community also made it easier for them to function. The phenomenon reached such proportions that in the 1850s the government was

[102] The historical literature offers only scant information about R. Menahem Nahum Rozynes and his son and about the latter's conflict with the local hasidim. See e.g. Blatman, 'Będzin/Bendin', 104; Rotenberg, 'Toledot bendin hayehudit', 218.

[103] AGAD, CWW 1481, p. 6.   [104] Ibid. 27–33; see also pp. 43–6.

[105] Kotik, *A Journey to a Nineteenth-Century Shtetl*, 142 (see also endnotes 90–1, p. 430). For an overview of Jewish informing in tsarist Russia see Gintsburg, 'Yehudim malshinim beyamim milefanim'.

Figure 6.6 Będzin in the 1880s or 1890s. Previously a rather insignificant town, it experienced an economic boom in the late nineteenth century and grew into an overcrowded industrial city. Photo by Holtz(?). Biblioteka Narodowa w Warszawie, Zbiory Ikonograficzne sygn. I.F.4044/IV-2

overwhelmed by the flood of denunciations and imposed severe penalties for false accusations.[106] Even after this, however, 'professional' informers functioned successfully in nearly every community, and were regarded as a recognized hazard. However, this is not the same as the informer and the communal rabbi being the same person. The appointment of such an individual as the communal rabbi of Będzin was a humiliation for the entire community, so almost from the very beginning there was widespread opposition to the appointment, led by local hasidim.

The energetic involvement of the hasidim and their leadership in the opposition to Rozynes can be explained in at least three ways. First, it appears that the Będzin hasidic group was relatively large; even Rozynes described it as 'this sect in Będzin, almost the largest group'.[107] Even though it is likely that he exaggerated the 'hasidic threat', the hasidic presence had been unmis-

[106] For an especially illustrative case from Łomża, where in the mid-1850s eleven individuals lived solely from blackmailing other Jews with denunciations, six of them being sentenced in 1855 to several months' imprisonment, see AGAD, CWW 1827, *passim*; KRSW 7319.
[107] AGAD, CWW 1481, p. 29.

takable in Będzin since at least the 1820s, and its scale was quite significant.[108] Since the hasidim were the largest organized group in the community, they were the natural leaders of the campaign against the universally hated rabbi/ informer.

A second reason for hasidic involvement could have been that the opposition candidate for the post of rabbi was the local hasidic leader Berek Hercygier, though we do not know whether his candidature was the cause of the hasidic involvement or rather its consequence. Regardless, once Hercygier was involved, the hasidim were doubly interested in removing Rozynes; first, to rid the community of an embarrassing rabbi, and second, to fill the post with their own man.

The third reason may well be the most interesting one as it touches on the sensitive issue of Polish Jewish patriotism. As an informer in the service of the Russian army and secret police, Rozynes had positioned himself unambiguously on the side of the tsarist authorities and therefore against Polish aspirations for independence. Furthermore, his appointment as rabbi, which was on the basis of the letter of recommendation written by the tsarist general, took place in 1835 or 1836, i.e. only four or five years after the collapse of the 1830–1 anti-tsarist uprising, which suggests that he was recruited as a tsarist spy precisely during the uprising. There was nothing unusual in this, since Jews were used as spies by nearly all the armies in eastern Europe, and there is ample evidence testifying to Jewish espionage on behalf of tsarist armies in the 1830–1 uprising (even though, obviously, slander and groundless accusations were proportionately more common).[109] Such ultra-loyalist attitudes on the side of Rabbi Rozynes, however, were resented by those who had Polish patriotic sympathies, or were merely unsympathetic to the Russian cause. There is actually strong evidence that such pro-Polish attitudes were not that unusual among Orthodox Jews in the nineteenth century. In fact, contrary to the erroneous assumptions of later historiography, which identified pro-Polish patriotism with pro-Polish acculturation or social integration and modernization, sympathy for the Polish yearning for independence was surprisingly common in traditional

---

[108] See e.g. AGAD, CWW 1433, pp. 116–17; AGAD, CWW 1445, pp. 223–32; see also APŁ, APRG 2494, pp. 681–1188. As early as the late 18th c., one of Będzin's *dayanim* (rabbinical judges) was Moses Hamburger, brother-in-law of Elimelekh of Leżajsk (Lyzhansk).

[109] See for example an action undertaken at the initiative of Jakub Tugendhold by the rabbis and elders of the Jewish community in Warsaw, including Solomon Lipschitz (Posner), Theodor Toeplitz, Judah Leib Bereksohn (Sonnenberg), and Józef Hayim Halberstam, fighting against Jewish spying during the 1831 Polish insurrection; AGAD, CWW 1435, pp. 112–28. On official awards given to several Jews of the Lublin voivodeship for their services to the intelligence of the Russian troops in 1831, see APL, AmL 2004, pp. 1–172. For a good account of the anti-Jewish accusations of spying during Polish uprisings, see Ringelblum, *Żydzi w powstaniu kościuszkowskiem*, 90–7.

Jewish circles in nineteenth-century Poland.[110] A contemporary memoirist mentions this, observing that 'not only of maskilim, assimilationists calling themselves "Poles" . . . but even hasidim, strictly observant Orthodox, devout Jews observing the religious laws and commandments—they are all Polish patriots'.[111] Examples of such positions are well known: Dov Berish Meisels, a famous Orthodox rabbi of Kraków and later of Warsaw, was the most acclaimed representative of such positions, but it is important to remember that he was not isolated among Orthodox Jews in his pro-Polish sympathies and pronouncements. Of course, very often the pro-Polish opinions expressed by representatives of the traditional Jewish community originated from concepts of 'Polishness' and the 'Polish state' very far from those nurtured by non-Jewish Poles, and were not even unanimously agreed upon by the Jews themselves. For some, the resurrection of the Polish state meant bringing back the legal and political framework of Jewish autonomy from the pre-modern Polish–Lithuanian Commonwealth. For others, pro-Polish political leanings were simply a reaction to the oppressive tsarist regime, commonly associated with all the 'calamities' the modern state had brought on the Jewish community. For still others, pro-Polish attitudes were entangled with messianic and mystical concepts. However, irrespective of these differences of opinion, they all resulted in pro-Polish, thus anti-Russian (or, more accurately, anti-tsarist), leanings and various speculations associated with the concept of Polish independence and a future Polish state.

Będzin seems to have been exceptional in the intensity of its pro-Polish patriotic sympathies: in the early 1860s it was one of the places most actively engaged in promoting 'Polish–Jewish brotherhood' in the insurrectionist cause. Stories of Jews, both traditional and more integrated, joining the ranks of the insurgents, as well as of voluntary financial assistance to the insurrectionist units, were still alive in Będzin in the twentieth century.[112] But Rozynes's appointment did not only meet with opposition because his pro-Russian sympathies were not shared by the community: it was opposed because it was the result of the intervention of non-Jewish authorities—in actuality, the tsarist army, which was a doubly alien authority—in internal community matters.

Moreover, it appears that the hasidim, more than any other Jews in Będzin, were among the fiercest opponents of the tsarist regime and

---

[110] See an interesting study on this matter by Gershon Bacon, 'Messianists, Pragmatists and Patriots'. See also a fascinating account in Kotik, *A Journey to a Nineteenth-Century Shtetl*, 201–10.   [111] Fridman, *Sefer zikhronot*, 263.

[112] Pinchas Szwajcer's memoirs from the 1831 insurrection in Będzin were published by Jacob Shatzky in 'Zikhrones fun a poylishn yidn', 174 (there is a Hebrew translation in 'Biyemei mered hapolanim be-1831': see *Pinkas bendin*, ed. Stein, 219). On 'Polish–Jewish brotherhood' and the pro-Polish tendencies of the Jewish community in Będzin see also Blatman, 'Bendzin/Będzin'; Jaworski, *Żydzi będzińscy*.

supporters of Polish national independence, so they had good reasons for nurturing a particular aversion to Rozynes. Surviving sources, albeit quite frag-mentary ones, indicate that they ascribed some sort of messianic meaning to Polish armed bids for independence. This was not by any means unusual in the context of the hasidic political tradition.[113] Strong anti-Russian and pro-Polish sentiments had already been expressed by an early hasidic leader, Pinhas of Korzec, who engaged in mystical acts aimed at preventing the Russian invasion of the Polish–Lithuanian Commonwealth shortly before the Second Partition (1793).[114] In later generations, many tsadikim were known for their outright hostility towards the tsarist regime and messianic speculations linking the rebirth of the Polish state with the advent of a mes-sianic era. Some of them expressed it in surprisingly strong pronouncements, such as that of Samuel Abba of Żychlin: 'it [i.e. the rebirth of Poland] touches very directly on the salvation of Israel, for it is known that Poland has great merit before God, may he be blessed, since it accepted Israel with open arms after expulsions from Germany and other lands. Therefore they deserve the reward of having a state once again, before the general salvation of all the children of Israel, with the coming of the messiah speedily and in our days.'[115]

Other leading Polish tsadikim, such as Menahem Mendel of Kock, Isaac Meir Alter of Góra Kalwaria, and Henokh Henikh Lewin of Aleksandrów, were also well-known critics of the tsarist regime and supporters of the Polish yearning for independence.[116] Possibly the most active among them was Isaac Meir Alter. According to hasidic tradition, his participation in organizing a national loan on behalf of the uprising government in 1831 was so significant that as a result of the defeat of the uprising he felt personally threatened; together with Menahem Mendel of Kock and Henokh Henikh of Aleksandrów he protected himself from potential repression by taking refuge in Brody, in the Habsburg province of Eastern Galicia.[117] Better documented are the pro-Polish leanings of his later political activities, including his efforts

[113] See AGAD, CWW 1481, pp. 407–18, esp. 408: 'for they own secret books where it is written that as long as the Russian empire exists, the messiah they are expecting cannot come, but when the Polish Kingdom begins to stir, this will be the great sign that the messiah is nigh'.

[114] See Heschel, *The Circle of the Baal Shem Tov*, 40–3.

[115] Zychlinski, *Sefer lahav esh*, 230–1, as cited in Bacon, 'Messianists, Pragmatists and Patriots', 21–2. Although the publication is relatively late and comes from the time of the independent Second Polish Republic, when making such statements was perfectly safe, there is an abundance of other hasidic testimonies about similar opinions expressed by R. Samuel Abba, thus making the tradition plausible. See e.g. *Sefer lahav esh*, 236–7.

[116] On the positions adopted by the tsadik Isaac Meir Alter during the period of 'Polish–Jewish fraternity' and the uprising, see Kandel, 'Kariera rabiniczna cadyka Icie-Majera'; Shatzky, *Geshikhte fun yidn in varshe*, iii. 356–62. Important data on the rapprochement between the tsadik and the Polish gentry can be found in Bałaban, 'Żydzi w powstaniu 1863 r.', 584–5.

[117] On this see Alfasi, *Gur: hameyased ḥidushei harim*, 88–9.

to improve Polish–Jewish relations from 1861 to 1863 during the period shortly before the next national uprising.[118] Moreover, a fascinating eschatological document coming from Gerer circles, possibly composed by either the second Gerer Rebbe, Judah Aryeh Leib Alter, or, more likely, by Isaac Meir Alter himself, also reveals that the expansion and future defeat of the Russian empire were interpreted in apocalyptic terms as the rise and fall of a demonic power, while Emperor Alexander II was perceived as the incarnation of the devil.[119] Support for the tsarist regime was thus analogous to an alliance with the devil.

All the opinions mentioned here were expressed by representatives of the rabbinical elite, but this should not be understood as proof of the limited circulation of such opinions; rather, it reflects the fact that traditional sources focus exclusively on the lives and thought of tsadikim and other leading figures. Scarce though it may be, there is certainly evidence that strong pro-Polish leanings were not limited to the rabbinical elite but were held by at least some ordinary hasidim. Thus Yekhezkel Kotik gives an account of a hasidic follower of Menahem Mendel of Kock, the only one living in Kotik's town of Kamieniec, being 'a true Polish patriot' and an ardent supporter of the Polish uprising of 1863–4.[120]

The anti-tsarist and pro-Polish stance taken by the hasidim in Będzin might reflect both the influence of Polish tsadikim such as Menahem Mendel of Kock and Isaac Meir Alter, who sympathized with Polish uprisings, and that of Israel of Różyn (Ruzhin), an influential hasidic leader during this period whose anti-tsarist attitude was widely known.[121] Significantly, the hasidic group from Będzin was in close contact with Israel of Różyn. According to Rozynes's testimony, Będzin hasidim sent an emissary, Mortkiele Kocker, to Israel of Różyn, asking the tsadik 'to write to his rabbinical colleagues [i.e. other tsadikim] exhorting them to say a prayer from the said book [not identified] included in the *maḥzor* [festival prayer book] and encourage everyone to do it, so that God would punish and condemn the

---

[118] On the appeal to religious teachers to introduce Polish language teaching, see *Jutrzenka*, 3 (1863), 381, cited in Borzymińska, *Szkolnictwo żydowskie w Warszawie*, 219–20; on an 1863 appeal for the Paschal documents for the sale of *ḥamets* (leaven), which is not permitted to be in a Jew's possession during Pesach, to be in Polish, see 'Wiadomości bieżące'; see also Shatzky, *Geshikhte fun yidn in varshe*, iii. 359.

[119] See Mark, '"Ein ben david ba ad shetitpashet malkhut aram armilus melekh rusiyah aleksander al kol ha'olam 9 ḥodashim"'. I am grateful to Zvi Mark for drawing my attention to this text and delivering other sources used in this section.

[120] Kotik, *A Journey to a Nineteenth-Century Shtetl*, 204–8.

[121] On the influence of the persecution of Israel of Różyn and the rise of anti-tsarist tendencies among hasidim, see Bacon, 'Messianists, Pragmatists and Patriots', 21–2. More on the anti-tsarist attitudes of the Ruzhiner Rebbe and their popular reception can be found in Assaf, *The Regal Way*, 121–4.

Person of His Majesty and send all kinds of calamities on his head for persecuting all Orthodox Jews, and if you pray hard, God will hear your prayer'.[122] An inquiry conducted during the following years confirmed some of the accusations and resulted in government-sanctioned harassment of that hasidic community. Regarding Menahem Mendel of Kock and Isaac Meir Alter, we do not possess strong evidence confirming their direct influence among the hasidim in Będzin at this time. From the fact, however, that at the later stage of the conflict the Będzin hasidim contacted Isaac of Warka, a close associate of both Menahem Mendel of Kock and Isaac Meir Alter, we may conclude that they stayed in contact with the representatives of the Przysucha school of hasidism, to which all the above-mentioned tsadikim belonged. Together with the fact that several decades later Będzin was one of the best-known strongholds of Ger hasidism, this allows us to hypothesize the possible influence of the tsadikim from Kock and Góra Kalwaria (Ger) among hasidic circles in Będzin.

All these factors contributed to the hasidim taking the lead in the campaign against Rozynes. Yet despite their massive campaign they failed to have him dismissed in 1836. Once more, the intercession of the former commander of the army in the Kraków voivoideship, who confirmed in writing that Rozynes provided many valuable services to the Russian army and deserved protection, proved decisive.[123] Under the influence of this statement, the ministerial authorities in Warsaw ignored the unfavourable evidence against the rabbi gathered in the earlier inquiry; they stopped the investigation, and Rozynes remained in post.

But the Będzin hasidim did not stop their campaign. In the next elections to the Jewish community board the hasidim gained control, an outcome certainly helped by the popularity engendered by their conduct in the Rozynes affair. In 1841 Dawid Erlich and Daniel Bugajer, both community elders and both hasidim, renewed their efforts to dismiss Rozynes. The strategy of this second attempt, however, was significantly different: the failure of their previous intervention prompted them to be better prepared, and they succeeded in enlisting the intercession of Rabbi Isaac and others influential in government circles in an effort to ensure that their efforts would not be blocked by the provincial or government authorities. Rozynes complained of this: 'I am loathed and accused of being a Russian spy . . . and I cannot get any protection from the government or any measure of justice because the hasidic rabbis, particularly the rabbi from Nadarzyn, who has great influence with the powerful Orthodox Jews in Warsaw, are trying to ruin me and to stain my reputation with the authorities and some high

---

[122] AGAD, CWW 1473, pp. 69–7.
[123] AGAD, CWW 1481, pp. 43–6. [124] Ibid. 404–5.

officials, even though they do not know me.'[124] The 'rabbi from Nadarzyn' was actually Isaac of Warka, who at that time was also formally carrying the title of rabbi in Nadarzyn (and, as we have seen, also of Czyżew).[125]

In his customary manner, Rabbi Isaac organized an extensive campaign. He directed his efforts at the central government institutions and used an argument to which the ministerial authorities proved sensitive: co-ordinated petitions highlighted the damage that Rozynes was doing not just to the Będzin Jewish community but also to the state Treasury and public order. This was, as we remember, the most typical of Rabbi Isaac's strategies: public order and finances were two major areas of government concern, so he always sought ways to bring them into the debate. Soon the government also received hostile reports about Rozynes from the mayors and rabbis of neighbouring communities. In consequence, the Government Committee for Internal and Religious Affairs came to adopt an exceptionally favourable attitude towards the petition of the Będzin hasidim. Doubtless an important factor here was a bribe; certainly the hasidim claimed to have spent the astronomical sum of 40,000 złoty (the equivalent of a hundred years' salary for a rabbi in a small town like Opatów, or twenty years' salary in a large town like Płock) to have Rozynes dismissed.[126] But this money would have been useless without the help of Rabbi Isaac, or rather his support team: its members were well connected in government circles and knew how and to whom such bribes should be directed and which argument could be effectively bolstered by a backhander.

It seems to me that this too points to the interdependence of 'high' and 'low' hasidic politics in the Kingdom of Poland. In a highly bureaucratized and centralized state—for such it was—gains in local politics were well nigh impossible without the help and support of the major players in the capital. This was so even where minor and purely local matters were concerned, as in the Będzin conflict. Bureaucratization and centralization, as well as ignorance, inertia, and the self-interest of the departments of state referred to earlier, resulted in a situation where often even very trivial matters passed through three or even four levels of government, and final decisions were made only at a high ministerial or government level. Thus local communities, both hasidic and non-hasidic, often felt helpless in the face of a state bureaucratic behemoth: without the professional help of a specialist *shtadlan* little could be achieved. Such help was not just limited to much-needed contacts with high government officials: even more important was knowledge of legal and administrative procedures that the local community simply lacked, including nuances of argument and rhetoric to which state authorities

---

[125] On Isaac's rabbinical post in Nadarzyn see [Zalmanov], *Sefer shemu'at yitshak*, 195.
[126] Ibid.

might be particularly responsive, or even ways of corrupting state officials. This was just the kind of help Rabbi Isaac provided to the hasidim from Będzin, just as he did in his interventions on behalf of the Czyżew rabbinate and in many other matters. The political, legal, and social situation in the Kingdom of Poland led not only to increased Jewish political activism at the state level but also to the need for competence in a wider range of areas, making it increasingly dependent on the expertise and professionalism of the new style of *shtadlan* such as Rabbi Isaac.

The professionalism of Rabbi Isaac, and indeed of any other new-style *shtadlan*, had benefits for both sides: this was why they were willing to sanction the involvement of an individual who did not actually have legal standing in the issue at stake. The assistance of a prominent *shtadlan* could offer significant benefits very quickly. In Będzin this meant the dismissal of Rabbi Rozynes from his post, something the community had tried unsuccessfully to engineer over many years but which was achieved very quickly once Rabbi Isaac got involved. Shortly afterwards Rozynes was expelled from the town and his real estate was confiscated. In Czyżew, Rabbi Isaac's intervention removed the threat of the nomination of an imposed rabbi from among the graduates of the Warsaw Rabbinical School. Each of these interventions in defence of local interests reinforced the prestige and authority of the tsadik, and indeed of the hasidic movement as whole, in the entire Jewish community. Both Będzin and Czyżew are perfect examples of this: following Rabbi Isaac's intervention, the post of rabbi (or a deputy rabbi carrying out rabbinical functions) was given to candidates supported by hasidism and remained in hasidic hands for at least several decades. Strangely, whereas an anti-hasidic denunciation claimed that a new hasidic rabbi was elected in Czyżew in 1858, the government insisted on denying this, stating that there was no rabbi in Czyżew, 'because the budget of the community makes no provision for one'.[127] The informal agreement imposed by Rabbi Isaac was thus still in force for all parties involved. Later, from 1878 to 1887, the post was occupied by Moses Joel Lipschitz Hagerman ben Jacob Salomon of Józefów Lubelski, himself a distinguished hasid of the tsadik of Kock.[128] As we remember, the nomination of a hasidic deputy rabbi happened in Czyżew immediately after the conflict during which the hasidim and their opponents found themselves in a stalemate and unable to settle on a candidate; Rabbi Isaac's intervention defused the conflict and removed the threat of the unwanted rabbi, but at the same time also deftly tipped the scales towards the hasidic movement that he represented.

This was fully analogous to the situation with interventions of hasidic

---

[127] See AGAD, CWW 1446, pp. 327–8; see also ibid. 171–2.
[128] Alfasi (ed.), *Entsiklopediyah laḥasidut*, iii. 349.

shtadlanim at the state level. In both cases, successful intervention strengthened the position of the hasidic movement, both at the state level and in individual communities.

6. Conclusions

Since the Kingdom of Poland was a highly bureaucratic and centralized state, no political undertakings could be classified as purely local or even provincial. Every intervention in a local matter required universal state-level competencies and triggered administrative procedures reaching the level of ministries or even the central government. This made local, communal politics dependent on state-level professional intercessors, which paved the way to the increasing professionalization of hasidic, and more generally Jewish, politics in the course of the nineteenth century. At the same time, there was a clear interdependence between the levels of communal and state politics. The local political actions played an analogous role to the hasidic ones in the sphere of great politics, as they served essentially the same goal of strengthening social support for the hasidic movement, either by spectacular interventions on the general level or by interventions on the communal level, more geographically limited but bringing more measurable, stronger, and more durable effects. One can say that local interventions by the new professional hasidic *shtadlanim* served to obtain support and to disseminate the influence of this movement by the use of mechanisms and competencies at the level of general politics. In the twentieth-century American catchphrase, 'all politics is local'. However, since in the case of Poland all local politics required involvement of bureaucrats at every level of the administrative hierarchy, the resolution of local problems required general competencies.

CHAPTER SEVEN

Haskalah and Government Policy towards Hasidism

POLISH MASKILIM engaged in political activism for the same reasons as other east European maskilim. It has often been shown that, throughout eastern Europe, the development of the Haskalah as a movement with its own institutions, networks, and so forth was connected to a certain rapprochement with government circles. The maskilim eagerly sought such a rapprochement since they believed that (*a*) it would achieve the objective of reforms in Jewish society that would genuinely improve the condition of the Jews in terms of their legal status, economic standing, and access to culture; (*b*) an enlightened government would readily collaborate with them, since it shared their belief in the need to reform Jewish society; and (*c*) government support would help them to achieve their objectives in a way that they could not do on their own.[1] The desire for rapprochement inevitably meant involvement in politics; although they saw themselves as an intellectual vanguard (a self-perception which was later reinforced by the historiography of the Haskalah movement), there is no doubt that the maskilim were deeply engaged in political activism of all sorts, including frequent interventions with the authorities, political publications, involvement in the struggle for communal power, and, above all, the implementation of various reform projects, as discussed below.

Apart from these general factors, which were common to all east European maskilim, local factors that were unique to specific social, political, and legal conditions of the Kingdom of Poland also played their part. It should be remembered that during the first half of the nineteenth century Poland was the only constitutional monarchy in eastern Europe. Although its rights were being violated and its autonomy gradually curtailed, it was, at least until 1831, the only state in this part of the continent where political opposition was legal, where an independent judiciary functioned, and, most

---

[1] Good accounts of the factors that drove the maskilim into an alliance with the state authorities are to be found in Stanislawski, *Tsar Nicholas I and the Jews*, 118–22; Lederhendler, *The Road to Modern Jewish Politics*, 86–110; Etkes, 'Hahaskalah bemizraḥ eiropah'; and id., 'Parashat hahaskalah'.

importantly, where heated and nearly free political debate could take place. One of the fiercest debates, which raged intermittently between 1815 and 1822, concerned the so-called Jewish Question, namely the project to reform Jewish society.[2] It is not surprising that the maskilim were drawn to participate.

Another reason why the leaders of the Haskalah in Poland were drawn to political activism is that many were in any case employed by the state, especially in education, and therefore had relatively easy access to the institutions determining or implementing government policy. This situation, which was true of almost all the prominent maskilim in Warsaw, and also of those in some of the other large towns, was clearly conducive to political activism in the realization of their objectives with regard to hasidism; it is to be expected that they would have used every political option open to them, and working in government institutions was clearly an advantage. Their proximity to decision-makers also meant that they were accessible for consultation, whether informally or in the context of commissioning formal reports. Examples of reports commissioned by the government have been discussed in previous chapters. Moreover, maskilim came to these issues with an awareness of the orientation of state politics that allowed them to have an important influence on government attitudes. Two questions, then, seem to be in order. First, how did maskilim influence the policies of the authorities towards hasidism? (By this I mean how did they attempt to exploit political tools to realize their own aims regarding hasidism, and to what extent did the government use their services in the investigations?) Second, how effective was the input of the maskilim—or to put it another way, to what extent was the politics of the Kingdom of Poland concerning hasidism the politics of the Haskalah? These two questions are the theme of this chapter. Of course, the scale and form of maskilic involvement in this area need to be examined in the broader context of the relationship of the Polish Haskalah to hasidism and its political activism more generally. However, as I have discussed both questions more extensively elsewhere,[3] my concern here is to provide only a broad understanding of the influence of the maskilim on the government's policies on hasidism. Where possible, I have included supplementary material with bibliographical references or short summaries in the footnotes.

[2] On the Jewish debate in the years 1815–22 see Gelber, 'She'elat hayehudim bepolin'; Mahler, *Divrei yemei yisra'el*, v. 167–72, 292–3; Eisenbach, *Emancypacja Żydów*, 196–212.

[3] On the attitude of the Polish maskilim towards hasidism see Wodziński, *Haskalah and Hasidism*; on the political activism of the Polish maskilim see Wodziński, 'Haskalah and Politics Reconsidered'.

1. The Role of Hasidism in the Political Activism of the Polish Maskilim

Maskilic political activism was by no means concerned only with hasidism; indeed it was far from being at the forefront of the maskilim's concerns. The reason for this is connected to the social and ideological development of both groups.

The activities and concerns of Polish maskilim were shaped to a significant degree by the possibilities of making a contribution to the numerous government projects for the reform of the Jewish people and to public debates on the Jewish Question and also, indirectly, by the strong pressure they felt to integrate (including the pressure to use the Polish language). This phenomenon was especially evident in the years known in Polish historiography as the 'constitutional period' (1815–30), though its results were also felt later. In other words, the maskilim of Poland were interested first and foremost in practical achievements and socio-political transformation; consequently, the focus on productivizing projects, such as turning Jews into farmers, was far greater than elsewhere in eastern Europe. This emphasis on the practical also shaped their attitude to hasidism, which they judged not in terms of an ideology representing a conceptually different world-view but merely as a possible barrier to (or perhaps an ally in) reforming the social order. In consequence hasidism was ignored until at least the 1830s because its influence was limited and it was not perceived as threatening; rather, the enemy was perceived to be the *kahal* and its traditional institutions. In so far as tsadikim and hasidism entered the consciousness of maskilim at all, they were perceived as part of the traditional Jewish world. But even this stance was not universal: some maskilim saw hasidim as potential allies in their struggle against the *kahal* and therefore supported their schismatic activity.

Understandably, the period before 1831 marked the peak time for maskilic political activism in Poland, in consequence of the large number of government initiatives at that time aimed at reforming Jewish society. The maskilim were justified in their assessment that this was a critical moment for achieving social change, and the multiplicity of reports commissioned by government institutions and other requests for advice convinced them that the government saw them as important partners. In this period, maskilim submitted close to a hundred extensive memoranda and reports to the Government Commission for Religious Denominations and Public Enlightenment, while additional reports were sent to other institutions. The reforms proposed ranged from such sweeping measures as the liquidation of the *kahal* and the rabbinate, through the control of registration of Jewish births, marriages, and burials, to the petty details of the *kahal*'s term of office and the remuneration of Jewish community board elders. It was the sheer scale of the involvement in state politics that distinguished the political activism of the Haskalah movement from that of other Jewish interest groups in this period; certainly no other social, ethnic, or religious group in the Kingdom of Poland engaged in political activism of this sort to anything like the same degree. Though the need for reform in the conditions of the peasantry or of cities attracted government interest no less than the reform of the Jewish people, in no other case was there such lively public engagement or such active authorship of reports and memoranda.

Interestingly, the point at which maskilic political activism began to decline in the 1830s was just when the scale of the potential threat posed by hasidism began to be understood. By this time the number of hasidim in the Kingdom of Poland had grown considerably. Their social activism, solidarity, excellent organization, and interest in involvement in community institutions (such as the Jewish community board and the rabbinate) made them natural rivals of the maskilim, who were also growing in number at this time. This frequently set the two movements in conflict and increased the antagonism between them, though, interestingly, there is no evidence of an increase in maskilic political interventions regarding hasidism at this time. It is not difficult to find the reason: the political activism of the Polish Haskalah declined dramatically after 1831 because the defeat of the anti-tsarist uprising was followed by strict censorship, political persecution, and hostility towards any civil initiative, which effectively paralysed public life by putting an end to free speech and to legal political activity. Although these measures were directed against Polish society and its insurrectionist tendencies they also took their toll on maskilic activism, even though there had been no real relationship between the maskilim and the insurgents.[4] In consequence the number of political interventions initiated by Polish maskilim fell dramatically in the early 1830s, and the emphasis shifted from advocacy of reform to the defence of traditional Jewish interests, or even the defence of individuals. As a result, the politics of the Polish Haskalah lost its reformist edge and came increasingly to resemble traditional *shtadlanut*. Jakub Tugendhold was especially active at this time, initiating dozens of defensive interventions.[5] The number of memoranda, reports, and articles in the press

[4] The only prominent maskil who was actively involved in the insurgent activities in 1830–1 was Jakub Tugendhold; he participated in the actions of the radical Patriotic Club, forced the Jewish community to announce a ban on Jews spying for the Russian army (see AGAD, CWW 1435, pp. 112–14), and published a series of articles and brochures supporting the uprising. For more on Jews in the uprising see Schiper, *Żydzi Królestwa Polskiego w dobie powstania listopadowego*.

[5] For instance, in 1833 Tugendhold submitted, together with Stern, a report insisting on the binding power of the Jewish law of divorce and demonstrating the innocence of the chief rabbi of Warsaw, Solomon Lipschitz, who had been charged with violating the state law on divorce

advocating social reform increased once more at the beginning of the 1860s, after Margrave Aleksander Wielopolski came to power as minister, and later prime minister. Jewish political activists turned again to the topic of Jewish reform, especially after the launch of the Polish Jewish weekly *Jutrzenka* ('Dawn') in 1861, but the authors were not now maskilim but rather a new generation of Jews entering the world of politics and calling for greater Polish–Jewish integration.

A final factor that may have significantly reduced the number of maskilic political interventions concerning hasidism is of a technical nature. Of the available forms of political intervention—apologetic and polemical tracts, memoranda sent directly to the government, and reports prepared at the request of the state administration—the maskilim generally restricted themselves to the last of these. There is considerable evidence that some maskilim believed them to be an especially effective tool,[6] and it seems they were justified in thinking so. It is true that the memorandum (meaning a formal submission, by an individual or a group of individuals, of a proposal of a general character and usually concerning large social groups rather than individuals or small groups) sometimes managed to provoke a reaction, but it seldom had any real effect, and even more rarely the intended effect. This is not surprising because memoranda had an existence of their own, quite independent of their authors' intentions. Because memoranda had not been commissioned but were submitted at their authors' initiative, the officials reviewing them were often suspicious of their motives and therefore unwilling to take them into consideration in making their decisions. Moreover, the attitude of such officials was often shaped less by the information included in a memorandum, which was usually in any case skimpy, than by stereotypes, prejudices, and their own views of the subject in question. Reports—i.e. formal opinions commissioned by the government or government agencies from prominent

---

(see AGAD, CWW 1448, pp. 396–9). In 1838 he refuted the charge that Jewish law allowed a person to perjure himself and to persecute converts (see AGAD, CWW 1435, pp. 407–17). In 1858 he defended the validity of a vow made by the Jewish soldier Pinkus Nenajdel, who married secretly and without the permission of his military superiors (see AGAD, CWW 1453, pp. 43–55).

[6] For instance, in 1824 the Committee for the Censorship of Hebrew Books and Manuscripts submitted to the government a report concerning hasidism. One member of this committee, Jakub Tugendhold, disagreed with his colleagues but did not come forward with a dissenting memorandum of his own. Instead he waited for a suitable occasion and a few months later, when asked for his opinion on some 'scandalous fragments' of Hebrew prayer, unknown to other Jews but possibly used by the hasidim, he embarked on a refutation of the committee's report, presenting his own view of the matter. In this report, he admitted that he had been waiting for a long time for the opportunity to express his own opinions on the subject, since 'he was otherwise unable to act upon this matter'. AGAD, CWW 1871, p. 164. See also Wodziński, 'Jakub Tugendhold and the First Maskilic Defence of Hasidism', 34–7.

maskilim—were an entirely different matter, primarily because the motiva-
tion of the authors was not suspect. Even in cases involving the same officials
and the same authors, the reactions to a memorandum and a report could
differ radically. Thus a memorandum by Ezekiel Hoge advocating the regulation of early Jewish marriages was rejected, mainly because Stanisław
Staszic suspected him of bias as his proposal called for Jews to be put in a
position of overseeing such matters; in other words, Jews should not have
influence on the course of the state regulations concerning Jews, 'which is
against the general rule'.[7] By contrast, a government commission headed by
Staszic had earlier accepted without objection Hoge's report on the right of
individual Jews to establish *shtiblekh* and *eruvin* and to regulate the *kahal's*
term of office.[8] Commissioned reports were more effective than memoranda
precisely because they *were* commissioned—that is, initiated by the government; since the issues had already been identified as deserving attention, the
measures they recommended were more likely to be adopted. Maskilic politics, then, was not to protest against government policy, but rather to exploit
every opportunity to influence it. This reflected a realistic assessment both
of their position and of the political mechanisms of their time, but it meant
that maskilic interventions were essentially limited to topics that the government had already identified as problematic. This was significant because, as
we have seen in previous chapters, hasidism was not at the forefront of government concerns (the various investigations into hasidism notwithstanding), so the number of reports commissioned from maskilim was small, and
their sphere of political activism in this area was similarly limited. To put it
another way, the relative lack of political interventions by maskilim on issues
relating to hasidim reflected the lack of government interest in this issue.
Thus the low level of such interventions after 1831 may be attributed to
caution concerning reformist tendencies after the failed insurrection and the
realization that responding to invitations to prepare commissioned reports
was a more successful political strategy than submitting memoranda.

2. The Role of Maskilim: Myth and Reality

The fact that the maskilim initiated relatively few interventions regarding
hasidism does not mean that they had no role in anti-hasidic investigations.
Quite the opposite. They were actively involved, for example, in the investigations of 1818, 1824, and 1834 discussed in previous chapters. This raises
some fundamental questions about the actual participation of maskilim in

[7] AGAD, CWW 1411, p. 27; Hoge's report, ibid. 17–19. See also AGAD, Sekretariat Stanu
Królestwa Polskiego 199, pp. 428–32.
[8] See, on *shtiblekh*, AGAD, CWW 1555, pp. 17–20; on *eruvin*, AGAD, CWW 1410, pp. 4–5;
and on *kahal* authorities, AGAD, CWW 1431, pp. 150–1.

initiating investigations, their role throughout the course of the investigations, and their eventual effectiveness.

2.1 Who Initiated the Investigations?

Few of the extant sources give specific information about the instigators of government investigations or the direct reasons for their initiation; this is certainly true of the most important incidents from 1818 in Płock and the 1823–4 investigation in Parczew. Even so, from the information that is available we can conclude that the investigations into hasidism were more frequently initiated by the *kahal* or other groups within traditional Jewish society than by maskilim. Thus it was a complaint by the *kahal* that instigated the anti-hasidic investigation in Połaniec in 1798, the first known investigation in central Poland, which in 1815 became part of the Kingdom of Poland.[9] Many of the incidents discussed in previous chapters followed a similar pattern—for example, the report that the *kahal* in Chęciny submitted in 1818 to the district commission regarding community members leaving the town during religious festivals; the letter of the *kahal* in Łask in 1820 requesting that hasidim be banned from holding separate services; or the report of Jakub Brüll against hasidim in Olkusz in 1817–18 (see Ch. 2). Moreover, the *kahal* authorities seem the most probable inspiration for those government investigations for which we do not know the source. Such was the case in the investigation in Płock in 1818, in which arguments raised by the president of the Voivodeship Commission, Florian Kobyliński, came from the arsenal of traditional accusations formulated against hasidic *shtiblekh* by the *kahal*, especially about the difficulty of communicating government decrees when hasidim did not attend the main synagogue and about the problem of donations made to their own funds diminishing community income. The great investigation of 1823–4 most probably stemmed from a complaint submitted by the Jewish community board or perhaps even by a rival group of hasidim. As news of the incident spread among hasidim, however, they attributed responsibility for it to maskilim—or as Alexander Zusya Kahana wrote, to 'hypocritical people' who 'do not observe Jewish law and are weak in religious belief'.[10] However, we know that the supposition was groundless; the participation of maskilim took place later and was quite marginal and completely different from what Kahana imagined, as described in Chapter 3. In reality, anti-hasidic investigations initiated by maskilim often concerned minor and very specific incidents.[11] The investigation of 1834 concerning complaints that the Polish market was being flooded by hasidic publications was

[9] Kuperstein, 'Inquiry at Polaniec'.

[10] See *11.42; AGAD, CWW 1871, pp. 65–9; there is further discussion in Ch. 3, §3 above.

[11] See for example the project by Moszkowski described in detail in Wodziński, *Haskalah and Hasidism*, 124–6, 279–81; see also AGAD, CWW 1436, pp. 215–33, and AGAD, KRSW 6630,

instigated not by Polish maskilim but by two Jewish printers from the Russian Pale of Settlement and the local teacher Aleksander I. Sawicki (see Ch. 4, §3). Moreover, in this case the maskilim Abraham Stern and Jakub Tugendhold actually defended the hasidim and countered the complaint brought by the two printers and Sawicki as a groundless argument that would benefit no one but the plaintiffs themselves.

As a rule, then, maskilim did not initiate anti-hasidic investigations, and when they did it was generally on marginal issues not linked to the root of the conflict between the two groups. Contrary to the image transmitted in Orthodox historiography, the incitement of state authorities against hasidim was generally not a maskilic tactic, and certainly never became an important tool. Reforms intended to check the growth of hasidism were indeed proposed to the authorities in the early years of the east European Haskalah by Menahem Mendel Lefin and Jacques Calmanson, but this approach was not continued in later years.

2.2 What Role Did the Maskilim Play in Anti-Hasidic Investigations?

If maskilim did not generally instigate government investigations into hasidism, the question remains about the role they did play in such investigations and their eventual significance in shaping government policy on this issue.

As already mentioned, the preferred form of maskilic political activism was submitting reports. This was true concerning hasidism as well: in almost every investigation, the involvement of maskilim was through reports commissioned by state institutions at different levels as part of ongoing investigations. Thus, the famous report of 1818 by Abraham Stern was commissioned as part of the investigation into events in Płock. Both known reports of the Kalisz maskil Dr Schönfeld stemmed from the request of the Voivodeship Commission of Kalisz concerning the conflicts in Łask and Częstochowa in 1820. In 1834, during an investigation of hasidic presses, maskilic involvement was limited to preparing reports commissioned by the government. There are more examples like this.

This form of political engagement brought with it both significant pos-

fo. 81. Another example comes from Łódź in 1848. An immediate reason for Icek Seidenman and ten other 'civilized Jews' to turn to government intervention was not an anti-hasidic offensive but a conflict with a hasidic tax collector and harassment they suffered from the hasidim. This was, thus, a strictly defensive undertaking. Moreover, Seidenman did not propose any regulation of hasidim as such but merely applied for the defence of his Reform prayer house against hasidic harassment. For more see my *Haskalah and Hasidism*, 138–40, and for the English translation of the interrogation protocol, see ibid. 282–5. See also AGAD, CWW 1712, pp. 38–73. For more on this topic, see J. Walicki, *Synagogues and Prayer Houses of Łódź*, 37–40.

sibilities and certain limitations. A very obvious limitation was that in the simplest cases there was no need for the opinions of external experts, so reports were simply not commissioned. In practice, the proportion of interventions connected to hasidim in which maskilim had a voice was relatively small. On the other hand, the fact that reports were commissioned in difficult, disputed, and exceptional cases offered significantly greater opportunities to exert real influence, because the commissioning of a report meant that the authorities were still trying to define their own position, so there was a significant possibility that its recommendations would be accepted. A report was therefore potentially a powerful political tool.

The maskilim were well aware of all this. Accordingly, evasive, noncommittal, and unco-operative reports were a rarity;[12] the great majority were relatively extensive and detailed, clearly formulating the question as the author saw it and suggesting a precise approach and specific recommendations. Thus Schönfeld's report on the *mikveh* in Częstochowa unequivocally condemned the position of the *kahal*, defended the right of hasidim to use the *mikveh*, and suggested a specific solution.[13] Abraham Stern's recommendations on banning hasidic gatherings were equally unequivocal, though his position on hasidism was indeed the diametrical opposite of Schönfeld's.[14] We can conclude that, although as a rule maskilim did not instigate investigations, they fully exploited any opportunity for intervention that might influence the authorities. Their reports not only gave detailed information about the phenomena under consideration but also proposed solutions.

The clearest example of this is the investigation concerning the smoking of tobacco by hasidim in the *beit midrash* in Międzyrzec Podlaski.[15] In 1840 the Government Commission for Internal and Religious Affairs received, at the same time, a petition from a representative of the non-hasidic majority in Międzyrzec demanding that smoking be banned in the *beit midrash*, and a petition from local hasidim, citing numerous religious sources, demanding that it be legalized.[16] Minister Aleksander Pisarev turned to the maskil Jakub

---

[12] This was the case in the report of the Jewish community board of Warsaw in 1823 regarding 'Hussites'. See *11.28; AGAD, CWW 1871, pp. 50–1; Schiper, *Żydzi Królestwa Polskiego w dobie powstania listopadowego*, 25.

[13] See *7.17; AGAD, KWK 702, pp. 73–86; see also Wodziński, *Haskalah and Hasidism*, 269–73; id., 'Chasydzi w Częstochowie', 295–8.

[14] See *4.07; AGAD, CWW 1871, pp. 43–6, and also AGAD, KWK 702, pp. 137–41; AGAD, KRSW 6634, fos. 239–42; Mahler, *Haḥasidut vehahaskalah*, 477–81; Wodziński, *Oświecenie żydowskie w Królestwie Polskim*, 268–71; id., *Haskalah and Hasidism*, 260–3.

[15] AGAD, CWW 1780, pp. 34–5. An excerpt from the complaint was published in Borzymińska, *Dzieje Żydów w Polsce*, 61–2; the case is described in Wodziński, *Haskalah and Hasidism*, 149.

[16] The letter from the Government Commission is in AGAD, CWW 1780, p. 37; Goldman's letter is ibid. 50–2.

Figure 7.1 Międzyrzec Podlaski: ruins of the central square after a fire.
Woodprint published in *Tygodnik Ilustrowany*, no. 387 (1875), p. 340.
Biblioteka Narodowa w Warszawie

Tugendhold for an opinion. Tugendhold wrote a comprehensive report that established the general significance of the issue, analysed the arguments presented by both sides, and provided critical comments on the sources to which the plaintiffs referred, while also adding sources of his own, and presented a very specific proposal for legislation:[17]

I respectfully submit that it would be very useful if the Honourable Government Commission for Internal and Religious Affairs would deign to put out a general recommendation with the following contents:

The Government Commission for Internal and Religious Affairs, extending its care to everything denominational in the Kingdom and seeking to dispel anything that would offend the solemnity of a location dedicated to the praise of God, and seeing that certain Jews allow themselves to smoke tobacco in the so-called *batei midrash*, about which Jews themselves have complained to the government, has decided to ban tobacco in such *batei midrash* which are generally the property of their respective communities and in which religious services take place daily both in the morning and in the evening and also on Saturdays and Jewish festivals.

---

[17] Ibid. 44–5. An excerpt from Tugendhold's opinion is in Borzymińska, *Dzieje Żydów w Polsce*, 62; the English translation is in Wodziński, *Haskalah and Hasidism*, 276–8. For more on the hasidic custom of smoking tobacco, see Jacobs, 'Tobacco and the Hasidim'.

Figure 7.2 Międzyrzec Podlaski. This early twentieth-century image testifies to the multi-ethnic and multi-religious character of Międzyrzec and many other hasidic localities in the eastern territories of the Kingdom of Poland: Jewish pedlars trade with Polish (Roman Catholic) and/or Byelorussian (Russian Orthodox) women near a Russian Orthodox church. Postcard, 1914/15. Private collection of the author

The report was impeccably prepared with a view to maximizing its effect. Aware of the suspicion with which government officials would read one Jew's opinion of another, Tugendhold accurately refuted opposing arguments, presented his own arguments logically and clearly, and at the same time explained the basis and source of all statements. To further strengthen the report and dispel any suspicion of bias, he also cited a report by two other Jews well known in government circles whose opinions therefore carried a certain weight. The first of these was the maskil Abraham Stern and the second was Hayim Dawidsohn, the chief rabbi of Warsaw and thus the highest authority in traditional Jewish society.[18] His thinking was that their names might actually convince the minister that the report expressed the views of the majority of Polish Jews and that its recommendations would therefore be widely accepted. Aware, too, of the inertia and ignorance of government bureaucrats, Tugendhold eased their task by actually formulating the ruling: all they had to do was to copy out the relevant sections and send them out to provincial authorities as new law—which happened soon afterwards. All this

[18] A brief note by Stern supporting Tugendhold's opinion was attached to the report: see AGAD, CWW 1780, p. 47. Dawidsohn's opinion is, in fact, not known, as the only document we have is Tugendhold's summary of their conversation on the matter.

Figure 7.3 A Polish hasid with a pipe in his hand. The widespread hasidic custom of smoking tobacco in virtually every location was one of the sources of anti-hasidic controversies in Jewish communities. From Leon Hollaenderski, *Les Israélites de Pologne* (Paris, 1846), illustration after p. 240. Zakład Narodowy im. Ossolińskich we Wrocławiu 102.891 I

is a good illustration of the efforts maskilim were prepared to make in writing commissioned reports and the impact that such reports could have.

Even so, one should not overestimate the influence that maskilim could have in this way: by definition, their advisory function limited their role and ended with the submission of a report. Perhaps there was subsequent informal contact with, or pressure on, the officials examining the issue, but the archives reveal almost no trace of such activity. There were, to be sure, exceptional situations in which maskilim were involved in the decision-making process of the state authorities in other than a purely advisory role, but these were a very small minority. The only example I have found of such a case concerning hasidism is the role of Jakub Tugendhold in the 1857 investigation into the Volhynian tsadik Abraham Twersky of Turzysk (Trisk). Tugendhold not only compiled the report about the tsadik's activity in the Kingdom of Poland[19] but was also involved in examining appeals from numerous individuals and Jewish communities interceding on Rabbi Abraham's behalf.[20] It seems that Tugendhold was allowed access to all the official documents, since we know that he read the appeals and added his own comments. In

---

[19] The English translation is in Wodziński, *Haskalah and Hasidism*, 287–8. For brief comments see ibid. 151.　　　[20] AGAD, CWW 1446, pp. 137–8, 221–3, 249–51.

Figure 7.4 Abraham Twersky of
Turzysk (Trisk) (1806–89), a hasidic
leader of the Chernobyl dynasty, who
travelled extensively in Volhynia and in
the eastern territories of the Kingdom
of Poland. From Samuel Abba
Horodezky, *Haḥasidut vehaḥasidim*
[Hasidism and Hasidim] (Tel Aviv,
1951), 4: illustration after p. 72.
Private collection of the author

effect, the decision to ban Rabbi Abraham's religious activities was in significant measure the work of Tugendhold,[21] but this was an exceptional situation.
In the overwhelming majority of cases, the all the maskilim did was to submit
a report. It seems that the maskilim were satisfied with their ascribed role;
only relatively rarely did they seek other ways of influencing the ongoing
investigations. This may be because they were convinced that their reports
were effective. But how effective were they really? Or to put in another way,
to what extent did government policy reflect the politics of the maskilim?

2.3 Effectiveness

The effectiveness of the maskilim's involvement in the investigations into
hasidism is difficult to determine because their opinions were frequently contradictory and their proposals at odds with each other—as, for example, in the
major investigation of 1823–4, in which Abraham Stern opposed the hasidim
and Jakub Tugendhold supported them. A further problem is that since we
often do not know the final decision in the question at issue we cannot
evaluate whether the maskilic adviser's report was effective; in other cases the

[21] AGAD, CWW 1446, pp. 252–63, 271–3; see also APL, AmL 1419, p. 156.

final decision is known, but we have too little information about the decision-making process to assess the influence of a given report. Excluding these cases, however, we can note that, in more cases than not, the decisions taken followed the recommendation of the maskilic adviser. At first glance this might suggest that the politics of the maskilim with regard to hasidism were effective, but closer examination highlights a certain pattern as to what was successful and what was not.

The reports submitted by Abraham Stern for the two most important investigations against hasidism, in 1818 and in 1823–4, are instructive. In both cases they were the only extensive source of information about hasidism available to the authorities; they were therefore read with attention, and Stern's reputation meant that they were considered authoritative. His recommendations were accepted by ministers Staszic and Potocki and by the Government Commission for Religious Denominations and Public Enlightenment, but they were eventually rejected by Viceroy Zajączek and had no long-lasting influence on government policies towards hasidism. Views he expressed in subsequent years were certainly given attention, but likewise did not have a significant influence; one politician even rejected his opinion totally, writing that Stern was 'stubborn' in his hatred of hasidim.[22] In contrast, Jakub Tugendhold, who was more positive in his attitude to hasidim, was significantly more influential. It was his report for the 1824 investigation that (among other factors) led to the rejection of Stern's anti-hasidic thesis, and on several occasions in subsequent years he prevented the imposition of anti-hasidic measures. It does not seem that this was only a question of their different political talents. In both the 1818 and 1824 investigations Stern's recommendations were implemented, but had the effect of escalating the conflict: the possible exit strategies were either to increase the restrictions placed on hasidim (which Stern himself did not want), or to abandon the restrictions and adopt a liberal policy towards them. The consequences of Stern's recommendations became particularly apparent in the period between February and July 1824 when as a result of his report a ban on hasidic *shtiblekh* was introduced. The immediate effect was to increase social conflict: as discussed elsewhere, mayors and voivodeship commissions began to flood the ministry with demands to use force to implement this decision.[23] It is not surprising, then, that the government eventually withdrew from Stern's recommendation and opted instead for a non-confrontational solution, which was of course to the hasidim's advantage. And so it was in many other cases: the overwhelming majority of the maskilic interventions that were actually implemented were those that benefited the hasidic movement. Or to

---

[22] See *11.60; AGAD, CWW 1871, pp. 124–9.
[23] See *11.40, *11.44, *11.45, *11.49; AGAD, CWW 1871, pp. 86, 97–106.

put it another way, the interventions of the maskilim in investigations into hasidism were most effective when they concurred with the general political intentions of the government.

This does not mean that maskilim achieved success only when they said what the government wanted to hear. Nor does it mean that they realized the government's political objectives rather than their own. Simply put, the political strategy of the maskilim evolved: after 1831 they increasingly abandoned the idea of reform and instead focused on protecting the interests of the Jewish community as a whole, meaning that their interests increasingly coincided with the government's political objective of relieving social conflict by not introducing measures that would antagonize hasidim. Moreover, as described above, the maskilim continued to introduce proposals which were then accepted by the authorities; so they did actually influence politics. Sometimes these proposals included measures that were anti-hasidic, requiring more attention to be given both to the method of implementation and to the likely consequences. Thus for example, Tugendhold's report on the conflict in Międzyrzec emphasized that his recommendations would be the best way to achieve the government's primary objectives of maintaining social order and minimizing social protest; that they did not stem from personal interests; and, above all, that they would demand only minimal bureaucratic involvement in their implementation. Of course, achieving such goals was impossible in the case of projects of reform, which by their nature entailed significant expenditure, major social changes, and potential tension. In consequence the overwhelming majority of the issues on which a report by a maskil effectively influenced the final decision were strictly limited in scope, marginal in their importance, and of narrow impact, and in general they were recommendations to adopt a laissez-faire approach rather than to actively oppose hasidic interests. In limiting their objectives in this way, the maskilim won in terms of influence what they lost in ambition and scale.

It should also be remembered that after 1831 the relations between the government and the Haskalah movement deteriorated. They remained polite but were no longer cordial. Paradoxically, this had its benefits: the need to evaluate the relationship with the authorities more critically led to greater realism in making proposals, which in turn increased their effectiveness as greater thought was given to what to write and how to write it.

Overall, a relatively large number of reports by maskilim made recommendations that were ultimately adopted. At one level they were therefore effective and successful. At the same time one should note that this success was limited, in that the recommendations that were adopted tended to be those that suggested compromise or conciliation; suggestions of reform, especially radical suggestions, had limited chances of success. Furthermore, to be effective a report had to be in conformity with the more general political approach of the government and take into consideration the prevailing bureaucratic inertia, ignorance, and reluctance to get involved in internal Jewish affairs. In combination these factors placed serious limits on the scope for political intervention, and success was determined more by external factors than by the competence of maskilic *shtadlanut*. The maskilim were successful in their political activism only in so far as it matched the realities of the situation. Accordingly, their influence on the politics of the authorities towards hasidism was quite limited, and they hardly ever defined its direction. But this is not surprising, since actually it had no clear direction.

3. How Did a Maskilic *Shtadlan* Differ from a Hasidic One?

The maskilim were not the only section of Jewish society to engage in politics. After emerging in the first half of the nineteenth century from the traditional sector of the Jewish community, the Orthodox camp became politically active in many regions of eastern Europe at roughly the same time as the maskilim did. Maskilic and Orthodox *shtadlanim* acted sometimes as rivals but more often as allies. They had much in common but differed in certain respects. In order to distinguish maskilic politics from Orthodox, and especially hasidic, *shtadlanut*, it is instructive to consider the tsadik Isaac of Warka, the most active representative of the Orthodox camp described in the previous chapters, as a point of reference. This will supply a convenient starting point to outline some essential characteristics of hasidic political activism and, by comparison or contrast, the maskilic model.

First, Rabbi Isaac often claimed to speak in the name of the entire Jewish community. He emphasized that he was 'a rabbi in whom the Jewish nation places its confidence' and 'whose true vocation is to watch over the religion as a whole', and who was therefore qualified to represent all Polish Jews. He sometimes supported this claim with the formal authorization granted to him by some Jewish community boards, and in one case by the rabbis of all the provincial capitals. The maskilim, by contrast, never claimed to represent the entire Jewish community. Occasionally they admitted that they represented only 'the more civilized' segment of Jewish society, but more often they spoke in their own name alone. The difference between their claims and those of Rabbi Isaac reflects the reality of the situation. The modernizing circles were no more than a small minority of the Jewish population, while the traditionalists were the overwhelming majority, so their representatives could claim to be identified with the entire Jewish community. Furthermore, Rabbi Isaac's conviction of his right to represent the entire Jewish population stemmed from the hasidic vision of the tsadik as a leader of the Jewish people in general. Nevertheless, neither he nor the maskilic *shtadlanim* ever received any official mandate from their respective constituencies. Rabbi Isaac was a self-appointed representative, though one should remember that there were in any case no political mechanisms of Jewish representation in Poland. Moreover, we have no means of knowing whether all traditional Jews were satisfied with what he achieved through his activism; there are some good reasons to doubt that they were. Rabbi Isaac was not so naive as to be ignorant of this, and nor were the maskilim so modest or so truthful as to refrain from claiming that they represented the Jewish majority when they believed that this would advance their cause. We should therefore look for other distinctions between the attitudes of Rabbi Isaac, on the one hand, and Jakub Tugendhold on the other.

Speaking in the name of the entire Jewish community implied the existence of a legally defined Jewish political entity. This, however, clashed with the fundamental maskilic belief that the Jewish collectivity could not be defined as an 'estate', a term which implied at least some degree of autonomy determined by legal or economic status. However much they emphasized their Jewish identity and their ethnic or historical affiliation and religious solidarity with the Jewish people, the maskilim thought that to speak in the name of the entire Jewish community could be politically dangerous. Moreover, their petitions to the government, especially during the earlier period, were based on the conviction that they were advancing a just cause rather than representing the will of the majority. The justice of their cause, they argued, rendered insignificant the misguided opinion of the majority, and the government was bound to agree with them, since their demands were not only entirely reasonable but also in tune with the historical progress of all mankind. They were convinced that their aspirations were compatible with the government's aims, since they sensed themselves to be riding the irreversible tide of progress, 'overtaken by the spirit of the time and . . . the will of the enlightened authority'.[24]

Unlike the maskilim, when Rabbi Isaac undertook to intervene politically on behalf of the Jewish community he could not assume that the government was favourably inclined towards him. He therefore needed strong arguments with which to counter opposition and force the state to comply with his recommendations. If he could show that his recommendations were in accord with the will of the traditional majority they would carry considerable weight, since by definition they would not threaten social harmony, whereas any ruling that ran counter to the will of the majority was liable to cause social unrest and be more difficult to implement. Rabbi Isaac understood this logic well and even stated it explicitly.[25] It was the foundation of all his interventions in the period of his greatest activism, i.e. after 1831. The maskilim, by contrast, neither needed nor were able to invoke the will of the majority in

[24] AGAD, CWW 1712, p. 49.   [25] AGAD, CWW 1412, pp. 192–3.

order to lend weight to their political interventions. The first difference between maskilic and hasidic *shtadlanut* may thus be described as a difference of imagined constituencies.

Another difference between Rabbi Isaac's *shtadlanut* and that of the maskilim was the stance that each adopted towards the government. Rabbi Isaac acted as an official spokesman, submitting formal petitions, exploiting formal procedures, and demanding formal decisions. He would challenge a decision reached at a low level of the administration by appealing to a higher level; he would demand to be informed of the legal basis on which a decision had been made, and he would force the authorities to see it through to full implementation. Activism of this type was entirely alien to the maskilim. Their memoranda, and even their reports, merely contained information and recommendations to be considered by others in a process over which they had no formal influence. They could not monitor, and certainly could not control, the progress of their proposals through the formal channels; the most they could do was to keep the topic on the agenda by means of repeat submissions. While Rabbi Isaac made demands, the maskilim only pleaded their case.

This difference between the formal petitions of the hasidim and the informal appeals of the maskilim was linked to another, perhaps the most striking, difference between their strategies. Rabbi Isaac usually employed a strictly legal line of argument, sometimes also pointing out the benefits that implementation of his strategy would bring to the government and the state. He invoked the constitution, civil codes, numerous royal decrees, and the decisions of the Administrative Council and various government ministries; he analysed and interpreted them in legal terms, highlighting every incoherence or internal contradiction. Argumentation of this type was almost entirely absent from maskilic submissions. Paradoxically, while Rabbi Isaac, a mystic and spiritual leader, employed primarily legal arguments and presented his activities as serving the material interests of the state, the maskilim tended to invoke mainly moral and religious arguments. This is clear from the different strategies adopted by Rabbi Isaac and by Jakub Tugendhold in defending the rights of Jewish prisoners. Rabbi Isaac quoted the detailed regulations issued by the Administrative Council on 31 January 1834 and 1 December 1837 (No. 12067) as well as the Kingdom's constitutional charter (the so-called Organic Statute).[26] Tugendhold, by contrast, explained the prisoners' right to rest on the sabbath in terms of the sanctity of religious law and the moral argument that if prison was to educate offenders and not only to punish them, then to force Jewish prisoners to work on the sabbath would be counterproductive since it would teach them to break religious law and behave immorally.[27] The difference in approach is particularly striking, given the

[26] AGAD, CWW 1435, pp. 424–5, 435.   [27] AGAD, CWW 1411, pp. 358–61.

conventional characterization of hasidism as mystical and of the Haskalah as rational.

The difference might be explained as a consequence of the maskilim's reluctance to engage in any formal dispute with the administration, a reluctance not shared by the hasidim. Rabbi Isaac's petitions frequently led to confrontation with the authorities, whereas the maskilim wished to avoid such conflict at all costs since they regarded the authorities as their strategic allies. One cannot exclude the possibility that the maskilim simply lacked the professional expertise required to advance their cause through formal administrative channels. While Rabbi Isaac's petitions were prepared by what I have termed his 'team'—a group of influential and legally skilled Jews among his circle of followers—the maskilim had no comparable pool of expert legal advice. Rabbi Isaac's petitions had the clearly defined aim of changing specific regulations or laws, so legal argumentation was the only possible approach. In contrast, the maskilim were not required to provide the legal basis for the opinions they expressed in their reports, but rather to assess the validity of the religious arguments invoked by conflicting sections of the Jewish community. Consequently, their reports were usually confined to moral rather than legal arguments—which was all that was expected of them.

These differences had far-reaching ramifications. Ostensibly, maskilic *shtadlanim* enjoyed a privileged relationship with the government, much more than the representatives of the Orthodox community did. They were personally acquainted with the prominent officials who were responsible for determining policy towards the Jews; they held positions that enabled them to become officially involved in shaping such policy; and the dozens of reports they were commissioned to produce gave them the opportunity directly to influence it. In time, they even learned to orientate themselves in the complexities of Polish politics, and to manipulate them to some effect. Nevertheless, they did not manage to dominate the Jewish political scene and, in the end, they turned out to be far less effective than their Orthodox rivals, especially those within the hasidic camp. Hasidic *shtadlanim* did not perceive themselves as being in ideological alliance with the government and therefore did not hesitate to confront it; they were thus more outspoken, and more effective in achieving their aims. They also understood better than the maskilim the changing political climate in the aftermath of 1831. They were thus better able to offer the new government the information and service it sought. The 1840s and 1850s turned out to be a period of triumph for hasidic *shtadlanut*, and this had a decisive effect not only on the parameters of the Jewish policy adopted by the Kingdom of Poland during this period but also on the development of both the Haskalah movement and Orthodoxy, especially the hasidic camp.

4. Conclusions

Comparing the scale of the maskilic contribution to the anti-hasidic politics of the government as confirmed by archival sources with the image of it projected in Orthodox historiography, one immediately realizes that the reality was significantly less picturesque, and above all more modest in scale, than hasidic stories of hostile maskilic intrigues would suggest. Though Polish maskilim were significantly involved in political activism, their interventions regarding hasidism were a strikingly small part of their activities. In any case, they rarely initiated investigations into hasidism; such participation as they had was usually as part of an ongoing investigation and at the request of state authorities, not the result of an independent initiative. This does not mean that supporters of modernization were completely uninterested in interventions regarding hasidism. Just the opposite: they saw the hasidic movement as one of the elements of the traditional social structure in need of reform, so such opportunities were scrupulously exploited. Accordingly, if invited to prepare a report they gladly did so, and provided extensive, well-argued texts. Their effectiveness, however, owed less to their content than it did to the complicated combined effect of general political factors and the nature of the report as a *modus operandi*. A commissioned report was by definition regarded as a credible document from an authoritative source, but the fact that its scope was limited to a pre-defined topic determined by the body commissioning it inevitably limited the potential for furthering a broader maskilic agenda. Similarly, while the close contacts between leading maskilim and representatives of the political elite facilitated the making of a decision in these circles of authority, it also limited their freedom to criticize or to develop their own solutions. While the effectiveness of maskilic interventions was proportionately quite high in terms of the number of interventions with a successful outcome, these strong external constraints meant that it was much less so when measured in terms of the issues addressed. In fact, maskilic interventions were really only effective in more marginal matters of lesser priority, or on topics where the issue at stake was the decision to abandon an effort at reform rather than to encourage it. With only slight exaggeration it might even be said that it was not the government that realized the maskilic vision of the political campaign regarding hasidism but the exact opposite—maskilic interventions were effective only in so far as they agreed with the more general conceptions and directions of the activities of the Polish political class. On balance, then, maskilic *shtadlanut* was, paradoxically, less effective than that of the hasidim. We may therefore discount the idea often expressed in traditional Jewish historiography to the effect that maskilim were behind the politics of the government of the Kingdom of Poland (and, by implication, of all the governments of eastern Europe) regarding hasidim. The maskilim played a supporting role, but rather a modest one. The real giants of this political confrontation were two underestimated forces: the politically maturing hasidic movement and the behemoth of the state bureaucracy.

Conclusion

O F T H E T H R E E P O L I T I C A L P L A Y E R S discussed in this book—the government, the hasidic activists, and the maskilic activists (who were by definition not directly involved in the confrontation between the state and hasidim)—the hasidim were clearly the most effective. Their astonishing success was due not only to the outstanding political talents of their leaders but also to their ability to identify and exploit the many significant weaknesses of the other players.

The weaknesses of others do not diminish the magnitude of the hasidic success but remind us of the nineteenth-century east European context in which it was achieved: a minority religious community of low social status and lacking civil rights facing a non-democratic state that determined the rules of the game. The state wielded a multitude of mechanisms of social control, ranging from what Pierre Bourdieu has called 'symbolic violence' to legislative power to direct force, but always holding the trump card: political dominance. Hasidic politics had to adapt itself to the space created for it, consciously or not, by the state's own politics. The fact that the playing field, as it were, was chosen by the state did not necessarily mean that the chances of success were loaded against the hasidim: the state was limited by its own internal weaknesses and conflicting goals, as well as by external factors. Most importantly, the imbalance between the state and the representatives of a small social movement created the possibility of the latter exploiting the situation to its own advantage, especially since the power of the authorities was not proportionally matched by knowledge about their opponents, whereas the hasidim, lacking power, built up a formidable arsenal of knowledge. When they deemed it politically appropriate, hasidim could simply pretend that they did not exist as a separate category; Alexander Zusya Kahana could maintain that he was not a hasid (as we saw in Płock in 1829), and the tsadik Abraham Twersky from Turzysk (Trisk) could claim that he was not a hasidic tsadik, just a merchant travelling for trade. The imbalance in relations is critical to understanding hasidic politics and its effectiveness: above all, it was the ability of the hasidic leaders to exploit the conditions created by state politics that determined their success, while the effectiveness of the state was significantly dependent on what the state itself did; though this does not mean that it was completely unaffected by the interaction with its hasidic interlocutors. On the contrary: the state's ability to achieve its objectives depended to a significant degree on appropriate recognition of the hasidic movement and on building good relations with its representatives. The imbalance of power offered the state the opportunity to achieve this, but success depended significantly on how this opportunity was exploited. What, then, did the politics of the state towards hasidism look like?

If we were seeking one sentence that would best characterize the politics of the Kingdom of Poland towards the hasidic movement, we would probably find it in the words of Tadeusz Czacki quoted earlier: 'It was expected in the Polish government that the hasidim would soon die out if nobody asked about them.'[1] Czacki, writing in 1807, was describing the attitude of the authorities towards hasidism in the pre-partition Polish–Lithuanian Commonwealth, a relatively early period in the development of hasidism. However, the statement holds true, with certain modifications, for the following decades, until the demise of the Polish administration after the anti-tsarist uprising of 1863–4. From 1815 on, both before the 1830–1 uprising in the Kingdom of Poland and subsequently, the authorities had tried to avoid recognizing the emergence of hasidism, or had downplayed its significance. The incompetent and poorly prepared bureaucracy was unable to handle a new phenomenon, even when it had long ceased to be new and indeed figured prominently in the conflicts within the Jewish community, complaints about which reached government bodies almost daily. Investigations into the complaints were undertaken without any understanding of the mutual relationships and contexts and without an attempt at a more general definition of the phenomenon, let alone an effort to become acquainted with it. This was entirely characteristic of the state's attitude to Jewish issues. The reasons were not hard to find: a lack of knowledge about hasidism (or indeed other kinds of Jewish religious life); a typical bureaucratic reluctance to undertake new challenges; a poorly functioning administration; and, above all, a generally hostile attitude to the Jewish community and its problems. The facts are quite shocking: although in this period (1815–64) Jewish issues arose with great frequency, the correspondence of the highest officials of the kingdom gave more attention to the purchase of two stallions for Viceroy Zajączek and to the death of the supplier of bulls to the royal court than to all the Jewish reforms and related legislation taken together.[2] The ignorance of the authorities regarding hasidism is palpable.

Not until around 1824 did the consciousness that hasidism was an important component of the social fabric of Polish Jewry penetrate the musty

---

[1] Czacki, *Rozprawa o Żydach i karaitach*, 106. See the discussion in Ch. 2 at n. 24 above.

[2] See the correspondence between Viceroy Józef Zajączek and the State Secretaries, first Ignacy Sobolewski and later Stefan Grabowski: AGAD, Sekretariat Stanu Królestwa Polskiego 3922, 3924.

offices and minds of the bureaucrats. The most distinguished among them, with Stanisław Staszic leading the way, then attempted to link government politics concerning hasidism with the broader issue known as the Jewish Question, that is, with the general plans to 'civilize' the Jews of Poland. In the most general sense, the 1824 investigation should be understood as a first serious attempt to come to grips with the existence of hasidism and its implications for the proposals to reform of the Jewish community. It was thus a turning-point both for the degree of recognition of the hasidic movement by the state and for the attempt to relate to it in plans for reform. The most visible result of this was the revitalization of the project for a government-sponsored rabbinical school in Warsaw, which was finally established shortly after the investigation. If the hasidic literature is to be believed in this matter, the establishment of the school sounded an alarm within hasidic circles; they saw it as a serious threat to traditional Jewish practice and immediately opposed it.[3] We also know that the government occasionally used the existence of the school and its graduates as an instrument of pressure on the Jewish community, a practice that Rabbi Isaac, the most illustrious of the hasidic *shtadlanim* of the time, famously countered (as we saw in Czyżew; see Ch. 6, §5).

Though effective in some senses, the isolated activities mentioned above had no real significance for the politics of the state concerning the hasidic movement. The long-envisaged reform of Jewish society was abandoned almost as soon the first opportunities for implementation occurred. The worsening political circumstances, the deaths of Viceroy Zajączek and Stanisław Staszic in 1826, and the outbreak and decline of the anti-tsarist uprising of 1830–1 shortly thereafter seriously limited the competence of the authorities and quashed their political ambitions; plans for the strategic reform of the Jewish community were rapidly abandoned. After 1831, the authorities consciously and deliberately initiated no actions against hasidim, though the latter figured with increasing frequency in reports and in the investigations resulting from these reports. At this point, the official politics concerning hasidism was effectively a lack of any kind of politics.

From the state's point of view, this was not without rational basis; in fact, it was entirely consistent with its fundamental goals at this time: because it minimized the need for involvement in social conflict at the local level, it lightened the burden on the state. Shorn of its ambitions for reform, the role of the state was merely to oversee the workings of society in such areas as tax collection, military recruitment, and policing. Even if the autocratic outrages of Nicholas I, all in line with his military vision of the world, effectively damaged the potential achievements of this politics (the decrees regarding

---

[3] See e.g. Bromberg, *Migedolei haḥasidut*, 41.

the change of dress and conscription were especially damaging blows), the state was quite consistent in following this self-limiting position.

Once the state had abandoned its plans to civilize the Jews, the issue of hasidism also became marginal to its concerns. The government was simply not interested in which liturgy Jews used, as long as it was not hostile to the state and the tsar, and the prayer book had been approved by the censor. It likewise did not care where hasidim prayed, or which ritual slaughterer they used, as long as all appropriate taxes were paid. Similarly insignificant was the exodus of Jews from their home towns to their 'miracle workers', provided this travel did not lead to social disturbances or illegal gatherings and anti-state activities. The only case known to me when pilgrimages to a tsadik were actually banned concerned those to Menahem Mendel of Kock for Rosh Hashanah in 1852—but cholera was rife that summer, and the government feared that 'about 5,000 people from communities near and far' descending on the town could cause the spread of disease.[4] The ban, then, had nothing to do with the reports of 'fanatical secret meetings' and Enlightenment plans to fight the 'hasidic ringleaders': the concern was to stop the spread of disease, not the spread of hasidism.

Students of hasidism know that the topics mentioned here—the prayer book and place of prayer, ritual slaughter, pilgrimage—are by no means an exhaustive list of those fundamental to the issue; but we have to remember that ideological questions fundamental to hasidic doctrine were not only incomprehensible to the state authorities but also essentially insignificant. Moreover, the protocols of the investigations I have discussed clearly show that by no means everyone among the non-hasidic, traditional Jewish community, or even all hasidim, were able to articulate these differences. Moreover, though it may seem paradoxical, the state withdrew from active politics concerning hasidism exactly when the movement experienced a surge of growth and thus increasingly became involved in the turbulent politics of community conflicts. From the point of view of the state, however, all this was immaterial: so long as hasidism did not appear to be politically threatening or a subversive social force, government officials lost no sleep over it.

The government's political stance of non-engagement in conflicts concerning hasidism was therefore due not only to the scaling back of its ambitions after 1831, but also to the recognition that it was of marginal importance to its strategic goals regarding Polish society, and even to the resolution of the so-called Jewish Question. The rationality of this recognition did not mean, however, that state politics regarding hasidism were effective, even relative to the very modest goals it set itself, because the source of failure was located elsewhere. Most striking in the history of the relationship of the authorities to hasidism was the fact that the key factor was not a

---

[4] See APP, AmP 883, pp. 109–13.

plan or comprehensive strategy but rather bureaucratic micro-management and the mentality of the bureaucrats at all levels, from the viceroy down to ministers, mayors, and the local police.

Bureaucratic practices were an especially important factor: irrespective of the strategic goals and laws enacted at the highest levels of state, implementation always rested on the low- and mid-level officials. With time, as the mechanisms of state administration faltered, bureaucratic autonomy increased; strategic goals became less clearly defined and procedures less consistent. As we have seen, the progressive decline of the administrative apparatus meant that, at least from the 1830s on, bureaucratic practices regarding hasidism were shaped less by strategic goals and the interests of the state than by inertia, ignorance, and self-interest. The maskil Jan Glücksberg wrote that Polish bureaucrats saw the law not as a way of facilitating daily life but rather as a way of harassing Jews on a daily basis and as institutionalizing 'the improper thought of greedy officials'.[5] This can certainly be seen in the painful experiences of those Polish Jews unabashedly exploited by numerous officials who saw them, first and foremost, as an easy source of bribes; but the greedy self-interest of the officials was only one of the factors operating here, and certainly not the most important one. Significantly more often, apathetic bureaucrats simply let issues take their own course. Given the government's abandonment of the active reform of the Jews, this laissez-faire attitude of low-level bureaucrats was not inconsistent with high-level policy decisions. In consequence, however, there ceased to be any mechanism to regulate relations between the state and hasidism. Paradoxically, this was sometimes a source of frustration for the administration because, in those rare situations when officials thought that intervention was warranted, they lacked the instruments for effective political action.

A good example of this occurred in the context of hasidic resistance to the laws governing Jewish dress in the 1840s and 1850s. This was actually the first major conflict between the Polish state and hasidism that could not be solved by the methods of subterfuge (see Ch. 6, §2) that had until then been used to good effect as a fundamental tool of hasidic politics. In the case of a law requiring Jews to wear regular European dress, such a tactic was impossible as non-compliance was clearly visible on the streets of every city. The law therefore set the state and the Jewish community at loggerheads in a way that resembled the situation brought about in the Pale of Settlement by the infamous military recruitment and cantonist system, an especially cruel system requiring Jewish communities to provide adolescent substitutes for adults who evaded military duty in the Russian army. In the Kingdom of Poland the law governing the conscription of Jews to the army was signifi-

---

[5] [Glücksberg], *Rzut oka na stan Izraelitów w Polsce*, 42.

cantly less fierce, so the flashpoint was not conscription but the law banning traditional Jewish dress, which proved to be a source of significant Jewish antagonism towards the state. The increasing repressiveness of the law as the window for exemption was narrowed and the penalties for infringement were raised, and indeed the use of force to compel compliance, escalated the conflict—a classic feature of the politics of tsar Nicholas I—causing hostility that was so great that any state would have taken steps to combat it.

A good example of how such conflict situations developed was the sermon delivered by Aryeh Leib (Lejbuś) Hirszberg, the rabbi of Pilica, on Rosh Hashanah in 1850, following the ban on Jewish dress. A hasid and a close collaborator of Menahem Mendel of Kock, Hirszberg allegedly announced: 'Gentlemen, the time is now! Rouse yourselves from the slavery of the government and monarchy, or they will take your children to the army, take our traditional clothing and tell us what to wear, and shave our beards. Today is the time our prayers before God will be heard. Wake from your great sadness and bitter tears and pray to God that the monarchy meet with misfortune and doom.'[6] When the authorities learned of this (through the infamous rabbi and informer Abraham Hersz Rozynes), Hirszberg was swiftly dismissed. Characteristically, though, the investigation ignored the significance of the issue for hasidim, even though Rozynes emphasized that the sermon was part of a more general hasidic opposition to the law requiring the change in dress. The administration was not, however, in a position to undertake any effective action, even when the necessity of such steps was clear; the authorities had to limit themselves to taking action against individuals. (Hirszberg was eventually pardoned some years later and reinstated.) A still clearer manifestation of the near-paralysis of the administration was the final effort to initiate active pro-hasidic politics in the 1860s (as discussed in Ch. 4, §6), which was a fiasco. The state was in no position to realize the goals of any political initiatives in this area, even when it tried.

The situation I am describing came about partly because the institutions and structure of the state were increasingly dysfunctional; the consequences of this were felt throughout society and not only in matters concerning hasidism or the Jewish community as a whole. An equally important factor, however, was specific to the politics regarding Jews: the influence of the bureaucratic mentality, or more precisely, the heady mix of xenophobic, irrational, and often barely articulated antisemitic prejudices, stereotypes, and phobias. The overwhelming influence of such factors was apparent from the time of the great investigation of 1823–4. The combination of anti-Jewish fears and prejudices with a contemptuous or paternalistic attitude to the Jewish community as a whole, and to 'fanatical hasidim' in particular, as

[6] AGAD, CWW 1473, pp. 69–76.

was common among the Polish power elite, had widespread negative consequences. Obviously it was damaging for the Jews themselves, but beyond that it also had a destructive influence, to a not insignificant degree, on those who held these views: they were incapable of freeing themselves from the limiting categories through which they perceived, organized, and understood the world. Moreover, these anti-Jewish fears, opinions, and resentments appeared not only in the views and activities of declared antisemites such as Wincenty Krasiński, Gerard Witowski, and Ludwik Janowski, but also among the ideas of thinkers and politicians trying to develop a calculated and responsible formulation of their vision of the world. Stanisław Staszic gradually edged towards an obsession with antisemitism that bordered on eliminationist fanaticism, leading him to articulate a vision of 'physical exclusivity' where Jews would live in closed districts under Christian supervision, a vision that he further articulated as 'separate living space, encircled by a physical barrier, which will not allow for their [i.e. the Jews'] space to touch the homes of other, native residents'—in today's terminology, a ghetto.[7] Tadeusz Mostowski often warned of the disastrous results of the emancipation of the Jews. The clear-headed Viceroy Zajączek, usually sympathetic to hasidim, publicly stated of Jews that 'these scoundrels will never be rid of scabies'.[8] Despite declaring the equality of all people, Julian Ursyn Niemcewicz published an angrily antisemitic story *Moszkopolis*, and throughout his life openly avoided any kind of personal contact with Jews (though he often explored Jewish themes in his work). A leading authority on nineteenth-century Polish culture, Maria Janion, describes this kind of attitude and these views as the foundation myth of Polish antisemitism.[9] More puzzling than the fanaticism of Staszic or Krasiński as ideologues is its popularity in broad circles of the Polish political and cultural elite for whom antisemitism was not a matter of ideology. Why did Zajączek, Niemcewicz, Czacki, or Radomiński not perceive a contradiction between the Enlightenment ideal of equality, which they notionally supported, and their attitude towards Jews, which was filled with fears, prejudices, and hostility? My conclusion is that their antisemitism was not, in reality, a doctrine, or even a conscious attitude; in broad circles of the Polish power elite and certainly throughout Polish society, such attitudes were part of an 'antisemitic habitus', that is, a set of automatic, culturally transmitted responses and unconscious ways of seeing the world and actions that were reproduced in daily life in each individual's way of thinking. Contact with a representative of the Jewish community (even if only through receiving a petition) invariably set off this 'antisemitic habitus' with its paternalistic feelings of superiority, and

---

[7] Staszic, 'O przyczynach szkodliwości Żydów', 238.   [8] Koźmian, *Pamiętniki*, iii. 22.

[9] Janion, 'Der Gründungsmythos des polnischen Antisemitismus'.

indeed contempt, mixed with vague fear and hostility. Though this habitus did not determine human actions, the blinkers it imposed greatly limited the spectrum of available codes of behaviour and created stereotypical responses. This perhaps explains the behaviour dominating the relationship of representatives of the Polish state towards the hasidic movement, behaviour which, though to a certain degree they benefited the official himself (because they bestowed a sense of social superiority), also induced a sense of frustration (because they limited the possibilities for appropriate action and reaction).

The consequences of this 'antisemitic habitus', or, perhaps simply xenophobic prejudice, affected not only hasidim but the entire Jewish community, and the same can be said of every other aspect of state politics concerning hasidim. Almost all the positions adopted on hasidism were only a specific application of more general positions of the state regarding the Jewish population. This is an important point: the analysis presented here of the politics towards hasidism has revealed a situation that is a microcosm of the politics towards the Jewish population as a whole, including the mechanisms, conditions, and limitations of that politics. Whereas previous studies of Polish attitudes towards Jews have focused on the analysis of great declarations, public debates, and key laws, the decision here to restrict the examination to a consideration of government policy on hasidism has led to a detailed explication of decision-making processes, micro-political mechanisms, and the influence of apparently less significant and extraneous factors. This highly unorthodox approach has produced insights that fundamentally change the image of the politics of the Kingdom of Poland concerning the Jewish community in the first half of the nineteenth century as described by Raphael Mahler and Artur Eisenbach.

The focus on government politics towards hasidim has also facilitated an understanding of the development of hasidic political engagement and its place within the history of the hasidic movement. As I have tried to show, hasidic political activity in the Kingdom of Poland cannot be divorced from the wider political context. From the earliest phase of defensive politics as practised by the circle of Berek Sonnenberg, to the development of a 'rabbinical shadow government' (meaning the involvement of rabbinical leaders in east European politics in mid-nineteenth century), to the political representations of Rabbi Isaac, each stage of hasidic activism was a factor in the political realities created by the state. Rabbi Isaac's activism was successful only because of his thorough understanding of the administrative procedures and weaknesses of the state bureaucracy and of the possibilities inherent in the political situation. He not only appropriated for hasidism the earlier prerogative of the *kahal* to represent the Jewish community; he also used it exceptionally well as a tool to influence state politics.

The successes achieved in this way by the political activism of Rabbi Isaac and other hasidic leaders (for example, Alexander Zusya Kahana, Meir of Opatów, Isaac Meir Alter of Góra Kalwaria (Ger), Jacob Aryeh of Radzymin, and Abraham Landau of Ciechanów) unquestionably influenced the status of hasidism in the Kingdom of Poland, and therefore the growth of the movement. Even if many tsadikim in other areas, such as Menahem Mendel Schneersohn or Israel of Różyn, showed a similar interest in political questions in the early nineteenth century, nowhere else could tsadikim boast such spectacular successes as those of Rabbi Isaac and his contemporaries, and nowhere else was an interest in politics so widespread. (Though from the 1860s the situation had changed and in fact Galicia became more important as a centre of hasidic political activism.) The factors contributing to this were, above all, the 'Jewish politics' of the state, which actually encouraged the co-operation of Jewish leaders with the state, and the administrative procedures of the Kingdom of Poland, which allowed effective legal intervention. The effectiveness of hasidic interventions in turn influenced the image of the movement in the wider Jewish community, which increasingly saw the hasidic leaders as its legal representatives and its most effective defenders. All of this left a significant imprint on the development of hasidism in the Kingdom of Poland, and on its ideological development.

The question posed in the Introduction regarding the place of hasidic political activity in the long-term development of Jewish politics—from pre-modern *shtadlanut* as practised by representatives of the Jewish community in the eighteenth century to modern forms of mass politics in the twentieth century—still remains. At first glance, nineteenth-century hasidic politics was neither pre-modern *shtadlanut* nor modern in the sense of appealing to a popular constituency; it cannot be described unequivocally as either. Was hasidic politics, then, a hybrid type of 'rabbinical shadow government'?[10] It seems not. Although the hasidic community consistently legitimized its political activism by drawing on traditional models such as the biblical figure of Mordecai, by mythologizing the figure of the tsadik, and by references to the model of the pre-modern *shtadlan*, hasidic political activism displayed so many modern characteristics that I would suggest that it is perhaps best considered not as a transitional form between old and new, but simply as the beginning of modern Jewish politics.[11]

[10] See Lederhendler, *The Road to Modern Jewish Politics*, 68–83.
[11] The politics practised by hasidim was not identical with the forms of political activity of modern parties and other mass political movements. However, considering that even today hasidic political activity displays many unique characteristics that distinguish it from the politics of the surrounding society, it may be time to question the assumed universality of accepted models.

We can thus see in some of these characteristics a hasidic adaptation to the political realities of a world that was becoming modern; one might say they are proof of hasidism being a modern movement in its own right. In the first place, the hasidic political activists of the nineteenth century differed from eighteenth-century *shtadlanim* in that they were self-appointed. Though they claimed to act in the name of the entire Jewish community, they were neither appointed by the community or its representatives nor did they have to consult the community regarding political objectives (though they often did so). In the case of Rabbi Isaac, the political dependence between the *shtadlan* and the community he represented was in a certain sense reversed: it was the hasidic *shtadlan*, and not the community, who became politically sovereign, as he himself determined both his constituency and his political goals. This seems to have been the result of two ongoing processes. The first was the evolution of hasidic political engagement and the adoption of forms of modern politics in a process I have termed 'defensive modernization'. As a result of this engagement, hasidic political representatives achieved an exceptional political competence, first in defending their own community and later, through elaborate interventions, broadening their sphere of influence in a way that allowed them to be relatively independent politically. The second is the Enlightenment and post-Enlightenment politics of the authorities of the Kingdom of Poland, which consistently aimed to limit the authority of traditional Jewish institutions; the vacuum this created meant that self-appointed representatives were free to act as relatively autonomous agents.

This did not mean that the hasidic *shtadlan* could simply dismiss the will and opinion of the broader Jewish community. It is true that he could act without the community's formal authorization, but the Jewish community was the basic point of reference in at least two ways. First, as we saw in Chapter 7, §3, one of the key claims of the hasidic *shtadlan* was that he represented the will of the entire Jewish community. For this claim to be effective, there had to be some truth to it; a *shtadlan* could not openly antagonize the community in terms of goals and methods. A second, and very important, reason was that hasidic *shtadlanut* aimed not only to realize political goals regarding non-Jewish centres of authority but also, and to an equal degree, to enhance the *shtadlan*'s own political reputation and thereby to generate support for hasidism within the Jewish community.

This nascent interdependence of political actors and the broader community was obviously still a far cry from modern electoral representative politics, but it certainly in some senses prefigured the forms of popular political participation that would develop at the end of the nineteenth century, or perhaps even suggested them. One such similarity is the assertion that the hasidic *shtadlan* represented the will of the entire Jewish community, and so (in the absence of earlier, pre-modern forms of Jewish autonomy), was the sole guarantee of peace and social order.

Of course, this interdependence of the *shtadlan* and his constituency was not synonymous with popular participation in politics such as we see in modern democratic parties. That type of political activity was simply impossible in the conditions of the Kingdom of Poland in the mid-nineteenth century, or in Austria, Prussia, or Russia. I would therefore suggest that hasidic stories such as the one of mass protests on the streets of Warsaw following the arrest of the Gerer Rebbe, Isaac Meir Alter, should be considered no more than fables.[12] Still, even the most autocratic government knew that ignoring the demands of the hasidic *shtadlan* could lead to social unrest, even if the *shtadlan* did not deliberately provoke such unrest. The government came to learn this through conflicts like that over Jewish dress, or (though significantly less so) over hasidic *shtiblekh* in 1824 (see Ch. 3), from which the government withdrew once it recognized the pointlessness of inflaming the social situation. One should also remember that the promise of maintaining peace and order became especially important after 1831, when it became a fundamental political goal of the authorities. Thus, the *shtadlanim*, like modern politicians, appealed to the support of a wider public to legitimize their activism.

Significantly, hasidic political representation appealed to the will of the community majority not only as a rhetorical argument in conflicts with government authorities, but also more broadly, for example when hasidic *shtadlanim* resolved social and political conflicts in Jewish communities where they did not reside and with which they had no formal ties. This fundamental characteristic distinguishing hasidic politics from pre-modern politics is what prompts me to say it may be considered a precursor of modern politics. In pre-modern Jewish politics, the link between the politician and his constituency—whether a single Jewish community or a supra-communal constituency—was almost always strictly defined by external modes of election, representation, and verification. Even if the early modern *shtadlan* sometimes engaged in matters of supra-regional or supra-community significance and sought broader political support, his reference group never went beyond the oligarchy of the community, the formal political representation empowered by the legal system of the pre-modern state.[13] By contrast, the fundamental principle of nineteenth-century hasidic *shtadlanut* in the Kingdom of Poland was consistently to appeal to a supra-local constituency, encompassing the

[12] The story about the imprisonment of tsadik Isaac Meir Alter of Góra Kalwaria (Ger), never corroborated by any archival evidence and in my opinion apocryphal, has been reported in numerous hasidic texts and has been accepted as reliable in historical literature; see e.g. Alfasi, *Gur: hameyased ḥidushei harim*, 304–5; Shatzky, *Geshikhte fun yidn in varshe*, ii. 93–5.

[13] See for example the well-known cases of Josel Rosheim and Baruch Yavan discussed in Stern, *Josel of Rosheim*, and Maciejko, 'Baruch Yavan and the Frankist Movement'.

entire Jewish community. Gaining the support of the whole community was, as we have seen, one of the fundamental goals of hasidic *shtadlanut*. The necessity of appealing to a reference point other than the community was, of course, partly because the great community and supra-community institutions of pre-modern times had either ceased to exist or were, to a greater or lesser degree, incapacitated. However, an equally important factor was that hasidic political representatives somehow invented their own constituency, a practice highly suggestive of modern mass politics. That this constituency was the entire Jewish community (or, more exactly, the males of that community) was not as clear in the conservative society of nineteenth-century eastern Europe as it seems today *ex post facto* from the perspective of modern civil society.

As important as the supra-local and popular nature of the ties between the hasidic activist and his developing constituency or reference group was its voluntary character. In the pre-modern Polish–Lithuanian Commonwealth, an ordinary Jew could participate in politics only through a formalized structure of community political representation approved by the state—just like the modern politician strictly and formally linked to his constituency. Electoral choices often came down to one or other member of the *kahal* oligarchy, that is, essentially the same pool of people. As a self-appointed and supra-local representative, the hasidic *shtadlan* in the nineteenth century was in a certain sense less dependent on the rank-and-file members of the community than were his pre-modern predecessors. At the same time, however, he sought the support of broad circles of the Jewish community independent of individual social status and position in the community, which potentially gave every Jew the right to political participation—the right to express passive or active support or opposition, or even to refrain from taking a position. In this sense, hasidic political representation adumbrates the political party, in which the link with members, sympathizers, or occasional allies depends on precisely this voluntary nature.

We can say, then, that nineteenth-century hasidic political engagement in the Kingdom of Poland in many respects heralded the birth of contemporary Jewish politics at the end of the century. Hasidic politics was modern in that it appealed to a broad mass constituency and used modern forms of political participation. Perhaps, then, the Zionist leader Nahum Sokołów was right when he said glibly in 1899 that hasidism was neither the tarnished superstition of dark Jewish masses nor, most certainly, the sweet angel from the nostalgic tales of Isaac Leib Peretz. Rather, he said, hasidism was the culmination of the deliberate goals of an active political party. This observation may hold true not only for 1899 but for earlier and later periods as well.

Bibliography

Archival Sources

Allgemeines Verwaltungsarchiv Wien
     Hofkanzleiprotokolle Galizien 1799

Archiwum Główne Akt Dawnych (AGAD)
     Centralne Władze Wyznaniowe (CWW)
     Kancelaria Senatora Nowosilcowa
     Komisja Rządowa Spraw Wewnętrznych (KRSW)
     Komisja Województwa Kaliskiego (KWK)
     Protokoły Rady Administracyjnej Królestwa Polskiego
     Sekretariat Stanu Królestwa Polskiego
     Rada Ministrów Księstwa Warszawskiego
     Rada Stanu i Rada Ministrów Księstwa Warszawskiego
     I Rada Stanu Królestwa Polskiego

Archiwum Państwowe w Częstochowie
     Akta miasta Częstochowy

Archiwum Państwowe w Katowicach
     Akta miasta Olkusza

Archiwum Państwowe w Kielcach (APK)
     Rząd Gubernialny Radomski (RGR)

Archiwum Państwowe Kielcach (APK), Oddział w Sandomierzu
     Akta miasta Sandomierza

Archiwum Państwowe w Lublinie (APL)
     Akta miasta Lublina (1809–1874) (AmL)

Archiwum Państwowe w Łodzi (APŁ)
     Akta miasta Pabianic
     Anteriora Piotrkowskiego Rządu Gubernialnego (APRG)

Archiwum Państwowe w Płocku (APP)
     Akta miasta Płocka (AmP)

Archiwum Państwowe w Radomiu
     Rząd Gubernialny Radomski I

Archiwum Państwowe w Toruniu, Oddział we Włocławku
     Akta miasta Włocławka
     Naczelnik Powiatu Włocławskiego

Printed Sources

AESCOLY, AHARON ZE'EV, *Haḥasidut bepolin* [Hasidism in Poland], ed. David Assaf (Jerusalem, 1998).

AGES, ARNOLD, 'Luigi Chiarini: A Case Study in Intellectual Anti-Semitism', *Judaica*, 37/2 (1981), 76–89.

AJNENKIEL, ANDRZEJ, BOGUSŁAW LEŚNODORSKI, and WŁADYSŁAW ROSTOCKI, *Historia ustroju Polski (1764–1939)* [History of the Polish State/ Political System, 1764–1939] (Warsaw, 1970).

ALFASI, YITSHAK, *Gur: hameyased ḥidushei harim, ḥayav, maḥshevotav vetorato* [Ger: The Founder Hidushei Harim (Israel Meir Alter)] (Tel Aviv, 1954).

——(ed.), *Entsiklopediyah laḥasidut: ishim* [Hasidic Encyclopedia: Personalities], 3 vols. (Jerusalem, 1986–2004).

ASKENAZY, SZYMON, 'Ze spraw żydowskich w dobie kongresowej' [On the Jewish Matters in the Period 1815–1830], *Kwartalnik poświęcony badaniu przeszłości Żydów w Polsce*, 1/3 (1913), 1–36.

ASSAF, DAVID, '"Money for Household Expenses": Economic Aspects of the Hasidic Courts', in Adam Teller (ed.), *Studies in the History of the Jews in Old Poland* (Jerusalem, 1998), 14–50 = *Scripta Hierosolimitana*, 38.

——*The Regal Way: The Life and Times of Rabbi Israel of Ruzhin*, trans. David Louvish (Stanford, Calif., 2002).

——and ISRAEL BARTAL, 'Shetadlanut ve'ortodoksiyah: tsadikei polin bemifgash im hazemanim haḥadashim' [Jewish Intercession and Orthodoxy: Polish Tsadikim Encounter Modern Times], in Rachel Elior, Israel Bartal, and Chone Shmeruk (eds.), *Tsadikim ve'anshei ma'aseh: meḥkarim beḥasidut polin* [Hasidism in Poland] (Jerusalem, 1994), 65–90.

BACON, GERSHON, 'Messianists, Pragmatists and Patriots: Orthodox Jews and the Modern Polish State', in Yaakov Elman, Ephraim Bezalel Halivni, and Zvi Arie Steinfeld (eds.), *Neti'ot ledavid: Jubilee Volume for David Weiss Halivni* (Jerusalem, 2004), 15–30.

——*The Politics of Tradition: Agudat Yisrael in Poland, 1916–1939* (Jerusalem, 1996).

——'Prolonged Erosion, Organisation and Reinforcement: Reflections on Orthodox Jewry in Congress Poland', in Yisrael Gutman (ed.), *Major Changes within the Jewish People in the Wake of the Holocaust* (Jerusalem, 1996), 71–91.

BAŁABAN, MAJER, 'Żydzi w powstaniu 1863 r. (Próba bibliografii rozumowanej)' [Jews in the 1863 Uprising (A Tentative Bibliography)], *Przegląd Historyczny*, 34 (1937–8), 564–99.

BANASZAK, MARIAN, 'Kapłaństwo Staszica—problem badawczy' [Priesthood of Staszic—a Research Agenda], in Janusz Olejniczak (ed.), *Stanisław Staszic* [Stanisław Staszic], papers from a conference held at Piła, 19–20 September 1995 (Piła, 1995), 91–100.

BARTAL, ISRAEL, 'Moses Montefiore: Nationalist before his Time, or Belated *Shtadlan?*', *Studies in Zionism*, 11/2 (1990), 111–25.

BEILIN, S., 'Iz istoricheskikh zhurnalov' [From the Historical Periodicals], *Evreiskaia Starina*, 3 (1911), 417–19.

BERGMAN, ELEONORA, 'The *Rewir* or Jewish District and the *Eyruv*', *Studia Judaica*, 5/1–2 (2002), 85–97.

BERGNER, HINDE, *On Long Winter Nights . . . : Memoirs of a Jewish Family in a Galician Township (1870–1900)*, trans. from the Yiddish, ed. and with an introduction by Justin Daniel Cammy (Cambridge, Mass., and London, 2005).

BIALE, DAVID, *Power and Powerlessness in Jewish History* (New York, 1986).

BILADI, YITSHAK, 'Toledotav shel tsadik' [History of the Tsadik], in id. (ed.), *Sifrei harabi shmelke minikolsburg* [Writings of R. Samuel Shmelke of Nikolsburg] (Jerusalem, 1998), 19–72.

BLATMAN, DANIEL, 'Bendzin/Będzin', in *Pinkas hakehilot: polin* [Encyclopedia of the Jewish Communities in Poland], vii: *Meḥozot lublin / kiyeltseh* [The Districts of Lublin and Kielce] (Jerusalem, 1999), 101–15.

BOIM, YEHUDA MENAHEM, *Harabi rebe bunem mipeshisḥa: toledot ḥayav, sipurim, minhagim, siḥot* [Rabbi Bunem of Przysucha], 2 vols. (Benei Berak, 1997).

BORZYMIŃSKA, ZOFIA, *Dzieje Żydów w Polsce: Wybór tekstów źródłowych. XIX wiek* [History of the Jews in Poland: Source Book, Nineteenth Century] (Warsaw, 1994).

——'Sprawa Rabiego Icchaka Meira Altera' [The Case of Isaac Meir Alter], *Biuletyn Żydowskiego Instytutu Historycznego*, 3 (2001), 367–77.

——*Szkolnictwo żydowskie w Warszawie 1831–1870* [Jewish Education in Warsaw, 1831–1870] (Warsaw, 1994).

BOURDIEU, PIERRE, *Reproduction in Education, Society and Culture*, trans. Richard Nice (Beverly Hills, Calif., 1977).

BRODOWSKA, HELENA, 'Stanisław Staszic 1755–1826', in Witold Jakóbczyk (ed.), *Wielkopolanie XIX wieku* [People of Wielkopolska in the Nineteenth Century] (Poznań, 1969), ii. 71–99.

BROMBERG, ABRAHAM I., *Migedolei haḥasidut: ha'admorim leveit vurke ve'amshinov* [Some of the Great Men of Hasidism: Tsadikim from the Dynasty of Warka and Mszczonów] (Jerusalem, 1982).

BRZEZINA, MARIA, *Polszczyzna Żydów* [Polish Language of the Jews] (Warsaw, 1986).

BUBER, MARTIN, *For the Sake of Heaven*, trans. L. Loewinson (Philadelphia, 1945).

BUCHNER, ABRAHAM, *Katechizm religijno-moralny dla Izraelitów—Yesodei hadat umusar hasekhel* [A Religious and Moral Catechism for Israelites], trans. into Polish by J. Rosenblum (Warsaw, 1836).

B[URSZTYŃSKI], J[AKUB], 'Russland und Polen: Czenstochau', *Allgemeine Zeitung des Judentums*, 5/40 (1841), 567–8.

BUTRYMOWICZ, MATEUSZ, 'Reforma Żydów' [Reform of the Jews], *MDSC* 118–28.

——'Sposób uformowania Żydów polskich w pożytecznych krajowi obywatelów' [The Way to Transform Polish Jews into Citizens Useful to the Country], *MDSC* 78–93.

CAŁA, ALINA, *Wizerunek Żyda w polskiej kulturze ludowej* [The Image of the Jew in Polish Folk Culture] (Warsaw, 1988); English translation: *The Image of the Jew in Polish Folk Culture* (Jerusalem, 1995).

CALMANSON, JACQUES, *Essai sur l'état actuel des Juifs de Pologne et leur perfectibilité* (Warsaw, 1796).

——*Uwagi nad niniejszym stanem Żydów polskich i ich wydoskonaleniem* [Essay on the Current State of the Polish Jews and their Betterment], trans. J[ulian] C[zechowicz] (Warsaw, 1797).

CHIARINI, LUIGI, *Théorie du judaisme, appliquée à la réforme des israélites de tous les pays de l'Europe*, 2 vols. (Paris, 1830).

CHIMIAK, ŁUKASZ, *Gubernatorzy rosyjscy w Królestwie Polskim: Szkic do portretu zbiorowego* [The Russian Governors in the Kingdom of Poland: Collective Portrait] (Wrocław, 1999).

CHRISTIAN, DAVID, 'Vodka and Corruption in Russia on the Eve of Emancipation', *Slavic Review*, 46 (1987), 471–88.

CHWALBA, ANDRZEJ, *Historia Polski 1795–1918* [History of Poland, 1795–1918] (Kraków, 2000).

——*Imperium korupcji w Rosji i Królestwie Polskim 1861–1917* [Empire of Corruption in Russia and the Kingdom of Poland, 1861–1917], 2nd edn. (Warsaw, 2001).

CZACKI, MICHAŁ, 'Refleksyje nad reformą Żydów' [On the Reform of the Jews], *MDSC* 206–12.

CZACKI, TADEUSZ, *Rozprawa o Żydach i karaitach* [Treatise on Jews and Karaites] (Vilna, 1807).

DAVIES, NORMAN, *God's Playground: A History of Poland*, 2 vols. (New York, 1982).

DEICH, GENRICH, *Tsarskoe pravitel'stvo i khasidskoe dvizhenie v Rossii: Arkhivnye dokumenty* [The Tsarist Government and the Hasidic Movement in Russia: Archival Documents] (n.p., 1994).

DEMBOWSKI, LEON, *Moje wspomnienia* [My Memories] (St Petersburg, 1898).

DEUTSCH, NATHANIEL, *The Maiden of Ludmir: A Jewish Holy Woman and her World* (Berkeley, 2003).

Diariusze sejmowe z wieku XVIII [Diet Protocols from the Eighteenth Century], ed. Władysław Konopczyński, 3 vols. (Warsaw, 1912–37).

'Dodatek z Prowincji', *Rozmaitości* [supplement to *Korespondent Warszawski*], 13 (1820), 49.

DUBNOW, SIMON, *Geschichte des Chassidismus*, 2 vols. (Berlin, 1931).

——'Vmeshatelstvo russkogo pravitel'stva v antichasidskuyu borbu (1800–1801)' [Participation of the Russian Authorities in the Anti-Hasidic Campaign, 1800–1801], *Evreiskaia Starina*, 2 (1910), 84–109, 253–82.

'Dwór Franka . . .' [Frank's Court], *MDSC* 176–82.

DYNNER, GLENN, 'How Many *Hasidim* Were There Really in Congress Poland? A Response to Marcin Wodziński', *Gal-ed*, 20 (2006), 91–104.

——*'Men of Silk': The Hasidic Conquest of Polish Jewish Society* (Oxford and New York, 2006).

——'Merchant Princes and Tsadikim: The Patronage of Polish Hasidism', *Jewish Social Studies*, 12/1 (2005), 64–110.

EISENBACH, ARTUR, *Emancypacja Żydów na ziemiach polskich 1785–1870 na tle europejskim* [The Emancipation of the Jews in Poland, 1785–1870] (Warsaw, 1989).

——*Kwestia równouprawnienia Żydów w Królestwie Polskim* [The Issue of the Emancipation of the Jews in the Kingdom of Poland] (Warsaw, 1972).

——JERZY MICHALSKI, EMANUEL ROSTWOROWSKI, and JANUSZ WOLAŃSKI (eds.), *Materiały do dziejów Sejmu Czteroletniego* [Sources on the History of the Four Year Sejm], vi (Wrocław, 1969).

ELIMELEKH OF LEŻAJSK (LYZHANSK), *No'am elimelekh* [A treatise on the idea of the tsadik] (Lwów, 1788).

ELYASHEVICH, DMITRY A., *Pravitel'stvennaya politika i evreiskaia pechat v Rasiyi 1797–1917: Ocherky istorii tsenzury* [Government Policy and Jewish Printing in Russia 1797–1917: Essays on the History of Censorship] (St Petersburg and Jerusalem, 1999).

ETKES, IMMANUEL, *Ba'al hashem: habesht—magiyah, mistikah, hanhagah* [The Besht—Magician, Mystic, and Leader] (Jerusalem, 2000); English translation: *The Besht: Magician, Mystic, and Leader*, trans. Saadya Sternberg (Hanover, NH, 2004).

——'Hahaskalah bemizraḥ eiropah: divrei mavo' [The Haskalah in Eastern Europe: Introduction], in id. (ed.), *Hadat vehaḥayim: tenu'at hahaskalah hayehudit bemizraḥ eiropah* [Religion and Life: The Jewish Haskalah Movement in Eastern Europe] (Jerusalem, 1993), 9–24.

——'The Historical Besht: Reconstruction or Deconstruction?', *Polin*, 12 (1999), 297–306.

——'Parashat hahaskalah mita'am vehatemurah bema'amad tenu'at hahaskalah berusiyah' [The Issue of Official Haskalah and the Development of the Haskalah Movement in Russia], in id. (ed.), *Hadat vehaḥayim: tenu'at hahaskalah hayehudit bemizraḥ eiropah* [Religion and Life: The Jewish Haskalah Movement in Eastern Europe] (Jerusalem, 1993), 167–216.

ETTINGER, SHMUEL, 'Hasidism and the *Kahal* in Eastern Europe', in Ada Rapoport-Albert (ed.), *Hasidism Reappraised* (London, 1996), 63–75.

——'The Modern Period', in Haim Hillel Ben-Sasson (ed.), *A History of the Jewish People* (Cambridge, 1994), 725–1096.

——'Takanot 1804' [Laws of 1804], in id., *Bein polin lerusiyah* [Between Poland and Russia] (Jerusalem, 1994), 234–56.

FEINKIND, MOJŻESZ, 'Dysputa żydowska za czasów Stanisława Staszica' [The Jewish Dispute at the Time of Stanisław Staszic], *Nasz Przegląd*, 4/41 (1926), 7.

——*Dzieje Żydów w Piotrkowie i okolicy od najdawniejszych czasów do chwili obecnej* [History of the Jews in Piotrków from the Beginning until Present Time] (Piotrków, 1930).

FELDMAN, WILHELM, 'Korespondencja "Izraelity"' [Correspondence], *Izraelita*, 22/1 (1887), 5.

——'Z piśmiennictwa' [From the Writings], *Izraelita*, 22/18 (1887), 145.

FIJAŁEK, JAN, 'Do zagadnienia szpitalnictwa żydowskiego w Piotrkowie Trybunalskim w połowie XIX w.' [The Jewish Hospitals in Piotrków Trybunalski in the Mid-Nineteenth Century], *Biuletyn Żydowskiego Instytutu Historycznego*, 10/3 (1959), 28–56.

FLATTO, SHARON, 'Hasidim and Mitnaggedim: Not a World Apart', *Journal of Jewish Thought and Philosophy*, 12/2 (2003), 99–121.

FLATTO, SHARON, *The Kabbalistic Culture of Eighteenth-Century Prague: Ezekiel Landau (the 'Noda Biyehudah') and his Contemporaries* (Oxford, 2010).

FORMISANO, RONALDO P., 'The Concept of Political Culture', *Journal of Interdisciplinary History*, 31/3 (2001), 393–426.

FRANKEL, JONATHAN, *Prophecy and Politics: Socialism, Nationalism and the Russian Jews* (Cambridge, 1981).

FREEZE, CHAERAN, 'Introduction: A Historiographical Survey', *Polin*, 18 (2005), 3–24.

——*Jewish Marriage and Divorce in Imperial Russia* (Hanover, NH, 2002).

FRENK, EZRIEL N., 'Yekhezkel Hoge oder "Haskel Meshumad"' [Ezekiel Hoge or 'Haskel the Apostate'], in id., *Meshumadim in poyln in 19ten yohrhundert* [Converts in Poland in the Nineteenth Century] (Warsaw, 1923), 38–110.

——and J. H. ZAGORODSKI, *Di familie Dawidsohn* [The Dawidsohn Family] (Warsaw, 1924).

FRIDMAN, ELIEZER ELIYAHU, *Sefer zikhronot (5618–5686)* [Memoirs, 1858–1926] (Tel Aviv, 1926).

FRIEDMAN, MENAHEM, 'Pashkevilim umoda'ot kir baḥevrah haḥaredit' [Libels and Wall Posters in the Haredi Orthodox Community], in *Pashkevilim: moda'ot kir ukherazot polmos bareḥov haḥaredi* [Libels: Posters and Polemical Announcements in the Haredi Orthodox Street] (Tel Aviv and Jerusalem, 2005), 8–37.

GĄSIOROWSKA, NATALIA, 'Cenzura żydowska w Królestwie Kongresowym' [Jewish Censorship in the Kingdom of Poland], *Kwartalnik poświęcony badaniu przeszłości Żydów w Polsce*, 1/2 (1912), 55–64.

——*Wolność druku w Królestwie Kongresowym 1815–1830* [Freedom of Print in the Kingdom of Poland, 1815–1830] (Warsaw, 1916).

GELBER, NATHAN M., *Hayehudim vehamered hapolani: zikhronotav shel ya'akov halevi levin miyemei hamered hapolani bishenat 1830–1831* [Jews and the Polish Uprising: Memoirs of Jacob Halevi Levin from the Polish Uprising of 1830–1831] (Jerusalem, 1953).

——*Die Juden und der Polnische Aufstand 1863* (Vienna, 1923).

——'Mendel lefin-satanover vehatsa'otav letikun oraḥ haḥayim shel yehudei polin bifnei haseim hagadol (1788–1792)' [Mendel Lefin Satanower and his Projects to Reform the Polish Jews at the Four Year Sejm (1788–1792)], in *Sefer yovel likhevod harav dr avraham veis* [Jubilee Volume for Abraham Weiss] (New York, 1964), 271–83.

——'She'elat hayehudim bepolin bishenot 1815–1830' [The Jewish Question in Poland, 1815–1830], *Zion*, 13–14 (1948–9), 106–43.

——'Di yidn-frage in kongres-poyln in di yorn 1815–1830' [The Jewish Question in the Kingdom of Poland in the Years 1815–1830], *Bleter far Geshikhte*, 1/3–4 (1948), 41–105.

——'Żydzi a zagadnienie reformy Żydów na Sejmie Czteroletnim' [Jews and the Question of the Reform of the Jews during the Four Year Sejm], *Miesięcznik Żydowski*, 1 (1931), 326–44, 429–40.

GERTNER, HAIM, 'Rabanut vedayanut begalitsiyah bamaḥatsit harishonah shel hame'ah hatesha-esreh: tipologiyah shel hanhagah masoratit bemashber' [Rabbis and Rabbinical Judges (*Dayanim*) in Galicia in the First Half of the

Nineteenth Century: A Typology of Traditional Leadership in Crisis] (Ph.D. diss., Hebrew University of Jerusalem, 2004).

GIDDENS, ANTHONY, *Modernity and Self-Identity: Self and Society in the Late Modern Age* (Cambridge, 1991).

GINTSBURG, SHAUL M., 'Yehudim malshinim beyamim milefanim' [Jewish Informers in the Old Times], in id., *Ketavim historiyim meḥayei hayehudim berusiyah bememshelet hatsarim* [Historical Writings from the Life of the Jews in Tsarist Russia], trans. J. L. Baruch (Tel Aviv, 1944), 168–78.

GLIŃSKI, WALDEMAR, *Komisja Rządowa Wyznań Religijnych i Oświecenia Publicznego wobec wspólnot religijnych w Królestwie Polskim w latach 1815–1820* [Government Commission for the Religious Denominations and Public Enlightenment in the Kingdom of Poland in the Years 1815–1820 and the Religious Communities] (Warsaw, 2002).

[GLÜCKSBERG, JAN], *Rzut oka na stan Izraelitów w Polsce, czyli Wykrycie błędnego z nimi postępowania, na aktach rządowych oparte* [A Cursory Glance at the State of the Israelites in Poland] (Warsaw, 1831).

GOLDBERG, JAKUB, 'The Changes in the Attitude of Polish Society toward the Jews in the Eighteenth Century', in Antony Polonsky (ed.), *From Shtetl to Socialism: Studies from Polin* (London and Washington, DC, 1993), 50–63.

——'Pierwszy ruch polityczny wśród Żydów polskich: Plenipotenci żydowscy w dobie Sejmu Czteroletniego' [First Political Movement among the Polish Jews: Jewish Plenipotentiaries in the Time of the Four Year Sejm], in Jerzy Michalski (ed.), *Lud żydowski w narodzie polskim* [Jewish People in the Polish Nation], papers from a conference held at Warsaw, 15–16 September 1992 (Warsaw, 1994), 45–63.

GRUSZCZYŃSKA, MARIANNA, 'Początki osadnictwa żydowskiego we Włocławku (1800–1845)' [Beginnings of the Jewish Settlement in Włocławek, 1800–1845], in Mirosław Krajewski (ed.), *Byli wśród nas: Żydzi we Włocławku oraz na Kujawach Wschodnich i w Ziemi Dobrzyńskiej* [Jews in Włocławek and the Eastern Part of Kujawy and Dobrzyń Region] (Włocławek, 2001), 12–36.

GRYNSZPAN, SHLOMO, 'Rabanim: kovets masot al rabanei plotsk' [Rabbis: Essays on the Rabbis of Płock], in Eliyahu Eizenberg (ed.), *Plotsk: toledot kehilah atikat-yomin bepolin* [Płock: History of the Old Polish Community] (Tel Aviv, 1967), 89–145.

GUESNET, FRANÇOIS, 'Die Politik der "Fürsprache"—Vormoderne jüdische Inter-essenvertretung', in Dan Diner (ed.), *Synchrone Welten: Zeiträume jüdischer Geschichte* (Göttingen, 2005), 67–92.

——'Politik der Vormoderne—*Shtadlanuth* am Vorabend der polnischen Teilungen', *Jahrbuch des Simon-Dubnow-Instituts*, 1 (2002), 235–55.

——*Polnische Juden im 19. Jahrhundert: Lebensbedingungen, Rechtsnormen und Organisation im Wandel* (Cologne, 1998).

HALPERIN, ISRAEL, 'Rabi levi-yitsḥak miberdichev ugezerot hamalkhut beyamav' [Rabbi Levi Isaac of Berdyczów (Berdichev) and the State Decrees of his Time], in id., *Yehudim veyahadut bemizraḥ eiropah* [Jews in Eastern Europe] (Jerusalem, 1968), 340–7.

HERTZBERG, ARTHUR, *The French Enlightenment and the Jews: The Origins of Modern Anti-Semitism* (New York, 1968).

HESCHEL, ABRAHAM JOSHUA, *The Circle of the Baal Shem Tov: Studies in Hasidism*, ed. Samuel H. Dresner (Chicago, 1985).

HORODEZKY, SAMUEL ABBA, *Haḥasidut vehaḥasidim* [Hasidism and Hasidim], 4 vols. (Tel Aviv, 1953).

HOROWITZ, BRIAN, 'A Portrait of a Russian-Jewish Shtadlan: Jacob Teitel's Social Solution', *Shofar*, 18/3 (2000), 1–12.

HUNDERT, GERSHON DAVID, *Jews in Poland-Lithuania in the Eighteenth Century: A Genealogy of Modernity* (Berkeley, 2004).

——*The Jews in a Polish Private Town: The Case of Opatów in the Eighteeenth Century* (Baltimore and London, 1992).

I[ZRAELSON], IA[KOV], 'Bor'ba pravitel'stva s khasidizmom (1834–1853 g.)' [Fight of the Government with Hasidism, 1834–1853], *Evreiskaia Starina*, 7 (1914), 90–102.

JACOBS, LOUIS, *Hasidic Prayer* (London, 1972).

——'Tobacco and the Hasidim', *Polin*, 11 (1998), 25–30.

JAGODZIŃSKA, AGNIESZKA, *Pomiędzy: Akulturacja Żydów Warszawy w drugiej połowie XIX wieku* [Between: Acculturation of the Warsaw Jews in the Second Half of the Nineteenth Century] (Wrocław, 2008).

JANION, MARIA, 'Der Gründungsmythos des polnischen Antisemitismus', in *Europäische Gesellschaften und der Holocaust* (Warsaw, 2004), 13–55.

[JANOWSKI, LUDWIK], *O Żydach i judaizmie czyli Wykrycie zasad moralnych tudzież rozumowania Izraelitów* [On Jews and Judaism; or, The Revealing of the Moral Principles and Thinking of the Jews] (Siedlce, 1820).

JASTROW, MARCUS, 'Bär Meisels, Oberrabbiner zu Warschau: Ein Lebensbild auf historischem Hintergrunde, nach eigener Anschauung entworfen', *Hebrew Leader* (1870), 15/25: 2; 15/26: 2; 16/1: 2; 16/2: 2; 16/3: 2; 16/4: 2; 16/5: 2; 16/6: 2; 16/7: 2; 16/8: 2; 16/9: 2; 16/10: 2; 17/1: 2.

JAWORSKI, WOJCIECH, *Żydzi będzińscy: Dzieje, zagłada* [Jews in Będzin: History, Destruction] (Będzin, 1993).

JEDLICKI, JERZY, *Jakiej cywilizacji Polacy potrzebują: Studia z dziejów idei i wyobraźni XIX wieku* [What Kind of Civilization Do Poles Need? On the Ideas and Concepts of the Nineteenth Century] (Warsaw, 1988).

JOZEFOWICZ, HERSZEL, 'Myśli stosowne do sposobu uformowania Żydów polskich w pożytecznych krajowi obywatelów' [Thoughts on Transforming the Polish Jews into Citizens Useful to the Country], *MDSC* 98–105.

KANDEL, DAWID, 'Kariera rabiniczna cadyka Icie-Majera' [The Rabbinic Career of the Tsadik Isaac Meir], *Kwartalnik poświęcony badaniu przeszłości Żydów w Polsce*, 1/2 (1912), 131–6.

——'Komitet Starozakonnych' [The Jewish Committee], *Kwartalnik poświęcony badaniu przeszłości Żydów w Polsce*, 1/2 (1912), 85–103.

——'Montefiore w Warszawie' [Montefiore in Warsaw], *Kwartalnik poświęcony badaniu przeszłości Żydów w Polsce*, 1 (1912), 74–94.

——'Żydzi w Królestwie Polskim po 1831 r.' [Jews in the Kingdom of Poland after 1831], *Biblioteka Warszawska*, 70/3 (1910), 542–58.

KARPIŃSKI, FRANCISZEK, *Pamiętniki* [Memoirs], foreword by Piotr Chmielowski (Warsaw, 1898).

'Katechizm o Żydach i neofitach' [Catechism on the Jews and Neophites], *MDSC* 466–80.

KATZ, JACOB, *Tradition and Crisis: Jewish Society at the End of the Middle Ages*, trans. Bernard D. Cooperman (New York, 1993).

KAUFMANN, DAVID, *Samson Wertheim, der Oberhoffactor und Landesrabbiner (1658–1724) und seine Kinder* (Vienna, 1888).

KEMLEIN, SOPHIA, *Żydzi w Wielkim Księstwie Poznańskim 1815–1848: Przeobrażenia w łonie żydostwa polskiego pod panowaniem pruskim* [Jews in the Grand Duchy of Poznań 1815–1848: The Transformation of Polish Jewry under Prussian Rule], trans. Zenona Choderny-Loew (Poznań, 2001).

KESTENBERG-GLADSTEIN, RUTH, *Neuere Geschichte der Juden in den böhmischen Ländern*, 2 vols. (Tübingen, 1969–2002).

Keter shem tov [The Crown of a Good Name] (Żółkiew, 1794).

KHITERER, VIKTORIA, 'Iosif Galperin, a Forgotten Berdichev Shtadlan', *Shvut*, 7 (1998), 33–47.

KIENIEWICZ, STEFAN, *Historia Polski 1795–1918* [History of Poland 1795–1918] (Warsaw, 1976).

——(ed.), *Polska XIX wieku: Państwo, społeczeństwo, kultura* [Poland in the Nineteenth Century: State, Society, Culture] (Warsaw, 1982).

KIRSZROT, JAKUB, *Prawa Żydów w Królestwie Polskim: Zarys historyczny* [Rights of the Jews in the Kingdom of Poland: A Historical Outline] (Warsaw, 1917).

KIZWALTER, TOMASZ, *Kryzys Oświecenia a początki konserwatyzmu polskiego* [The Crisis of Enlightenment and the Beginnings of Polish Conservatism] (Warsaw, 1987).

KLAUSNER, ISRAEL, 'Hagezerah al tilboshet hayehudim, 1844–1850' [The Decree on Jewish Dress, 1844–1850], *Gal-ed*, 6 (1982), 11–26.

——*Vilna bitekufat haga'on: hamilḥamah haruḥanit vehaḥevratit bekehilat vilna bitekufat hagra* [Vilna in the Time of the Gaon] (Jerusalem, 1942).

KLIER, JOHN D., *Imperial Russia's Jewish Question, 1855–1881* (Cambridge, 1995).

——'Krug Ginzburgov i politika shtadlanuta v imperatorskoi Rossii' [The Gintsburg Circle and the Jewish Intercession in Imperial Russia], *Vestnik Evreiskogo universiteta v Moskve*, 3/10 (1995), 38–55.

——*Russia Gathers Her Jews: The Origins of the Jewish Question in Russia, 1772–1825* (DeKalb, Ill., 1985).

KOŁŁĄTAJ, HUGO, *Listy anonima i prawo polityczne narodu polskiego* [Anonymous Letters and Political Rights of the Polish Nation], 2 vols. (Warsaw, 1954).

KOTIK, YEKHEZKEL, *A Journey to a Nineteenth-Century Shtetl: The Memoirs of Yekhezkel Kotik*, ed. David Assaf, trans. Margaret Birstein (Detroit, 2002).

KOŹMIAN, KAJETAN, *Pamiętniki* [Memoirs], 3 vols. (Wrocław, 1972).

[KRASIŃSKI, WINCENTY], *Aperçu sur les Juifs de Pologne par un officier général polonois* (Warsaw, 1818).

KRASZEWSKI, JÓZEF IGNACY, *Wspomnienia Wołynia, Polesia i Litwy* [Memoirs from Volhynia, Polesie, and Lithuania] (Warsaw, 1985).

KRUSZYŃSKI, JÓZEF, *Stanisław Staszic a kwestia żydowska* [Stanisław Staszic and the Jewish Question] (Lublin, 1926).

KUPERSTEIN, ISAIAH, 'Inquiry at Polaniec: A Case Study of a Hassidic Controversy in 18th Century Galicia', *Bar-Ilan Annual*, 24–5 (1989), 25–39.

KUWAŁEK, ROBERT, 'Chasydzkie domy modlitwy w Lublinie w XIX–XX wieku' [Hasidic Prayerhouses in Lublin in the Nineteenth to Twentieth Centuries], in Konrad Zieliński and Monika Adamczyk-Garbowska (eds.), *Ortodoksja. Emancypacja. Asymilacja: Studia z dziejów ludności żydowskiej na ziemiach polskich w okresie rozbiorów* [Orthodoxy, Emancipation, Assimilation: On the History of the Polish Jews in the Period of Partitions] (Lublin, 2003), 49–78.

——'Pomiędzy tradycją a asymilacją: Walka o wpływ i władzę w lubelskiej gminie żydowskiej między ortodoksami i asymilatorami w latach 1862–1915' [Between Tradition and Assimilation: The Fight for Power in the Lublin Jewish Community between the Orthodox and Assimilationists in the Years 1862–1915], in Krzysztof Pilarczyk (ed.), *Żydzi i judaizm we współczesnych badaniach polskich* [Jews and Judaism in Contemporary Polish Research], papers from a conference held at Kraków, 21–23 November 1995 (Kraków, 1997), 227–47.

——'Urzędowi rabini lubelskiego Okręgu Bożniczego 1821–1939 (Przyczynek do dziejów Gminy Żydowskiej w Lublinie)' [Official Rabbis in Lublin, 1821–1939 (On the History of the Jewish Community in Lublin)], in Tadeusz Radzik (ed.), *Żydzi w Lublinie: Materiały do dziejów społeczności żydowskiej Lublina* [Jews in Lublin: On the History of Jewish Society in Lublin] (Lublin, 1995), 27–65.

LANGER, JIŘI, *Nine Gates to the Chassidic Mysteries*, trans. Stephen Jolly (New York, 1961).

LASK ABRAHAMS, BETH-ZION, 'Stanislaus Hoga—Apostate and Penitent', *Jewish Historical Society of England: Transactions*, 15 (1939–45), 121–49.

LEDERHENDLER, ELI, *The Road to Modern Jewish Politics: Political Tradition and Political Reconstruction in the Jewish Community of Tzarist Russia* (New York and Oxford, 1989).

[LEFIN, MENAHEM MENDEL], 'Essai d'un plan de réforme ayant pour objet d'éclairer la nation juive en Pologne et de redresser par là ses mœurs', *MDSC* 409–21.

LEŚNIEWSKI, CZESŁAW, *S. Staszic: Jego życie i ideologia* [Staszic: His Life and Ideas] (Warsaw, 1925).

LESZCZYŃSKI, ANATOL, *Sejm Żydów Korony, 1623–1764* [Council of the Four Lands, 1623–1764] (Warsaw, 1994).

LEVINE, HILLEL, '"Should Napoleon Be Victorious . . . ": Politics and Spirituality in Early Modern Jewish Messianism', in Rachel Elior (ed.), *The Sabbatian Movement and its Aftermath: Messianism, Sabbatianism and Frankism*, Jerusalem Studies in Jewish Thought 17 (Jerusalem, 2001), ii. 65*–83*.

LEWIN, IZAAK, 'Staszic a Żydzi' [Staszic and the Jews], in id., *Przez pryzmat historii* [Through the Lens of History] (Warsaw, 1994), 49–56.

LEWIN SABINA, 'Beit-hasefer lerabanim bevarshah bashanim 1826–1863' [The Warsaw Rabbinical School, 1826–1863], *Gal-ed*, 11 (1989), 35–58.

LEWIS, JUSTIN JARON, '"Eydele, the Rebbe": Shifting Perspectives on a Jewish Gender Transgressor', *Journal of Modern Jewish Studies*, 6/1 (2007), 21–40.

LINDE, SAMUEL B., *Słownik języka polskiego* [Dictionary of the Polish Language], 5 vols. (Lwów, 1854).

'List przyjaciela Polaka' [A Letter from a Polish Friend], *MDSC* 169–75.

LÖBEL, ISRAEL, 'Glaubwürdige Nachricht von der in Polen und Lithauen befindlichen Sekte: Chasidim genannt', *Sulamith*, 1/2, no. 5 (1807), 308–33.

LOEWENTHAL, NAFTALI, '"Daughter/Wife of Hasid" or "Hasidic Woman"?', *Jewish Studies*, 40 (2000), 21–8.

——'Women and the Dialectic of Spirituality in Hasidism', in Immanuel Etkes et al. (eds.), *Bema'agelei ḥasidim: kovets meḥkarim lezikhro shel profesor mordekhai vilenski* [Within Hasidic Circles: Studies in Hasidism in Memory of Mordecai Wilensky] (Jerusalem, 2000), *7–*65.

ŁUKASIŃSKI, WALERIAN, *Uwagi pewnego oficera nad uznaną potrzebą urządzenia Żydów w naszym kraju i nad niektórymi pisemkami w tym przedmiocie teraz w druku wyszłemi* [Remarks of an Officer on the Need to Settle the Rights of Jews in our Country] (Warsaw, 1917).

LURIE, ILIA, *Edah umedinah: ḥasidut ḥabad ba'imperiyah harusit 5588–5643* [The Habad Movement in Tsarist Russia, 1828–1882] (Jerusalem, 2006).

MACIEJKO, PAWEŁ, 'Baruch Yavan and the Frankist Movement: Intercession in an Age of Upheaval', *Jahrbuch des Simon-Dubnow-Instituts*, 4 (2005), 333–54.

MĄCZAK, ANTONI, *Klientela: Nieformalne systemy władzy w Polsce i Europie XVI–XVIII w.* [Clientele: Informal Systems of Power in Poland and Europe, Sixteenth to Eighteenth Centuries] (Warsaw, 1994).

MAHLER, RAPHAEL, *Divrei yemei yisra'el: dorot aḥaronim* [History of the Jews in Modern Times], 6 vols. (Merhavia, 1952–76).

——*Haḥasidut vehahaskalah (begalitsiyah uvepolin hakongresa'it bamaḥatsit harishonah shel hame'ah hatesha-esreh, hayesodot hasotsi'aliyim vehamediniyim)* [Hasidism and the Haskalah in Galicia and Poland in the First Half of the Nineteenth Century] (Merhavia, 1961).

——*Hasidism and the Jewish Enlightenment: Their Confrontation in Galicia and Poland in the First Half of the Nineteenth Century*, trans. Eugene Orenstein, Aaron Klein, and Jenny Machlowitz Klein (Philadelphia, 1985).

——*A History of Modern Jewry, 1780–1815* (New York, 1971).

MAJMON, SALEZY, 'Luźne kartki: Z dziejów rozkrzewienia się u nas chasydyzmu' [From the History of the Expansion of Hasidism], *Izraelita*, 29 (1894), 329.

MANEKIN, RACHEL, 'Hasidism and the Habsburg Empire, 1788–1867', *Jewish History* (forthcoming).

——'Tsemiḥatah vegibushah shel ha'ortodoksiyah hayehudit begalitsiyah: ḥevrat "maḥazikei hadat", 1867–1883' [The Emergence and Formulation of Jewish Orthodoxy in Galicia: The Mahazikei Hadat Society, 1867–1883] (Ph.D. diss., Hebrew University of Jerusalem, 2000).

MARK, ZVI, '"Ein ben david ba ad shetitpashet malkhut aram armilus melekh rusiyah aleksander al kol ha'olam 9 ḥodashim": tikvot meshiḥiyot beḥasidut gur' ['The Son of David Shall Not Come until the Kingdom of Armilus Alexander, King of Russia, Expands its Rule over the Whole World for Nine Months': Messianic Expectations in Gur Hasidism], *Tarbiz*, 77/2 (2008), 295–324.

MENDELSOHN, EZRA (ed.), *Jews and the State*, Studies in Contemporary Jewry 19 (Jerusalem, 2003).

MEVORACH, BARUCH, 'The Imperial Court-Jew Wolf Wertheimer as Diplomatic Mediator (during the War of the Austrian Succession)', *Scripta Hierosolimitana*, 23 (1972), 184–213.

MICHALSKI, JERZY, 'Sejmowe projekty reformy położenia ludności żydowskiej w Polsce w latach 1789–1792' [Projects to Reform the Status of the Jewish People in Poland in the Years 1789–1792], in id. (ed.), *Lud żydowski w narodzie polskim* [Jewish People in the Polish Nation], papers from a conference held at Warsaw, 15–16 September 1992 (Warsaw, 1994), 20–44.

MICHELSON, MORDEKHAI MOTELE, *Ma'amar mordekhai* [Article of Mordecai] (Piotrków, 1907).

MICHELSON, TSEVI YEKHEZKEL, 'Kuntres mareh kohen vehu toledot rabenu hameḥaber' [History of the Writer], in Alexander Zusya Kahana, *Sefer torat kohen* [Book of the Priestly Torah] (Warsaw, 1939), vol. ii, separately paginated.

Mikhtavim ve'igerot kodesh, ed. David Abraham Mandelbaum [Letters and Holy Epistles] (New York, 2003).

MOCHNACKI, BAZYLI, *Sprawa Birnbauma jako dowód jednej z wielu innych uciążliwości przez Polaków wycierpianych—w krótkości z akt sądowych wyciągniona* [The Case of Birnbaum as an Example of Persecutions Suffered by the Poles] (Warsaw, 1830).

MOSZKO JANKIELE [JULIAN URSYN NIEMCEWICZ], *Pamiętnik Warszawski*, 1/3 (1815), 546–7.

MYCIELSKI, MACIEJ, *Marcin Badeni (1751–1824): Kariera kontuszowego ministra* [Marcin Badeni: Career of an Old-Style Minister] (Warsaw, 1994).

NADLER, ALLAN, *The Faith of the Mithnagdim: Rabbinic Responses to Hasidic Rapture* (Baltimore and London, 1997).

Napoleon utekufato: reshumot ve'eduyot ivriyot benei hador [Napoleon and his Times: Hebrew Sources from the Period], ed. Baruch Mevorach (Jerusalem, 1968).

NATHANS, BENJAMIN, *Beyond the Pale: The Jewish Encounter with Late Imperial Russia* (Berkeley, 2002).

NELSON, DALE C., 'Ethnicity and Socioeconomic Status as Sources of Participation: The Case of Ethnic Political Culture', *American Political Science Review*, 73 (1979), 1024–38.

NIEMCEWICZ, JULIAN URSYN, *Lejbe i Sióra czyli Listy dwóch kochanków. Romans* [Lejbe and Sióra: Letters of Two Lovers. A Novel], 2 vols. (Warsaw, 1821).

——*Rok 3333, czyli Sen niesłychany* [Year 3333, or an Unbelievable Dream] (Warsaw, 1913).

See also MOSZKO JANKIELE

O srzodkach aby reforma Żydów w Polsce mogła bydź skuteczną, przez Mowszę Jankielewicza [On the Means to Make the Reform of the Jews Effective] (Warsaw, 1819).

'O Żydach w Polszcze' [On the Jews in Poland], *Rozmaitości* [supplement to *Korespondent Warszawski*], 20 (1818), 89–91.

OPALSKI, MAGDALENA, and ISRAEL BARTAL, *Poles and Jews: A Failed Brotherhood* (Hanover, NH, 1992).

[PAWLIKOWSKI, JÓZEF], *Myśli polityczne dla Polski* [Political Thoughts for Poland] (Warsaw, 1789).

PECZENIK, GINDA, *Glücksbergowie: Karta z dziejów drukarstwa i księgarstwa warszawskiego w pierwszej połowie XIX w.* [The Glücksberg Family: From the History of the Printing Industry in Warsaw in the First Half of the Nineteenth Century] (Warsaw, n.d.), copy in Archiwum Żydowskiego Instytutu Historycznego, Majer Bałaban Collection 117/46.

PEDAYA, HAVIVA, 'Bikoret al i. etkes *Ba'al hashem: habesht—magiyah, mistikah, hanhagah*' [Review of Immanuel Etkes, *Ba'al hashem*], *Zion*, 70 (2005), 248–65.

——'Bikoret al m. rosman *Habesht: mehadesh hahasidut*' [Review of Moshe Rosman, *Habesht*], *Zion*, 69 (2004), 515–24.

——'Teguvah liteguvato shel moshe rosman' [Response to the Response of Moshe Rosman], *Zion*, 70 (2005), 546–51.

PETROVSKY-SHTERN, YOHANAN, 'The Drama of Berdichev: Levi Yitshak and his Town', *Polin*, 17 (2004), 83–95.

Pinkas bendin [Memorial Book of Będzin], ed. Abraham S. Stein (Tel Aviv, 1959).

Pinkas bialistok: grunt-materialn tsu der geshikhte fun di yidn in bialistok biz nokh der ershter velt-milkhame [The Book of Białystok: Materials for the History of the Jews in Białystok up to the First World War], ed. Yudl Mark, 2 vols. (New York, 1949).

Pinkas hakehilot: polin [Encyclopedia of the Jewish Communities in Poland], iv: *Varshah vehagalil* [Warsaw and Surroundings] (Jerusalem, 1989); vii: *Mehozot lublin / kyeltseh* [Provinces of Lublin and Kielce] (Jerusalem, 1999).

POLEN, NEHEMIA, 'Miriam's Dance: Radical Egalitarianism in Hasidic Thought', *Modern Judaism*, 12/1 (1992), 1–21.

Polski słownik biograficzny [Polish Biographical Dictionary], 42 vols. to date (Kraków, 1935–).

[POTOCKI, STANISŁAW K.], *Żyd nie żyd? Odpowiedź na głos ludu izraelskiego* [Jew, Non-Jew? Response to the Voice of the Jewish People] (Warsaw, 1818).

PRZYBYLSKI, RYSZARD, *Krzemieniec: Opowieść o rozsądku zwyciężonych* [Krzemieniec] (Warsaw, 2003).

PUTNAM, ROBERT D., 'Studying Elite Political Culture: The Case of Ideology', *American Political Science Review*, 65 (1971), 651–81.

'Rabanim ugedolei torah be'olkush' [Rabbis and Torah Sages in Olkush], in Tsevi Yasheev (ed.), *Olkush (elkish): sefer zikaron likehilah shehukhhadah basho'ah* [Olkusz: Memorial Book for the Community of Olkusz] (Tel Aviv, 1972), 21–30.

RABINOWICZ, HARRY MORDKA, 'Sir Moses Montefiore and Chasidism', *Le'ela*, 36 (1993), 35–8.

RABINOWICZ, TSEVI M., *Bein peshisha lelublin: ishim veshitot behasidut polin* [Between Przysucha and Lublin: Personalities and Ideas in Polish Hasidism] (Jerusalem, 1997).

——'Toledot radomsk' [History of Radomsko], in L. Losh (ed.), *Sefer yizkor likehilat radomsk vehasevivah* [Memorial Book for the Community of Radomsko and its Surroundings] (Tel Aviv, 1967).

[RADOMIŃSKI, JAN ALOJZY], *Co wstrzymuje reformę Żydów w kraju naszym i co ją przyspieszyć powinno?* [What Is Hampering the Reform of the Jews in our Country and What Could Hasten It?] (Warsaw, 1820).

RAKOVSKY, PUA, *My Life as a Radical Jewish Woman: Memoirs of a Zionist Feminist in Poland*, ed. Paula E. Hyman, trans. from the Yiddish by Barbara Harshav with Paula E. Hyman (Bloomington, Ind., 2002).

RAPOPORT-ALBERT, ADA, 'The Emergence of a Female Constituency in Twentieth-Century Habad Hasidism', in David Assaf and Ada Rapoport-Albert (eds.), *Yashan mipenei ḥadash*, i: *Ḥasidim uva'alei musar* [Let the Old Make Way for the New, i: Hasidism and the Musar Movement] (Jerusalem 2009), 7–68* (English section).

—— 'Hagiography with Footnotes: Edifying Tales and the Writing of History in Hasidism', in ead. (ed.), *Essays in Jewish Historiography* (Ottawa, 1991), 119–59.

—— 'Hasidism after 1772: Structural Continuity and Change', in ead. (ed.), *Hasidism Reappraised* (London, 1996), 76–140.

—— 'On Women in Hasidism: S. A. Horodecky and the Maid of Ludmir Tradition', in Ada Rapoport-Albert and Steven J. Zipperstein (eds.), *Jewish History: Essays in Honour of Chimen Abramsky* (London, 1988), 495–525.

RASKIN, DWOJRA, *Ks. profesor Alojzy Ludwik Chiarini w Warszawie (ze szczególnym uwzględnieniem jego stosunku do Żydów)* [Luigi Chiarini in Warsaw: His Attitude towards Jews], copy in Archiwum Żydowskiego Instytutu Historycznego, Majer Bałaban Collection 117/47 (also in CAHJP, HM7426).

RAVITZKY, AVIEZER, 'Munkács and Jerusalem: Ultra-Orthodox Opposition to Zionism and Agudaism', in Shmuel Almog, Jehuda Reinharz, and Anita Shapira (eds.), *Zionism and Religion* (Hanover, NH and London, 1998), 67–89.

REDDAWAY, W. F., J. H. PENSON, O. HALECKI, and R. DYBOSKI (eds.), *The Cambridge History of Poland from Augustus II to Piłsudski, 1697–1935* (Cambridge, 1941).

'Reforma Żydów: Projekt od deputacji do tego wyznaczonej' [Reform of the Jews: Project by the Deputation], *MDSC* 215–28.

RINGELBLUM EMANUEL, 'Khsides un haskole in varshe in 18-tn yorhundert' [Hasidism and the Haskalah in Warsaw in the Eighteenth Century], *YIVO-Bleter*, 13 (1938), 124–32.

—— *Projekty i próby przewarstwienia Żydów w epoce stanisławowskiej* [Projects and Attempts at Reforming the Jews in the Period of Stanisław Poniatowski] (Warsaw, 1934).

—— 'Reshime fun yidishe doktoyrim, mediker un farmatsevtn, bateylikte inem oyfshtand fun yor 1863' [List of Jewish Doctors and Pharmacists in the 1863 Uprising], *Sotsyale Meditsin*, 10/1–2 (1937), 23–9; 10/3–4 (1937), 23–7.

—— 'Yidishe doktoyrim un mediker in oyfshtand fun yor 1863' [Jewish Doctors in the 1863 Uprising], *Sotsyale Meditsin*, 9/1–12 (1936), 23–6.

—— *Żydzi w powstaniu kościuszkowskiem* (Warsaw, 1938).

ROSMAN, MOSHE, 'Al nashim vaḥasidut: he'arot lediyun' [Observations on Women and Hasidism], in David Assaf and Ada Rapoport-Albert (eds.), *Yashan mipenei ḥadash*, i: *Ḥasidim uva'alei musar*, [Let the Old Make Way for the New, i: Hasidism and the Musar Movement] (Jerusalem 2009), 151–64.

——*Founder of Hasidism: A Quest for the Historical Baal Shem Tov* (Berkeley, 1996).

——'Hasidism as a Modern Phenomenon—The Paradox of Modernization without Secularization', *Jahrbuch des Simon-Dubnow-Instituts/Simon Dubnow Institute Yearbook*, 6 (2007), 215–24.

——'The History of Jewish Women in Early Modern Poland: An Assessment', *Polin*, 18 (2005), 25–56.

——'Lemeḥkar bikorti al habesht hahistori—teguvah' [On the Critical Research into the Historical Besht—Response], *Zion*, 70 (2005), 537–45.

——*The Lords' Jews: Magnate–Jewish Relations in the Polish–Lithuanian Commonwealth during the Eighteenth Century* (Cambridge Mass., 1990).

ROSTOCKI, WŁADYSŁAW, *Korpus w gęsie pióra uzbrojony: Urzędnicy warszawscy, ich życie i praca w Księstwie Warszawskim i Królestwie Polskim do roku 1851* [Corps Armed with Writing Pens: The Officials of Warsaw, their Life and Work in the Duchy of Warsaw and the Kingdom of Poland until 1851] (Warsaw, 1972).

——*Pochodzenie społeczne, kwalifikacje i przebieg kariery urzędników Komisji Województwa Mazowieckiego w czasach Królestwa Polskiego* [Social Background, Qualifications, and Careers of the Officials of the Voivodeship Commission of Mazovia in the Times of the Kingdom of Poland] (Warsaw, 2002).

ROTENBERG, S., 'Toledot bendin hayehudit' [History of Jews in Będzin], in *Pinkas bendin* [Memorial Book of Będzin], ed. Abraham S. Stein (Tel Aviv, 1959), 216–19.

RUBINSTEIN, ABRAHAM, 'Reshitah shel haḥasidut bepolin hamerkazit' [The Beginnings of Hasidism in Central Poland] (Ph.D. diss., Hebrew University of Jerusalem, 1960).

SALMON, YOSEF, *Religion and Zionism: First Encounters* (Jerusalem, 2002).

SAWICKI, ARON, 'Szkoła Rabinów w Warszawie (1826–1862) (na podstawie źródeł archiwalnych)' [The Warsaw Rabbinical School (1826–1862) (based on archival materials)], *Miesięcznik Żydowski*, 3/1 (1933), 244–74.

SCHATZ UFFENHEIMER, RIVKA, *Hasidism as Mysticism: Quietistic Elements in Eighteenth-Century Hasidic Thought*, trans. Jonathan Chipman (Princeton and Jerusalem, 1993).

SCHIPER, IGNACY, *Przyczynki do dziejów chasydyzmu w Polsce* [Studies in the History of Hasidism in Poland], ed. Zbigniew Targielski (Warsaw, 1992).

——'Samorząd żydowski w Polsce na przełomie wieku 18 i 19-go (1764–1831)' [Jewish Self-Government at the Turn of the Eighteenth Century, 1764–1831], *Miesięcznik Żydowski*, 1/1 (1931), 513–29.

——*Żydzi Królestwa Polskiego w dobie powstania listopadowego* [Jews of the Kingdom of Poland in the Period of the November Uprising] (Warsaw, 1932).

SCHNEERSOHN, JOSEPH, *The 'Tzemach Tzedek' and the Haskala Movement*, trans. Zalman I. Posner (New York, 1969).

SCHWARZFUCHS, SIMON, *Napoleon, the Jews and the Sanhedrin* (London, 1979).

Sefer me'ir einei hagolah [Book of the Light of the Exile], 2 vols. (Brooklyn, 1970).

Sejmy i sejmiki koronne wobec Żydów: Wybór tekstów źródłowych [Diets and Dietines of the Polish Crown on the Jews: Selection of Sources], ed. Anna Michałowska-Mycielska (Warsaw, 2006).

SEREJSKI, MARIAN HENRYK, 'Początki i dzieje słów "kultura" i "cywilizacja" w Polsce' [Beginnings and History of the Terms 'Culture' and 'Civilization' in Poland], in id., *Przeszłość a teraźniejszość: Szkice i studia historiograficzne* [Past and Present: Historiographical Essays] (Wrocław, 1965), 237–49.

SHAMRI, ARYEH, 'Rabonim, rabeim un parneysim in der kehile kalushin' [Rabbis, *Rebbes*, and Community Leaders in Kałuszyn], in id. et al. (eds.), *Sefer kalushin: geheylikt der khorev gevorener kehile* [Kałuszyn Memorial Book] (Tel Aviv, 1962), 85–100.

SHATZKY, JACOB, 'Avraham Yakov Shtern (1768–1842)', in *The Joshua Starr Memorial Volume: Studies in History and Philology* (New York, 1953), 203–18.

——*Geshikhte fun yidn in varshe* [History of the Jews in Warsaw], 3 vols. (New York, 1947–53).

——*Yidishe bildungs-politik in poyln fun 1806 biz 1866* [Jewish Educational Politics in Poland 1806–1866] (New York, 1943).

——'Zikhrones fun a poylishn yidn vegn di oyfshtandn fun 1831 un 1863' [Memoirs of Polish Jews from the Uprisings of 1831 and 1863], *YIVO-Bleter*, 5 (1933), 174–8.

SHMERUK, CHONE, 'Chasydyzm i kahał' [Hasidism and the *Kahal*], in *Żydzi w Dawnej Rzeczypospolitej* [Jews in Old Poland], papers from a conference held at Kraków, 22–26 September 1986 (Wrocław, 1991), 59–65.

——'Hasidism and the Kehilla', in Antony Polonsky, Jakub Basista, and Andrzej Link-Lenczowski (eds.), *The Jews in Old Poland, 1000–1795* (London, 1993).

——'Mashma'utah haḥevratit shel hasheḥitah haḥasidit' [The Social Significance of Hasidic *Sheḥitah*], *Zion*, 20 (1955), 47–72.

SHNEUR ZALMAN OF LYADY, *Likutei amarim* [Collection of Teachings] (Sławuta, 1796).

SHOCHAT, AZRIEL, 'Ligezerot hagiyusim shel nikolai harishon' [On the Conscription Decrees of Nicholas I], in A. Even-Shoshan et al. (eds.), *Sefer shalom sivan* (Jerusalem, 1980), 307–18.

——*Mosad 'harabanut mita'am' berusiyah: parashat bema'avak hatarbut bein ḥaredim levein maskilim* [The Institution of 'Crown Rabbinate' in Russia: A Chapter in the Struggle between the Haredi Orthodox and the Maskilim] (Haifa, 1975).

SINKOFF, NANCY B., *Out of the Shtetl: Making Jews Modern in the Polish Borderlands* (Providence, RI, 2004).

——'Strategy and Ruse in the Haskalah of Mendel Lefin of Satanow', in Shmuel Feiner and David Sorkin (eds.), *New Perspectives on the Haskalah* (London, 2001), 86–102.

SŁOWIKOWSKI, ADAM, 'Wspomnienia szkoły krzemienieckiej' [Recollections from the Krzemieniec School], in Stanisław Makowski (ed.), *Krzemieniec: Ateny Juliusza Słowackiego* [Krzemieniec: The Athens of Juliusz Słowacki] (Warsaw, 2004), 471–83.

SMOCZYŃSKI, A., 'Krótki rys historyczny Żydów z dołączeniem uwag o ich cywilizacji' [A Short Historical Outline on the Jews], *Gazeta Wiejska*, 48–9 (1818), 375–82, 389–90.

SOKOŁÓW, NAHUM, 'Do pracy i zgody!' [To Work and Unity!], *Izraelita*, 34/24 (1899), 259–60.

——*Zadania inteligencji żydowskiej: Szkic programu* [Responsibilities of the Jewish Intelligentsia: Outline of the Programme] (Warsaw, 1890).

Sr. k.k. Majestät Franz des Zweyten politische Gesetze und Verordnungen für Oester-reichischen, Böhmischen und Galizischen Erbländer, 14 vols. (Vienna, 1793–1816).

STAMPFER, SHAUL, 'The Controversy over Sheḥitah and the Struggle between Hasidim and Mitnagedim', in id., *Families, Rabbis and Education: Traditional Jewish Society in Nineteenth-Century Eastern Europe* (Oxford, 2010), 342–55.

——'The Missing Rabbis of Eastern Europe', in id., *Families, Rabbis and Education: Traditional Jewish Society in Nineteenth-Century Eastern Europe* (Oxford, 2010).

STANISLAWSKI, MICHAEL, *Tsar Nicholas I and the Jews: The Transformation of Jewish Society in Russia 1825–1855* (Philadelphia, 1983).

STASZIC, STANISŁAW, 'O przyczynach szkodliwości żydów i środkach usposobienia ich, aby się społeczeństwu użytecznemi stali' [On the Reasons for the Harmfulness of the Jews and How to Make them Useful to Society'], in id., *Dzieła* [Works], iv (Warsaw, 1816).

——*Ród ludzki* [The Human Race], 3 vols. (Warsaw, 1959).

STERN, SELMA, *The Court Jew* (Philadelphia, 1950).

——*Josel of Rosheim, Commander of Jewry in the Holy Roman Empire of the German Nation*, trans. Gertrude Hirschler (Philadelphia, 1965).

[ŚWITKOWSKI, PIOTR], 'Uwagi względem reformy Żydów uprojektowanej przez jw. Butrymowicza' [Remarks on the Reform of the Jews Projected by Butrymowicz], *MDSC* 135–41.

SZACKA, BARBARA, *Stanisław Staszic: Portret mieszczanina* [Stanisław Staszic: Portrait of a Townsman] (Warsaw, 1962).

SZMULEWICZ, RYWKA, *Dzieje Komitetu Starozakonnych w Warszawie 1825–1837* [History of the Jewish Committee in Warsaw, 1825–1837] (Warsaw, n.d.), copy in Archiwum Żydowskiego Instytutu Historycznego, Majer Bałaban Collection 117/1.

SZTERNKRANC, DORA, *Zniesienie kahałów i utworzenie dozorów bóźniczych w pierwszych latach Królestwa Polskiego* [The Abolition of *Kahals* and Creation of Jewish Community Boards in the Early Years of the Kingdom of Poland] (Warsaw, n.d.), copy in Archiwum Żydowskiego Instytutu Historycznego, Majer Bałaban Collection 117/5.

SZTOMPKA, PIOTR, *The Sociology of Social Change* (Oxford, 1993).

TAZBIR, JANUSZ, 'Conspiracy Theories and the Reception of *The Protocols of the Elders of Zion* in Poland', *Polin*, 11 (1998), 171–82.

TELLER, ADAM, 'Hasidism and the Challenge of Geography: The Polish Background to the Spread of the Hasidic Movement', *AJS Review*, 30/1 (2006), 1–29.

THURSH, KATHRIEL F., and ME'IR KORZEN (eds.), *Vlotslavek vehasevivah: sefer zikaron* [Włocławek and Surroundings: Memorial Book] (Tel Aviv, 1967).

TORTE, H.-J., 'Das russische Beamtentum in der ersten Hälfte des 19. Jahrhunderts', *Forschungen zur Osteuropäischen Geschichte*, 13 (1967), 7–345.

Transactions of the Parisian Sanhedrim, or Acts of the Assembly of Israelitisch Deputies of France and Italy, trans. M. Diogene Tama (London, 1807).

TSEDERBAUM, ALEXANDER HALEVI, *Keter kehunah, o divrei hayamim lekohanei ha'emunah ha'isra'elit uvenoteiha* [The Crown of the Priesthood: History of the Priests of the Jewish Faith] (Odessa, 1867).

'Tsenzura evreiskich knig v tsarstvovanie imperatora Nikolaia I' [Censorship of Jewish Books during the Reign of Nicholas I], *Voskhod*, 6 (1903), 131–40.

UNGER, MENASHE, 'Der sar montefiore un der vurker rebe' [Sir Montefiore and the Tsadik of Warka], in *Vurkah: sefer zikaron—vurke yizkor bukh* [Warka: Memorial Book] (Tel Aviv, 1976), 28–35.

URY, SCOTT, 'The *Shtadlan* of the Polish–Lithuanian Commonwealth: Noble Advocate or Unbridled Opportunist?', *Polin*, 15 (2002), 267–99.

VAN LUIT, RIETY, 'Hasidim, Mitnaggedim and the State in M. M. Lefin's *Essai d'un Plan de Réforme*', *Zutot*, 1 (2001), 188–95.

WALDEN, MOSHE MENAHEM, *Ohel yitshak* [The Tent of Isaac] (Piotrków, 1914).

WALFISH, BARRY DOV, *Esther in Medieval Garb: Jewish Interpretation of the Book of Esther in the Middle Ages* (New York, 1993).

WALICKI, ANDRZEJ, *Philosophy and Romantic Nationalism: The Case of Poland* (Notre Dame, Ind., 1994).

WALICKI, JACEK, *Synagogues and Prayer Houses of Łódź (to 1939)*, trans. Guy Russel Torr (Łódź, 2000).

WANDYCZ, PIOTR, *The Lands of Partitioned Poland, 1795–1918* (Seattle, 1974).

WARSZAWSKI, YESHIYA, 'Yidn in kongres-poyln (1815–1831)' [Jews in the Kingdom of Poland, 1815–1830], *Historishe shriftn fun YIVO*, 2 (1937), 322–54.

WEBER, MAX, *On Law, Economy and Society*, ed. M. Rheinstein (Cambridge, Mass., 1954).

WEEKS, THEODORE R., *From Assimilation to Antisemitism: The 'Jewish Question' in Poland, 1850–1914* (DeKalb, Ill., 2006).

WEHLER, HANS ULRICH, *Deutsche Gesellschaft*, i: *1700–1815* (Munich, 1987).

WERBLOWSKY, RAPHAEL JUDAH ZVI, 'Faith, Hope and Trust: A Study in the Concept of Bittahon', *Papers of the Institute of Jewish Studies, London* (Jerusalem, 1964), 95–139.

WERSES, SHMUEL, 'Hasifrut ha'ivrit bepolin: tekufot vetsiyunei derekh' [Hebrew Literature in Poland: Periods and Directions], in Israel Bartal and Israel Gutman (eds.), *Kiyum veshever: yehudei polin ledoroteihem*, ii: *Ḥevrah, tarbut, le'umiyut* [The Broken Chain: Polish Jewry through the Ages, ii: Society, Culture and Nationalism] (Jerusalem, 2001), 161–90.

WERTHEIM, AARON, *Law and Custom in Hasidism*, trans. Shmuel Himelstein (Hoboken, NJ, 1992).

'Wiadomości bieżące: Suum cuique [To Each His Own]', *Jutrzenka*, 3 (1863), 152.

WILENSKY, MORDECAI, *Ḥasidim umitnagedim: letoledot hapolmos shebeineihem 1772–1815* [Hasidim and Mitnagedim: A Study of the Controversy between Them, 1772–1815], 2 vols. (Jerusalem, 1970).

——'Hassidic Mitnaggedic Polemics in the Jewish Communities of Eastern Europe: The Hostile Phase', in Gershon D. Hundert (ed.), *Essential Papers on Hasidism: Origins to Present* (New York, 1991), 244–71.

WISHNITZER, M. L., 'Proekty reformy evreyskago byta v Gertsogstve Varshavskom i Tsarstve Polskom' [Projects of the Reform of the Jewish Life in the Duchy of Warsaw and the Kingdom of Poland], *Perezhitoe*, 1 (1909), 164–221.

[WITOWSKI, GERARD], *Sposób na Żydów czyli środki niezawodne zrobienia z nich ludzi uczciwych i dobrych obywateli: Dziełko dedykowane posłom i deputowanym na Sejm 1818 r.* [A Means of Dealing with the Jews; or, Sure Methods by which They Can Be Made into Honest People and Good Citizens] (Warsaw, 1818).

WODZIŃSKI, MARCIN, 'Blood and the Hasidim: On the History of Ritual Murder Accusations in Nineteenth-Century Poland', *Polin*, 22 (2009), 273–90.

——'Chasydzi w Częstochowie: Źródła do dziejów chasydyzmu w centralnej Polsce' [Hasidim in Częstochowa: Sources for the History of Hasidism in Central Poland], *Studia Judaica*, 8 (2005), 279–301.

——'Chasydzkie konwersje? Czy chasydyzm był sektą i co z tego wynika' [Hasidic Conversions? Hasidism as a Sect], in Agnieszka Jagodzińska (ed.), *W poszukiwaniu religii doskonałej? Konwersja a Żydzi* [In Search of a Perfect Religion? Conversion and the Jews] (Wrocław, 2012), 135–56.

——'"Civil Christians": Debates on the Reform of the Jews in Poland, 1789–1830', in Benjamin Nathans and Gabriella Safran (eds.), *Culture Front: Representing Jews in Eastern Europe* (Philadelphia, 2008), 62–8.

——'Good Maskilim and Bad Assimilationists: Toward a New Historiography of the Haskalah in Poland', *Jewish Social Studies*, 10/3 (2003–4), 87–122.

——'Hasidism, *Shtadlanut*, and Jewish Politics in Nineteenth Century Poland: The Case of Isaac of Warka', *Jewish Quarterly Review*, 96/2 (2005), 290–320.

——*Haskalah and Hasidism in the Kingdom of Poland: A History of Conflict*, trans. Sarah Cozens (Oxford, 2005).

——'Haskalah and Politics Reconsidered: The Case of the Kingdom of Poland, 1815–1860', in David Assaf and Ada Rapoport-Albert (eds.), *Yashan mipenei ḥadash*, ii: *Maskilim, mitnagedim verabanim*, [Let the Old Make Way for the New, ii: Haskalah, Orthodoxy, and the Opposition to Hasidism] (Jerusalem 2009), 163–97* (English section).

——'How Many *Hasidim* Were There in Congress Poland? On the Demographics of the Hasidic Movement in Poland during the First Half of the Nineteenth Century', *Gal-ed*, 19 (2004), 13–49.

——'How Should We Count *Hasidim* in Congress Poland? A Response to Glenn Dynner', *Gal-ed*, 20 (2006), 105–21.

——'Jakub Tugendhold and the First Maskilic Defence of Hasidism', *Gal-ed*, 18 (2001), 13–41.

——*Oświecenie żydowskie w Królestwie Polskim wobec chasydyzmu: Dzieje pewnej idei* [The Jewish Enlightenment in the Kingdom of Poland and Hasidism: History of an Idea] (Warsaw, 2003).

——'Rząd Królestwa Polskiego wobec chasydyzmu: Początki "polityki chasydzkiej" w Królestwie Kongresowym (1817–1818)' [The Beginnings of the 'Hasidic Policy' in the Congress Kingdom, 1817–1818], in Krzysztof Pilarczyk (ed.), *Żydzi i judaizm we współczesnych badaniach polskich* [Jews and Judaism in Contemporary Polish Research], iii (Kraków, 2003), 65–77.

WODZIŃSKI, MARCIN, 'Sprawa chasydymów: Z materiałów do dziejów chasydyzmu w Królestwie Polskim' [The Case of the Hasidim: From Materials on the
History of Hasidism in Central Poland], in Krystyn Matwijowski (ed.), *Z historii
ludności żydowskiej w Polsce i na Śląsku* [History of the Jews in Poland and Silesia],
Acta Universitatis Wratislaviensis 1568 (Wrocław, 1994), 227–42; French
translation: 'L'Affaire des "Chasydymów": Matériaux pour l'histoire des Has-
sidim dans le Royaume de Pologne', *Tsafon. Revue d'études juives du Nord*, 29
(1997), 35–58.

——'Tsavato shel berek zonenberg: hakarierah hamaftiyah shel nadvan al korḥo'
[The Testament of Berek Sonnenberg: The Strange Career of a Philanthropist
in Spite of Himself], *Gal-ed*, 22 (2010), 167–82.

——'Women and Hasidism: A "Non-Sectarian" Perspective', *Jewish History*, 27
(forthcoming).

WOLFOWICZ, SZYMEL, 'Więzień w Nieświeżu do Stanów Sejmujących o potrzebie
reformy Żydów' [A Prisoner in Nieśwież to the Debating Estates], *MDSC*
141–53.

Z dziejów gminy starozakonnych w Warszawie w XIX stuleciu [From the History of the
Jewish Community in Warsaw in the Nineteenth Century], i: *Szkolnictwo* [Edu-
cation] (Warsaw, 1907).

ZAIONCHKOVSKY, A., *Pravitel'stvennyi apparat samoderzhavnoy Rossii w XIX v.* [State
Administation of Autocratic Russia] (Moscow, 1978).

ZALKIN, MORDECAI, 'Hahaskalah hayehudit bepolin: kavim lediyun' [The
Haskalah in Poland: An Outline for Discussion], in Israel Bartal and Israel
Gutman (eds.), *Kiyum veshever: yehudei polin ledoroteihem*, ii: *Ḥevrah, tarbut,
le'umiyut* [The Broken Chain: Polish Jewry through the Ages, ii: Society,
Culture, and Nationalism] (Jerusalem, 2001), 391–413.

[ZALMANOV, SHRAGA], *Sefer shemu'at yitsḥak: likutei imrot tehorot . . . maran rabenu
yisra'el yitsḥak admor hazaken mivarka* [Book of Isaac's Sayings: Collection of
Pure Sayings of Rabbi Israel Isaac of Warka] (Benei Berak, 2006).

ZDRADA, JERZY, *Historia Polski 1795–1914* [History of Poland, 1795–1914]
(Warsaw, 2005).

ZIENKOWSKA, KRYSTYNA, 'Citizens or Inhabitants? The Attempt to Reform the
Status of the Polish Jews during the Four Years' Sejm', *Acta Poloniae Historica*, 76
(1997), 31–52.

ZINBERG, ISRAEL, *A History of Jewish Literature*, trans. Bernard Martin, 16 vols.
(Cincinnati and New York, 1972–8).

*Źródła do dziejów chasydyzmu w Królestwie Polskim, 1815–1867, w zasobach polskich
archiwów państwowych / Archival Sources on the History of Hasidism in the Kingdom
of Poland, 1815–1867, in the Polish State Archives*, ed. Marcin Wodziński (Kraków
and Budapest, 2011).

1815–1867, in the Polish State Archives], ed. Marcin Wodziński (Kraków 2011).

'Zwierciadło polskie dla publiczności' [A Polish Mirror for the Public], *MDSC*
235–68.

ZYCHLINSKI, EPHRAIM MEIR GAD, *Sefer lahav esh* [Book of the Flame of Fire]
(Piotrków, 1935).

Index

Page numbers referring to illustrations are in italics.

Printed and bound by CPI Group (UK) Ltd, Croydon, CR0 4YY

09/06/2025

14685812-0005